4th International Workshop on Computational Approaches to Historical Language Change (LChange 2023)

Singapore
6 December 2023

ISBN: 978-1-7138-8601-3

Printed from e-media with permission by:

Curran Associates, Inc.
57 Morehouse Lane
Red Hook, NY 12571

Some format issues inherent in the e-media version may also appear in this print version.

Association for Computational Linguistics
209 N. Eighth Street
Stroudsburg, Pennsylvania 18360

Phone: 1-570-476-8006
Fax: 1-570-476-0860

acl@aclweb.org

Additional copies of this publication are available from:

Curran Associates, Inc.
57 Morehouse Lane
Red Hook, NY 12571 USA
Phone: 845-758-0400
Fax: 845-758-2633
Email: curran@proceedings.com
Web: www.proceedings.com

LChange 2023

4th International Workshop on Computational Approaches to Historical Language Change 2023

Proceedings of the Workshop

December 6, 2023

The LChange organizers gratefully acknowledge the support from the following sponsors.

Gold

Order copies of this and other ACL proceedings from:

Association for Computational Linguistics (ACL)
209 N. Eighth Street
Stroudsburg, PA 18360
USA
Tel: +1-570-476-8006
Fax: +1-570-476-0860
acl@aclweb.org

Preface by the General Chair

Welcome to the 4th International Workshop on Computational Approaches to Historical Language Change (LChange'23) co-located with EMNLP 2023. LChange is held on December 6th, 2023, as a hybrid event with participation possible both virtually and on-site in Singapore.

Characterizing the time-varying nature of language will have broad implications and applications in multiple fields including linguistics, artificial intelligence, digital humanities, computational cognitive and social sciences. In this workshop, we bring together the world's pioneers and experts in **computational approaches to historical language change with a focus on digital text corpora**. In doing so, this workshop carries out the triple goals of disseminating state-of-the-art research on diachronic modeling of language change, fostering cross-disciplinary collaborations, and exploring the fundamental theoretical and methodological challenges in this growing niche of computational linguistic research.

In response to the call, we received 28 submissions. Each of them was carefully evaluated by at least two members of the Program Committee, whom we believed to be most appropriate for each paper. Based on the reviewers' feedback we accepted 17 full and short papers as oral or poster presentations. We had two distinguished keynote presentations: the first by Gemma Boleda (Research Professor in the Department of Translation and Language Sciences of the Universitat Pompeu Fabra, Spain) who presented a talk entitled "What does semantic change have to do with Hello Kitty? Referring as the source of change", and the second by Mario Giulianelli (a postdoctoral fellow at ETH Zurich) with the talk "Neural language models for word usage representation and analysis". Finally, we invited five EMNLP'23 Findings papers to be presented as posters, which are not included in the workshop proceedings.

To further support the community, we offered five student scholarships to cover registration fees. We also offered mentoring for four young researchers on their research topic in the field of language change, either during the workshop or virtually.

We hope that you will find the workshop papers insightful and inspiring. We would like to thank the keynote speakers for their stimulating talks, the authors of all papers for their interesting contributions, and the members of the Program Committee for their insightful reviews. Our special thanks go to the emergency reviewers who stepped in to provide their expertise. We also express our gratitude to the EMNLP 2023 workshop chairs for their kind assistance during the organization process. Finally, our thanks go to our gold sponsor iguanodon.ai, as well as the research project "Towards Computational Lexical Semantic Change Detection" (Swedish Research Council, contract 2018-01184) and the research program "Change is Key!" (Riksbankens Jubileumsfond, contract M21-0021).

Nina Tahmasebi, workshop chair, University of Gothenburg (Sweden)
Syrielle Montariol, EPFL (Switzerland)
Haim Dubossarsky, Queen Mary University of London and University of Cambridge (United Kingdom)
Andrey Kutuzov, University of Oslo (Norway)
Simon Hengchen, iguanodon.ai and University of Geneva (Switzerland)
David Alfter, University of Gothenburg (Sweden)
Francesco Periti, University of Milan (Italy)
Pierluigi Cassotti, University of Gothenburg (Sweden)

LChange'23 Workshop Chairs

Organizing Committee

General Chair

Nina Tahmasebi, University of Gothenburg, Sweden

Program Chairs

Syrielle Montariol, École polytechnique fédérale de Lausanne, Switzerland
Haim Dubossarsky, Queen Mary University of London and University of Cambridge, United Kingdom
Andrey Kutuzov, University of Oslo, Norway
Simon Hengchen, iguanodon.ai and University of Geneva, Switzerland
David Alfter, University of Gothenburg, Sweden
Francesco Periti, University of Milan, Italy
Pierluigi Cassotti, University of Gothenburg, Sweden

Program Committee

Program Chairs

David Alfter, University of Gothenburg
Pierluigi Cassotti, University of Gothenburg
Haim Dubossarsky, Queen Mary University of London and University of Cambridge
Simon Hengchen, iguanodon.ai and University of Geneva
Andrey Kutuzov, University of Oslo
Syrielle Montariol, Ecole Polytechnique Fédérale de Lausanne
Francesco Periti, University of Milan
Nina Tahmasebi, University of Gothenburg

Reviewers

Nikolay Arefyev, University of Oslo
Ehsaneddin Asgari, University of California, Berkeley, Data Lab, Volkswagen Group and Helmholtz Center for Infection Research
Pierpaolo Basile, University of Bari
Christin Beck, Universität Konstanz
Aleksandrs Berdicevskis, Gothenburg University
Pierluigi Cassotti, University of Gothenburg
Paul Cook, University of New Brunswick
Stefano De Pascale, Vrije Universiteit Brussel and KU Leuven
Chiara Di Bonaventura, King's College London, University of London
Clémentine Fourrier, HuggingFace
Karlien Franco, QLVL | KU Leuven & FWO Vlaanderen
Mario Giulianelli, University of Amsterdam
Mauricio Gruppi, Villanova University
Simon Hengchen, iguanodon.ai and University of Geneva
Valentin Hofmann, University of Oxford
Abhik Jana, IIT Bhubaneswar
Adam Jatowt, The University of Tokyo, Tokyo Institute of Technology
Andres Karjus, Tallinn University
Andrey Kutuzov, University of Oslo
Barbara McGillivray, King's College London, University of London
Syrielle Montariol, Ecole Polytechnique Fédérale de Lausanne
Paul Nulty, Birkbeck College, University of London and University College Dublin
Lidia Pivovarova, University of Helsinki
Martin Pömsl, School of Computer Science, McGill University
Taraka Rama, University of Gothenburg
Angelika Romanou, Ecole Polytechnique Fédérale de Lausanne
Eyal Sagi, University of St. Francis
Asad B. Sayeed, University of Gothenburg
Dominik Schlechtweg, Institute for Natural Language Processing, University of Stuttgart
Stephen Eugene Taylor, University of West Bohemia
Samia Touileb, University og Bergen, Norway
Ekaterina Vylomova, The University of Melbourne
Melvin Wevers, University of Amsterdam

Frank D. Zamora-Reina, University of Chile

Keynote Talk: What does semantic change have to do with Hello Kitty? Referring as the source of change

Gemma Boleda
University Pompeu Fabra

Abstract: It has long been noted that lexical semantic change is rooted in specific utterances, specific reference acts: for instance, in Old English deor"(deer") meant wild animal", and it acquired its current meaning probably via hunting, deer being the favorite animal of the chase".[1] However, traditional historical linguistics lacked the tools to explore the process from reference to semantic change on a large scale. Current methods in computational linguistics, as well as the increasing availability of large-scale linguistic resources, afford precisely that. In this talk, I will present work that links reference to change by examining different phenomena (production of referring expressions, regular polysemy) at different timescales (language development, synchronic use, language evolution), using quantitative and computational methods.

[1] https://www.etymonline.com/search?q=deer

Bio: Gemma Boleda is a Research Professor in the Department of Translation and Language Sciences of the Universitat Pompeu Fabra (Barcelona, Spain) and co-director of the Computational Linguistics and Linguistic Theory (COLT) research group. She is a linguist who uses quantitative and computational methods to investigate how language works. She is in particular interested in how people convey meaning through language.

Keynote Talk: Word usage representations from neural language models

Mario Giulianelli
ETH Zurich

Abstract: Neural language models are powerful tools for language scientists interested in studying word usage and its evolution over time. Drawing from a series of recent findings, I will argue that contemporary neural language models can infer contextually appropriate word interpretations which are predictive of human comprehension behaviour, and that they allow for quantitative yet interpretable comparisons between word usages. I will discuss methods to engage with language models for obtaining word representations, including the collection of neural representations generated during the processing of word usage examples, and the direct input of natural language instructions to induce human-readable word definitions. These approaches hold significant relevance for examining shifts and variations in word usage across the temporal and spatial dimensions.

Bio: Mario is a postdoctoral researcher at ETH Zurich, where he works with the Rycolab in the Institute for Machine Learning, Department of Computer Science; and a member of the ELLIS Society. Previously, he was a PhD student at the University of Amsterdam in the Institute for Logic, Language and Computation. He studies language use and evolution using tools from computer science, linguistics, and cognitive science.

Table of Contents

Program

Wednesday, December 6, 2023

09:15 - 09:30 *Introduction*

09:30 - 10:30 *Keynote Mario Giulianelli*

10:30 - 11:00 *Coffee Break*

11:00 - 12:00 *Session 1*

EvoSem: A database of polysemous cognate sets
Mathieu Dehouck, Alex François, Siva Kalyan, Martial Pastor and David Kletz

Semantic Shifts in Mental Health-Related Concepts
Naomi Baes, Nick Haslam and Ekaterina Vylomova

Scent and Sensibility: Perception Shifts in the Olfactory Domain
Teresa Paccosi, Stefano Menini, Elisa Leonardelli, Ilaria Barzon and Sara Tonelli

12:00 - 13:30 *Lunch Break*

13:30 - 14:30 *Keynote Gemma Boleda*

14:30 - 15:30 *Session 2*

Political dogwhistles and community divergence in semantic change
Max Boholm and Asad B. Sayeed

Automating Sound Change Prediction for Phylogenetic Inference: A Tukanoan Case Study
Kalvin Chang, Nathaniel Romney Robinson, Anna Cai, Ting Chen, Annie Zhang and David R Mortensen

Domain-Adapting BERT for Attributing Manuscript, Century and Region in Pre-Modern Slavic Texts
Piroska Lendvai, Uwe Reichel, Anna Jouravel, Achim Rabus and Elena Renje

Wednesday, December 6, 2023 (continued)

15:30 - 16:30 *Poster Session*

ChiWUG: A Graph-based Evaluation Dataset for Chinese Lexical Semantic Change Detection
Jing Chen, Emmanuele Chersoni, Dominik Schlechtweg, Jelena Prokic and Chu-Ren Huang

Changing usage of Low Saxon auxiliary and modal verbs
Janine Siewert, Martijn Wieling and Yves Scherrer

Towards Detecting Lexical Change of Hate Speech in Historical Data
Sanne Hoeken, Sophie Jasmin Spliethoff, Silke Schwandt, Sina Zarrieß and Özge Alacam

From Diachronic to Contextual Lexical Semantic Change: Introducing Semantic Difference Keywords (SDKs) for Discourse Studies
Isabelle Gribomont

Multi-lect automatic detection of Swadesh list items from raw corpus data in East Slavic languages
Ilia Afanasev

Literary Intertextual Semantic Change Detection: Application and Motivation for Evaluating Models on Small Corpora
Jackson Ehrenworth and Katherine A. Keith

A longitudinal study about gradual changes in the Iranian Online Public Sphere pre and post of 'Mahsa Moment': Focusing on Twitter
Sadegh Jafari, Amin Fathi, Abolfazl Hajizadegan, Amirmohammad Kazemeini and Sauleh Eetemadi

16:30 - 17:30 *Session 3*

Representing and Computing Uncertainty in Phonological Reconstruction
Johann-Mattis List, Nathan Hill, Robert Forkel and Frederic Blum

Anchors in Embedding Space: A Simple Concept Tracking Approach to Support Conceptual History Research
Jetske Adams, Martha Larson, Jaap Verheul and Michael Boyden

GHisBERT – Training BERT from scratch for lexical semantic investigations across historical German language stages
Christin Beck and Marisa Köllner

Wednesday, December 6, 2023 (continued)

17:30 - 17:45 *Closing Remarks*

Literary Intertextual Semantic Change Detection: Application and Motivation for Evaluating Models on Small Corpora

Jackson Ehrenworth
Williams College
jne1@williams.edu

Katherine A. Keith
Williams College
kak5@williams.edu

Abstract

Lexical semantic change detection is the study of how words change meaning between corpora. While Schlechtweg et al. (2020) standardized datasets and evaluation metrics for this shared task, for those interested in applying semantic change detection models to small corpora—e.g., in the digital humanities—there is a need for evaluation involving much smaller datasets. We present a method and open-source code pipeline for downsampling the SemEval-2020 Task 1 corpora while preserving gold standard measures of semantic change. We then evaluate several high-performing unsupervised models on these downsampled corpora, and find that the models experience both dramatically decreased performance (average 67% decrease) and high variance. Finally, we propose a novel application to the digital humanities: *literary intertextual semantic change detection*, the production of a ranked list of words by degree of semantic change between two books. We then provide a case study of this application to Fanon's *The Wretched of the Earth* and Hartman's *Scenes of Subjection* and find that semantic change detection models—even with their current limited performance on small corpora—may still produce fruitful avenues of exploration for literary scholars.

1 Introduction

Semantic meaning is fluid. The word *plane*, for instance, underwent a dramatic semiotic shift around the early 1900s from the sense of "flat geometric surface" to the sense of "aeroplane" (oed). The last ten years have seen the rise of computational linguistic approaches that attempt to provide unsupervised detection of lexical semantic change (Kutuzov et al., 2018; Tahmasebi et al., 2021). Applications include discovering laws of semantic change (Xu and Kemp, 2015; Hamilton et al., 2016b; Dubossarsky et al., 2017; Boleda, 2020), investigating the evolution of harmful stereotypes (Garg et al., 2018), or determining how societal relationships to certain concepts experience diachronic drift (Kozlowski et al., 2019), among others.

The majority of these fields involve studying *large* conglomerate corpora as proxies for societal beliefs. In the burgeoning literary digital humanities (Gold, 2012; Kirschenbaum, 2016; Eve, 2022), among other fields, however, one is often invested in studying *small* corpora, where each corpus is on the order of 150k tokens (about the size of a single authored English fiction novel). Schlechtweg et al. (2020) standardized evaluation metrics and datasets for unsupervised semantic change detection, but Schlechtweg et al.'s smallest corpus contains over 1.7 million tokens, and their largest over 110 million. In this work, we investigate the degree of performance degradation of semantic change detection models when evaluated on small corpora. We expect this setting to be challenging for the evaluated models due to the limited number of examples of each target word in context available to them.

To further motivate the importance of evaluating semantic change detection models on small corpora, we focus on applying these models to aid literary studies. In the context of literary criticism, investigating subtle differences in language between two books often provides the building blocks for broader comparative literary insight. In this work, then, we propose a novel application—*literary intertextual semantic change detection*, the production of a ranked list of words by degree of semantic change between two books—as an exploratory tool to suggest words that may be of literary interest and suitable for extended investigation (e.g., through comparative close-reading by humans). In this setting, corpora sizes are limited by the length of the books under consideration.

Finally, as a case study for how, and, importantly to us, whether, current semantic change detection models can be employed to produce fruitful avenues of inquiry for literary scholars, we apply the best performing English model evaluated in Sec-

Proceedings of the 4th Workshop on Computational Approaches to Historical Language Change, pages 1–14
December 6, 2023

tion 5.1 to two books—*The Wretched of the Earth* (Fanon, 1961/2021) and *Scenes of Subjection* (Hartman, 1997/2022)—which we suspected may have interesting intertextual semantic changes due to prior domain knowledge. We find that there is reason to be optimistic that semantic change detection can be used in an exploratory manner to aid literary critics.

To summarize, our primary contributions are the following:

- We create an evaluation framework that enables the downsampling of the SemEval-2020 Task 1: Unsupervised Lexical Semantic Change Detection datasets presented by Schlechtweg et al. (2020) while preserving ground truth data.[1]
- We evaluate a few of the best-performing semantic change detection models on downsampled corpora and find both dramatic decreases in performance (average 67% decrease) and high variance, opening the door to future work building models specifically for this low-resource setting.
- We propose a novel application of semantic change detection to the digital humanities—*literary intertextual semantic change detection*—and, through a case study of two books (*The Wretched of the Earth* (Fanon, 1961/2021) and *Scenes of Subjection* (Hartman, 1997/2022)) demonstrate the usefulness of these types of models for literary criticism.

2 Related Work

2.1 Methods for Semantic Change Detection

Methods for semantic change detection can be loosely categorized into four groups, the majority of which use cosine similarity between word embeddings created from two corpora as a proxy for semantic change. First, there are count-based methods that rely on explicit co-occurence matrices or their derivatives (Sagi et al., 2009; Cook and Stevenson, 2010; Gulordava and Baroni, 2011). There has been a general shift away from these initial methods towards the use of prediction-based models—such as those based on Continuous Skip gram with negative sampling (Mikolov et al., 2013, SGNS)—for the creation of word embeddings, with various strategies for aligning embeddings across time steps (Kim et al., 2014; Kulkarni et al., 2015; Dubossarsky et al., 2019). Recently, the use of contextualized word embeddings, derived predominantly from the BERT (Devlin et al., 2019) or ELMo (Peters et al., 2018) architectures, have seen a surge in popularity in the field. Generally, contextualized word embeddings are created by finetuning pre-trained language models on the corpora under consideration and then extracting and clustering or averaging hidden layer weights (Giulianelli et al., 2020; Martinc et al., 2020; Montariol et al., 2021; Rosin et al., 2022; Rosin and Radinsky, 2022). Separately, there are also probabilistic or dynamic methods that use both context-free (Bamler and Mandt, 2017; Rosenfeld and Erk, 2018) and context-based (Hofmann et al., 2021) mechanisms.

2.2 Applications of Word Embeddings to Small Corpora Tasks

While we are not aware of any research quantitatively evaluating semantic change detection models on small corpora, word embeddings that perform well on tasks involving small corpora have applications to, and have been studied in, a variety of fields.[2] Word embeddings have been used in psychology to detect formal thought disorder in transcribed or written statements (Voleti et al., 2020; Sarzynska-Wawer et al., 2021) and studied for their ability to capture word associations in dream reports (Altszyler et al., 2017; Elce et al., 2021). In the field of philosophy, meanwhile, domain-expertise has been used to investigate whether word embeddings can cluster related concepts in large single authored corpora with domain-specific content (Betti et al., 2020; Oortwijn et al., 2021). And political scientists have developed methods to support significance testing for use in contexts where corpora are large but target words are domain-specific and generally rare (Rodriguez et al., 2023).

Despite the broad interest in investigating the ability of word embeddings to capture semantic meaning even when data is scarce—a literature that this paper compliments—we are not aware of any attempts to evaluate the approaches surveyed in Section 2.1 on semantic change detection tasks for small corpora, nor are we aware of any annotated

[1] All experiments and code are available at `https://github.com/jnehrenworth/small-corpora-scd`.

[2] While Montariol and Allauzen (2019) have studied semantic change detection models in the context of scarce data, their research occurred before Schlechtweg et al. (2020) and, because of this, was limited to empirical evaluation on corpora without gold-standard data.

test sets for semantic change detection covering corpora small enough to simulate single books.

2.3 Applications of Semantic Change Detection to the Digital Humanities

Semantic change detection applied to the digital humanities is still nascent. Nevertheless, this intersection has previously been hinted at as a direction for future work by authors working in the field of semantic change detection (Tahmasebi and Risse, 2017; Kutuzov et al., 2018; Tahmasebi et al., 2021), and there is other prior work at this intersection. Semantic change detection has been used to track semantic innovation in abolitionist newspapers (Soni et al., 2021), investigate a debate about compositional shifts in a single authored series of Danish historical works (Nielbo et al., 2019), study evolving representations and stereotypes of Jewish people in 19th century France (Sullam et al., 2022), track the transformation of tropes in a large curated corpus of German poetry (Haider and Eger, 2019), and attempt to model character relations in the *Harry Potter* series (Volpetti et al., 2020; K et al., 2020).

While the exploratory use of semantic change detection in the digital humanities is not novel, we are not aware of any papers that suggest using semantic change detection directly to produce a ranked list of words by intertextual semantic change as an avenue for comparative literary analysis.[3]

3 Datasets

3.1 Overview

The standard datasets and shared tasks for semantic change detection were presented by Schlechtweg et al. (2020) in "SemEval-2020 Task 1: Unsupervised Lexical Semantic Change Detection." Schlechtweg et al. (2020) released corpora in four languages—English, German, Latin, and Swedish—each of which are bifurcated diachronically at some time period. The released corpora are genre-balanced year to year. Abbreviated summary statistics of these corpora are given in Table 1.

For each pair of corpora in a given language, call them C_1 and C_2, Schlechtweg et al. (2020) present two subtasks: 1. binary classification, and 2. ranking the degree of semantic change. Our work is exclusively focused on Subtask 2, where the the goal is to determine the amount of semantic shift that a list of target words have undergone between C_1 and C_2 by proxy of ranking them according to their degree of semantic shift (e.g., "gay" has changed more than "cell" which has changed more than "peer"). For one, it seems intuitively likely (and the results presented by Schlechtweg et al. (2020) tend to bear this out) that high performance on Subtask 2 is indicative of high performance on Subtask 1. It also seems to us as if Subtask 2 captures more about the subtle movement of language that literary critics are generally interested in. For instance, a polysemous word may not experience a binary sense change between C_1 and C_2 while still shifting from primarily one sense type to another. The production of a ranked list of words carries another, perhaps ancillary, benefit: it provides a literary critic the ability to easily prioritize which words to investigate more thoroughly. We believe this ability to be especially relevant because of how onerous we found it in our case study (Section 6) to determine for a given word: a) what the semantic change was, and b) whether the semantic change had literary relevance.

For each language, Schlechtweg et al. (2020)

	C_1 Tokens	C_2 Tokens	Target Words
English	6.5M	6.7M	37
German	70.2M	72.3M	48
Swedish	71.0M	110.0M	31

Table 1: Summary statistics for SemEval-2020 Task 1 corpora, abbreviated from Schlechtweg et al. (2020). C_1 and C_2 are time-specific corpora. *Target Words* indicate the number of evaluation words to be ranked by degree of semantic change between C_1 and C_2.

	C_1			C_2		
	Gold	Random	Total	Gold	Random	Total
English	138k	12k	150k	94k	56k	150k
German	156k	0k	156k	125k	25k	150k
Swedish	107k	43k	150k	95k	55k	150k

Table 2: Summary statistics for downsampled corpora, where: *Gold* is the number of tokens selected from lines used in the manual annotation process, as found in the usage graphs of Schlechtweg et al. (2021), *Random* is the number of tokens from lines randomly sampled until 150k total tokens were included, and *Total* is the total number tokens included.

[3] Our proposed application can be considered a near special-case of Lexical Semantic Change Discovery (Kurtyigit et al., 2021), except that our use-case is focused on graded change rather than that of binary classification (see Section 3.1 for more details).

released gold standard data for a subset of target words balanced for part of speech and frequency: via a manual annotation process, each target word was assigned a label between 0 and 1 denoting degree of semantic change (0 means no change has taken place, 1 is the maximum amount of change).

3.2 Downsampling Method

This paper focuses on downsampling the datasets presented by Schlechtweg et al. (2020) while preserving the gold standard data obtained via manual annotation. The annotation process, described in detail by Schlechtweg et al. (2021), involved selectively annotating pairs of word uses to create a sparsely connected usage graph. As randomly sampling a certain number of sentences from the SemEval-2020 Task 1 corpora until a target token amount is met would destroy this usage graph, we preserved it via the following steps:

1. After pre-processing and cleaning the text (see Appendix A), we used exact matching, to cross-reference the context text of each raw annotated use—presented in Schlechtweg et al. (2021)—used to create the SemEval-2020 Task 1 gold standard data with its counterpart in the SemEval-2020 Task 1 corpora (Schlechtweg et al., 2020).[4]

2. We programmatically selected all lines from the SemEval-2020 Task 1 corpora that were part of the manual annotation process.

3. We then took a random sample of additional lines until a desired token threshold was reached.

For the experiments presented in this paper, a token threshold of 150k was used. The German C_1 corpus had 156k tokens already present from the annotated sentences, so no additional random sampling occurred. For summary information about the downsampled corpora see Table 2.

4 Evaluating Existing Methods on Small Corpora

In this paper we evaluate three models that present a range of different architectures, from static (non-contextual) embeddings to contextual embeddings, and are, to our knowledge, among the highest performing open-source models for unsupervised semantic change detection:

1. Pražák et al. (2020), the winning submission on SemEval-2020 Task 1, Subtask 1. The authors train static (non-contextual) embeddings using SGNS, align them using orthogonal Procrustes, and then use cosine distance to compare aligned embeddings.

2. Pömsl and Lyapin (2020), the winning submission on SemEval-2020 Task 1, Subtask 2. The authors train static (non-contextual) embeddings using SGNS, align them using orthogonal Procrustes, and then take Euclidean distance as their metric when comparing aligned embeddings.[5]

3. Rosin and Radinsky (2022), the highest performing open-source contextualized semantic shift detection model on Subtask 2 we are aware of (Montanelli and Periti, 2023). The authors propose a temporal self-attention mechanism as a modification to the standard transformers architecture. They use a pre-trained BERT model, fine-tune it on diachronic corpora using their proposed temporal attention mechanism, and then create time-specific representations of target words by extracting and averaging hidden-layer weights. These representations are then averaged at the token level and compared using cosine similarity.[6]

We have used the models essentially as-is from their respective GitHub repositories. Hyperparameters for all models were chosen based on those reported in each paper. Note that both Pražák et al. (2020) and Pömsl and Lyapin (2020) learn static (non-contextual) embeddings from scratch on the target corpora, while the contextualized model of Rosin and Radinsky (2022) is already pre-trained and only fine-tuned on the target corpora.

[4]We used the lemmatized versions of both the SemEval-2020 Task 1 corpora and the annotated uses for this matching procedure. Due to larger inconsistencies in formatting between the Latin annotated uses and the SemEval-2020 Task 1 corpora, we were unable to successfully devise a way to cross-reference Latin annotated uses (see Appendix A). For that reason, the Latin corpora was excluded from this study.

[5]Note that although Pömsl and Lyapin describe ensemble and models with contextualized embeddings in their paper, their winning submission used static (non-contextual) embeddings and is what we have chosen to evaluate.

[6]For the purposes of this study, we use the best tested version of BERT (Devlin et al., 2019) for each language from HuggingFace's repository, as reported by the authors (`bert-tiny` for English and `bert-base-german-cased` for German).

Model	SemEval-Small Avg.	EN	DE	SV	SemEval Avg.	EN	DE	SV	Δ
Pražák et al. (2020)	0.269	0.106	0.361	0.340	0.481	0.367	0.697	0.604	−44%
Pömsl and Lyapin (2020)	0.049	0.060	0.022	0.066	0.527	0.422	0.725	0.547	−90%
Rosin and Radinsky (2022)	0.226	0.320	0.132		0.695	0.627	0.763		−67%

Table 3: Summary view of mean performance across 500 downsampled corpora (SemEval-Small), measured using Spearman's ρ, along with best performance as reported by Schlechtweg et al. (2020) or by Montanelli and Periti (2023) (SemEval). Δ refers to average percent decrease in performance between the SemEval corpora and the downsampled corpora, while EN, DE, and SV denote performance on the English, German, and Swedish corpora, respectively.

We do not intend for this to be an exhaustive evaluation of all possible methods in the field. Instead, we hope to open the door for future research to evaluate other methods for semantic change detection — perhaps Nonce2Vec (Herbelot and Baroni, 2017), LSA+SVD (Deerwester et al., 1990), or PPMI+SVD (Levy et al., 2015), all of which some literature suggest may perform well on tasks involving small corpora (Hamilton et al., 2016a; Altszyler et al., 2017; Oortwijn et al., 2021). Other than models specifically targeting smaller corpora, more recent SemEval-style shared tasks in Russian and Spanish (RuShiftEval (Kutuzov and Pivovarova, 2021) and LSCDiscovery Zamora-Reina et al. (2022)) have shown that Word-in-Context (WiC) and Word Sense Disambiguation (WSD) models tend to have quite high performance on the task of semantic change detection. The WiC models "DeepMistake" (Arefyev et al., 2021; Agarwal and Nenkova, 2022) or XL-LEXEME (Cassotti et al., 2023), or the WSD model "GlossReader" (Rachinskiy and Arefyev, 2021, 2022) may be ideal candidates for future evaluation.

5 Results and Evaluation

For each model described in Section 4, we ran experiments to evaluate performance on downsampled datasets (Section 5.1), quantify variability across bootstrap resamples (Section 5.2), and analyze performance across corpora size (Section 5.3). All reported results are Spearman's rank-order correlation coefficient ρ between the predicted and gold-standard lists of target words ranked by degree of semantic change, as is standard across the literature (Schlechtweg et al., 2020).

5.1 Downsampled Results

We downsampled the SemEval-2020 Task 1 corpora five hundred different times according to the method proposed in Section 3 across all languages and evaluated the models discussed in Section 4 on these downsampled corpora.[7]

We found that Pražák et al.'s model performs the best on average across languages ($\rho = 0.269$), although the gap is small to the model of Rosin and Radinsky (2022) ($\rho = 0.226$), while Pömsl and Lyapin's model, which won the SemEval Subtask 2 shared competition, performs quite poorly, with essentially no correlation demonstrated between predicted and gold standard degree of semantic change lists ($\rho = 0.049$). Interestingly, while Rosin and Radinsky's model performed worse that that of Pražák et al. (2020) when evaluated against the German corpora ($\rho = 0.132$ vs. $\rho = 0.361$), it performed significantly better with the English corpora ($\rho = 0.320$ vs. $\rho = 0.106$). We hypothesize that the difference in performance across these two languages could be due to differing performance in the underlying base models—`bert-tiny` vs. `bert-based-german-cased`—though we leave to future work ablation studies confirming these differences.

Full results are presented in Table 3. On average, there was a 67% decrease in performance compared to the full SemEval corpora, indicating the need for improved methods for detecting semantic change on small corpora.

5.2 Variance Results

In an ideal world, semantic change detection models should display low performance variance: when evaluated on similar datasets they should not have radically different performance. To test whether the models described in Section 4 have this property, we measured the variability in Spearman's ρ across the 500 English downsamples. In these downsamples, only the randomly selected lines change (see

[7]Note that Rosin and Radinsky do not support semantic change detection in Swedish, so we report results only from English and German for their model.

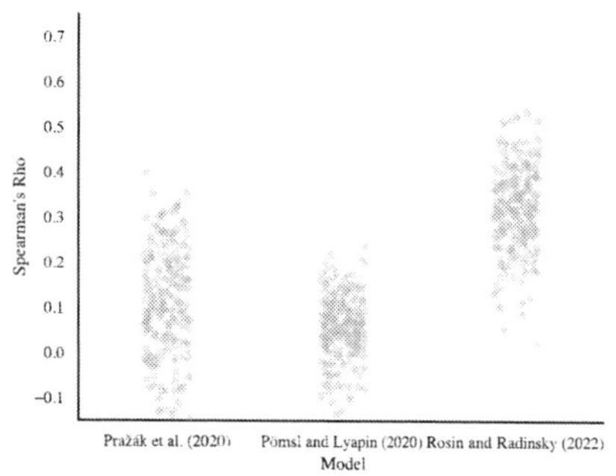

Figure 1: Scatter plot demonstrating the high variance in performance exhibited by each tested model. Each dot represents Spearman's ρ evaluated for a given model on a particular 150k-token downsample of the SemEval English corpus.

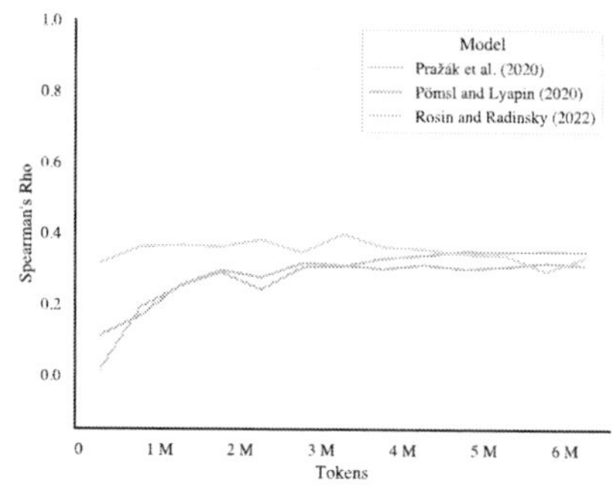

Figure 2: Mean Spearman's ρ across 50 downsamples of the SemEval English corpora plotted against corpus size of both downsampled corpora. The performance of the BERT-based temporal attention model (Rosin and Radinsky, 2022) was essentially stable across corpora sizes, while the performance of the SGNS-based models (Pražák et al., 2020; Pömsl and Lyapin, 2020) improved as corpora size increased.

Table 2) and the gold-standard lines remain the same. Thus, the target words in any two downsampled corpora should present similar degrees of semantic change.

Our results, presented in Figure 1, suggest that all tested models demonstrate startlingly high performance variance. We report the mean performance in the EN column in Table 3, and the standard deviation was: 0.108 for Pražák et al. (2020), 0.075 for Pömsl and Lyapin (2020), and 0.091 for Rosin and Radinsky (2022). This kind of test and result supports the literature studying stability of word embeddings which suggest that small data is especially challenging for the consistency of prediction-based models (Antoniak and Mimno, 2018; Bloem et al., 2019).

5.3 Corpora Size Results

Finally, we evaluated each model across varying sizes of the English corpora. We downsampled the English corpora to individual corpus target token amounts from 250k to 6.25M, with jumps of 500k tokens. We downsampled the corpora 50 times at each token level, with mean Spearman's ρ shown in Figure 2.

For the SGNS-based models of Pömsl and Lyapin (2020) and Pražák et al. (2020), performance improved most dramatically at smaller corpora sizes, although it did generally continue to increase, albeit more slowly, at larger corpora sizes. This was perhaps the expected result, as we believed that more data would improve static embeddings learned from the corpora under consideration. We hypothesize that the reason the performance of the temporal attention model of Rosin and Radinsky (2022) was essentially stable across corpora sizes is due to the author's fine-tuning approach: because the model did not require training from scratch we expected its performance to depend far less on corpus size.[8] These results suggest a model's pre-training could be very influential for semantic change detection performance.

6 Case Study in Literary Intertextual Semantic Change Detection

In the setting of literary criticism, one is often interested in conducting close readings based on subtle differences of language between two books—be they at the level of theoretical motifs, grammatical structures, or single word semiotic shifts—that can then be woven into broader processes of argumentation or productions of comparative meaning (Richards, 1929; Derrida, 1968/2013; Smith, 2016).[9] We propose the application of *literary in-*

[8]The performance of the temporal attention model was not as high as expected nearer to the full SemEval English corpora (at 6.25M tokens mean ρ = 0.336 vs. the ρ = 0.627 reported in Rosin and Radinsky (2022) on the SemEval English corpora). Despite re-implementing the steps of their paper to the best of our ability, and corresponding with the authors, we were unable to reproduce best reported results from Rosin and Radinsky (2022).

[9]These citations may appear strange to a literary critic, for the study of fluidity in language is embedded in essentially all modern-day literary criticism. We've chosen to cite Richards as *Practical Criticism*'s impact on New Criticism arguably lead to the modern practice of close reading, Derrida because the investigation of slippage in language and

tertextual semantic change detection—the production of a ranked list of words by degree of semantic change between two books—as an exploratory technique to aid literary scholars in finding single word differences that may be of literary interest and suitable for extended investigation (e.g., through comparative close-reading).

As a case study for how, and, importantly to us, whether, current semantic change detection models can be employed to create fruitful avenues of inquiry for literary scholars, we applied the best performing English model evaluated in Section 5.1 (Rosin and Radinsky, 2022) to two books—*The Wretched of the Earth* (Fanon, 1961/2021) and *Scenes of Subjection* (Hartman, 1997/2022). We chose these two novels because we suspected—based on our prior domain knowledge—that they may have interesting intertextual semantic changes (see Section 6.1 for further elaboration). Our research question was: how well does an intrinsic evaluation metric of $\rho = 0.320$ translate to usefulness in an external literary task?

6.1 Case Study Selection

We picked Frantz Fanon's *The Wretched of the Earth* and Saidiya Hartman's *Scenes of Subjection* because we suspected that the word "violence" may have experienced a non-obvious intertextual semantic shift of literary importance. Fanon and Hartman are two black authors writing in a similar literary tradition but whose distinct contexts and research interests shape their interactions with, and study of, violence. To see why this is the case, we will sketch a brief primer of their works.

In 1961, during the Algerian War of Independence, Fanon produced *The Wretched of the Earth*, a searing collection of essays on the psychological effects of colonialism, the effectiveness and cathartic power in violence as a strategy for decolonialization, and the project of post-colonial nation building. Fanon's most radical claims in *The Wretched of the Earth* revolve around his advocacy of physical violence as a productive, beneficial part of decolonialization, a "cleansing force [that] rids the colonized of their inferiority complex, of their passive and despairing attitude [...] emboldens them, and restores their self-confidence" (Fanon, 1961/2021, p. 51).

Hartman, in *Scenes of Subjection*, is interested in a very different kind of violence. She excavates the seemingly small moments of terror and performance that constituted subjection in slavery, what she describes as "the ordinary terror and habitual violence that structured everyday life and inhabited the most mundane and quotidian practices": the ambivalent nature of pleasure mediated in a context of forced performance, the songs enslaved people were made to sing to simulate the appearance of happiness leading up to a coffle, the inability of black bodies to legally bear witness (Hartman, 1997/2022, p. xxx).[10]

We believe, then, that the word "violence" has experienced an intertextual semantic shift suggesting a broader thematic movement of literary significance. If a semantic change detection model can highlight such a shift, then it demonstrates that these systems can be used to suggest avenues of inquiry leading to genuine literary insight. So, our (more specific) research question is: will the model of Rosin and Radinsky (2022) uncover the semantic shift of the word "violence" between *The Wretched of the Earth* and *Scenes of Subjection*? We are also interested in what other terms the model will describe as having experienced semantic shift, and in qualitatively evaluating whether any of those terms have literary importance.

6.2 Literary Validity

Both books were lemmatized and stripped of punctuation. Then non-stopwords that had been used more than 50 times in both books were ranked via the temporal attention model of Rosin and Radinsky (2022) by degree of semantic change.[11] Violence, appearing 367 times across both books, was ranked the tenth most changed word. The top ten words are given in Table 4, as are a small hand-selected series of example sentences we believe suggest the intertextual semantic change that has occurred in the word "violence" between *The*

play in semiotics may have reached its apotheosis with deconstruction and "Plato's Pharmacy", and Smith for her quite lucid article—specifically with a digital humanities audience in mind—on the history and praxis of close reading.

[10]We are essentializing both Hartman's and Fanon's messages for the sake of clarity. Hartman, for instance, is certainly also interested in extreme forms of degradation and violence embedded inside the institutions of slavery, while Fanon was trained as a psychologist and intimately aware of the ways in which colonialism operates as a form of linguistic and cultural violence. Nevertheless, one of Hartman's most impactful contributions was to raise awareness of quotidian forms of violence, and it is difficult to state how impactful Fanon's focus on overt violence remains in academic and radical circles.

[11]For the computational experiment, we used digitized private copies of both books. We cannot make these public due to copyright, but please contact us if interested in reproducibility.

Top-10 words: however, see, since, **political**, new, order, subject, say, life, **violence**

word	Examples from *The Wretched of the Earth*	Examples from *Scenes of Subjection*
violence	the most brutal aggressiveness and impulsive **violence** are channeled, transformed, and spirited away (p. 19).	Songs, jokes, and dance transform wretched conditions into a conspicuous [. . .] display of contentment. This [. . .] itself becomes an exercise of **violence** (p. 53).
	Colonialism is [. . .] naked **violence** and only gives in when confronted with greater **violence** (p. 23).	The most invasive forms of slavery's **violence** lie [. . .] in what we don't see [. . .] mundane [. . .] forms of terror (p. 66).
political	The nationalist **political** parties never insist on the need for confrontation (p. 22).	a notion of the **political** inseparable from [. . .] the ability [. . .] to effect hegemony (p. 109).
	it is not the **political** parties who called for the armed insurrection (p. 32).	What form does the **political** acquire for the enslaved? (p. 109)

Table 4: **Top row:** Top-10 words ranked by degree of intertextual semantic change (greatest first) between *The Wretched of the Earth* and *Scenes of Subjection* according to the temporal attention model of Rosin and Radinsky (2022). **Bottom table:** Hand-selected example sentences demonstrating the semantic change that occurred for "violence" and "political." See Section 6.2 for qualitative interpretation of these semantic shifts.

Wretched of the Earth and *Scenes of Subjection*. Our qualitative evaluation is that in these examples Fanon uses violence to mean *raw physical force producing bodily harm*, while Hartman's use suggests a gentler, though no less injurious, definition: *insidious psychological harm*. As hinted at in footnote 10, these uses are by no means universal throughout the entirety of their respective books, but they do point to what we believe is the broader shift in the way the two authors discuss violence.

Some of the words in the top ten do not seem to have experienced a semantic shift at all. For instance, "however" is ranked the most changed word but seems to be used in a nearly identical and remarkably quotidian way by both Fanon and Hartman. For other words, after conducting close readings of the sentences in which they occur in both novels, we conclude that the shift is unremarkable or mainly an artifact of the distributional hypothesis. "Subject" is a good example. By both Fanon and Hartman, we observe that it is used predominantly to refer to *a person that is discussed, conducted, or investigated*, but Fanon uses it almost exclusively co-occuring with "colonized," as in "colonized subject," while Hartman's more generally uses "subject" to refer to enslaved individuals. Any system based on the distributional hypothesis will determine that "subject" has experienced a semantic shift based on Hartman's lack of use of the term "colonized subject," but it is debatable whether this is an example of semantic shift of literary interest.

More promisingly, the system was able to suggest directions of study which previously we had not considered. "Political," appearing 164 times across both books and ranked the fourth most changed word by the model, is one example of this. Despite having worked with both books extensively, we had not considered "political" as a word or concept with an interesting intertextual semantic difference.

We summarize Fanon's use of "political" primarily in the sense of *in relation to an arm of the administration of the state*, as in "political party," which he uses often. This fits with Fanon's strategic focus, which is at least partly driven by a desire to create a blueprint for actionable political revolution with the aim of divesting unified, anti-democratic political power from colonial governmental regimes. We find that Hartman, in contrast, more often than not uses "political" as a noun signifying *the complex of entanglements existing between a citizen and the state*, as in "the political." Unlike Fanon, there is a somewhat subtle notion in which Hartman questions whether political frameworks are even the right tools through which to understand practices of resistance available to subaltern individuals. She writes that the "traditional notions of the political [. . .] the unencumbered self, the citizen, the self-possessed individual, and the volitional and autonomous subject" are made fraught under slavery, for "Slaves are not consensual and willful actors, the state is not a vehicle for advancing their claims, they are not citizens, and their status as persons is contested" Hartman (1997/2022, p. 103, 109). The effect of this is that transgressive practices by enslaved individuals—practices of resistance—are made obscure when measured against "traditional notions of the political," for those spheres were not available to and did not encompass slaves. This causes her to both question the suitability of politics as an interpretive device for understanding practices of resistance, and "reimagine the political in toto" Hartman (1997/2022, p. 103, 108). While outside the scope of this work, one could imagine a fruitful investigation and comparative literary paper based on this proposed semantic difference.

6.3 Case Study Discussion

That "violence" was ranked in the top ten most changed words is quite encouraging. For it shows that even with relatively poor performance on the task of determining degree of semantic change in small corpora, as demonstrated in Section 5.1, a semantic change detection system may still produce avenues for investigation that prove viable after sustained literary analysis. Of course, here we already suspected that "violence" had experienced intertextual semantic change. But we did not previously know about the intertextual differences in the word "political." Indeed, "political" is a case study for how we imagine such a system being deployed: take two books, use a semantic change detection system to produce a list of words ranked by intertextual semantic change, and then conduct close readings based on the top ranked words.

We suspect that literary intertextual semantic change detection will be exploratory rather than confirmatory at the ranking stage. One will—and should—always have to return to the text to interrogate whether any suggested word has experienced intertextual semantic change that is both real and of literary interest. We also suspect that to an extent a literary critic must be discerning in order to find words that have interesting intertextual semantic changes. Of the top ten ranked words given in Table 4, only four—political, order, subject, and violence—strike us as being suitable for literary analysis, and some, such as "however," do not seem to us to have experienced any intertextual semantic change at all. It is difficult to know whether this is a product of the relatively poor intrinsic evaluation metrics ($\rho = 0.320$) demonstrated through Section 5.1, a challenge of models based on distributional semantics that have limited ability to understand important surrounding context (be it because of a fixed context window or breaking at the sentence level), or simply one of the impediments of studying unigrams which cannot capture the full spectrum of contextual meaning that literary critics are most interested in studying. Finally, it was extremely labor intensive to determine for each word in the ranked list: a) what the semantic change was, and b) whether the semantic change had literary relevance. This interpretability challenge is perhaps a weakness in existing methods, and an opportunity for future work specifically designed to provide more interpretable output for use in cultural analytics.

We hope as novel methods are developed and intrinsic performance is improved on Experiment 5.1, extrinsic performance on real-world tasks such as this one will become easier and more impactful. Regardless, our case study provided evidence that current semantic change detection systems—even with low intrinsic performance on small corpora—may unveil avenues of investigation in small corpora yielding genuine literary insight.

7 Conclusion

In this paper, we presented—to our knowledge, at least—the first evaluation of semantic change detection models on small corpora (approximately 150k tokens). We found that several high-performing semantic change detection models perform significantly worse on standard tasks evaluated on these smaller corpora, on average experiencing a 67% decrease in performance, and demonstrate remarkably high variance across bootstrap resamples. Overall, for those in the digital humanities there is a clear need for novel and stable methods that are able to accurately detect lexical semantic changes between small corpora, and we hope that our evaluation framework encourages focus on this low-resource setting. However, through a novel literary application and case study, we also demonstrated that there is reason to be optimistic that semantic change detection can be used in an exploratory manner to aid literary critics.

References

plane, n.5. In *OED Online*. Oxford University Press.

Oshin Agarwal and Ani Nenkova. 2022. Temporal effects on pre-trained models for language processing tasks. *Transactions of the Association for Computational Linguistics*, 10:904–921.

Edgar Altszyler, Sidarta Ribeiro, Mariano Sigman, and Diego Fernández Slezak. 2017. The interpretation of dream meaning: Resolving ambiguity using latent semantic analysis in a small corpus of text. *Consciousness and Cognition*, 56:178–187.

Maria Antoniak and David Mimno. 2018. Evaluating the stability of embedding-based word similarities. *Transactions of the Association for Computational Linguistics*, 6:107–119.

Nikolay Arefyev, Daniil Homskiy, Maksim Fedoseev, Adis Davletov, Vitaly Protasov, and Alexander Panchenko. 2021. Deepmistake: Which senses are hard to distinguish for a wordincontext model. In *Computational linguistics and intellectual technologies: Papers from the annual conference Dialogue.*

Robert Bamler and Stephan Mandt. 2017. Dynamic word embeddings. In *Proceedings of the 34th International Conference on Machine Learning*, volume 70 of *Proceedings of Machine Learning Research*, pages 380–389. PMLR.

Arianna Betti, Martin Reynaert, Thijs Ossenkoppele, Yvette Oortwijn, Andrew Salway, and Jelke Bloem. 2020. Expert concept-modeling ground truth construction for word embeddings evaluation in concept-focused domains. In *Proceedings of the 28th International Conference on Computational Linguistics*, pages 6690–6702, Barcelona, Spain (Online). International Committee on Computational Linguistics.

Jelke Bloem, Antske Fokkens, and Aurélie Herbelot. 2019. Evaluating the consistency of word embeddings from small data. In *Proceedings of the International Conference on Recent Advances in Natural Language Processing (RANLP 2019)*, pages 132–141.

Gemma Boleda. 2020. Distributional semantics and linguistic theory. *Annual Review of Linguistics*, 6(1):213–234.

Pierluigi Cassotti, Lucia Siciliani, Marco DeGemmis, Giovanni Semeraro, and Pierpaolo Basile. 2023. XL-LEXEME: WiC pretrained model for cross-lingual LEXical sEMantic changE. In *Proceedings of the 61st Annual Meeting of the Association for Computational Linguistics (Volume 2: Short Papers)*, pages 1577–1585, Toronto, Canada. Association for Computational Linguistics.

Paul Cook and Suzanne Stevenson. 2010. Automatically identifying changes in the semantic orientation of words. In *Proceedings of the Seventh International Conference on Language Resources and Evaluation (LREC'10)*, Valletta, Malta. European Language Resources Association (ELRA).

Scott Deerwester, Susan T Dumais, George W Furnas, Thomas K Landauer, and Richard Harshman. 1990. Indexing by latent semantic analysis. *Journal of the American society for information science*, 41(6):391–407.

Jacques Derrida. 1968/2013. Plato's pharmacy. In *Dissemination*. Bloomsbury, London.

Jacob Devlin, Ming-Wei Chang, Kenton Lee, and Kristina Toutanova. 2019. BERT: Pre-training of deep bidirectional transformers for language understanding. In *Proceedings of NAACL-HLT*.

Haim Dubossarsky, Simon Hengchen, Nina Tahmasebi, and Dominik Schlechtweg. 2019. Time-out: Temporal referencing for robust modeling of lexical semantic change. In *Proceedings of the 57th Annual Meeting of the Association for Computational Linguistics*, pages 457–470, Florence, Italy. Association for Computational Linguistics.

Haim Dubossarsky, Daphna Weinshall, and Eitan Grossman. 2017. Outta control: Laws of semantic change and inherent biases in word representation models. In *Proceedings of the 2017 Conference on Empirical Methods in Natural Language Processing*, pages 1136–1145, Copenhagen, Denmark. Association for Computational Linguistics.

Valentina Elce, Giacomo Handjaras, and Giulio Bernardi. 2021. The language of dreams: Application of linguistics-based approaches for the automated analysis of dream experiences. *Clocks & Sleep*, 3(3):495–514.

Martin Paul Eve. 2022. *The Digital Humanities and Literary Studies*. Oxford University PressOxford.

Frantz Fanon. 1961/2021. *The Wretched of the Earth*, 60th anniversary edition edition. Grove Press, New York.

Nikhil Garg, Londa Schiebinger, Dan Jurafsky, and James Zou. 2018. Word embeddings quantify 100 years of gender and ethnic stereotypes. *Proceedings of the National Academy of Sciences*, 115(16):E3635–E3644.

Mario Giulianelli, Marco Del Tredici, and Raquel Fernández. 2020. Analysing lexical semantic change with contextualised word representations. In *Proceedings of the 58th Annual Meeting of the Association for Computational Linguistics*, pages 3960–3973, Online. Association for Computational Linguistics.

Matthew K Gold. 2012. *Debates in the digital humanities*. U of Minnesota Press.

Kristina Gulordava and Marco Baroni. 2011. A distributional similarity approach to the detection of semantic change in the Google Books ngram corpus. In *Proceedings of the GEMS 2011 Workshop on GEometrical Models of Natural Language Semantics*, pages 67–71, Edinburgh, UK. Association for Computational Linguistics.

Thomas Haider and Steffen Eger. 2019. Semantic change and emerging tropes in a large corpus of new high german poetry. In *Proceedings of the 1st International Workshop on Computational Approaches to Historical Language Change*, pages 216–222.

William L. Hamilton, Jure Leskovec, and Dan Jurafsky. 2016a. Cultural shift or linguistic drift? comparing two computational measures of semantic change. In *Proceedings of the 2016 Conference on Empirical Methods in Natural Language Processing*, pages 2116–2121, Austin, Texas. Association for Computational Linguistics.

William L. Hamilton, Jure Leskovec, and Dan Jurafsky. 2016b. Diachronic word embeddings reveal statistical laws of semantic change. In *Proceedings of the 54th Annual Meeting of the Association for Computational Linguistics (Volume 1: Long Papers)*, pages 1489–1501, Berlin, Germany. Association for Computational Linguistics.

Saidiya Hartman. 1997/2022. *Scenes of Subjection: Terror, Slavery, and Self-Making in Nineteenth-Century America*, 25th anniversary edition edition. Oxford University Press, New York, USA.

Aurélie Herbelot and Marco Baroni. 2017. High-risk learning: acquiring new word vectors from tiny data. In *Proceedings of the 2017 Conference on Empirical Methods in Natural Language Processing*, pages 304–309, Copenhagen, Denmark. Association for Computational Linguistics.

Valentin Hofmann, Janet Pierrehumbert, and Hinrich Schütze. 2021. Dynamic contextualized word embeddings. In *Proceedings of the 59th Annual Meeting of the Association for Computational Linguistics and the 11th International Joint Conference on Natural Language Processing (Volume 1: Long Papers)*, pages 6970–6984, Online. Association for Computational Linguistics.

Vani K, Simone Mellace, and Alessandro Antonucci. 2020. Temporal embeddings and transformer models for narrative text understanding. In *Proceedings of the Text2Story'20 Workshop*.

Yoon Kim, Yi-I Chiu, Kentaro Hanaki, Darshan Hegde, and Slav Petrov. 2014. Temporal analysis of language through neural language models. In *Proceedings of the ACL 2014 Workshop on Language Technologies and Computational Social Science*, pages 61–65, Baltimore, MD, USA. Association for Computational Linguistics.

Matthew G Kirschenbaum. 2016. What is digital humanities and what's it doing in english departments? In *Defining digital humanities*, pages 211–220. Routledge.

Austin C Kozlowski, Matt Taddy, and James A Evans. 2019. The geometry of culture: Analyzing the meanings of class through word embeddings. *American Sociological Review*, 84(5):905–949.

Vivek Kulkarni, Rami Al-Rfou, Bryan Perozzi, and Steven Skiena. 2015. Statistically significant detection of linguistic change. In *Proceedings of the 24th International Conference on World Wide Web*, WWW '15, pages 625–635, Republic and Canton of Geneva, CHE. International World Wide Web Conferences Steering Committee.

Sinan Kurtyigit, Maike Park, Dominik Schlechtweg, Jonas Kuhn, and Sabine Schulte im Walde. 2021. Lexical semantic change discovery. In *Proceedings of the 59th Annual Meeting of the Association for Computational Linguistics and the 11th International Joint Conference on Natural Language Processing (Volume 1: Long Papers)*, pages 6985–6998, Online. Association for Computational Linguistics.

Andrey Kutuzov, Lilja Øvrelid, Terrence Szymanski, and Erik Velldal. 2018. Diachronic word embeddings and semantic shifts: a survey. In *Proceedings of the 27th International Conference on Computational Linguistics*, pages 1384–1397, Santa Fe, New Mexico, USA. Association for Computational Linguistics.

Andrey Kutuzov and Lidia Pivovarova. 2021. Rushifteval: a shared task on semantic shift detection for russian. *Computational linguistics and intellectual technologies:*.

Omer Levy, Yoav Goldberg, and Ido Dagan. 2015. Improving distributional similarity with lessons learned from word embeddings. *Transactions of the Association for Computational Linguistics*, 3:211–225.

Matej Martinc, Petra Kralj Novak, and Senja Pollak. 2020. Leveraging contextual embeddings for detecting diachronic semantic shift. In *Proceedings of the Twelfth Language Resources and Evaluation Conference*, pages 4811–4819, Marseille, France. European Language Resources Association.

Tomas Mikolov, Kai Chen, Greg Corrado, and Jeffrey Dean. 2013. Efficient estimation of word representations in vector space. In *Proceedings of the International Conference on Learning Representations (ICLR'13)*.

Stefano Montanelli and Francesco Periti. 2023. A survey on contextualised semantic shift detection. *arXiv preprint arXiv:2304.01666*.

Syrielle Montariol and Alexandre Allauzen. 2019. Empirical study of diachronic word embeddings for scarce data. In *Proceedings of the International Conference on Recent Advances in Natural Language Processing (RANLP 2019)*, pages 795–803, Varna, Bulgaria. INCOMA Ltd.

Syrielle Montariol, Matej Martinc, and Lidia Pivovarova. 2021. Scalable and interpretable semantic change detection. In *Proceedings of the 2021 Conference of the North American Chapter of the Association for Computational Linguistics: Human Language Technologies*, pages 4642–4652, Online. Association for Computational Linguistics.

Kristoffer Laigaard Nielbo, Mads Linnet Perner, Christian Larsen, Jonas Nielsen, and Ditte Laursen. 2019. Automated compositional change detection in saxo grammaticus' gesta danorum. In *Proceedings of the Digital Humanities in the Nordic Countries 4th Conference, Copenhagen, Denmark, March 5-8, 2019*, volume 2364 of *CEUR Workshop Proceedings*, pages 320–332. CEUR-WS.org.

Yvette Oortwijn, Jelke Bloem, Pia Sommerauer, Francois Meyer, Wei Zhou, and Antske Fokkens. 2021. Challenging distributional models with a conceptual network of philosophical terms. In *Proceedings of the 2021 Conference of the North American Chapter of the Association for Computational Linguistics: Human Language Technologies*, pages 2511–2522, Online. Association for Computational Linguistics.

Matthew E. Peters, Mark Neumann, Mohit Iyyer, Matt Gardner, Christopher Clark, Kenton Lee, and Luke Zettlemoyer. 2018. Deep contextualized word representations. In *Proceedings of the 2018 Conference of the North American Chapter of the Association for Computational Linguistics: Human Language Technologies, Volume 1 (Long Papers)*, pages 2227–2237, New Orleans, Louisiana. Association for Computational Linguistics.

Martin Pömsl and Roman Lyapin. 2020. CIRCE at SemEval-2020 task 1: Ensembling context-free and context-dependent word representations. In *Proceedings of the Fourteenth Workshop on Semantic Evaluation*, pages 180–186, Barcelona (online). International Committee for Computational Linguistics.

Ondřej Pražák, Pavel Přibáň, Stephen Taylor, and Jakub Sido. 2020. UWB at SemEval-2020 task 1: Lexical semantic change detection. In *Proceedings of the Fourteenth Workshop on Semantic Evaluation*, pages 246–254, Barcelona (online). International Committee for Computational Linguistics.

Maxim Rachinskiy and Nikolay Arefyev. 2021. Zeroshot crosslingual transfer of a gloss language model for semantic change detection. In *Computational linguistics and intellectual technologies: Papers from the annual conference Dialogue*, volume 20, pages 578–586.

Maxim Rachinskiy and Nikolay Arefyev. 2022. GlossReader at LSCDiscovery: Train to select a proper gloss in English – discover lexical semantic change in Spanish. In *Proceedings of the 3rd Workshop on Computational Approaches to Historical Language Change*, pages 198–203, Dublin, Ireland. Association for Computational Linguistics.

I. A. Richards. 1929. *Practical Criticism*. Harcourt Brace & Company, New York City.

Pedro L. Rodriguez, Arthur Spirling, and Brandon M. Stewart. 2023. Embedding regression: Models for context-specific description and inference. *American Political Science Review*, pages 1–20.

Alex Rosenfeld and Katrin Erk. 2018. Deep neural models of semantic shift. In *Proceedings of the 2018 Conference of the North American Chapter of the Association for Computational Linguistics: Human Language Technologies, Volume 1 (Long Papers)*, pages 474–484, New Orleans, Louisiana. Association for Computational Linguistics.

Guy Rosin and Kira Radinsky. 2022. Temporal attention for language models. In *Findings of the Association for Computational Linguistics: NAACL 2022*, pages 1498–1508.

Guy D. Rosin, Ido Guy, and Kira Radinsky. 2022. Time masking for temporal language models. In *Proceedings of the Fifteenth ACM International Conference on Web Search and Data Mining*, WSDM '22, page 833–841, New York, NY, USA. Association for Computing Machinery.

Eyal Sagi, Stefan Kaufmann, and Brady Clark. 2009. Semantic density analysis: Comparing word meaning across time and phonetic space. In *Proceedings of the Workshop on Geometrical Models of Natural Language Semantics*, pages 104–111, Athens, Greece. Association for Computational Linguistics.

Justyna Sarzynska-Wawer, Aleksander Wawer, Aleksandra Pawlak, Julia Szymanowska, Izabela Stefaniak, Michal Jarkiewicz, and Lukasz Okruszek. 2021. Detecting formal thought disorder by deep contextualized word representations. *Psychiatry Research*, 304:114135.

Dominik Schlechtweg, Barbara McGillivray, Simon Hengchen, Haim Dubossarsky, and Nina Tahmasebi. 2020. SemEval-2020 task 1: Unsupervised lexical semantic change detection. In *Proceedings of the Fourteenth Workshop on Semantic Evaluation*, pages 1–23, Barcelona (online). International Committee for Computational Linguistics.

Dominik Schlechtweg, Nina Tahmasebi, Simon Hengchen, Haim Dubossarsky, and Barbara McGillivray. 2021. DWUG: A large resource of diachronic word usage graphs in four languages. In *Proceedings of the 2021 Conference on Empirical Methods in Natural Language Processing*, pages 7079–7091.

Barbara Herrnstein Smith. 2016. What was "close reading"? a century of method in literary studies. *The Minnesota Review*, 2016(87):57–75.

Sandeep Soni, Lauren F. Klein, and Jacob Eisenstein. 2021. Abolitionist networks: Modeling language change in nineteenth-century activist newspapers. *Journal of Cultural Analytics*, 6(1).

Simon Levis Sullam, Giorgia Minello, Rocco Tripodi, and Massimo Warglien. 2022. Representation of jews and anti-jewish bias in 19th century french public discourse: Distant and close reading. *Frontiers in Big Data*, 4.

Nina Tahmasebi, Lars Borin, Adam Jatowt, Yang Xu, and Simon Hengchen, editors. 2021. *Computational approaches to semantic change*. Number 6 in Language Variation. Language Science Press, Berlin.

Nina Tahmasebi and Thomas Risse. 2017. On the uses of word sense change for research in the digital humanities. In *Research and Advanced Technology for Digital Libraries*, pages 246–257, Cham. Springer International Publishing.

Rohit Voleti, Julie M. Liss, and Visar Berisha. 2020. A review of automated speech and language features for assessment of cognitive and thought disorders. *IEEE Journal of Selected Topics in Signal Processing*, 14(2):282–298.

Claudia Volpetti, K. Vani, and Alessandro Antonucci. 2020. Temporal word embeddings for narrative understanding. In *Proceedings of the 2020 12th International Conference on Machine Learning and Computing*, ICMLC 2020, pages 68–72, New York, NY, USA. Association for Computing Machinery.

Yang Xu and Charles Kemp. 2015. A computational evaluation of two laws of semantic change. In *CogSci*.

Frank D. Zamora-Reina, Felipe Bravo-Marquez, and Dominik Schlechtweg. 2022. LSCDiscovery: A shared task on semantic change discovery and detection in Spanish. In *Proceedings of the 3rd Workshop on Computational Approaches to Historical Language Change*, pages 149–164, Dublin, Ireland. Association for Computational Linguistics.

A Pre-processing and Cleaning for Cross-Reference

To cross-reference the context text of each annotated use with its SemEval-2020 Task 1 counterpart, we first pre-processed and cleaned the datasets. This was required prior to exact matching due to formatting differences that make straightforward comparisons—and fuzzy matching—inaccurate. We should note that this cleaning procedure was used only to cross-reference. Once a cleaned line from one of the SemEval corpora was matched with the cleaned context text for an annotated use, we inserted the unaltered SemEval line into our downsampled corpora to preserve the properties of the original dataset.

For instance, the English SemEval line:

> period of its greatest activity be towards the middle of the day the hour at which student generally which unfortunate class be most obnoxious to its attack_nn – be unwilling to be disturb.

corresponds to the annotated use:

> period of its greatest activity be towards the middle of the day , the hour at which student generally , - - which unfortunate class be most obnoxious to its attack , – be unwilling to be disturb .

This is a relatively simple example, where stripping punctuation, part of speech tags, and spaces would allow an exact match to be used. However, there are other instances where OCR artifacts[12] or inconsistent formatting made the cross-referencing task slightly more difficult. For example, there was inconsistent formatting in German corpora dealing with the letter “x” in the context of an example like“2x4” (sometimes it is removed, sometimes it is not). To clean our data for cross-referencing, then, we stripped punctuation, OCR artifacts, duplicate and trailing spaces, _nn and _vb part of speech tags, and finally the letter “x” from both the lemmatized context text for each annotated use and each line from the lemmatized SemEval corpora.

We found only one exception that couldn't be cross-referenced with this procedure and manually included it in the final dataset. The SemEval line:

> so after the famous christmas-dinner with its nice roast-meats and pudding and pie after the game of romp with her father and the ride on the rocking-horse with her brother who at last from mere mischief have tip_vb her off and send her cry to her mother begin to think about go there

corresponds to the following context text surrounding the word “tip”:

> so , after the famous christmas dinner with its nice roast-meats , and pudding , and pie , - - after the game of romp with her father , and the ride on the rocking-horse with her brother , who , at last , from mere mischief , have tip her off , and send her cry to her mother , —she begin to think about go there .

The discerning reader will notice that there is one word missing ("her mother begin to think" vs. "her mother , —she begin to think") in the SemEval corpora.

[12]We provide examples of these OCR artifacts in our code repository `https://github.com/jnehrenworth/small-corpora-scd`.

We attempted to develop similar heuristics for the Latin dataset, but we were unable to do so because of larger formatting and content inconsistencies between Latin context text and SemEval lines. For more detailed documentation, visit `downsample.py` of our repository: `https://github.com/jnehrenworth/small-corpora-scd`.

Domain-Adapting BERT for Attributing Manuscript, Century and Region in Pre-Modern Slavic Texts

Piroska Lendvai
Dept. of Digital Humanities
Bavarian Academy of Sciences
Munich, Germany
piroska.lendvai@badw.de

Uwe Reichel
audEERING GmbH, Germany &
Hungarian Research Centre for Linguistics
Budapest, Hungary
ureichel@audeering.com

Anna Jouravel and **Achim Rabus** and **Elena Renje**
Department of Slavic Languages and Literatures
University of Freiburg, Germany
anna.jouravel,achim.rabus,elena.renje@slavistik.uni-freiburg.de

Abstract

Our study presents a stratified dataset compiled from six different Slavic bodies of text, for cross-linguistic and diachronic analyses of Slavic Pre-Modern language variants. We demonstrate unsupervised domain adaptation and supervised finetuning of BERT on these low-resource, historical Slavic variants, for the purposes of provenance attribution in terms of three downstream tasks: manuscript, century and copying region classification. The data compilation aims to capture diachronic as well as regional language variation and change: the texts were written in the course of roughly a millennium, incorporating language variants from the High Middle Ages to the Early Modern Period[1], and originate from a variety of geographic regions. Mechanisms of language change in relatively small portions of such data have been inspected, analyzed and typologized by Slavists manually; our contribution aims to investigate the extent to which the BERT transformer architecture and pretrained models can benefit this process. Using these datasets for domain adaptation, we could attribute temporal, geographical and manuscript origin on the level of text snippets with high F-scores. We also conducted a qualitative analysis of the models' misclassifications.

1 Introduction

One of the prerequisites of diachronic linguistic research is the chronological and geolocational attribution of historical texts. Establishing the provenance of textual material incorporates two interwoven research areas: language history and textual history. For language history, reliable provenance attribution enables determining and categorizing linguistic features corresponding to specific time periods that can thereby uncover language change; for textual history, it facilitates the tracking of the traditions of text creation (copying and handing down) employed in manuscripts, and thereby the reconstruction of a text's archetype.

Chronological and geolocational attribution of historical texts is a laborious process that can benefit from recent advances in natural language processing (NLP): to this end, in a collaborative project between Slavic studies and language technology, we apply domain adaptation and finetuning of BERT (Devlin et al., 2019) on historical Slavic data. Our focus material consists of six bodies of text that originate from medieval and early modern manuscripts and early printings, created in South-Eastern and Eastern Europe. They had been manually transcribed and dated between the 10th-18th centuries on the manuscript level, based on codicological, linguistic and paleographical aspects. The manuscripts and early printings we examined use Cyrillic script and non-normalized orthography[2]. They pertain to the written genre of non-vernacular language and to the broader domain of religion.

The texts encompass language varieties ranging from Old Church Slavic to its later recensions; these are known to have developed under influences of a.o. geographically constrained cultural areas. Variants were formed by factors that gave rise to orthographic, lexical and morphosyntactic changes, e.g. via modernising tendencies that adapted to the vernacular usage at the geographic area where the texts got copied and compiled, but also reverse ten-

[1]According to Western classification.

[2]Written in *scriptio continua* customary for that time, where spaces are occasionally used in an unsystematic way to mark breath pauses, but our transcribed texts are word segmentated either during transcription or during HTR.

Proceedings of the 4th Workshop on Computational Approaches to Historical Language Change, pages 15–21
December 6, 2023 ©2023 Association for Computational Linguistics

dencies in the form of stylistic archaizing, reintroducing specific linguistic properties characteristic of South Slavic; this was in trend at the turn of the 14th/15th centuries in certain Rus'ian literary schools, called the Second South Slavic influence (Talev, 1973).

The above heterogeneity of change-inducing factors impacted various linguistic levels, as reflected by our historical data. This poses uncharted challenges to provenance attribution, which we tackled in three downstream text classification tasks: the attribution of the properties *manuscript*, *century* and *region* performed with BERT models on texts segmented into sentence-like snippets. We also used the data for domain adaptation of BERT models, evaluating its impact on the downstream tasks.

In related work in NLP, large language models and transformer architectures have been put to use for some historical languages (Bamman and Burns, 2020; Schweter et al., 2022; Gabay et al., 2022; Manjavacas, 2022; Lendvai and Wick, 2022), but we are not aware of studies using this technology for treating historical Slavic data; Kutuzov and Pivovarova (2021) reported on a shared task for assessing semantic change for selected lexical items but based on Modern Russian data starting from the 18th century. Use cases similar to ours are described in recent studies, e.g. on chronological attribution of text with deep learning methods on historical languages (Assael et al., 2019; Liebeskind and Liebeskind, 2020; Rastas et al., 2022). Further related downstream tasks include language identification, i.e. discriminating closely related languages or varieties, where studies report on the compilation of corpora specifically for this purpose and on methods that range from classical machine learning e.g. based on frequency of character n-grams, lexical frequency and exclusivity, part-of-speech and morphology information, to deep learning approaches, a.o. based on character embeddings (Islam et al., 2011; Zampieri et al., 2019; Wu et al., 2019; Bernier-Colborne et al., 2019).

Our contributions in this paper are the following: Introducing six Pre-Modern Slavic bodies of text (henceforth: datasets) and their employment in deep learning experiments with BERT (Section 2); Describing our experimental matrix in terms of BERT models, domain adaptation procedure and setup of downstream tasks (Section 3); Evaluating and analyzing the performance scores and misclassifications of the models and sketching ongoing work (Section 4); Discussing our pilot study in terms of limitations (Section 5).

2 Data and class labeling

Table 1 presents an overview of the six datasets we used. The first three columns correspond to our three downstream text classification tasks that each designate a small set of coarse-grained target labels. In effect, we partition the same data into different subsets along a specific property, the first one *manuscript*, where BERT needs to assign to each text snippet from which manuscript this snippet comes from. For attributing the *century*, we have three classes: '10–12', '15–16' and '18': we binned data from the first two datasets; resp. from the third and fourth, resp. from the last two. For attributing the property of *region* of the texts, two classes

Manuscript	Century	Region	Place of Copying	Language	Main genre	# Snippets
Codex Suprasliensis	10-11	South	Eastern Old Bulgaria	Old Church Slavic; South Slavic recension	hagiographical-homiletic	4,831
Cyril of Jerusalem's Catechetical Lectures	11-12	East	Kyivan Rus'	Old Church Slavic; South Slavic recension; Transmitted version used: East Slavic recension	dogmatic	4,282
Dionisio corpus (printed)	15-16	South	Serbia, Macedonia	Serbian Church Slavic; South Slavic recension	liturgical	10,685
Apostolos (from the Uspensky version of the Great Menaion Reader)	16	East	Muscovy	Russian Church Slavic; East Slavic recension	gospel	14,058
Sluzhabnik 'service book'	18	South	Serbia	Serbian Church Slavic; South Slavic recension	liturgical	3,350
Elizabeth Bible (printed)	18	East	Muscovy	Russian Church Slavic; East Slavic recension	Bible translation	11,796

Table 1: Data characteristics. Online information about each body of text is available by clicking on its name.

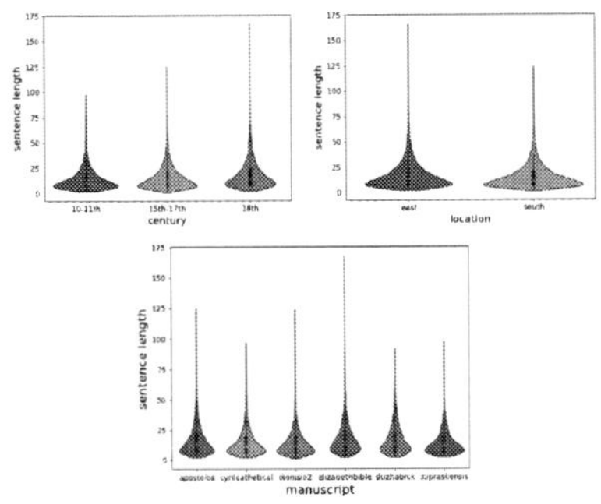

Figure 1: Violin plots showing the distribution of snippet lengths in the datasets per downstream task.

are distinguished, since the transmitted versions of manuscripts that we use have emerged either in the Southern Slavic or in the Eastern Slavic language area. It is important to see that partitioning along the spatial property (i.e., downstream task: *region* attribution) entails that the classes for that task will comprise temporally heterogeneous data (i.e., diachronic versions of the languages in that geographical area) and vice versa. In the downstream task of *manuscript* attribution, the data feature a specific combination of temporal and spatial properties that are unique to the given manuscript, etc.

The texts were available to us in transcribed form. For sentence segmentation we used Stanza (Qi et al., 2020) with *Old Church Slavonic* set as language. The segmented material qualifies as text snippets rather than syntactically complete sentences: some contain only punctuation or are very short. We discarded snippets with character length (including whitespace) less than 15 in order to remove semantically rather unintelligible strings. In Figure 1 we show the resulting distribution of snippet lengths in the respective datasets per downstream task.

For all downstream tasks the aggregated dataset was split the same way into training, development, and test partition by the ratios 80/10/10. The split was stratified on the manuscripts and was made disjunct on manuscript paragraphs, aiming to reduce potential topic overlap between partitions. For the preceding domain adaptation step the training set was further split by 90/10 into a masked language modeling (MLM) training and development set.

3 BERT experiments

For the domain adaption and finetuning experiments we report on the usage of three pretrained models; all were available in the Hugging Face repository: the multilingual model *bert-base-multilingual-uncased*, and the specifically Cyrillic models *KoichiYasuoka/bert-base-slavic-cyrillic-upos* and *anon-submission-mk/bert-base-macedonian-bulgarian-cased*. We have run a matrix of 93 model trainings: as shown in Figure 2, we compared direct finetuning of the pretrained models (henceforth also referenced as the base models) on the downstream tasks vs. domain adapting the pretrained models plus their subsequent finetuning. The pretrained models serve as baseline for each downstream task, i.e. baseline results are obtained via the experiments along the right arrow.

3.1 Domain adaptation

Vocabulary extension For domain adaptation we extended the tokenizers' vocabularies with the lexical content of the manuscripts by adding the union of the 100 most frequent words of each manuscript of at least five characters that were yet unknown to the tokenizer. We restricted the vocabulary extension in order to avoid catastrophic forgetting in the subsequent masked language modeling task.

Masked Language Modeling Subsequently, each pretrained model was domain-adapted, i.e. finetuned on the MLM task. We added the standard *BertForMaskedLM* head provided by Hugging Face for the MLM training, in effect domain-adapting the encoder weights of each pretrained model. We trained the models on the MLM task in 10 epochs with a learning rate of $2e-5$, the AdamW optimizer with a Cross Entropy loss, and a batch size of 16. We kept the best model in terms of the lowest loss on the development set. We did not perform next sentence prediction (NSP) since our current downstream tasks do not require the understanding of sentence pair relations; classification operates on the level of single text snippets and we use mean pooling for the downstream tasks. For both masked LM and subsequent finetuning on the downstream tasks, we set the maximum number of tokens to 128.

3.2 Finetuning on downstream tasks

For each of the downstream tasks we finetuned the off-the-shelf as well as the domain-adapted (see above) variants of the three pretrained models in the same way: we added a classification head to the encoder consisting of one feed-forward hidden layer with a *tanh* activation function, and a final linear output projection layer to the respective number

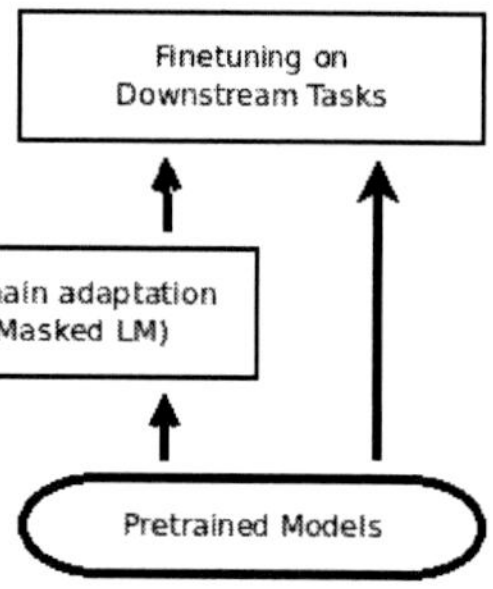

Figure 2: Experimental setup: we compared direct finetuning of the pretrained models on the downstream tasks vs. domain adapting the pretrained models and their subsequent finetuning.

of classes. Input to this head was the mean pooling over the hidden states of the last encoder layer to which we applied a dropout with probability 0.1.

Model finetuning was conducted in four epochs, by training on the training data and validating on the development data with a learning rate of $3e-5$, the AdamW optimizer with a weighted Cross Entropy loss, a batch size of 16 and without freezing the encoder layers. After the four epochs were completed we selected the model that performed best on the development set out of the four, in terms of Unweighted Average Recall (UAR), i.e. the mean value of the class-wise true positive rate; we subsequently evaluated this model on the held-out test data for the respective downstream task. Each such finetuning pass was repeated five times with different random seeds for each downstream task. Via the weighted loss for class balancing as well as via the UAR metric we aimed to address the imbalanced class distributions in our data.

4 Results

Table 2 reports for each BERT model the performace in terms of unweighted average F-score (UAF), in particular its mean and standard deviation over the five random seeds. F-score is the standard evaluation metric in NLP for classification tasks, and UAF expresses the class-wise averaged harmonic mean of precision and recall. We observed that the ranking of the models is similar regardless of expressing the performance scores in terms of UAF or UAR metric, i.e. the trend stays the same: domain-adapted models outperform their underlying pretrained model, i.e. the baseline. Domain adaptation (expressed by the *From-Adapted* column in the table) proved beneficial for all tested language models. If we compare these results with those obtained by the baseline models (expressed by the *From-Pretrained* column), we see that all models profited from domain adaptation roughly to the same extent. The overall low standard deviation values indicate that the findings are independent of the seed and thus robust.

BERT reached top performance on the three attribution tasks that are complex and thus time-consuming for human Slavist experts. The universal model *bert-base-multilingual-uncased* yielded very high performance and in two out of three tasks the best results. It was not outperformed by the two other models that had been created specifically for Cyrillic texts. The universal model is likely highly competitive due to drawbacks of the two Cyrillic models: the uncased *bert-base-slavic-cyrillic-upos* model was trained for token classification (part-of-speech tagging), so it performed suboptimal on our downstream tasks which need to operate on the basis of sequence classification; *bert-base-macedonian-bulgarian-cased* is based on a cased tokenizer, but casing is not consistent in our historical datasets.

4.1 Analysis of misclassifications

We assessed the classification output qualitatively, manually inspecting misclassifications made by *bert-base-multilingual-uncased.* In terms of attributing *region*, we saw that text snippets from East Slavic datasets got misclassified as South Slavic when they contained a token – e.g. вънезаапоу 'suddenly' – that already occurs in Old Church Slavic manuscripts dated to the 11th century, i.e. is of South Slavic origin, cf. Kurz (1958). Yet, what from a technical perspective is a misclassification, can have a significant value from the philological point of view: it might indicate – and in this particular case it indeed does – that a text snippet in a manuscript handed down in an East Slavic context has its roots in the South Slavic region. This is not surprising, given that the majority of Slavic religious texts were translations from Greek made on South Slavic soil and copied later in other regions.

In turn, a text snippet containing the token таже ('the same') was misclassified into the East Slavic region, but this word is indeed seen in both East Slavic and South Slavic texts, even in the earliest manuscripts, cf. Kurz (1958), despite its diachronical variation between East and South Slavic. During linguistic-historical development, the Proto-Indo-European cluster **dj* changed its phonetic

Task	Model	From-Pretrained	From-Adapted
manuscript	KoichiYasuoka/bert-base-slavic-cyrillic-upos	0.922 (0.004)	0.941 (0.003)
manuscript	anon-submission/mk-bert-base-macedonian-bulgarian-cased	0.935 (0.002)	0.961 (0.001)
manuscript	bert-base-multilingual-uncased	0.945 (0.002)	**0.962** (0.003)
century	KoichiYasuoka/bert-base-slavic-cyrillic-upos	0.952 (0.002)	0.965 (0.001)
century	anon-submission/mk-bert-base-macedonian-bulgarian-cased	0.961 (0.001)	**0.977** (0.002)
century	bert-base-multilingual-uncased	0.959 (0.001)	0.976 (0.001)
region	KoichiYasuoka/bert-base-slavic-cyrillic-upos	0.96 (0.002)	0.976 (0.001)
region	anon-submission/mk-bert-base-macedonian-bulgarian-cased	0.968 (0.001)	0.984 (0.001)
region	bert-base-multilingual-uncased	0.979 (0.002)	**0.986** (0.001)

Table 2: Performance scores on the three downstream tasks on directly finetuned models (*From-Pretrained*) that we regard as baseline vs. domain-adapted and subsequently finetuned models (*From-Adapted*), in terms of Unweighted Average F-score arithmetic mean values and standard deviations (in brackets) obtained from five random seeds.

form, in East Slavic languages developing into the simple consonant ж [ʒ] – a voiced post-alveolar fricative as in viSion –, cf. Trunte (2001), p. 186, while in South Slavic languages it remained with the cluster, realized as жд [ʒd] so that in South Slavic manuscripts one encounters the form тажде but the form таже is similarly common there.

Regarding chronological variation, 15th–16th and 18th century data misclassified as 10th–12th century contained phrasings (e.g. того ради и рече 'and it is that for/for this reason that he says'), which with regard to grammar and lexicon may actually be traced back to the 11th century. However, this specific string occurs with high-frequency and appears in numerous copied Church Slavic texts, and thereby has less profound interpretive implications. Concerning 11th century snippets misclassified as 15th-16th or 18th century material, we can exemplify the token пристоупиша ('they approached') that occurs in a snippet from a text translated in ca. 9th–10th cc., handed down in a manuscript hitherto dated to the last quarter of the 11th century and located in the Kyivan Principality. Since the orthography of the ending -а in the given grammatical form (*3PlAorIndAkt*) is more common in younger East Slavic manuscripts – the orthographical variant that had been in use in Old Church Slavic manuscripts was the *little yus'* grapheme ѧ, cf. Trunte (2001), p. 185 –, its attribution as 15th–16th century is comprehensible, but since this spelling was not unusual for manuscripts of the 11th–12th cc. either, the dating to the 15th-16th cc. cannot be postulated on the basis of this form.

Yet another example for variation involves the writing of the reflexive postfix -сѧ that can stand either directly adjacent to the word form or can be separated from it by a space; this variation however depends on modern editorial principles rather than on scribal usus, given the medieval *scriptio continua* practice. In particular, while adjacency is used in the contemporary edition of the 16th century *Apostolos* (ed. Besters-Dilger (2014)) as well as in the 18th century printed Elizabeth Bible (ed. 1751), likely influenced by its modern Russian (i.e. Eastern Slavic) continuation, we see that spacing is used in the modern edition of the *Codex Suprasliensis*, in line with typographical separation from the verbal stem in modern South Slavic languages. This orthographic discrepancy certainly implies some bias, implying that BERT's classification strategy is getting influenced by contemporary editorial principles represented in parts of the data.

4.2 Conclusions and future work

Our current pilot study set out to investigate the extent to which BERT can be used for provenance attribution on Pre-Modern Slavic manuscript data in terms of three coarse-grained text classification tasks that characterise temporal-spatial dimensions of historical, mainly liturgical and religious, language data. The aggregated dataset we employed in this study contains three axes of variation – time, region, manuscript –, allowing to perform analyses for identifying patterns between multiple variables that can play a role in language change. We experimented with domain adaptation of pretrained BERT models and reached overall high performance on the downstream text classification tasks. The results provide plausible insights into how BERT makes use of the data, even though we are aware that our initial approach bears limitations for comprehensive linguistic analyses: we showed examples that shed light on why temporal and regional variation in the texts lead to errors in the classification. For further studies on language change, we aim to make the trained models classify finer-grained phenomena and the labeled data more representative and then release these resources.

5 Limitations

Our current goal was to investigate the extent to which a generic BERT approach on the level of text snippets would be able to utilize data characteristics that encode in a heterogeneous way the provenance characteristics we are after. Such an approach is deliberately coarse-grained and is likely to be predominantly semantically-oriented. Our downstream tasks had classes that we were directly able to generate from the manuscript level. Since we lack ground truth provenance labels attributed on sub-manuscript level, we were aware that the current experimental setup would be suboptimal for acquiring results that would be describing linguistic specificities pointing out phonological, morphological, etc. features of linguistic change.

It is indeed the goal of our project to generate such expert labels in a data-driven way; for example, our task setup is getting extended to the token and to the character levels. We are also working on better token segmentation and expansion of the data in order to minimise potential manuscript biases in terms of orthography and content.

Ethics Statement

The authors fully acknowledge the ACL Ethics Policy and strongly commit to using their skills for the benefit of society, its members and the environment surrounding them.

Acknowledgements

The QuantiSlav project is funded from the EU's Recovery and Resilience Facility and by the Federal Ministry of Education and Research in accordance with the guidelines for funding projects to strengthen the data skills of young scientists (Grant number: 16DKWN123B).

References

Yannis Assael, Thea Sommerschield, and Jonathan Prag. 2019. Restoring ancient text using deep learning: a case study on Greek epigraphy. In *Proceedings of the 2019 Conference on Empirical Methods in Natural Language Processing and the 9th International Joint Conference on Natural Language Processing (EMNLP-IJCNLP)*, pages 6368–6375, Hong Kong, China. Association for Computational Linguistics.

David Bamman and Patrick J. Burns. 2020. Latin BERT: A contextual language model for classical philology.

Gabriel Bernier-Colborne, Cyril Goutte, and Serge Léger. 2019. Improving cuneiform language identification with BERT. In *Proceedings of the Sixth Workshop on NLP for Similar Languages, Varieties and Dialects*, pages 17–25, Ann Arbor, Michigan. Association for Computational Linguistics.

Juliane Besters-Dilger. 2014. *Kommentierter Apostolos. Volume 1.* Otto Sagner, Freiburg i. Br.

Jacob Devlin, Ming-Wei Chang, Kenton Lee, and Kristina Toutanova. 2019. BERT: Pre-training of deep bidirectional transformers for language understanding. In *Proceedings of the 2019 Conference of the North American Chapter of the Association for Computational Linguistics: Human Language Technologies, Volume 1 (Long and Short Papers)*, pages 4171–4186, Minneapolis, Minnesota. Association for Computational Linguistics.

Simon Gabay, Pedro Ortiz Suarez, Alexandre Bartz, Alix Chagué, Rachel Bawden, Philippe Gambette, and Benoît Sagot. 2022. From FreEM to D'AlemBERT: a Large Corpus and a Language Model for Early Modern French.

Md. Zahurul Islam, Roland Mittmann, and Alexander Mehler. 2011. Multilingualism in ancient texts: Language detection by example of old high german and old saxon. In *GSCL conference on Multilingual Resources and Multilingual Applications.*

Joseph Kurz. 1958. *Slovník jazyka staroslovenského: Lexikon linguae palaeoslovenicae.* Nakladatelství Českovlovenské Akademie ved, Prague.

Andrey Kutuzov and Lidia Pivovarova. 2021. RuShiftEval: a shared task on semantic shift detection for Russian. In *Computational linguistics and intellectual technologies: Papers from the annual conference Dialogue.*

Piroska Lendvai and Claudia Wick. 2022. Finetuning Latin BERT for Word Sense Disambiguation on the Thesaurus Linguae Latinae. In *Proc. of the Workshop Cognitive Aspects of the Lexicon (CogALex), co-located with Asia-Pacific Chapter of the Association for Computational Linguistics (AACL) and 10th International Joint Conference on Natural Language Processing (IJCNLP).*

Chaya Liebeskind and Shmuel Liebeskind. 2020. Deep learning for period classification of historical hebrew texts. *Journal of Data Mining & Digital Humanities*, 2020.

E. M. A. Manjavacas. 2022. Adapting vs. pre-training language models for historical languages. *Journal Of Data Mining & Digital Humanities, NLP4DH*, pages 1–19.

Peng Qi, Yuhao Zhang, Yuhui Zhang, Jason Bolton, and Christopher D. Manning. 2020. Stanza: A Python natural language processing toolkit for many human languages. In *Proceedings of the 58th Annual Meeting of the Association for Computational Linguistics: System Demonstrations.*

Iiro Rastas, Yann Ciarán Ryan, Iiro Tiihonen, Mohammadreza Qaraei, Liina Repo, Rohit Babbar, Eetu Mäkelä, Mikko Tolonen, and Filip Ginter. 2022. Explainable publication year prediction of eighteenth century texts with the BERT model. In *Proceedings of the 3rd Workshop on Computational Approaches to Historical Language Change*, pages 68–77, Dublin, Ireland. Association for Computational Linguistics.

Stefan Schweter, Luisa März, Katharina Schmid, and Erion Çano. 2022. hmBERT: Historical multilingual language models for named entity recognition.

Ilya Talev. 1973. *Some Problems of the Second South Slavic Influence in Russia*. Otto Sagner.

Nicolina Trunte. 2001. *Slavenskij jazyk: ein praktisches Lehrbuch des Kirchenslavischen in 30 Lektionen; zugleich eine Einführung in die slavische Philologie. Bd. 2, Mittel- und Neukirchenslavisch.* Slavistische Beiträge (494), Munich.

Nianheng Wu, Eric DeMattos, Kwok Him So, Pin-zhen Chen, and Çağrı Çöltekin. 2019. Language discrimination and transfer learning for similar languages: Experiments with feature combinations and adaptation. In *Proceedings of the Sixth Workshop on NLP for Similar Languages, Varieties and Dialects*, pages 54–63, Ann Arbor, Michigan. Association for Computational Linguistics.

Marcos Zampieri, Shervin Malmasi, Yves Scherrer, Tanja Samardžić, Francis Tyers, Miikka Silfverberg, Natalia Klyueva, Tung-Le Pan, Chu-Ren Huang, Radu Tudor Ionescu, Andrei M. Butnaru, and Tommi Jauhiainen. 2019. A report on the third VarDial evaluation campaign. In *Proceedings of the Sixth Workshop on NLP for Similar Languages, Varieties and Dialects*, pages 1–16, Ann Arbor, Michigan. Association for Computational Linguistics.

Representing and Computing Uncertainty in Phonological Reconstruction

Johann-Mattis List
MCL Chair / DLCE
University of Passau / MPI-EVA
Passau / Leipzig, Germany

Nathan W. Hill
Trinity Centre for Asian Studies
University of Dublin
Dublin, Ireland

Robert Forkel
DLCE
MPI-EVA
Leipzig, Germany

Frederic Blum
DLCE
MPI-EVA
Leipzig

Abstract

Despite the inherently fuzzy nature of reconstructions in historical linguistics, most scholars do not represent their uncertainty when proposing proto-forms. With the increasing success of recently proposed approaches to automating certain aspects of the traditional comparative method, the formal representation of proto-forms has also improved. This formalization makes it possible to address both the representation and the computation of uncertainty. Building on recent advances in supervised phonological reconstruction, during which an algorithm learns how to reconstruct words in a given proto-language relying on previously annotated data, and inspired by improved methods for automated word prediction from cognate sets, we present a new framework that allows for the representation of uncertainty in linguistic reconstruction and also includes a workflow for the computation of fuzzy reconstructions from linguistic data.

1 Introduction

Phonological reconstruction refers to the techniques that linguists use to reconstruct the phonological and phonetic shape of word forms or morphemes in unattested ancestral languages. Although the results are inherently provisional (as witnessed by the changes in the fable by Schleicher 1868 over the last decades, cf. Lühr 2008), linguists typically present their results in the form of discrete phonological units, giving the impression of exactitude and rigor. Thus, although phonological reconstructions change with time as the knowledge or assumptions about a language family change, scholars typically provide the results as if they were final. By focusing on the uncertainty of phonological reconstructions, we aim to provide a new framework by which uncertainty in phonological reconstruction can be a) represented (in etymological databases or etymological dictionaries), and b) computed (from etymological datasets). Representation and computation have several benefits. On the one hand, improved representations allow for a more refined reconstruction practice that more directly and consistently indicates the weak points in a reconstruction. On the other hand, computing the uncertainty of a given reconstruction system allows scholars to refine their reconstructions by helping them to identify weak points and potential errors in their cognate judgments or correspondence patterns.

The traditional techniques for phonological reconstruction, by which ancestral word forms are reconstructed from observed words with the help of the comparative method, are of crucial importance for historical language comparison. Despite the inherently fuzzy nature of reconstructions, most scholars have so far hesitated to systematically represent their uncertainty when proposing proto-forms (for an exception see Baxter and Sagart 2014), and discussions of uncertainty are very spurious in the literature. With the increasing success of recently proposed techniques by which certain aspects of the traditional comparative method can be automated, the formal representation of words, morphemes, cognate sets, and proto-forms has also improved. This makes it possible to address the problems of both the representation and the computation of uncertainty. Supervised approaches have led to major advances in automated phonological reconstruction; scholars provide a partially annotated dataset in which a certain number of proto-forms are already provided, and an algorithm is then trained on the data in order to propose new proto-forms for so far unobserved cognate sets. This task is very similar to the task of cognate reflex prediction, in which the word forms which

Proceedings of the 4th Workshop on Computational Approaches to Historical Language Change, pages 22–32
December 6, 2023 ©2023 Association for Computational Linguistics

have to be predicted are not proto-forms, but word forms from descendant languages, and algorithms have to predict the reflex of a cognate set in a given language based on the sound correspondence patterns and the reflexes of the cognate set in related languages. In the past decade, scholars have proposed quite a few new methods for both cognate reflex prediction and supervised phonological reconstruction.

Meloni et al. (2021) tested recurrent neural networks on a dataset of Romance languages originally compiled by Ciobanu and Dinu (2013), reporting very promising results on supervised approaches. This study was later extended by Kim et al. (2023), who used a Transformer architecture (Vaswani et al., 2017) and additionally tested the approach on a dataset of Chinese dialect varieties. List et al. (2022b) proposed a new framework based on support vector machines to predict proto-forms from phonetic alignments, which they tested on six different datasets covering several different language families. In a recently organized Shared Task on cognate reflex prediction (List et al., 2022c), Kirov et al. (2022) proposed two methods that outperformed alternative approaches, one originally designed for the handling of place name pronunciations in Japan (Jones et al., 2022), and one designed for the restoration of digital images in which pixels are missing (Liu et al., 2018). All in all, the most successful methods in the shared task all showed good performance: when retaining 90% of the data for training, the methods differed on average by one sound from the attested word forms.

While the task of unsupervised phonological reconstruction, where algorithms would reconstruct a proto-language from cognate sets from scratch, has not been sufficiently investigated so far (an early approach by Bouchard-Côté et al. 2013 was only tested on Austronesian languages with the code never published), we can see that phonological reconstruction in a supervised setting has become a real option and could be integrated into computer-assisted workflows, in which scholars first annotate parts of their data, then compute new reconstructions automatically, and later refine them again.

With respect to the representation of uncertainty in reconstruction, linguists typically adopt ad-hoc solutions for individual language families or individual enterprises. In Indo-European studies, scholars express their uncertainty with respect to the three laryngeals ($*h_1$, $*h_2$ or h_3) by writing a capital **H*. In their reconstruction of Old Chinese, Baxter and Sagart (2014) employ a complex notation system that puts uncertain parts of their reconstruction into brackets (with *-[n]* meaning, for example, that the reconstruction could be either the final *-n* or to *-r*). In other cases, scholars mention alternative reconstructions only in comments. While both manual and automated methods are inherently fuzzy with respect to phonological reconstruction, so far, few methods have explicitly embraced fuzziness, trying to present uncertainty in reconstructions explicitly. An exception was the method of List (2019), which offered degrees of uncertainty in the imputation of missing sounds in aligned cognate sets, but the fuzzy reconstructions were not further evaluated or inspected.

2 Materials

We work with three etymological datasets which are coded in Cross-Linguistic Data Formats (`https://cldf.clld.org`, Forkel et al. 2018; Forkel and List 2020), following the Lexibank workflow for the handling of multilingual wordlists (List et al., 2022a). The Burmish dataset consists of 8 Burmish languages, and 269 etymologies that are reflected in at least two descendant languages with a total of 1,442 reflexes. The data was originally compiled by Gong and Hill (2020) and later converted to CLDF formats by List and Forkel (2022) and further refined for the present study. It is accessible online at `https://github.com/lexibank/hillburmish`. The Karen dataset consists of 10 Karenic languages, and offers 365 etymologies originally proposed by Luangthongkum (2019), which are reflected in at least 2 languages with a total of 2,866 reflexes. The data was also compiled for the study by List and Forkel (2022) and slightly refined for this study. It is accessible online at `https://github.com/lexibank/luangthongkumkaren`. The Panoan dataset consists of 20 Panoan languages, and includes the reconstruction of 514 cognate sets across 470 concepts proposed by Oliveira (2014). In total, the dataset features 7,305 reflexes. During the digitization of this dataset, all cognate sets were manually aligned (Blum and Barrientos, 2023). It is accessible online at `https://github.com/pano-tacanan-history/oliveiraprotopanoan`.

Reconstruction	Initial	Nucleus	Coda	Tone
Predictor 1	d	u	-	^{2}
Predictor 2	d	u	-	^{1}
Predictor 3	d	u	-	^{1}
Predictor 4	d	u	-	^{4}
Predictor 5	d	u	-	^{4}
Predictor 6	d	u	-	^{4}
Predictor 7	d	u	-	^{4}
Predictor 8	d	u	-	^{4}
Predictor 9	d	u	-	^{4}
Predictor 10	^{ʔ}t	u	-	^{4}
Summary	d:90|^{ʔ}t:10	u:100	-:100	^{4}:80|^{1}:20|^{2}:10
Proto-Form	d	u		^{2}

Table 1: Predictions for "belly" (cognate set 80) in Burmish. The table contrasts predicted word forms for all 10 different predictors, along with the aggregated representation (row Summary) and contrasted with the reconstruction provided by the experts (Proto-Form).

3 Methods

3.1 Representing Fuzzy Reconstructions

We follow Bodt and List (2022) who represent multiple options for the prediction of an individual sound by using the pipe symbol | as a separator for the different options. The symbol is often used in the meaning of "or" in regular expressions, which makes it particularly apt to represent uncertainty, since we can interpret a fictitious proto-form like [p a|i t] as a kind of a regular expression that matches both the form [p a t] and [p i t]. Note that this notation needs to be used with some care when more than one sound is treated as uncertain, since the resulting expression will always match the Cartesian product of the uncertain sounds. Thus, a fictitious proto-form [p a|i t|d] would match four distinct proto-forms, namely the forms [p a t], [p i t], [p a d], and [p i d]. If scholars want to explicitly propose two different proto-forms only, e.g. [p a t] vs. [p i d], our notation cannot be used. We recommend instead to assume two distinct forms, which can both be proposed as possible proto-forms for a given cognate set. Our fuzzy notation is thus only reserved for cases where the uncertainty is independent of contextual information that could be derived from the proto-form.

3.2 Computing Fuzzy Reconstructions

Our method for the creation of fuzzy reconstructions is straightforward. We expand the framework for supervised phonological reconstruction proposed by List et al. (2022b), by drawing several samples from the same data, in which different parts of the forms are intentionally ignored. While the framework of List et al. starts from a training set in which proto-forms are provided and then a model is trained that can be used to predict proto-forms for data that has not been seen before, we draw multiple samples, drop a certain number of words from each sample, and use the method by List et al. to train the "classifier" that can be used to predict proto-forms from aligned cognate sets. Since we drop data in each of the samples, each sample will produce slightly different proto-forms, depending on the data which has been randomly ignored. The different proto-forms offered may point to problems in the original data, or reveal cognate sets that in fact underspecify the proto-form.

While fuzziness could of course also be directly computed from the direct output of most approaches to supervised phonological reconstruction (since most of them work in a probabilistic manner that allows one to return not only the one and only best result, but also a certain range of candidates, see also Fourrier et al. 2021), our approach of using subsets of the original data has the clear advantage that it does not take the correctness of the original data for granted. When taking all data at once, it is difficult to spot irregularities in the data itself. When taking subsets, however, we test the robustness of the reconstructions for individual cognate sets. If the reconstruction, for example, depends on only one reflex, but this reflex is then discarded due to the subsampling in one particular

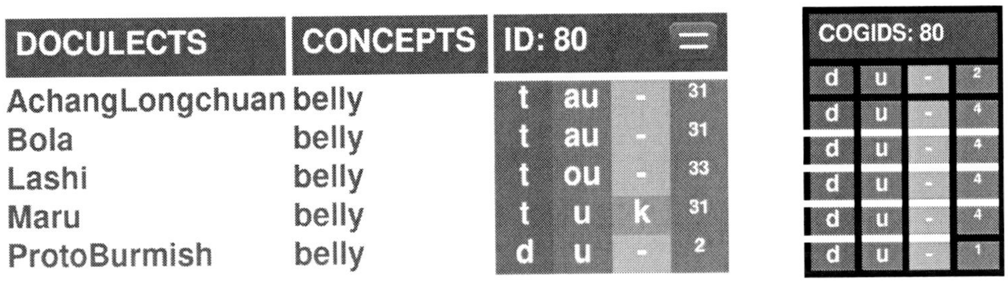

(a) Phonetic alignment of all word forms (including the proto-form). (b) Quintile representation.

Figure 1: Contrasting the alignment representation with the quintile representation of the fuzzy reconstruction in the EDICTOR tool.

run, the resulting reconstruction may turn out to be different, and this particular difference would then be accounted for in this trial and surface as an uncertainty.

In the default settings of our method, we create 10 proto-form predictors from the annotated data and remove 10% of the word forms in each of the samples. When creating an individual reconstruction, we feed our method with a concrete cognates set and then use all 10 predictors to predict proto-forms. The predictions are then summarized, and we count for each position in the original alignment how often which proto-sound occurs. These fuzzy reconstructions are then represented in the form of a sequence in which a column of the alignment is represented by at least one sound, and each possible sound is provided with the frequency in which it occurs in our 10 samples. Table 1 provides an example from the Burmish data for the fuzzy prediction procedure and the specific output produced by our method.

Since certain irregularities in the input data may be filtered from the different samples, irregular patterns which could lead an algorithm to propose erroneous proto-forms will be filtered out, and in this way the overall robustness of individual reconstruction can be tested.

3.3 Visualizing Fuzzy Reconstructions

Apart from the technical representation shown above, we have experimented with different ways to represent uncertainty or "fuzziness" in the tools we use to annotate etymological data. Since the manual curation of the cognate sets was carried out with the help of EDICTOR (List 2023, `https://digling.org/edictor`), a web-based tool for the creation and curation of etymological datasets, we extended the EDICTOR representation of phonetic alignments by adding a representation which we call quintile-representation. In this representation, we represent the frequencies observed in the ten predictions with the help of a table with five rows, in which each row represents the attested symbols (converted from 10 to 5, to keep the table representation neat). This is shown in Figure 1.

3.4 Implementation

The method of fuzzy reconstruction is implemented as Version 1.4.1 of the LingRex software package (`https://pypi.org/project/lingrex`, List and Forkel 2023b, which is itself an extension of the LingPy software package for quantitative tasks in historical linguistics (`https://pypi.org/project/lingpy`, List and Forkel 2023a). The quintile visualization is implemented as part of Version 2.2 of the EDICTOR tool (`https://digling.org/edictor`, List 2023). The supplementary material shows how the package can be used and applied to the data, it is curated on GitHub (`https://github.com/lingpy/fuzzy/releases/tag/v1.1`) and has been archived with Zenodo (`https://doi.org/10.5281/zenodo.10007475`).

4 Evaluation

Since we do not have a clear account on what constitutes a good "fuzzy reconstruction" and what constitutes a bad one, we closely analyzed the fuzzy reconstructions proposed for the three datasets and further investigated the results both quantitatively and qualitatively. In the following, we will thus report on the proportion of fuzzy reconstructions per datasets, the most frequently confused sounds in fuzzy reconstructions, and then report on major problems in the original data revealed through a

Dataset	Prediction	Count	Proportion	Alignment Size
Burmish	correct	154	0.57	4.13
	false	115	0.43	4.29
	certain	199	0.74	4.13
	uncertain	70	0.26	4.39
Karen	correct	246	0.65	4.03
	false	133	0.35	4.27
	certain	310	0.82	4.05
	uncertain	69	0.18	4.41
Panoan	correct	405	0.79	4.25
	false	109	0.21	5.14
	certain	465	0.90	4.37
	uncertain	49	0.10	5.14

Table 2: Summary scores for the Burmish, Karenic, and Panoan predictions. Correct predictions refer to all those predictions which are identical with the reconstruction in the gold standard and which show no uncertainty. False predictions are those which show uncertainty or which are not identical with the proposed predictions in the gold standard. Certain predictions are those in which all ten trials on differently distorted data show the same results for a given proto-form. Uncertain predictions are those, accordingly, in which we observe differences. Alignment size refers to the size of the alignment of the cognate sets (conducted automatically).

close inspection of the fuzzy reconstructions proposed for the Burmish dataset.

4.1 Proportion of Fuzzy Reconstructions

As a first test of our approach, we computed fuzzy reconstructions from the three datasets and then compared whether (a) the reconstructions were fuzzy at all, and (b) to what extent they diverged from the proposed reconstructions. We explicitly chose a setting where we train and test the method on the same dataset, since we were not interested in the evaluation of the reconstruction method (which performs fairly well, but not perfect) but in the degree to which conclusions were based on the data in its entirety or different parts of it. For each proto-form in the three datasets, we computed fuzzy reconstructions, from which we created consensus reconstructions using the notation shown in Table 1. For each proposed reconstruction we tested (a) if the reconstruction had conflicts (i.e. if it was "fuzzy"), and (b) if it was not fuzzy, if it coincided with the reconstruction proposed by the linguist.

For the Burmish data, consisting of a total of 269 reconstructions, we arrived at the results reported in Table 2 (top). As can be seen from the table, the proportion of words reconstructed correctly by the approach and proportion of words that were reconstructed as "certain" (with no variation) is much larger than the proportion of false or uncertain reconstructions. Since a correct reconstruction has to be certain, it is not surprising that these numbers are similar, but the small difference of 57% vs. 74% shows that only a small part of the reconstructions identified as "certain" are also wrong. We find a small difference with respect to the alignment size (the number of words of which alignments for individual proto-forms are reconstructed) between correctly and falsely reconstructed proto-form, but due to the restricted syllable structure of Burmish languages, we do not find huge differences here. Additional studies are needed to find out what influences the certainty of automated reconstructions.

The results for the Karen data, consisting of 365 cognate sets, are shown in Table 2 (middle). As can be seen here, the number of correctly reconstructed proto-forms as well as the number for certain proto-forms are both higher than in the case of the Burmish data. One factor which may have contributed to this is that exceptional reflexes in this dataset have been manually identified and marked as such (as part of ongoing research), which means that certain irregularities in the data did not negatively impact the predictions. In contrast to the Burmish data, the differences in alignment size for correct vs. false proto-forms and certain vs. uncertain ones are more pronounced in this dataset.

The results for the Panoan data in Table 2 show some interesting differences. Of the total of 514 cognate sets, 405 (79%) are reconstructed correctly, a considerably higher number than for the other

Burmish			Karen			Panoan		
Sound A	**Sound B**	**Freq.**	**Sound A**	**Sound B**	**Freq.**	**Sound A**	**Sound B**	**Freq.**
^{4}	^{1}	14	n	n̥	18	n	r^{n}	24
^{4}	^{3}	9	n	ɴ	14	k	-	13
i	e	8	ɴ	ŋ	10	r^{n}	~	10
ŋ	-	7	^{55}	^{0}	9	-	t^{r}	10
^{2}	^{3}	7	l	l̥	8	n	-	9
-	ʔ	7	m̥	m	6	r^{n}	-	6
^{ʔ}s	s	6	-	ʔ˺	6	k	t^{r}	6
^{ʔ}k	g	6	^{1}	^{0}	5	t	t^{r}	5
^{2}	^{4}	6	k	g	5	t	-	5
r	j	6	ʔ˺	ʔ	4	r^{n}	r	5

Table 3: Frequently confused sounds in the three datasets. Frequency refers to the number of cognate sets in which the automated reconstruction proposed alternative proto-sounds.

datasets. The number of reconstructions that are provided as "certain" is also higher (90%) than for the other datasets. There is also a considerable difference in alignment size: The alignment size for correct (4.25) and "certain" (4.37) reconstructions is much lower than for false (5.14) and "uncertain" (5.14) reconstructions. Here, a larger alignment size arises as a possible source influencing the correctness and certainty of automated reconstructions. This illustrates that it may be worthwhile to investigate more closely how the reconstructions differ between different language families and between alignments of different sizes within the language families.

4.2 Frequently Confused Sounds

Each fuzzy reconstruction proposes at least two alternative sounds for one proto-segment in a given proto-form. Investigating these more closely in order to understand which sounds are frequently confused by the analysis, allows us to gain insights into those sounds in the proto-languages which are particularly difficult to reconstruct. Table 3 provides the 10 most frequently confused sound pairs in both datasets (our workflow reports all of them).

As can be seen from the individual results for the Karen and Burmish data, the particular problems are quite different across both datasets and cannot be directly compared with each other. A major difficulty in the Karenic data is the reconstruction of voiceless sonorants ([n̥], [l̥], [m̥], etc.), which the author proposes on the basis of the tonal development in some of the descendant languages (Luangthongkum, 2019). Since there are quite a few exceptions with respect to the tonal development, we find that the original reconstruction itself cannot always indicate clearly whether a proto-sound should be voiced or voiceless, which is at times marked by putting the h, which is used to mark a sonorant as voiceless in parentheses (resulting in forms like (h)n-, ibid.). The confusion of the tone marked as [^{0}] with other tones results from our annotation practice of certain weak syllables, in which originally no tone was reconstructed. Since we wanted to indicate a tone nevertheless, to fill the slot in our alignment, the [^{0}] thus marks an underspecified value, which – as the fuzzy reconstructions show – might just as well be given a more concrete reconstruction.

In the Burmish data, on the other hand, we find three major types of confusion. The first relates to the reconstruction of tones. The reconstruction here is often predicted by the nature of the final consonants, which are not actively used in the automated reconstruction method. This may explain the confusion in this case. The second case relates to the reconstruction of gaps (marked by the symbol [-]), which are often confused with sounds occurring in coda position, such as [ŋ], [r], or [ʔ]. The confusion of pre-glottalized initials like [^{ʔ}s] and [^{ʔ}k] and their non-glottalized counterparts also results from the fact that the reconstruction of pre-glottalized initials depends on the vowels that appear as reflexes in certain Burmish languages. Since this information was not taken into account by our automated method, it is not surprising that results may vary here. The confusion resulting from information that is not represented in the individual column of an alignment but in other parts shows

Achang	m̥	ʐ	a	ŋ	^{31}
Old Burmese	k^{h}	j	i	j	^{5}
Fuzzy Proto-Form	^{ʔ}m:70|^{ʔ}k:30	r:50|j:30|-:20	i:80|a:20	-:100	^{2}:100
Proto Burmish	^{ʔ}k	j	i		^{2}

(a) Erroneous cognate judgments in cognate set #288 “dung (horse)” for Achang.

Achang	s	ɔ	ʔ	^{55}
Atsi	p	a	n	^{21}
Bola	x	a	ʔ	^{55}
Lashi	ʃ	ɔ̱	ʔ	^{55}
Maru	s	o	ʔ	^{55}
Rangoon	tθ	ɑ	-	^{53}
Xiandao	s	ɔ	ʔ	^{55}
Fuzzy Proto-Form	^{ʔ}s:70|s:30	a:100	k:100	^{4}:100
Proto Burmish	^{ʔ}s	a	k	^{4}

(b) Context-dependency of individual patterns in cognate set #536 “shy, be / bashful”.

Achang	ts	ɔ	-	^{31}
Atsi	s	i	k	^{55}
Bola	t	a	-	^{31}
Lashi	l	ə	ŋ	^{55}
Maru	ts	ɔ	-	
Old Burmese	c	a	-	^{55}
Rangoon	s^{h}	ɑ̃	-	^{53}
Xiandao	s	ɔ	ŋ	^{55}
Fuzzy Proto-Form	dz:100	a:100	-:90|ŋ:10	^{2}:100
Proto Burmish	dz	a	-	^{2}

(c) Deep and unclear etymologies in cognate set #93 “granddaughter”.

Atsi	m	j	i̱	-	^{55}
Bola	m	-	ə̱i	-	^{31}
Lashi	m	j	e̱:i	-	^{53}
Old Burmese	m	-	i	j.ʔ	^{3}
Rangoon	m	-	i	-	^{53}
Xiandao	n	-	i	-	^{35}
Fuzzy Proto-Form	m:100	-:100	e:90|i:10	-:100	^{3}:100
Proto Burmish	m	-	i	-	^{3}

(d) Systematic ambiguities in particular languages in cognate set #414 “forget”.

Table 4: Examples for causes of fuzziness in Burmish reconstructions.

that additional analyses in which we take the vowel information in the Burmish languages and the tonal information in the Karenic languages into account would be useful in the future.

The confused sounds for the Panoan data fall mainly into two groups, (a) word-final stops [k], [t], and [tʳ], and (b) word-final nasal and liquid consonants [n], [rⁿ], and [r]. Interestingly, those cases are either described as uncertain due to missing data by the original author (word-final nasals), or are the most debated feature of the reconstruction (word-final stops instead of three-syllabic words with an open syllable). The word-final sonorants are described by the author of the dataset as being uncertain due to the lack of reflexes in Kaxararí, a nearly undescribed Panoan language which retains the contrast of word-final [r] and [n]. This is the main source of confusion for [n], [rⁿ], and [r], but also for some of the word-final stops. Here, the confusion primarily arises because the reconstructions are proposed based on reflexes of only a few languages, which often do not provide sufficient evidence for identifying the phonemic nature of the reflex in the proto-language. Our method thus correctly identifies the cases in which the provided reconstructions should be considered "fuzzy", given their uncertain nature. It also validates the large part of correct reconstructions.

4.3 Detailed Examples for Burmish

A closer inspection of discrepancies in the Burmish data reveals four major kinds of problems, namely (1) problems resulting from problematic cognate judgments in our data, (2) problems resulting from the context-dependency of reconstructions which our automated reconstruction method does not (yet) account for, (3) problems resulting from deep etymologies which are not (yet) well understood, and (4) problems resulting from some systematic and so far not clearly understood ambiguities in particular languages.

4.3.1 Problematic Cognate Judgments

The method allows us to identify quite a few cases where individual cognate judgments turned out to be erroneous and should be modified in future versions of our data. As an example, consider cognate set #288 "dung (horse)" in our Burmish data, shown in Table 4 (a). That erroneous cognate judgments occur in larger etymological projects is inevitable to some degree. Here, our method for the reconstruction of "fuzzy" proto-forms directly helps us to identify and eliminate these problems in future releases of our data.

4.3.2 Context-Dependency of Reconstructions

While phonological reconstruction can, in the majority of the cases, be successfully carried out by considering individual correspondence patterns alone, there are certain cases where it is not enough to look at a pattern in isolation. What needs to be done instead is to evaluate the pattern in combination with other patterns from the same alignment. Although our method for automatic phonological reconstruction was designed in such a way that it can in theory account for this context-dependency of individual reconstructions, we did not take specific and known processes of sound change in the Burmish and the Karenic data into account, when applying our method to the data. This was done intentionally, since we wanted to see how far we can get with a unified approach. Individual reconstruction errors and cases of uncertainty in the automated reconstruction, however, show that context-dependency should be accounted for in future applications of our approach.

As an example for the problems resulting from ignoring context-dependencies, Table 4 (b) shows the reconstruction for the cognate set #536 "shy, be / bashful" in the Burmish data. As we can see, Lashi has a tense vowel (indicated by the bar under the vowel, shaded in gray in the table). Tense vowels are taken as evidence for the reconstruction of pre-glottalized initials in Proto-Burmish, while the correspondence pattern of the initial itself does not provide concrete evidence for the presence or absence of pre-glottalization. As a result, we can see that the automated method is uncertain, proposing a pre-glottalized initial in 70% of the cases, and a plain initial in 30%.

List and Forkel (2022) have described in detail, how context-dependency can be accounted for by means of "extended alignments" or "multi-tiered sequence representations". Future studies are needed to test how well these work to handle the Burmish (and also the Karenic) data.

4.3.3 Etymologies with Unclear Variation

There are a couple of cognate sets where we have in principle no doubts that the words in question are cognates, but we have problems to understand the etymological processes in full. These deep etymologies with unclear variation are usually of great importance when it comes to advancing existing reconstruction systems. However, since they may well reflect processes predating the history of the language family in question, the solution may only be achieved when taking more languages from higher clades of the language family in question into account.

As an example, consider Table 4 (c), showing alignments and reconstructions for cognate set #93 "granddaughter". While it is possible that all forms are cognate, it is hard to decide for sure, given that individual languages show reflexes which do not follow our expectations. Thus the initial [l-] in Lashi does not fit the pattern at all, and from the pattern, we have evidence for three different finals in the data. Future work may either show that we have to refine the cognate assignment of individual words in this pattern, or we may find solutions in certain etymological processes that counteract regular sound change.

4.3.4 Systematic Ambiguities in Languages

As a final type of difficulty, there are cases where we have clear ambiguities in individual languages which we cannot (yet) resolve and explain. As an example, Table 4 (d) shows ambiguities for the reconstruction of the vowel nucleus in the cognate set #414 "forget", where our reconstruction proposes **i*, while the automated method sees more evidence for **e* (90%) and less evidence for **i* (10%). The evidence from the correspondence pattern is difficult to interpret. While Old Burmese points to an **i*, Bola and Lashi point to an **e*. The fuzzy reconstruction approach thus correctly points to the ambiguity of the pattern in the light of our data.

5 Conclusion

In this study, we have introduced some novel ideas regarding the handling of uncertainty in phonological reconstruction in historical linguistics. We have tried to show that it may be useful to transparently record uncertainty not only in classical reconstructions but also in reconstructions proposed by automated approaches.

These considerations resulted in the proposal of a new framework for fuzzy reconstructions that allows one to compute fuzzy reconstructions from annotated comparative wordlists. Applying this framework to three datasets, two from the Sino-Tibetan language family (Burmish and Karenic), as well as on the Panoan language family, we have shown how the framework can be used to compute the degree of uncertainty in a given dataset, how frequently confused sounds can be computed, and how an individual inspection of the data reveals major classes of errors in the original data.

In the future, we hope to refine our current approach in three ways. First, we want to enhance the individual automatic reconstructions for the Burmish data and the Karenic data by taking the context of important sounds into account. Second, we want to enhance our data by correcting cases where we identified problematic cognate judgments. Third, we want to apply our method to more data from other language families in order to see how the approach performs there.

Supplementary Material

Supplementary material needed to replicate the experiments shown here, including data and code, has been curated on GitHub (`https://github.com/lingpy/fuzzy/releases/tag/v1.1`) and archived with Zenodo (`https://doi.org/10.5281/zenodo.10007475`).

Limitations

Our approach comes with some limitations. First, since the computation depends on the original data, fuzzy cognates do not only reflect true cases of uncertainty (where scholars would assess that the evidence is not enough to decide for one particular among several sounds) but can also be due to errors in the originally coded data. Second, since we use a specific procedure of grouping sounds in those cases where a proto-sound does not correspond to any sound in the descendant data,[1] our automated reconstruction approach currently may reconstruct phonotactically incorrect proto-forms. These forms may consist, for example, of two identical finals. Third, as also discussed in the study, context-dependencies which are not explicitly handled in the reconstruction procedure may yield ambiguities even in those cases, where we know they should not occur. Fourth, so far, our experiments have only been dealing with alignments that were computed automatically. Manually annotated alignments have not yet been tested.

[1] This is labelled *trimming* in List et al. 2022b, but the term does not seem a good choice, given that trimming in biology refers to cases where entire columns in an alignment are dropped, see Blum and List 2023.

Ethics Statement

Our data are taken from publicly available sources. There are no ethical issues or conflicts of interest in this work that we would know of at the time of writing.

Acknowledgements

This project was supported by the ERC Consolidator Grant ProduSemy (PI Johann-Mattis List, Grant No. 101044282, see https://doi.org/10.3030/101044282) and the Max Planck Research Grant CALC³ (https://calc.digling.org, PI Johann-Mattis List). Views and opinions expressed are however those of the author(s) only and do not necessarily reflect those of the European Union or the European Research Council Executive Agency (nor any other funding agencies involved). Neither the European Union nor the granting authority can be held responsible for them. We thank the anonymous reviewers for helpful comments and all people who share their data openly, so we can use it in our research.

References

William H. Baxter and Laurent Sagart. 2014. *Old Chinese. A new reconstruction.* Oxford University Press, Oxford.

Frederic Blum and Carlos Barrientos. 2023. A new dataset with phonological reconstructions in CLDF. *Computer-Assisted Language Comparison in Practice*, 6(6).

Frederic Blum and Johann-Mattis List. 2023. Trimming phonetic alignments improves the inference of sound correspondence patterns from multilingual wordlists. In *Proceedings of the 5th Workshop on Research in Computational Linguistic Typology and Multilingual NLP*, pages 52–64, Dubrovnik, Croatia. Association for Computational Linguistics.

Timotheus Adrianus Bodt and Johann-Mattis List. 2022. Reflex prediction. a case study of western kho-bwa. *Diachronica*, 39(1):1–38.

Alexandre Bouchard-Côté, David Hall, Thomas L. Griffiths, and Dan Klein. 2013. Automated reconstruction of ancient languages using probabilistic models of sound change. *Proceedings of the National Academy of Sciences of the United States of America*, 110(11):4224–4229.

Alina Maria Ciobanu and Liviu P. Dinu. 2013. Automatic detection of cognates using orthographic alignment. In *Proceedings of the 52nd Annual Meeting of the Association for Computational Linguistics (Short Papers)*, pages 99–105.

Robert Forkel and Johann-Mattis List. 2020. Cldfbench. give your cross-linguistic data a lift. In *Proceedings of the Twelfth International Conference on Language Resources and Evaluation*, pages 6997–7004, Luxembourg. European Language Resources Association (ELRA).

Robert Forkel, Johann-Mattis List, Simon J. Greenhill, Christoph Rzymski, Sebastian Bank, Michael Cysouw, Harald Hammarström, Martin Haspelmath, Gereon A. Kaiping, and Russell D. Gray. 2018. Cross-Linguistic Data Formats, advancing data sharing and re-use in comparative linguistics. *Scientific Data*, 5(180205):1–10.

Clémentine Fourrier, Rachel Bawden, and Benoît Sagot. 2021. Can cognate prediction be modelled as a low-resource machine translation task? In *Findings of the Association for Computational Linguistics: ACL-IJCNLP 2021*, pages 847–861, Online. Association for Computational Linguistics.

Xun Gong and Nathan W. Hill. 2020. *Materials for an Etymological Dictionary of Burmish.* Zenodo, Geneva.

Llion Jones, Richard Sproat, and Haruko Ishikawa. 2022. Helpful neighbors: Leveraging geographic neighbors to aid in placename pronunciation. In preparation.

Young Min Kim, Kalvin Chang, Chenxuan Cui, and David R. Mortensen. 2023. Transformed protoform reconstruction. In *Proceedings of the 61st Annual Meeting of the Association for Computational Linguistics (Volume 2: Short Papers)*, pages 24–38, Toronto, Canada. Association for Computational Linguistics.

Christo Kirov, Richard Sproat, and Alexander Gutkin. 2022. Mockingbird at the SIGTYP 2022 Shared Task: Two types of models for the prediction of cognate reflexes. In *The Fourth Workshop on Computational Typology and Multilingual NLP*, Online. Association for Computational Linguistics.

Johann-Mattis List. 2019. Automatic inference of sound correspondence patterns across multiple languages. *Computational Linguistics*, 45(1):137–161.

Johann-Mattis List. 2023. *EDICTOR. A web-based tool for creating, editing, and publishing etymological datasets [Software, Version 2.1.0].* MCL Chair at the University of Passau, Passau.

Johann-Mattis List and Robert Forkel. 2022. Automated identification of borrowings in multilingual wordlists [version 3; peer review: 4 approved]. *Open Research Europe*, 1(79):1–11.

Johann-Mattis List and Robert Forkel. 2023a. *LingPy. A Python library for quantitative tasks in historical linguistics [Software Library, Version 2.6.11].* Max Planck Institute for Evolutionary Anthropology, Leipzig.

Johann-Mattis List and Robert Forkel. 2023b. *LingRex: Linguistic reconstruction with LingPy [Software, Version 1.4.2]*. Max Planck Institute for Evolutionary Anthropology, Leipzig.

Johann-Mattis List, Robert Forkel, Simon J. Greenhill, Christoph Rzymski, Johannes Englisch, and Russell D. Gray. 2022a. Lexibank, a public repository of standardized wordlists with computed phonological and lexical features. *Scientific Data*, 9(316):1–31.

Johann-Mattis List, Nathan W. Hill, and Robert Forkel. 2022b. A new framework for fast automated phonological reconstruction using trimmed alignments and sound correspondence patterns. In *Proceedings of the 3rd Workshop on Computational Approaches to Historical Language Change*, pages 89–96, Dublin. Association for Computational Linguistics.

Johann-Mattis List, Ekatarina Vylomova, Robert Forkel, Nathan Hill, and Ryan D. Cotterell. 2022c. The SIGTYP shared task on the prediction of cognate reflexes. In *Proceedings of the 4th Workshop on Computational Typology and Multilingual NLP*, pages 52–62, Seattle. Association for Computational Linguistics, Max Planck Institute for Evolutionary Anthropology.

Guilin Liu, Fitsum A. Reda, Kevin J. Shih, Ting-Chun Wang, Andrew Tao, and Bryan Catanzaro. 2018. Image inpainting for irregular holes using partial convolutions. In *Proceedings of the 15th European Conference on Computer Vision (ECCV 2018)*, pages 89–105, Munich, Germany. Springer International Publishing. Preprint.

Theraphan Luangthongkum. 2019. A view on proto-karen phonology and lexicon. *Journal of the Southeast Asian Linguistics Society*, 12(1):i–lii.

Rosemarie Lühr. 2008. Von Berthold Delbrčk bis Ferdinand Sommer: Die Herausbildung der Indogermanistik in Jena [From Berthold Delbrück to Ferdinand Sommer: The Development of Indo-European Studies in Jena]. Vortrag im Rahmen einer Ringvorlesung zur Geschichte der Altertumswissenschaften (09.01.2008, FSU-Jena).

Carlo Meloni, Shauli Ravfogel, and Yoav Goldberg. 2021. Ab antiquo: Neural proto-language reconstruction. In *Proceedings of the 2021 Conference of the North American Chapter of the Association for Computational Linguistics: Human Language Technologies*, pages 4460–4473, Online. Association for Computational Linguistics.

Sanderson Castro Soares de Oliveira. 2014. *Contribuições para a reconstrução do Protopáno*. Ph.D. thesis, Universidade de Brasília, Brasília.

August Schleicher. 1868. Eine fabel in indogermanischer sprache. In A. Kuh and August Schleicher, editors, *Beiträge zur vergleichenden Sprachforschung auf dem Gebiete der arischen, celtischen und slawischen Sprachen*, 5, pages 206–208. Ferdinand Dümmler, Berlin.

Ashish Vaswani, Noam Shazeer, Niki Parmar, Jakob Uszkoreit, Llion Jones, Aidan N Gomez, Ł ukasz Kaiser, and Illia Polosukhin. 2017. Attention is all you need. In *Advances in Neural Information Processing Systems*, volume 30, pages 1–11. Curran Associates.

GHisBERT – Training BERT from scratch for lexical semantic investigations across historical German language stages

Christin Beck
University of Konstanz
University of Tübingen
christin.beck@uni-konstanz.de

Marisa Köllner
University of Tübingen
marisa.koellner@uni-tuebingen.de

Abstract

While static embeddings have dominated computational approaches to lexical semantic change for quite some time, recent approaches try to leverage the contextualized embeddings generated by the language model BERT for identifying semantic shifts in historical texts. However, despite their usability for detecting changes in the more recent past, it remains unclear how well language models scale to investigations going back further in time, where the language differs substantially from the training data underlying the models. In this paper, we present GHisBERT, a BERT-based language model trained from scratch on historical data covering all attested stages of German (going back to Old High German, c. 750 CE). Given a lack of ground truth data for investigating lexical semantic change across historical German language stages, we evaluate our model via a lexical similarity analysis of ten stable concepts. We show that, in comparison with an unmodified and a fine-tuned German BERT-base model, our model performs best in terms of assessing inter-concept similarity as well as intra-concept similarity over time. This in turn argues for the necessity of pre-training historical language models from scratch when working with historical linguistic data.

1 Introduction

In historical linguistics, studying semantic change and the evolution of word senses has a long-standing tradition (e.g., Paul, 1880; Ullmann, 1942; Stern, 1964; Lehmann, 1992; Bybee, 2015). However, in NLP and computational linguistics, researchers only recently began to take an interest in the topic, focusing on the task of 'shift detection' (cf. Giulianelli et al., 2020), i.e., the identification of changes in word meaning over time. The task has been taken up in a SemEval challenge on identifying lexical semantic change in English, German, Swedish and Latin (SemEval-2020; Schlechtweg et al., 2020), whose success has inspired several follow-up challenges focusing on different sets of languages, e.g., Italian (Basile et al., 2020), Russian (Pivovarova and Kutuzov, 2021), and Spanish (Zamora-Reina et al., 2022). The interest in the topic is fueled by the possibility to address the task of identifying lexical semantic change via pre-trained neural language models. In particular, recent work addresses the task via methodologies based on contextualized embeddings as generated by the state-of-the-art language model BERT (Devlin et al., 2019), exploring methodologies for how to measure, quantify and evaluate semantic change on the basis of these embeddings (see, e.g., Giulianelli et al., 2020; Martinc et al., 2020; Laicher et al., 2021; Kutuzov et al., 2022).

Despite this recent surge of computational methodologies developed for lexical semantic change detection (LSCD), there are still many historical linguistic research questions related to LSCD which have not yet been touched upon computationally. From a historical linguistic perspective, one of the major shortcomings is the lack of temporal depth. That is, most computational studies focus on identifying change in the more recent past, within one language stage, e.g., comparing English data from the 19th century with data from the 20th century CE. While this renders feasible the application of pre-trained language models such as BERT, which have been trained on contemporary data, and might be of interest for information retrieval applications, this is in general not what is of interest to the historical linguist. In historical linguistics, change is usually investigated across longer periods of time of more temporal depth, with change being assessed across language stages, e.g., from Old English (5th-11th century CE) to Middle English (12th-15th century CE), in order to be able to track sense evolutions in more detail (cf. Stern, 1964). Yet, given that prototypically, the language use as well as the orthography in the historical language stages deviate strongly from

Proceedings of the 4th Workshop on Computational Approaches to Historical Language Change, pages 33–45
December 6, 2023

the contemporary language, this casts doubt on the applicability of the readily available pre-trained language models to research questions related to significantly older language stages.

In this paper, we address this methodological gap by developing our own historical BERT-based language model for German: GHisBERT. GHisBERT is trained from scratch on corpus data covering all attested stages of historical German, i.e., Old High German (c. 750-1050 CE, OHG), Middle High German (c. 1050-1350 CE, MHG), Early New High German (c. 1350-1650, ENHG), and New High German (from 1650 onwards, NHG) (see, e.g., Nübling et al. (2008) on the German periodization scheme). We illustrate the usability of our model for research questions related to lexical semantics in historical German by conducting a lexical similarity experiment across three language stages, MHG, ENHG, and NHG. Our experiment is based on measuring the cosine similarity between BERT embeddings produced for ten concepts extracted from the Swadesh (1955) list, i.e., culturally stable concepts which should occur frequently in each of the language stages. To test our model, we assess both, the intra-concept similarity over time as well as inter-concept similarites at each of the investigated time periods. In addition, we compare GHisBERT's performance with a fine-tuned German BERT-base model using the same training data and use the unmodified German model for baseline comparisons. We show that GHisBERT performs better than the other models with respect to capturing intra-concept similarities over time as well as capturing lexical semantic interrelations between the investigated concepts. This highlights the usability of BERT-based models for historical linguistic research questions related to lexical semantics, while at the same time emphasizing the necessity of pre-training language models with the relevant historical data.

2 Related Work

2.1 Lexical semantic change detection

By now, it has become standard to use semantic vector space approaches based on pre-trained neural language models for detecting lexical semantic change (see, e.g., Tahmasebi et al., 2018; Kutuzov et al., 2018; Schlechtweg et al., 2020; Montanelli and Periti, 2023). These approaches can be grouped into (i) type-based approaches (e.g., Hamilton et al., 2016; Hellrich and Hahn, 2016; Schlechtweg et al., 2019), i.e., approaches which use static word embeddings, e.g., word2vec/SGNS (Mikolov et al., 2013) or GloVe (Pennington et al., 2014) embeddings, generating one global vector for each word in a corpus, and (ii) token-based approaches (Hu et al., 2019; Beck, 2020; Giulianelli et al., 2020; Martinc et al., 2020; Montariol et al., 2021; Kurtyigit et al., 2021; Montanelli and Periti, 2023), i.e., approaches based on contextualized word embeddings, e.g., BERT embeddings, which provide one separate context-dependent vector for each occurrence of a word in a corpus.

While LSCD has been previously dominated by type-based approaches and static embeddings (see, e.g., Kaiser et al., 2020; Laicher et al., 2020), recent research efforts move towards producing state-of-the-art results for LSCD based on contextualized BERT embeddings (see, e.g., Kurtyigit et al., 2021; Kutuzov et al., 2022). Several different metrics have been proposed to assess change on the basis of contextualized embeddings and we introduce the most relevant ones in the following.

2.2 Distance-based metrics

Prototypically, for assessing change (and stability) with contextualized word embeddings, distance-based metrics are used which compare the token embeddings computed for a target word across two (or more) corpora from different time periods. Currently, average pair-wise distance (APD) and inverted cosine-similarity over prototypes (PRT) are standardly employed (see, e.g., Giulianelli et al., 2020; Laicher et al., 2020; Kutuzov et al., 2022).

APD Given two corpora C_1 and C_2 representing two different time periods t_1 and t_2, APD represents the average of the distances between all possible pairs of token embeddings, with one embedding per pair representing a target word occurrence in C_1 and the other embedding corresponding to a target word occurrence in C_2. With $U_w^{t_1}$ and $U_w^{t_2}$ referring to the usage matrices of a target word w in t_1 and t_2 respectively,

$$\text{APD}(U_w^{t_1}, U_w^{t_2}) = \frac{1}{N_w^{t_1} \cdot N_w^{t_2}} \sum_{x_i \in U_w^{t_1}, x_j \in U_w^{t_2}} d(x_i, x_j) \quad (1)$$

N corresponds to the number of occurrences of w in each time period, and d is the cosine distance (1-cosine similarity). High APD values are taken to be indicative of strong semantic change, and low values are to be interpreted as weak change.

PRT Based on the same definitions, but using cosine similarity c instead of d, PRT is the inverted cosine similarity between the average token embedding of all target word occurrences (i.e., the protoype embedding) in C_1 and the protoype embedding in C_2:

$$\text{PRT}(U_w^{t_1}, U_w^{t_2}) = \frac{1}{c(\frac{\sum_{x_i \in U_w^{t_1}} x_i}{N_w^{t_1}}, \frac{\sum_{x_{ij} \in U_w^{t_2}} x_j}{N_w^{t_2}})} \quad (2)$$

Inverted cosine similarity is used instead of cosine similarity to produce higher values for stronger changes (see Kutuzov and Giulianelli, 2020). Accordingly, higher values indicate stronger semantic change, lower values indicate weaker changes.

The distance-based estimates are generally evaluated against a human-annotated gold standard, usually with respect to a gold rank where target words are ordered according to their degree of change (see, e.g., subtask 2 of SemEval-2020). In a systematic comparison, Kutuzov et al. (2022) show that averaging the APD and PRT estimates (ensemble method) provides for robust results with respect to predicting the correct rank of target words in terms of change degrees, performing better than using just individual strategies.

In rare cases, the metrics are used for binary change classification, i.e., to classify whether target words are changing over time or not (cf. subtask 1 of SemEval-2020), which requires additional mechanisms. For example, Kurtyigit et al. (2021) propose to use a thresholding technique based on mean and standard deviation values of cosine distances between embeddings and Liu et al. (2021) introduce an approach using permutation-based statistical testing in combination with cosine distances for binary change detection.

2.3 Historical language models

Despite the increasing success of using BERT for LSCD, it remains unclear whether a model trained mostly on contemporary data, e.g., the original BERT-base model is trained on the Google BooksCorpus (800M words) and English Wikipedia (2,500M words), can be readily applied to historical texts. Without having seen any of the relevant historical data during training, the language model might not be able to represent the historical usages of a word adequately.

Addressing this issue, Qiu and Xu (2022) present HistBERT, a BERT-based model which is pre-trained further (i.e., fine-tuned) on the balanced Corpus of Historical American English (COHA; Davies, 2012), adding high-quality balanced historical data going back to the 1820s. They show that, in comparison with the original BERT model, HistBERT provides for improved performances in word similarity tasks and a semantic shift analysis where the underlying data stems from the historical periods covered by the COHA data. Likewise, in earlier work, Martinc et al. (2020) successfully used fine-tuning of a BERT model on the historical corpora under investigation for performance improvement. In addition to further pre-training, Rosin and Radinsky (2022) propose to use a time-aware self-attention mechanism, which encloses temporal information about the text sequences during the extended learning process.

Yet, while fine-tuning on historical data improves lexical semantic change detection, the strong prevalence of the contemporary data used for training BERT might still skew the fine-tuned model towards modern-day language use. Manjavacas and Fonteyn (2022a) show that for historical English (with data going back to 1473 CE), pre-training a BERT model from scratch on the relevant historical data provides for a stronger background model than just fine-tuning the original BERT model with respect to a variety of downstream tasks. In addition, Manjavacas and Fonteyn (2022b) show that historically pre-trained models, i.e., MacBERTh for historical English (1450-1950 CE) and GysBERT for historical Dutch (1500-1950 CE), perform significantly better with respect to non-parametric word sense disambiguation than the corresponding modern models.[1] [2]

Addressing the task of Named Entity Recognition in historical texts, Schweter et al. (2022) pre-train a historical multilingual BERT model (hmBERT) with historical data from German (1683-1949), French (1814-1944), English (1800-1899), Finnish and Swedish (each 1900-1910), establishing a new state-of-the-art via their model.[3]

However, while these models highlight the usefulness of pre-training historical language models, the training data of these models does not support investigations of data exceeding the most recent

[1] https://macberth.netlify.app/

[2] GysBERT and GHisBERT are accidental namesakes.

[3] https://huggingface.co/dbmdz/bert-base-historic-multilingual-cased

historical language stages. It is unclear how well these models scale to data going back further in time, i.e., to data stemming from another historical language stage, where the language differs even more substantially. To our knowledge, there exists no contextualized language model which covers the historical stages of German which we investigate in the present study.

3 GHisBERT: A historical German language model

In this paper, we present **GHisBERT** (**G**erman **His**torical **BERT**), a BERT-based model trained from scratch on historical German data, covering all attested stages of the language, i.e., OHG, MHG, ENHG, and NHG, with data going back to 750 CE.[4]

3.1 Training data

The training data for our model stems from two different sources. More precisely, we extracted all sentences from the *Referenzkorpora zur deutschen Sprachgeschichte* 'Reference Corpora of Historical German', which contain subcorpora for OHG (Referenzkorpus Altdeutsch, ReA, 750-1050 CE; Zeige et al., 2022), MHG (Referenzkorpus Mittelhochdeutsch, ReM, 1050-1350 CE; Klein et al., 2016), and ENHG (Referenzkorpus Frühneuhochdeutsch, ReF, 1350-1650 CE; Herbers et al., 2021).[5] This resulted in 3,227 sentences for OHG, 245,880 sentences for MHG , and 106,988 sentences for ENHG. Sentence splitting was performed based on the presence of modern punctuation markers indicating sentence boundaries (*!.?*) as well as specific historical sentence boundaries, e.g., the middle dot (·), following the respective corpus guidelines.[6] To further balance the training data and to extend the data with contemporary German data, we added data from the *Deutsches Textarchiv* (DTA, Textarchiv, 2023), which is already split into sentences, extracting 100,000 randomly sampled sentences for each of the following periods: 1400-1599, 1600-1799, and 1800-1999. An overview of the data is given in Table 1.

Corpus	Period	Time Span	Sentences	Words
ReA	OHG	750-1050	3 227	18 424
ReM	MHG	1050-1350	245 880	2.3M
ReF	ENHG	1350-1650	106 988	3.7M
DTA1	ENHG	1400-1599	100 000	2.6M
DTA2	NHG	1600-1799	100 000	2.1M
DTA3	NHG	1800-1999	100 000	1.6M
Total	All	750-1999	656 095	12.3M

Table 1: Overview of the training data for GHisBERT.

3.2 Model training

Following Manjavacas and Fonteyn's (2022a) work on historical English, we use the hyperparameterization of the BERT-base configuration and the HuggingFace implementation for training GHisBERT from scratch on historical German data.[7] This corresponds to 12 hidden layers with a hidden size of 768, 12 attention heads, a maximum length of 512 for position embeddings and a vocabulary size of 32,000 tokens. Likewise, we use the masked language modeling (MLM) objective for optimization during training. We trained over 10 epochs, using small batches of size 8 (to avoid memory issues) and gradient accumulation.

For comparison, we further pre-train a modern German BERT-base model via MLM with the same data used for GHisBERT, i.e., we continue training from the last checkpoint of dbmdz/BERT-base-german-cased (henceforth BERT-german), fine-tuning the pre-trained model with historical data.[8] BERT-german was originally trained on over 2 billion words extracted from contemporary texts, e.g., Wikipedia dumps and the EU Bookshop Corpus (Skadiņš et al., 2014).[9] Fine-tuning was performed using the same parameters, but only over 4 epochs as per the recommendations of the original BERT paper (Devlin et al., 2019). We refer to the historically fine-tuned version of BERT-german as BERT-fine. We did not use the multilingual historical model developed by Schweter et al. (2022), i.e.,

[4]GHisBERT is available as a huggingface repository under `https://huggingface.co/christinbeck/GHisBERT`.

[5]`https://www.deutschdiachrondigital.de/`

[6]We are aware that identifying sentence boundaries based on punctuation might not always be correct in historical German. Nonetheless, this approximation gives us the relevant context which is needed for training a BERT model.

[7]`https://huggingface.co/docs/transformers/model_doc/bert`

[8]`https://huggingface.co/dbmdz/bert-base-german-cased`

[9]Alternatively, we could have used the German BERT variant provided by deepset (`https://www.deepset.ai/german-bert`). Our choice between the two variants was arbitrary. The dbmdz model is trained on a larger variety of text sources, but whether this presents an advantage over the deepset model still needs to be experimentally defined. We plan to experiment with further model variants and architectures in the future.

hmBERT, which also contains historical German data, in our experiment, because for one, the historical German data used for training hmBERT still only represents the NHG language stage and for another, having multiple training languages renders a direct comparison with our model more difficult.

In order to be able to deal with the historical orthography and word forms present in our data, we train our own BERT tokenizer on our historical data. This tokenizer is used for tokenization before feeding the historical data into any of the models.[10]

4 Lexical similarity and stability across language stages

To test the applicability of our model to investigations of lexical semantic change in historical language stages, we conduct a case study which investigates whether the lexical semantic stability of ten Swadesh concepts is captured adequately over time, i.e., across three consecutive historical language stages: MHG, ENHG, and NHG. To do so, we compare GHisBERT with BERT-fine and BERT-german via a lexical similarity analysis, assessing the inter-concept similarity at each time stage as well as the intra-concept similarity of each concept across time.

4.1 Target concepts

Most existing computational studies on LSC in German base their investigations on the 48 German target words which were part of the SemEval-2020 challenge (see, e.g., Kurtyigit et al., 2021). However, only very few of these NHG target words can be found in the historically older language stages. We therefore selected ten target words which occur in all three language stages from the 200-word list of basic vocabulary introduced by Swadesh (1955). These concepts are well distributed throughout the list according to Swadesh's stability ranking: VOGEL 'bird', HUND 'dog', EI 'egg', FISCH 'fish' (among the first 50 most stable concepts); BERG 'mountain', FUSS 'foot, KOPF 'head' (among the 50-100 most stable concepts); FRAU 'woman', BAUM 'tree', SONNE 'sun' (among the 100-200 most stable concepts). The basic vocabulary list was both narrowed and extended in recent studies in the course of the establishment of different databases (see, e.g., Dellert and Buch, 2018; Holman et al., 2008), but since the estimation of a concept stability ranking is highly data-dependent, it differs with regard to the languages under investigation. We therefore use the stability ranking of the well-established 200-word Swadesh list, provided by Dellert and Buch (2018), for the selection of the target words. While the concepts themselves are expected to be stable across languages and time, the corresponding word forms are not excluded from undergoing lexical semantic change. However, given their concept stability, we expect the word forms to be relatively stable within one language and within our examined time range.

4.2 Data

For our investigation, we extract all sentences from the 'Reference Corpora of Historical German' in which one of our targets occurs, using the same sentence generation principles as given in Section 3.1. This proportion of the data covers the MHG and ENHG period in our study (via the ReM and ReF corpora). To cover the NHG period, we extract all sentences from the DTA in which the target concepts occur in the time span 1700-1999. Overall, this results in 148,306 sentences, with 3,942 MHG sentences, 6,009 ENHG sentences, and 138,355 NHG sentences.[11]

While the concepts are assumed to be stable parts of the language, occurring in all three stages, the word forms themselves are subject to change over time, undergoing phonological and morphological changes (see, e.g., Nübling et al., 2008). To be able to track the concepts as target words over the language stages, we first had to identify the relevant historical lemmas of our concepts, forming 'etymological chains' assigning the historical word forms of each concept to their contemporary counterparts.

4.3 Etymological chains

We build our etymological chains based on information extracted from Kluge (2012), an etymological dictionary which provides OHG and MHG correspondences of NHG words. For example, *fuoz* is given as the OHG form and *vuoz* as the MHG form of NHG *Fuß* 'foot' in Kluge (2012) (see Table 3 in Appendix A for a full list of lemma correspondences and the respective occurrence frequencies across stages). We searched for all possible correspondences of our target concepts in the lemmatized versions of each of the corpora under inves-

[10]The source code used for tokenization, model training and fine-tuning is available at `https://github.com/christinschaetzle/GHisBERT`.

[11]We excluded the OHG period from our investigation since our target concepts only rarely occurred in this stage, see Table 3 in Appendix A for the relevant occurrence frequencies.

tigation, and extracted the respective sentences in their non-lemmatized form.[12]

4.4 Concept embeddings

For each of the sentences in which our target concepts occur, we generate target word embeddings using our different model versions in the following way. First, we replace the target word representing one of our concepts with the NHG lemma version of the concept, e.g., *vuoz* is replaced with *Fuß*, to mitigate the word form bias reported by Laicher et al. (2021). That is, we use the non-lemmatized, original, sentences to produce concept embeddings, but replace the target word form by its modern concept lemma. After tokenization, we pass the sentences to the model and extract the corresponding sentence embeddings at the second-to-last layer. We use the second-to-last layer, since this layer has been shown to provide the most context-specific embeddings (Ethayarajh, 2019).[13] Next, we compute the word embeddings of each target concept occurrence by averaging over the respective wordpiece embeddings, as is standard procedure.

4.5 Lexical similarity analysis

In order to generate insights into whether our model is able to be used for systems investigating lexical semantic change across language stages, we investigate whether GHisBERT is able to produce adequate results in a lexical similarity analysis of our stable target concepts. That is, we assess the inter-concept similarity of each concept at each language stage, by computing the cosine similarity (COS) between the average embedding of a concept to the average embeddings of all other concepts at a given stage. Additionally, we measure the intra-concept similarity of each concept over time, by comparing the average embeddings of each concept separately between language stages via COS. Ideally, a concept should show significantly greater simliarities to itself over time than to other concepts at each language stage. In addition, the best model should show the largest differences (i.e., lowest similarities) across concepts, capturing the lexical semantic interrelations between the target concepts. To test this, we compute paired t-tests testing for significant differences between the inter-similarity distribution of a concept and the intra-similarity of a concept over time.

Overall, there is still no consensus on which metrics to use for identifying lexical semantic change (and stability in turn) based on BERT embeddings. We experimented with several of the distance-based metrics introduced in Section 2.2, including APD, COS, PRT, and the ensemble method, which averages APD and PRT. Overall, we found that COS, with its value boundedness between 0 and 1, provides for the most interpretative measure with respect to both, intra-concept similiarity over time as well as inter-concept similiarity.[14]

4.6 Evaluation

Most existing work on LSCD ranks the target words under investigation with respect to a quantitative estimate indicating the degree of change of a word between two time periods. This ranking is then usually evaluated against a gold dataset, where the same target words have been ranked on the basis of a detailed, extensive manual annotation process. As this is the first research enterprise setting out to track lexical semantic change based on contextualized embeddings across historical language stages of German, there exists yet no gold data that goes back far enough in time to be compatible with our investigated data. Therefore, we were not able to perform a comparable ground truth evaluation. Instead, we calculate t-tests for assessing similarities and differences between the results produced by the individual models. In addition, we perform qualitative cross-checks of the underlying data via a manual inspection of 50 randomly sampled sentences per concept and language stage.

5 Results

Inter-concept similarity The inter-concept similarity at each time stage shows how similar the average embedding of each concept is to the average embeddings of all other concepts. In terms of the inter-concept similarity at each stage, GHisBERT provides for the best results, presenting similarities that range between 0.18 and 1, representing low and high similarities between concepts adequately, while BERT-fine and BERT-german provide much

[12] In addition, we considered further spelling variants to cover as much data as possible, e.g., *bërg* is used for BERG 'mountain' in ReM, while Kluge (2012) gives *berc* for MHG.

[13] We also experimented with concatenation of the embeddings of the last four layers, averaging over the embeddings of the last four layers, and summing the embeddings of the last four layers. The differences between those approaches are marginal, but concatenation and the second-to-last layer approach produce slightly stronger similarity values.

[14] We provide the code for our experiment under `https://github.com/christinschaetzle/GHisBERT`.

	GHisBERT			BERT-fine			BERT-german		
Concept	COS_{ME}	COS_{EN}	COS_{avg}	COS_{ME}	COS_{EN}	COS_{avg}	COS_{ME}	COS_{EN}	COS_{avg}
BAUM	0.90	0.96	0.93***	0.95	0.94	0.95***	0.98	0.99	0.99***
BERG	0.92	0.97	0.95***	0.94	0.93	0.94***	0.98	0.99	0.99***
EI	**0.70**	**0.92**	**0.81*****	**0.73**	**0.92**	**0.82***	0.94	0.98	0.96***
FISCH	0.85	0.87	0.86***	0.94	0.93	0.93***	0.99	0.99	0.99***
FRAU	0.95	0.95	0.95***	0.95	0.91	0.93***	0.99	0.99	0.99***
FUSS	0.88	0.89	0.89***	0.94	0.89	0.92**	0.97	0.99	0.98***
HUND	0.87	0.95	0.91***	0.91	0.93	0.92***	0.98	0.98	0.98***
KOPF	**0.85**	**0.94**	**0.90*****	0.93	0.94	0.93***	0.98	0.99	0.98***
SONNE	0.89	0.95	0.92***	0.93	0.93	0.93***	0.98	0.99	0.98***
VOGEL	0.92	0.96	0.94***	0.94	0.94	0.94***	0.97	0.98	0.97***

Table 2: Cosine similarities between average concept embeddings from MHG and ENHG (COS_{ME}) and ENHG and NHG (COS_{EN}), as well as the average of these similarities (COS_{avg}). Statistically significant differences between inter- and intra-concept similarity are calculated via t-tests (p<0.001***, p<0.01**, p<0.05*).

higher similarities, see the heatmaps in Figure 1. In particular, BERT-german produces very high similiarity values between concepts at each stage, i.e., values ranging between 0.87 and 1, not being able to capture the differences between the concepts.

Overall, GHisBERT gives the most pronounced representation of synchronic inter-concept similarities. At the MHG stage, EI 'egg' shows the lowest similarity to all other concepts with all three models. This is an interesting text effect which is borne out in particularly by the GHisBERT embeddings: in the MHG proportion of the data, EI only occurs in Latin texts, referring to the 3rd person masculine pronoun *ei* 'he', and not to 'egg'. As such, it is no surprise that it differs from all other concepts. Other lexical semantic similarities which are neatly captured by GHisBERT at all stages are the relationship between animal concepts, e.g., FISCH 'fish', VOGEL 'bird', and HUND 'dog' show high simliarities to one another, and the interrelation between body parts, e.g., KOPF 'head' and FUSS 'foot'. In addition, FRAU 'woman', which is the only human, sentient concept, shows lower similarities than the other concepts to one another (with EI being an exception here).

Intra-concept similarity across time Table 2 shows the cosine similarities between the average concept embeddings across language stages, i.e., between MHG and ENHG (COS_{ME}), between ENHG and NHG (COS_{EN}), and the average across the two distributions (COS_{avg}) for each of the three models. Despite the high inter-concept similarities reported for BERT-german, all three models show highly statistically significant differences between the average inter-concept similarity distributions and the average intra-concept similarity over time (COS_{avg}), see Table 2. Yet again, for BERT-fine and BERT-german, the similarity values are less nuanced than for GHisBERT. In particular, the comparably large change for EI, which is due to the Latin influence in MHG that is not present in the ENHG and NHG data for EI, is most pronounced for GHisBERT. However, the similarity values for EI are similar with GHisBERT and BERT-fine, despite a lower significance in terms of the difference between EI's inter- and intra-concept similarity for BERT-fine. Overall, the COS_{avg} distributions of GHisBERT and BERT-fine do not show a statistically significant difference, whereas the difference between GHisBERT and BERT-german is significant (as is the difference between BERT-fine and BERT-german, both with p<0.001).

Yet, what is striking, is that GHisBERT adequately estimates a larger difference, i.e., a lower similarity, between MHG and ENHG than between ENHG and NHG, while this is not the case for the other two models, with a significant difference between the COS_{ME} distributions of GHisBERT to the other models (p<0.001). GHisBERT's results are in line with broader linguistic developments in historical German (see, e.g., Nübling et al., 2008; Fleischer and Schallert, 2011), for which MHG can be characterized as a major period of change, with a considerably freer word order and several strong phonological and morphological changes (e.g., vowel reduction), leading to the ENHG period, thus reflecting a stronger change between MHG and ENHG than between ENHG and NHG.

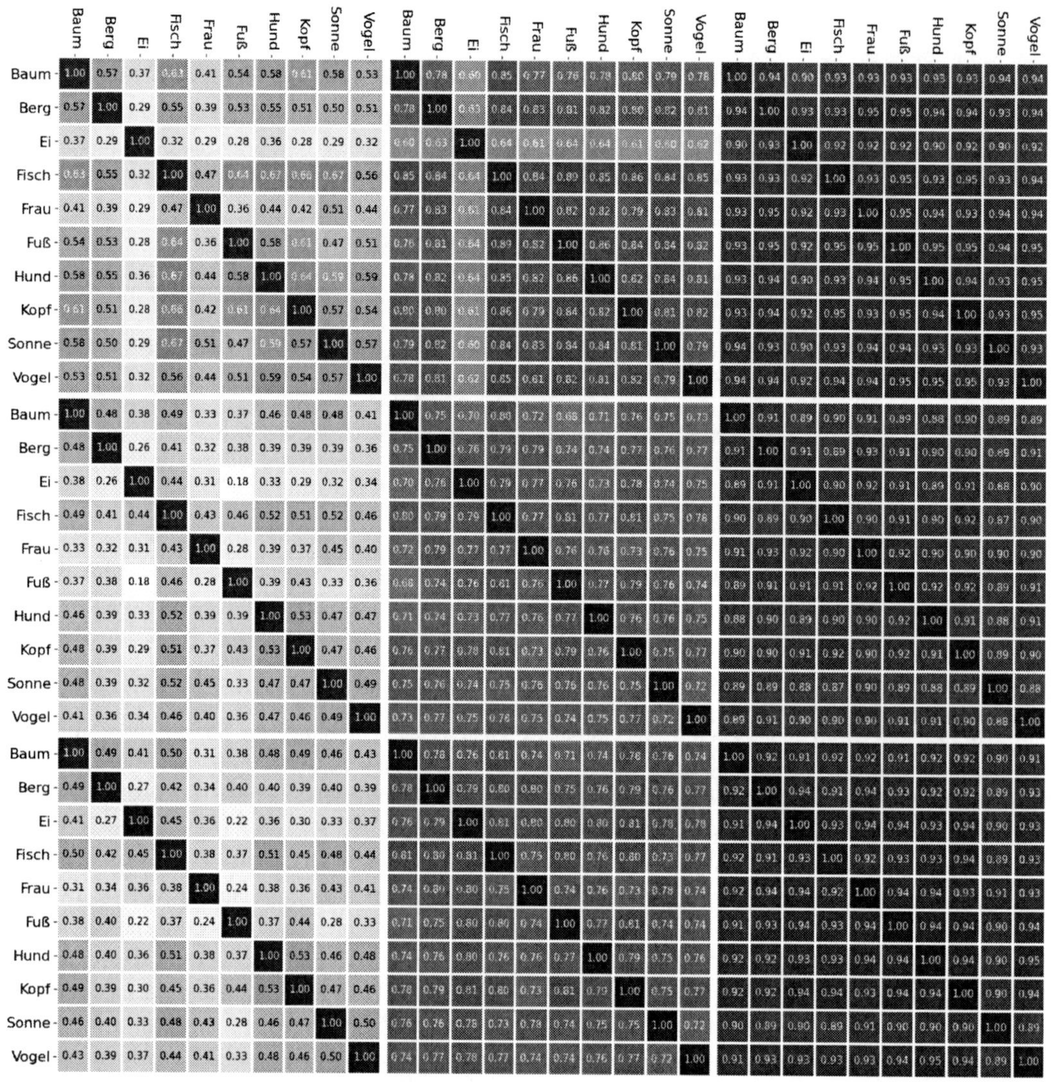

Figure 1: Heatmaps showing the inter-concept similarities at the MHG (top), ENHG (middle), NHG (bottom) stage as calculated via embeddings from GHisBERT (left), BERT-fine (center), and BERT-german (right).

In addition, several of our qualitative observations fit well with the results produced by GHisBERT. For one, concepts which show lower similarities with respect to both COS_{ME} and COS_{EN}, i.e., FISCH 'fish' and FUSS 'foot', show polysemy in the corpora from all three language stages, with FUSS 'foot' referring to the body part, the 'foot' (bottom) of a mountain, and its usage as a measure of length. FISCH 'fish' in turn is found in its biological as well as astrological usage and additionally occurs often in biblical contexts. For another, KOPF 'head', which shows a comparably low COS_{ME} but a large COS_{EN} similarity, seems to be undergoing change between MHG and ENHG: in MHG, KOPF is still mainly found in its historically older use as 'drinking vessel, cup' (cf. Kluge, 2012; Pfeifer et al., 1993), which differs strikingly from the usage in ENHG and NHG as 'head', and is no longer found in modern German. While this development stands out with GHisBERT, it is less evident with the other models, see Table 2.

In sum, our lexical similarity analysis shows that GHisBERT provides for the best results in terms of capturing the lexical semantic relationships between our ten target concepts in the historical language stages. The results produced by GHisBERT present a more nuanced picture of synchronic as well as diachronic interrelations between target concepts than the results achieved via the unmodified and the fine-tuned BERT-german models. Overall, these findings are in line with our manual qualitative cross-checks of the underlying data.

6 Conclusion

This paper provides evidence for the usability of BERT-based models for investigations of lexical semantic change going beyond the contemporary language stage. More precisely, we show via a lexical similarity analysis that BERT embeddings can be used for assessing inter- and intra-concept similarities across three historical German language stages, Middle High German, Early New High German, and New High German. In a systematic comparison, we show that pre-training a BERT-based model from scratch with the relevant historical data provides for more adequate results than fine-tuning alone. This in turn highlights the relevance of pre-training neural language models with language-specific data for lexical semantic investigations.

Limitations

While our paper presents the first research endeavor (that we know of) which investigates lexical semantics in historical German going beyond the NHG stage using BERT embeddings, it also points out the necessity of more ground truth data for evaluation. The lack of a gold standard for evaluation is the strongest limitation of our paper, leading to a lack of a true quantitative evaluation. Annotating data from historical language stages is notoriously difficult and time-consuming, requiring expert knowledge of the language stages (see, e.g., Beck et al., 2020). Therefore, we first set out to investigate whether GHisBERT potentially is a useful tool for investigating lexical semantic change across language stages in this paper before manually annotating data, but definitely plan to do so in the future (together with expert annotators). Along with this, we intend to evaluate our model with respect to further lexical semantic tasks in the future.

A further limitation is the large computational power and time which is generally needed for training a BERT model from scratch: this might not always be feasible for researchers with a more historical linguistic background, which might be lacking the necessary infrastructure. It is thus unclear how well our methodology is transferable to studies seeking to understand lexical semantic developments in the history of other languages and with respect to different datasets. A related issue is that most studies on LSC focus on using BERT embeddings, but it remains unclear how well more recent large language models, e.g., GPT-4 (OpenAI, 2023), and different model architectures scale to the task of investigating LSC across language stages, and, in turn, how these play out the computational issues.

We moreover leave frequency effects and extra-linguistic factors, such as different text genres and dialects, aside in this paper, but intend to look further into this as part of future work.

Ethics Statement

This paper does not present a risk or produce any liabilities for individuals and/or groups of individuals and we do not expect any negative consequences. We provide full transparency of our methodology by open-sourcing our source codes and models. The corpus data underlying our approach in this paper is available as open source and we do not select data based on any ethnic restrictions. We either use all the available data or randomly select individual data points. Having stated this, historical data is generally not equally distributed with respect to regional and social aspects (as well as many other factors), and it is to be expected that certain varieties of speakers will be underrepresented in the data. This is a general problem of historical linguistic work, which we were not able to mitigate in this paper.

Acknowledgements

We thank the Deutsche Forschungsgemeinschaft (DFG, German Research Foundation) for funding our research within DFG FOR 2237: Project "Words, Bones, Genes, Tools: Tracking Linguistic, Cultural, and Biological Trajectories of the Human Past" (both authors) and within Project D02 "Evaluation Metrics for Visual Analytics in Linguistics" – Project-ID 251654672 – TRR 161 (Christin Beck). In addition, we would like to thank Fadhl Al-Eryani for helping us with the corpus work and Chundra Cathcart for setting up the Kluge chains and discussing various aspects of this work with us.

References

Pierpaolo Basile, A. Caputo, Tommaso Caselli, Pierluigi Cassotti, and Rossella Varvara. 2020. DIACR-Ita @ EVALITA2020: Overview of the EVALITA2020 diachronic lexical semantics (DIACR-Ita) task.

EVALITA Evaluation of NLP and Speech Tools for Italian - December 17th, 2020.

Christin Beck. 2020. DiaSense at SemEval-2020 task 1: Modeling sense change via pre-trained BERT embeddings. In *Proceedings of the Fourteenth Workshop on Semantic Evaluation*, pages 50–58, Barcelona (online). International Committee for Computational Linguistics.

Christin Beck, Hannah Booth, Mennatallah El-Assady, and Miriam Butt. 2020. Representation problems in linguistic annotations: Ambiguity, variation, uncertainty, error and bias. In *Proceedings of the 14th Linguistic Annotation Workshop*, pages 60–73, Barcelona, Spain. Association for Computational Linguistics.

Joan Bybee. 2015. *Language Change*. Cambridge University Press.

Mark Davies. 2012. Expanding horizons in historical linguistics with the 400-million word corpus of historical american english. *Corpora*, 7(2):121–157.

Johannes Dellert and Armin Buch. 2018. A new approach to concept basicness and stability as a window to the robustness of concept list rankings. *Language Dynamics and Change*, 8(2):157 – 181.

Jacob Devlin, Ming-Wei Chang, Kenton Lee, and Kristina Toutanova. 2019. BERT: Pre-training of deep bidirectional transformers for language understanding. In *Proceedings of the 2019 Conference of the North American Chapter of the Association for Computational Linguistics: Human Language Technologies, Volume 1 (Long and Short Papers)*, pages 4171–4186, Minneapolis, Minnesota. Association for Computational Linguistics.

Kawin Ethayarajh. 2019. How Contextual are Contextualized Word Representations? Comparing the Geometry of BERT, ELMo, and GPT-2 Embeddings. In *Proceedings of the 2019 Conference on Empirical Methods in Natural Language Processing and the 9th International Joint Conference on Natural Language Processing (EMNLP-IJCNLP)*, pages 55–65, Hong Kong, China. Association for Computational Linguistics.

Jürg Fleischer and Oliver Schallert. 2011. *Historische Syntax des Deutschen. Eine Einführung*. Narr Verlag, Tübingen.

Mario Giulianelli, Marco Del Tredici, and Raquel Fernández. 2020. Analysing lexical semantic change with contextualised word representations. In *Proceedings of the 58th Annual Meeting of the Association for Computational Linguistics*, pages 3960–3973, Online. Association for Computational Linguistics.

William L. Hamilton, Jure Leskovec, and Dan Jurafsky. 2016. Diachronic word embeddings reveal statistical laws of semantic change. In *Proceedings of the 54th Annual Meeting of the Association for Computational Linguistics (Volume 1: Long Papers)*, pages 1489–1501, Berlin, Germany. Association for Computational Linguistics.

Johannes Hellrich and Udo Hahn. 2016. Bad Company—Neighborhoods in neural embedding spaces considered harmful. In *Proceedings of COLING 2016, the 26th International Conference on Computational Linguistics: Technical Papers*, pages 2785–2796, Osaka, Japan. The COLING 2016 Organizing Committee.

Birgit Herbers, Sylwia Kösser, Ilka Lemke, Ulrich Wenner, Juliane Berger, Sarah Kwekkeboom, and Frauke Thielert. 2021. Dokumentation zum Referenzkorpus Frühneuhochdeutsch und Referenzkorpus Deutsche Inschriften. *Bochumer Linguistische Arbeitsberichte*, 24.

Eric W Holman, Søren Wichmann, Cecil H Brown, Viveka Velupillai, André Müller, Dik Bakker, et al. 2008. Advances in Automated Language Classification. *Quantitative Investigations in Theoretical Linguistics*.

Renfen Hu, Shen Li, and Shichen Liang. 2019. Diachronic sense modeling with deep contextualized word embeddings: An ecological view. In *Proceedings of the 57th Annual Meeting of the Association for Computational Linguistics*, pages 3899–3908, Florence, Italy. Association for Computational Linguistics.

Jens Kaiser, Dominik Schlechtweg, and Sabine Schulte im Walde. 2020. OP-IMS @ DIACR-Ita: Back to the Roots: SGNS+OP+CD still rocks Semantic Change Detection. In *Proceedings of the 7th evaluation campaign of Natural Language Processing and Speech tools for Italian (EVALITA 2020)*, Online. CEUR.org.

Thomas Klein, Klaus-Peter Wegera, Stefanie Dipper, and Claudia Wich-Reif. 2016. Referenzkorpus Mittelhochdeutsch (1050-1350). Version 1.0. https://www.linguistics.ruhr-uni-bochum.de/rem/.

Friedrich Kluge. 2012. *Etymologisches Wörterbuch der deutschen Sprache*. De Gruyter.

Sinan Kurtyigit, Maike Park, Dominik Schlechtweg, Jonas Kuhn, and Sabine Schulte im Walde. 2021. Lexical semantic change discovery. In *Proceedings of the 59th Annual Meeting of the Association for Computational Linguistics and the 11th International Joint Conference on Natural Language Processing (Volume 1: Long Papers)*, pages 6985–6998, Online. Association for Computational Linguistics.

Andrey Kutuzov and Mario Giulianelli. 2020. UiO-UvA at SemEval-2020 task 1: Contextualised embeddings for lexical semantic change detection. In *Proceedings of the Fourteenth Workshop on Semantic Evaluation*, pages 126–134, Barcelona (online). International Committee for Computational Linguistics.

Andrey Kutuzov, Lilja Øvrelid, Terrence Szymanski, and Erik Velldal. 2018. Diachronic word embeddings and semantic shifts: a survey. In *Proceedings of the 27th International Conference on Computational Linguistics*, pages 1384–1397, Santa Fe, New Mexico, USA. Association for Computational Linguistics.

Andrey Kutuzov, Erik Velldal, and Lilja Øvrelid. 2022. Contextualized embeddings for semantic change detection: Lessons learned. In *Northern European Journal of Language Technology, Volume 8*, Copenhagen, Denmark. Northern European Association of Language Technology.

Severin Laicher, Gioia Baldissin, Enrique Castaneda, Dominik Schlechtweg, and Sabine Schulte im Walde. 2020. CL-IMS @ DIACR-Ita: Volente o Nolente: BERT does not outperform SGNS on Semantic Change Detection. In *Proceedings of the 7th evaluation campaign of Natural Language Processing and Speech tools for Italian (EVALITA 2020)*, Online. CEUR.org.

Severin Laicher, Sinan Kurtyigit, Dominik Schlechtweg, Jonas Kuhn, and Sabine Schulte im Walde. 2021. Explaining and improving BERT performance on lexical semantic change detection. In *Proceedings of the 16th Conference of the European Chapter of the Association for Computational Linguistics: Student Research Workshop*, pages 192–202, Online. Association for Computational Linguistics.

Winfried P. Lehmann. 1992. *Historical Linguistics: An Introduction*. Holt. 3rd edition, first published in 1962.

Yang Liu, Alan Medlar, and Dorota Glowacka. 2021. Statistically significant detection of semantic shifts using contextual word embeddings. In *Proceedings of the 2nd Workshop on Evaluation and Comparison of NLP Systems*, pages 104–113, Punta Cana, Dominican Republic. Association for Computational Linguistics.

Enrique Manjavacas and Lauren Fonteyn. 2022a. Adapting vs. Pre-training Language Models for Historical Languages. *Journal of Data Mining & Digital Humanities*, NLP4DH.

Enrique Manjavacas and Lauren Fonteyn. 2022b. Non-parametric word sense disambiguation for historical languages. In *Proceedings of the 2nd International Workshop on Natural Language Processing for Digital Humanities*, pages 123–134, Taipei, Taiwan. Association for Computational Linguistics.

Matej Martinc, Petra Kralj Novak, and Senja Pollak. 2020. Leveraging contextual embeddings for detecting diachronic semantic shift. In *Proceedings of the Twelfth Language Resources and Evaluation Conference*, pages 4811–4819, Marseille, France. European Language Resources Association.

Tomas Mikolov, Ilya Sutskever, Kai Chen, Greg Corrado, and Jeffrey Dean. 2013. Distributed representations of words and phrases and their compositionality. *Advances in Neural Information Processing Systems*, 26:3111–3119.

Stefano Montanelli and Francesco Periti. 2023. A survey on contextualised semantic shift detection. ArXiv:2304.01666.

Syrielle Montariol, Matej Martinc, and Lidia Pivovarova. 2021. Scalable and interpretable semantic change detection. In *Proceedings of the 2021 Conference of the North American Chapter of the Association for Computational Linguistics: Human Language Technologies*, pages 4642–4652, Online. Association for Computational Linguistics.

Damaris Nübling, Antje Dammel, Janet Duke, and Renata Szczepaniak. 2008. *Historische Sprachwissenschaft des Deutschen. Eine Einführung in die Prinzipien des Sprachwandels*, 2nd edition. Gunter Narr Verlag, Tübingen.

OpenAI. 2023. Gpt-4 technical report. *arXiv preprint arXiv:2303.08774*.

Hermann Paul. 1880. *Principien der Sprachgeschichte*. Niemeyer, Tübingen.

Jeffrey Pennington, Richard Socher, and Christopher D. Manning. 2014. GloVe: Global vectors for word representation. In *Proceedings of the 2014 Conference on Empirical Methods in Natural Language Processing*, pages 1532–1543.

Wolfgang Pfeifer, Wilhelm Braun, Gunhild Ginschel, Gustav Hagen, Anna Huber, Heinrich Petermann Klaus Müller, Gerlinde Pfeifer, Dorothee Schröter, and Ulrich Schröter. 1993. *Etymologisches Wörterbuch des Deutschen*. Digitalisierte und von Wolfgang Pfeifer überarbeitete Version im Digitalen Wörterbuch der deutschen Sprache, https://www.dwds.de/d/wb-etymwb.

Lidia Pivovarova and Andrey Kutuzov. 2021. RuShiftEval: a shared task on semantic shift detection for Russian. In *Computational linguistics and intellectual technologies: Papers from the annual conference Dialogue*.

Wenjun Qiu and Yang Xu. 2022. HistBERT: A pretrained language model for diachronic lexical semantic analysis. *CoRR*, abs/2202.03612.

Guy D. Rosin and Kira Radinsky. 2022. Temporal attention for language models. In *Findings of the Association for Computational Linguistics: NAACL 2022*, pages 1498–1508, Seattle, United States. Association for Computational Linguistics.

Dominik Schlechtweg, Anna Hätty, Marco Del Tredici, and Sabine Schulte im Walde. 2019. A wind of change: Detecting and evaluating lexical semantic change across times and domains. In *Proceedings of the 57th Annual Meeting of the Association for Computational Linguistics*, pages 732–746, Florence, Italy. Association for Computational Linguistics.

Dominik Schlechtweg, Barbara McGillivray, Simon Hengchen, Haim Dubossarsky, and Nina Tahmasebi. 2020. SemEval-2020 Task 1: Unsupervised Lexical Semantic Change Detection. In *To appear in Proceedings of the 14th International Workshop on Semantic Evaluation*, Barcelona, Spain. Association for Computational Linguistics.

Stefan Schweter, Luisa März, and Erion Çano. 2022. hmBERT: Historical multilingual language models for named entity recognition. In *Experimental IR Meets Multilinguality, Multimodality, and Interaction - Proceedings of the Eleventh International Conference of the CLEF Association (CLEF 2022)*.

Raivis Skadiņš, Jörg Tiedemann, Roberts Rozis, and Daiga Deksne. 2014. Billions of parallel words for free: Building and using the EU bookshop corpus. In *Proceedings of the Ninth International Conference on Language Resources and Evaluation (LREC'14)*, pages 1850–1855, Reykjavik, Iceland. European Language Resources Association (ELRA).

Gustaf Stern. 1964. Meaning and change of meaning, with special reference to the English language. In *Indiana University Studies in the History and Theory of Linguistics*. Indiana University Press, Bloomington. First published in 1931.

Morris Swadesh. 1955. Towards greater Accuracy in Lexicostatistic Dating. *International Journal of American Linguistics*, 21(2):121–137.

Nina Tahmasebi, Lars Borin, and Adam Jatowt. 2018. Survey of computational approaches to diachronic conceptual change. *CoRR*, abs/1811.06278.

Deutsches Textarchiv. 2023. *Grundlage für ein Referenzkorpus der neuhochdeutschen Sprache*. Berlin-Brandenburgischen Akademie der Wissenschaften, Berlin. https://www.deutschestextarchiv.de/.

Stephen Ullmann. 1942. The range and mechanism of changes of meaning. *The Journal of English and German Philology*, 61:46–52.

Frank D. Zamora-Reina, Felipe Bravo-Marquez, and Dominik Schlechtweg. 2022. LSCDiscovery: A shared task on semantic change discovery and detection in Spanish. In *Proceedings of the 3rd Workshop on Computational Approaches to Historical Language Change*, pages 149–164, Dublin, Ireland. Association for Computational Linguistics.

Lars Erik Zeige, Gohar Schnelle, Martin Klotz, Karin Donhauser, Jost Gippert, and Rosemarie Lühr. 2022. Deutsch Diachron Digital. Referenzkorpus Altdeutsch. Humboldt-Universität zu Berlin. http://www.deutschdiachrondigital.de/rea/.

A Appendix A: Target concepts

	NHG		ENHG		MHG		OHG		
Concept	lemma	*n*	lemma	*n*	lemma	*n*	lemma	*n*	Total *n*
BAUM 'tree'	*Baum*	181	*Baum*	300	*boum*	8 845	*boum*	0	9 326
BERG 'mountain'	*Berg*	423	*Berg*	647	*berc*	14 020	*berg*	0	15 090
EI 'egg'	*Ei*	5	*Ei*	129	*ei*	7 385	*ei*	0	7 519
FISCH 'fish'	*Fisch*	110	*Fisch*	344	*visch*	5 331	*fisc*	1	5 786
FRAU 'woman'	*Frau*	2 050	*Frau*	2 935	*vro(u)we*	3 7702	*frouwa*	0	42 687
FUSS 'foot'	*Fuß*	487	*Fuß*	65	*vuoz*	21 999	*fuoz*	3	22 554
HUND 'dog'	*Hund*	110	*Hund*	269	*hunt*	8 070	*hunt*	0	8 449
KOPF 'head'	*Kopf*	29	*Kopf*	223	*kopf*	16 067	*kopf, kupf*	0	16 319
SONNE 'sun'	*Sonne*	396	*Sonne*	914	*sunne*	11 293	*sunna*	3	12 606
VOGEL 'bird'	*Vogel*	151	*Vogel*	183	*vogel*	7 643	*fogal*	0	7 977
All		3 942		6 009		138 355		7	148 313

Table 3: Target concepts and the occurrence frequencies of the corresponding lemmas at each language stage.

A longitudinal study about gradual changes in the Iranian Online Public Sphere pre and post of 'Mahsa Moment': Focusing on Twitter

Sadegh Jafari
Iran University of Science and Technology
sadegh_jafari@comp.iust.ac.ir

Amin Fathi
Iran University of Science and Technology
aminbaybon@gmail.com

Abolfazl Hajizadegan
University of Tehran
a.hajizadegan@ut.ac.ir

Amirmohammad Kazameini
Vector Institute
Amirmohammad.kazemeini@vectorinstitute.ai

Sauleh Eetemadi
Iran University of Science and Technology
sauleh@iust.ac.ir

Abstract

Mahsa Amini's death shocked Iranian society. The effects of this event and the subsequent tragedies in Iran not only in realspace but also in cyberspace, including Twitter, were tremendous and unimaginable. We explore how Twitter has changed after Mahsa Amini's death by analyzing the sentiments of Iranian users in the 90 days after this event. Additionally, we track the change in word meaning and each word's neighboring words. Finally, we use embedding clustering methods for topic modeling.

1 Introduction

Clashes broke out throughout Iran after Mahsa Amini, a 22-year-old Kurdish Iranian woman, died on 16 September 2022 after being detained by "morality police" and taken to a "re-education center" allegedly for not abiding by the country's conservative dress code. Although Iranian officials have said that Mahsa Amini died of a heart attack, according to a United Nations report, Amini collapsed at a detention center in Tehran on 13 September 2022, in the custody of Iran's morality police and then died three days later after being transferred to a hospital. The report said Amini was "severely beaten" by Iranian authorities during her detention. (UN, 2022)
During a crisis, people and the media take over the flow of information, process it, and react to it. The effects of this situation may harm the mental health of the affected population. Mahsa Amini's death caused widespread reactions on several social networks among Iranian and non-Iranian users; for example, although Twitter is banned in Iran and people are having trouble accessing it, MahsaAmini and its Persian-translated hashtag became one of the most repeated hashtags on Twitter and broke a historical record.(BBC, 2022)

The content effects of this tragic incident on Twitter, especially among Iranian users during the 90-day period following Mahsa Amini's death, were analyzed. Twitter data, including tweets with the hashtag "#mahsa_amini" and relevant hashtags, were collected from September 21, 2022, through December 19, 2022. The dataset comprises a total of 1,944,056 tweets in various languages, primarily Persian and English. After preprocessing the tweets, the Persian dataset was utilized to assess the sentiment of Iranian users and illustrate how events during this period, such as the onset of executions, impacted the emotions of Iranian Twitter users. Subsequently, word embeddings were examined to assess the extent to which the meaning of Persian words in tweet content evolved due to the societal changes triggered by Mahsa Amini's death. Cosine similarity was computed between the embedding vector of each word using the original BERT(Devlin et al., 2018) model and a fine-tuned BERT model for this purpose.

Moreover, an analysis of neighboring words for each word before and after Mahsa Amini's death was conducted. The findings concerning the key protest slogan in Iran, "woman, life, freedom," revealed significant changes in the neighboring words of "woman" and "life" on Twitter following Mahsa Amini's death. However, this incident did not lead to notable alterations in the neighboring words of "freedom." The paper's final section employed topic modeling as an unsupervised machine-learning technique to automatically cluster words within the English and Persian tweet datasets obtained from Twitter.

2 Related Works

Previously, researchers have computationally investigated diachronic language change in various ways. Sagi et al. (2009) use a variation of latent semantic analysis to identify semantic change of specific words from early to modern English. Mihalcea and Nastase (2012) take a supervised learning approach and predict the time period to which a word belongs given its surrounding context. Kim et al.

Proceedings of the 4th Workshop on Computational Approaches to Historical Language Change, pages 46–52
December 6, 2023 ©2023 Association for Computational Linguistics

Language	Number of tweets
Persian	1,445,537
English	317,046
Arabic	54,106
Urdo	28,880
German	13,919

Table 1: the number of tweets of the five most frequent languages in the dataset.

(2014) use word2vec (Mikolov et al., 2013) to assay the change of words across time. Hamilton et al. (2016) develop a robust methodology for quantifying semantic change by evaluating word embeddings (PPMI (Marek et al., 2011), SVD (Stewart, 1993), word2vec) against known historical changes. Xie et al. (2020) investigate the change in moral sentiment among the public using longitudinal corpora. We use a transformer base language model to calculate word embeddings to specify our dataset's context. Also, we use a model to predict the semantics of sentences, which can help us find the reason for the change of words.

3 Data

We use the "snscrape" python library to crawl Twitter data tweets "mahsa_amini" and relevant hashtags from 2022-9-21 through 2022-12-19 . Our dataset contains about 2 million tweets in different languages. To pre-process the tweets, we removed usernames, hashtags, and URLs. According to this pre-processed dataset and the results obtained from the "langdetect" python library, the number of tweets of the five most frequent languages in the dataset is illustrated in Table 1.

4 Sentiment analysis

For this aim, we use "persiannlp/mt5-small-parsinlu-sentiment-analysis" transformer-based model (Daniel Khashabi, 2020) to predict the sentiment of sentences in Persian tweets; the chart of the results is shown in figure 1. The events that have happened have led to the growth of negative feelings among Iranian Twitter users. For example, as can be seen in the chart, negative sentiments among Iranian users increased significantly from December 5 until December 10. Calls for strikes and protests on December 5, 6, and 7, as well as the media coverage of the execution of "Mohsen Shekari", who was the first known executed person over anti-government protests, on December 8,

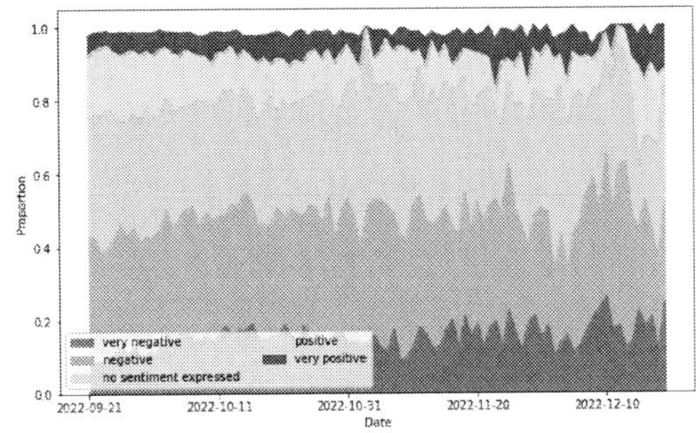

Figure 1: Illustration of result chart for sentiment analysis, the horizontal axis represents 90 days after Mahsa Amini's dead, and the vertical axis represents the population percentage. In the above chart, red, orange, gray, pale green, and deep green, respectively, represent "very negative sentiment", "negative sentiment", " no sentiment expressed", "positive sentiment" and "very positive sentiment".

caused a wave of negative emotions among Iranian users so that the proportion of negative emotions in Persian tweets reached its maximum level in these 90 days. There are also some impulses in the chart at certain times; for example, on November 25, videos of shooting protesters in Zahedan city and anti-riot police forces celebration in the streets after the victory of the Iranian national football team against Wales in Qatar's world cup provoked many adverse reactions on Twitter.

5 Word embedding analysis

In this section, the analysis of word embeddings after and before Mahsa Amini's death is undertaken. First, we calculate the embedding of the Persian tweets using the "HooshvareLab/BERT-base-parsBERT-uncased" (Mehrdad Farahani, 2020) transformer-based model, we use BERT because it offers contextualized embeddings, enabling us to analyze how various word senses change in meaning across different contexts. BERT model calculate the context-aware embedding, so each word can have multiple embeddings depending on the context of the text. We calculate the average of all these word embeddings to get each word's unique embedding.

5.1 Find embedding of words before fine-tuning the model

First, we calculate embedding for each word in the corpus and then remove the tokens that are stop-words or function-words, or subwords(BERT creates some subwords in its tokenizer, for example, ##ing). After that, we choose the 1000 most frequent tokens.

5.2 Find embedding of words after fine-tuning the model

Then we fine-tune the BERT model with a sample of 300,000 Persian tweets from 2022-9-21 through 2022-12-19 for three epochs with learning-rate=2e-5 and weight-decay=0.01. After that, we repeat step 5.1 and calculate the embeddings of each word.

5.3 Calculate self-similarity

Finally, due to this method's popularity, we calculate the cosine similarity between the embedding vector of the word with the original BERT model (known as emb_{before}) and the embedding vector of the word with a fine-tuned BERT model (known as emb_{after}). The similarity metric is defined as

$$sim = \frac{emb_{before} \cdot emb_{after}}{||emb_{before}|| \; ||emb_{after}||}. \quad (1)$$

If the self-cosine similarity of a word is 1, that word is not changed at all. However, if the self-cosine similarity of a word is near 0, it shows that it is changed so much after this period. Considering the interconnected relationship between language and culture in every society, tracking the changes in the meaning of words is essential for analyzing society's culture. The most significant changes were in profanity; for example, the function of the sexual slurs changed, and Twitter users used them in a political context throughout these 90 days. During emotionally charged periods, like protests or reactions to tragic events such as Mahsa Amini's death, individuals may vividly express their emotions, occasionally resorting to profanity. Emotions such as anger, frustration, and grief can increase online profanity usage, allowing individuals to vent their feelings. Furthermore, the transformation of profanity's role from a personal expression to a tool in political protests highlights language's adaptability to shifting societal dynamics. This linguistic evolution mirrors the changing landscape of public discourse amid social and political unrest, with individuals increasingly using strong language to underscore their positions on contentious issues. Also, the meaning of words such as "woman", "life", "freedom" and "protest" changed a lot. Table 2 displays words with the most significant meaning changes according to the self-cosine similarity metric.

Persian word	English translation	cosine similarity value
ژیان	life (in Kurdish)	0.394
شیش	six	0.440
کون	ass	0.496
گای	f*ck	0.526
کیر	d*ck	0.530
خایه	male balls	0.535
ژن	woman (in Kurdish)	0.549
نذاری	don't allow	0.559
جنده	bitch	0.562
آبادی	prosperity	0.567

Table 2: Ten words with the lowest self-cosine similarity scores, which are derived from a pool of the 1000 most frequently used words.

Persian word	English translation	NSV value
ژیان	life (in Kurdish)	0.045
ژن	woman (in Kurdish)	0.043
گای	f*ck	0.041
پشم	fur	0.035
صدا	voice	0.035
عن	sh*t	0.035
آبادی	prosperity	0.035
گوز	fart	0.035
کون	ass	0.034
کیر	d*ck	0.034

Table 3: Among the 1000 most frequently used words, ten words with the highest NSV scores are identified. The NSV metric typically ranges from 0 to 1. However, for these ten words in the table, their NSV values are extremely low, nearing 0. This is due to the NSV metric's nature, as it calculates a word's similarity to itself. When used to compare two nearly unrelated words, the metric's value significantly increases.

5.4 Calculate neighbor square value

In this section, we want to use another way to measure each word's embedding space changes. The problem with self-cosine similarity is that a word and its neighbors might move to new same neighborhood points in the embedding space, so in this situation, self-cosine similarity shows this word changed, but we know that only our coordinate is changed. We should compare embeddings in the same coordinate using a new metric, NSV (neighbor square value).

In algorithm 1, we want to find k words most similar to the desired word. First, we calculate the cosine similarity for all words with input words and then save them in the neighbors dictionary(the key is a word, and the value is cosine similarity). Finally, we return the k words with the highest cosine similarity with our word.

Persian word	English translation	NSV rank	cosine similarity rank
شصت	sixty	981	77
هفتاد	seventy	951	91
سی	thirty	973	128
هشتاد	eighty	918	89
دویست	two hundred	888	100
سیصد	three hundred	882	103
نود	ninety	854	78
چهارصد	four hundred	876	118
بیست	twenty	915	160
پنجاه	fifty	863	137

Table 4: Rankings pertain to the 1000 most commonly used words, as evidenced by the substantial semantic changes observed at higher ranks within the cosine similarity matrix. In contrast, the NSV rank positions these words at the bottom, indicating minimal semantic alterations.

Algorithm 1 Find k nearest neighbors

Input: word, embeddings, k
Output: neighbors
$neighbors \leftarrow \emptyset$
for token **to** embeddings.tokens **do**
  $cs \leftarrow CosineSimilarity(word, token)$
  $neighbors \cdot add((token, cs))$
end for
return $neighbors \cdot SortByValue(k)$

Algorithm 2 get neighbor cosine similarity matrix

Input: word, embeddings, k
Output: matrix

$$matrix_{kk} = \begin{bmatrix} 0 & \cdots & 0 \\ \vdots & \ddots & \vdots \\ 0 & \cdots & 0 \end{bmatrix}$$

$neighbors \leftarrow FindNearestNeighbors(word, embeddings, k)$

for i=0 **to** k **do**
  for j=0 **to** k **do**
    $vector_i \leftarrow neighbors[i] \cdot vector$
    $vector_j \leftarrow neighbors[j] \cdot vector$
    $matrix[i][j] \leftarrow CosineSimilarity(vector_i, vector_j)$
  end for
end for
return $matrix$

<table>
<tr><th rowspan="2">Word</th><th colspan="2">Neighboring words</th></tr>
<tr><th>before</th><th>after</th></tr>
<tr><td>(Woman) زن</td><td>(women) زن‌ها
(man) مرد
(girl) دختر
(lady) خانم
(sister) خواهر</td><td>(man) مرد
(life) زندگی
(women) زن‌ها
(woman in Kurdish) ژن
(girl) دختر</td></tr>
<tr><td>(Life) زندگی</td><td>(future) آینده
(home) خانه
(woman) زن
(family) خانواده
(country) وطن</td><td>(woman) زن
(homeland) میهن
(life in Kurdish) ژیان
(man) مرد
(prosperity) آبادی</td></tr>
<tr><td>(Freedom) آزادی</td><td>(liberation) آزادی
(free) آزاد
(justice) عدالت
(peace) صلح
(victory) پیروزی</td><td>(liberation) آزادی
(free) آزاد
(victory) پیروزی
(justice) عدالت
(peace) صلح</td></tr>
</table>

Table 5: Analyzing the top 5 neighboring words for 'woman,' 'life,' and 'freedom' before and after Mahsa Amini's death reveals significant changes.
While 'woman' and 'life' were influenced, 'freedom' remained consistent. This reflects the historical significance of freedom movements in Iran, dating back to the 1979 revolution. Before her passing, Twitter discussions about 'woman' covered diverse topics, including lifestyle and relationships. After her death, the focus shifted to critical subjects related to her case and women's rights. 'Women in Kurdish' among the related words shows the broader discussion encompassing regional and ethnic aspects.

In algorithm 2, we want to find the neighbor cosine similarity matrix. Each element of this matrix shows the cosine similarity between $neighbor_i$ and $neighbor_j$ of the input word.

$$NSV = \frac{\sum_{i=0}^{k}\sum_{j=0}^{k}(m_b[i][j] - m_a[i][j])^2}{k^2} \quad (2)$$

Finally, we calculate the NSV. m_b is matrix before finetuning and m_a is matrix after finetuning. NSV is between 0 to 1. 0 means that the embedding space of our word does not change, and 1 means that our word has completely changed. Table 3 displays words with the most significant meaning changes according to the NSV metric. Comparing the two methods, as discussed earlier, makes it clear that the NSV metric provides more consistent results. For instance, as seen in table 4, the self-cosine-similarity metric for numeric words suggests significant changes, implying that numeric words undergo substantial alterations. However, the NSV values for numeric words are remarkably low, indicating minimal changes, aligning with our expectations.

6 Topic Modeling

For topic modeling, we used the LDA (Blei et al., 2003) technique for English tweets and HDBSCAN (McInnes et al., 2017) for Persian tweets; the reason for this is the better performance of the LDA method on English tweets and the HDBSCAN method on Persian tweets. We remove the numbers, double spacing, and stopwords to clean the tweet dataset using the NLTK library. After that, we convert the text tweets into vectors. We also filtered any words that appeared in more than 90% tweets or less than 25 tweets. For the number of clusters, we ran the model for k = 5,7,10 clusters for English tweets and k = 4, 6,9 clusters for Persian tweets, and the results showed better performance on k=7 for English tweets and on k=4 for Persian tweets, which are illustrated in table 6 and table 7 .

For English tweets, the first topic related to the news about what has passed during this period, which is why the words Republic and Islam (which represent the Islamic Republic) are at the top of this topic. "massacre," "rape," "torture" and "shoot" are also among the frequent words of this cluster. The second topic expresses gratitude for the support of the international community; as seen in table 6, the words "thank" and "support" are among the five most used words in this category. Other keywords in this cluster are "love," "need," "dear," and "appreciate".Topic number 3, more than anything, deals with asking for help from the international community; the words "help", "us", "internet", "human", "right", "world" and "support" are among the most frequent words in this topic.

Topic number 4 is also related to the context and motto of what happened in Iran, as can be seen in table 6, "woman", "life" and "freedom" are in the five most frequent words in this cluster, "brave", "right", "together" and "free" are other key words of this cluster. The fifth topic expresses violence and oppression, "arrest", "beaten", "execute", "gestapo", "moral", "police" and "danger" are the most repeated words of this topic. The sixth topic expresses a more general aspect of protests; words such as "prison", "student", "IRGC", "university", "dictator", and "street" are among the other frequent words of this cluster of words. And finally, the last topic that discussed the death of Mahsa Amini, words such as "sharia", "hijab", "mandatory", "moral", "police", "kill", "Mahsa", "Amini" and "murder" are the most repeated words in this cluster of words.

topic1	topic2	topic3	topic4	topic5	topic6	topic7
Islam	thank	people	freedom	arrest	protest	police
republic	Iranian	Iranian	woman	Islam	Iran	kill
kill	support	please	Iran	beaten	force	Iranian
people	people	human	life	secure	Islam	brutal
regime	voice	help	fight	hijab	death	girl

Table 6: 5 most frequent words for each topic in English tweets.

topic1	topic2	topic3	topic4
(woman) زن	(hope) آرزو	(Mahsa) مهسا	(people) مردم
(life) زندگی	(victory) پیروزی	(my sister) خواهرم	(blood) خون
(freedom) آزادی	(free) آزاد	(Amini) امینی	(life) زندگی
(man) مرد	(Iran) ایران	(Iran) ایران	(war) جنگ

Table 7: 4 most frequent words for each topic in Persian tweets, also, in the results, there was a topic related to tweets of numbers that are not mentioned in the table above; Twitter users have used these numbers for purposes such as mentioning the number of people killed and the days that have passed since Mahsa Amini's death.

In the results obtained in Persian tweets, the first topic contains tweets with the main slogans of the protesters, such as "woman, life, freedom" The second topic has hopeful content for the future, "hope", "victory" and "free" are among the most frequent words in this topic. The third topic included tweets directly related to Mahsa Amini's death and the last topic deals with Persian Twitter users' protests regarding Iran's current situation.

7 Conclusion and feuture work

So far, we have focused on textual analysis of Iranian Twitter accounts before and after 'Mahsa Moment'. We will complete these analyses in the future. In addition, another longitudinal study - as a complementary method – has been left for the future due to a lack of time. After completing and updating our databases about different characteristics of Iranian 'users' and 'influencers' on Twitter, we will test the significance of changes on both sides of 'Mahsa Moment'. The variables that we are gathering are as follows: location, gender, political tendency, number of followers and join date. In the next step, we will analyze the relationship network between the influencers. For this purpose, by using Gephi (Bastian et al., 2009), the relationships graph will be visualized, and the main communities within the Iranian space of Twitter will be detected according to the Louvain (Blondel et al., 2008) method. We also intend to calculate a topic prevalence chart, similar to the one presented in the study by Ebadi et al. (2021), and analyze its findings. We will employ DeLong et al. (2023) method instead of cosine similarity because this paper serves as a more accurate predictor than cosine similarity based on embeddings when using BERT in a sense-disambiguation related task. We also aim to conduct our analysis on the entire dataset of 2 million entries to ensure more accurate results.

Limitations

The research struggled with many limitations. One of the most important ones was the lack of access to appropriate computing resources such as GPU, especially for sentiment analysis (we only analyzed a sample of 100,000 tweets, while the total available tweets were almost 2 million, and the analysis of the embedding space was on 300,000 tweets and we were not able to analyze the whole data). Also, we were looking for gender analysis. For that, we need to crawl new data. But, we could not do this because of financial transaction restrictions due to Iran sanctions. Another limitation was the internet shutdown by the government after the protests which led to slowness and frequent interruptions of the research process.

References

Mathieu Bastian, Sebastien Heymann, and Mathieu Jacomy. 2009. Gephi: an open source software for exploring and manipulating networks. In *Proceedings of the international AAAI conference on web and social media*, volume 3, pages 361–362.

BBC. 2022. hashtags, a viral song and memes empower iran's protesters.

David M Blei, Andrew Y Ng, and Michael I Jordan. 2003. Latent dirichlet allocation. *Journal of machine Learning research*, 3(Jan):993–1022.

Vincent D Blondel, Jean-Loup Guillaume, Renaud Lambiotte, and Etienne Lefebvre. 2008. Fast unfolding of communities in large networks. *Journal of statistical mechanics: theory and experiment*, 2008(10):P10008.

Siamak Shakeri Pedram Hosseini Pouya Pezeshkpour Malihe Alikhani Moin Aminnaseri Marzieh Bitaab Faeze Brahman Sarik Ghazarian Mozhdeh Gheini Arman Kabiri Rabeeh Karimi Mahabadi Omid Memarrast Ahmadreza Mosallanezhad Erfan Noury Shahab Raji Mohammad Sadegh Rasooli Sepideh Sadeghi Erfan Sadeqi Azer Niloofar Safi Samghabadi Mahsa Shafaei Saber Sheybani Ali Tazarv Yadollah Yaghoobzadeh Daniel Khashabi, Arman Cohan. 2020. ParsiNLU: a suite of language understanding challenges for persian. *arXiv*.

Katherine A DeLong, Sean Trott, and Marta Kutas. 2023. Offline dominance and zeugmatic similarity normings of variably ambiguous words assessed against a neural language model (bert). *Behavior research methods*, 55(4):1537–1557.

Jacob Devlin, Ming-Wei Chang, Kenton Lee, and Kristina Toutanova. 2018. Bert: Pre-training of deep bidirectional transformers for language understanding. *arXiv preprint arXiv:1810.04805*.

Ashkan Ebadi, Pengcheng Xi, Stéphane Tremblay, Bruce Spencer, Raman Pall, and Alexander Wong. 2021. Understanding the temporal evolution of covid-19 research through machine learning and natural language processing. *Scientometrics*, 126:725–739.

William L Hamilton, Jure Leskovec, and Dan Jurafsky. 2016. Diachronic word embeddings reveal statistical laws of semantic change. *arXiv preprint arXiv:1605.09096*.

Yoon Kim, Yi-I Chiu, Kentaro Hanaki, Darshan Hegde, and Slav Petrov. 2014. Temporal analysis of language through neural language models. *arXiv preprint arXiv:1405.3515*.

Kenneth Marek, Danna Jennings, Shirley Lasch, Andrew Siderowf, Caroline Tanner, Tanya Simuni, Chris Coffey, Karl Kieburtz, Emily Flagg, Sohini Chowdhury, et al. 2011. The parkinson progression marker initiative (ppmi). *Progress in neurobiology*, 95(4):629–635.

Leland McInnes, John Healy, and Steve Astels. 2017. hdbscan: Hierarchical density based clustering. *J. Open Source Softw.*, 2(11):205.

Marzieh Farahani Mohammad Manthouri Mehrdad Farahani, Mohammad Gharachorloo. 2020. Parsbert: Transformer-based model for persian language understanding. *ArXiv*, abs/2005.12515.

Rada Mihalcea and Vivi Nastase. 2012. Word epoch disambiguation: Finding how words change over time. In *Proceedings of the 50th Annual Meeting of the Association for Computational Linguistics (Volume 2: Short Papers)*, pages 259–263.

Tomas Mikolov, Kai Chen, Greg Corrado, and Jeffrey Dean. 2013. Efficient estimation of word representations in vector space. *arXiv preprint arXiv:1301.3781*.

Eyal Sagi, Stefan Kaufmann, and Brady Clark. 2009. Semantic density analysis: Comparing word meaning across time and phonetic space. In *Proceedings of the Workshop on Geometrical Models of Natural Language Semantics*, pages 104–111.

Gilbert W Stewart. 1993. On the early history of the singular value decomposition. *SIAM review*, 35(4):551–566.

UN. 2022. un experts demand accountability for death of mahsa amini, call for end to violence against women.

Jing Yi Xie, Renato Ferreira Pinto Jr, Graeme Hirst, and Yang Xu. 2020. Text-based inference of moral sentiment change. *arXiv preprint arXiv:2001.07209.*

Political dogwhistles and community divergence in semantic change

Max Boholm* and **Asad Sayeed**[†]
*Gothenburg Research Institute (GRI), [†]Dept. of Philosophy, Linguistics and Theory of Science
University of Gothenburg
{max.boholm, asad.sayeed}@gu.se

Abstract

We test whether the development of political dogwhistles can be observed using language change measures; specifically, does the development of a "hidden" message in a dogwhistle show up as differences in semantic change between communities over time? We take Swedish-language dogwhistles related to the on-going immigration debate and measure differences over time in their rate of semantic change between two Swedish-language community forums, *Flashback* and *Familjeliv*, the former representing an in-group for understanding the "hidden" meaning of the dogwhistles. We find that multiple measures are sensitive enough to detect differences over time, in that the meaning changes in *Flashback* over the relevant time period but not in *Familjeliv*. We also examine the sensitivity of multiple modeling approaches to semantic change in the matter of community divergence.

1 Introduction

As a type of manipulative communication, a political dogwhistle is a message with a controversial (or extreme) in-group meaning that is hidden to most of the public and only apprehended by a limited proportion of its audience, but at the same time communicates a less controversial (less extreme) out-group meaning to the wider audience who does not grasp the in-group meaning of the message (Haney-López, 2014; Stanley, 2015). An example is "inner city", which has a general meaning of "central section of a city" but has also been used with concealed derogatory racial reference to an area with a poor, African American population (Saul, 2018). Dogwhistles enable attracting some part of its audience who are appealed to by the extreme view, while at the same time not offending others (who do not get the hidden message). With concealed meanings, communicators can avoid accountability for expressing and approving of controversial views. Therefore dogwhistle communication can pose problems for representative democracy (Goodin and Saward, 2005; Stanley, 2015) and speech moderation online (Gavidia et al., 2022; Schmidt and Wiegand, 2017; Zhu and Bhat, 2021).[1]

By design, in-group meanings of dogwhistles evolve in parallel to existing out-group interpretations. Therefore semantic change is essential to the concept of the dogwhistle. However, little systematic attention has, in fact, been devoted to semantic change in dogwhistle expressions. This paper sets out to study this under-explored temporal dimension of dogwhistles through techniques from Natural Language Processing (NLP) to detect lexical semantic change (LSC). More precisely, the aim of this paper is to explore the role of community in the semantic change of set of known-to-be Swedish dogwhistle expressions (DWEs), identified in other work (Åkerlund, 2022; Hertzberg, 2022; Lindgren et al., 2023), including *kulturberika* (culture enrich) and *globalist* (described in more detail below).

In this work, we address the role of community in semantic change by studying the semantic change of DWEs in two online communities (Åkerlund, 2022; Bhat and Klein, 2020): *Flashback*, which is a discussion forum that is known for hosting controversial topics of discussion and for expression of controversial societal opinions (Åkerlund, 2021; Blomberg and Stier, 2019; Malmqvist, 2015); and *Familjeliv* ("family life" in English), which is a discussion forum that is expected to be very different from *Flashback*, with its focus on topics of parenting and family life, but also include discussions on politics and society (Hanell and Salö, 2017). We test *the isolated change of DWEs hypothesis*, i.e., that meaning change of dog-

[1]In democracies, political leaders get a mandate to govern through general elections. They get (re-)elected or replaced by their official proposals for collective action and policies. Dogwhistles obscure this legitimacy of the political mandate given by elections, since the promises are not what they seem to be.

Proceedings of the 4th Workshop on Computational Approaches to Historical Language Change, pages 53–65
December 6, 2023

whistles is *community-dependent*. Here, this expectation is more precisely tested under the following formulation:

H1: The degree of semantic change of (selected) DWEs observed in the (highly politically polarized) online community *Flashback* is different from the degree of semantic change of the same terms (at the same period of time) in the (less polarized) community *Familjeliv*.

In recent years, several different approaches have been developed for modeling of LSC (Kutuzov et al., 2018; Tahmasebi and Dubossarsky, 2023; Tahmasebi et al., 2021; Tang, 2018). For a robust testing of H1, we test and compare results modeled by three different approaches: (1) the **SGNS** approach, which uses word embeddings built through a skip-gram with negative sampling (SGNS) model (Mikolov et al., 2013); (2) the **SBERT-PRT** approach which averages over contextual token embeddings from Sentence-BERT (SBERT) (Reimers and Gurevych, 2019), so called "prototypes" (PRT) (Kutuzov and Giulianelli, 2020; Martinc et al., 2020a); and (3) the **SBERT-CLT** approach which, like the previous approach, uses contextual embeddings from SBERT, but instead of averaging, clusters token embeddings and compare distribution over clusters over time. We test H1 with respect to all three approaches (described in more detail below).

2 Related work

2.1 The meaning of dogwhistles

Quaranto (2022) argues for the importance of linguistic practices in understanding dogwhistles. Essential to this account is the notion of community, since linguistic practices are defined in relation to some community who uphold the practice. At some level of analysis, the speech act of dog whistling *depends on specific lexical forms* embedded in particular linguistic practices (Henderson and McCready, 2018; Quaranto, 2022). While every usage of such DWEs does not perform a dogwhistle speech act – additional criteria are involved in performing the act of dogwhistling (Quaranto, 2022; Saul, 2018) – specific linguistic forms are necessary for conveying the in-group meaning.[2] As such, the link between DWEs and their in-group meanings are upheld by linguistic communities. Dogwhistle meanings in general and the meaning change of dogwhistles in particular are expected to be *community-dependent*. A stronger claim is that the semantic changes of DWEs observed in one community is unlikely to be observed in another community. Here, this expectation is discussed as *the isolated change of DWEs hypothesis*, which is more precisely tested under the formulation in H1. Note that the isolated change of DWEs hypothesis is a special case of a more general thesis that any lexical meaning and therefore also LSC more generally depends on the linguistic communities in which words are used (Clark, 1996).

2.2 Lexical semantic change detection

In accordance with the distributional hypothesis (Firth, 1957; Harris, 1954; Sahlgren, 2008), existing computational methods to analyze LSC apply unsupervised techniques to build numerical vector representations of words at different periods of time and then compare those vectors to determine how much, when and in what way words change (Tahmasebi et al., 2021). For the first two questions (how much and when), the semantic change of a word w in a transition from t_i to t_j, $\Delta_{t_i,t_j}(w)$, is the distance of w's vector at t_i ($\overrightarrow{w}_{t_i}$) and its vector at t_j ($\overrightarrow{w}_{t_j}$):

$$\Delta_{t_i,t_j}(w) = distance(\overrightarrow{w}_{t_i}, \overrightarrow{w}_{t_i})$$

Both *static* word embeddings, such as Word2Vec (Mikolov et al., 2013) and GloVe (Pennington et al., 2014), and *contextualized* word embeddings, such as ELMo (Peters et al., 2018) and BERT (Devlin et al., 2019) have been used to vectorize words in LSC. With static word embeddings, w's meaning is represented by *one* vector that generalizes over its usages. There are two common measures of the distance of static word embeddings: cosine distance (Hamilton et al., 2016) and angular distance (Kim et al., 2014). With contextualized word embeddings, the procedure for word representations over time is somewhat more elaborate than for static embeddings (Giulianelli et al., 2020; Kutuzov and Giulianelli, 2020; Martinc et al., 2020a; Vani et al., 2020). First, contextual word embeddings, such as BERT and ELMo, are multi-layered, multidimensional representations that for every token have a $L \times N$ vector representations, where L is the number of layers and N is the number of dimensions. Selecting the top layer or averaging over (top) layers

[2]This might be too strong a claim, since symbols other than words have been claimed to function as dogwhistles, as exemplified by the Willie Horton campaign (Mendelberg, 1997).

is usually applied when comparing vectors over time. Second, with contextualized embeddings, there is no single representation of w at each time period to be compared. Rather, a word is associated with sets of token vectors at t_i and t_j. In order to arrive at a single measure of change of a word in transition from t_i to t_j, there are two main solutions. In a *prototype approach* the distance between the average token vectors at t_i and t_j is measured by cosine distance or angular distance. These average token vectors are referred to as "prototypes" in previous work. In a *clustering approach* token vectors in t_i and t_j are clustered and then the distance of the distributions of clusters are compared by some measure for comparing probability distributions, for example, Jensen-Shannon distance (Giulianelli et al., 2020; Kutuzov and Giulianelli, 2020; Martinc et al., 2020b; Vani et al., 2020).

Comparisons of methods for LSC detection show mixed findings. The best performing models of SemEval-2020 shared task on unsupervised LSC detection used static word embeddings (Schlechtweg et al., 2020). However, reported findings include contextualized approaches outperforming static embeddings (Kutuzov and Giulianelli, 2020); clustering of contextual embeddings performing worse than approaches that average contextual embeddings (Laicher et al., 2021) and approaches with static embeddings (Martinc et al., 2020b); and clustering contextualized embeddings performing better than averaging over them (Martinc et al., 2020a). Moreover, performance is often different for different languages (Kutuzov and Giulianelli, 2020; Martinc et al., 2020b; Vani et al., 2020). Performance on Swedish data is sometimes found to be worse than, for example, English and German (Laicher et al., 2021; Martinc et al., 2020b), sometimes better (Vani et al., 2020).

3 Data

3.1 Data sets

Two online communities are explored here: *Flashback* and *Familjeliv*. As mentioned above, *Flashback* is a discussion forum on a wide range of topics organized in "threads" under 15 general sections (e.g., drugs, economy, lifestyle and politics). As of 3 August, 2023, the website claims to have over 1.5 million members and almost 80 million posts. *Flashback* support anonymity of users, which enables discussion of controversial topics and expression of controversial opinions, including discrimination and racism (Åkerlund, 2021; Blomberg and Stier, 2019; Malmqvist, 2015). While threats and hate speech are not allowed by the rules of *Flashback*, the website clearly contains offensive language. In a recent survey from 2021, 26% of male and 21% of female social media users in Sweden reported using *Flashback* within the last 12 months (Internetstiftelsen, 2021).

The discussion forum *Familjeliv* is organized in threads of 20 general categories (with several subtopics), where most topics focus on family and parenting (e.g., adoption, pregnancy, and pets), but also include topics of society, economy and law. In 2014, *Familjeliv* had about 700 000 visitors every week (Hanell and Salö, 2017). The forum is explicitly claimed to be a meeting place for women (Hanell and Salö, 2017), which is confirmed by survey data from 2021: 4% of male and 8% of female social media users in Sweden reported using *Familjeliv* within the last 12 months (Internetstiftelsen, 2021).

The corpora we use are collected from the Swedish national language data processing infrastructure Språkbanken Text.[3] The *Flashback* data hosted by them range from 2000 to 2022. In total, *Flashback* data contain 49M sentences (posts) and 785M words. On average, there are 2.1M sentences (SD = 1.4M) and 34.1M words (SD = 21.7M) per year. The *Familjeliv* data range from 2003 to 2022 and contain 19M sentences (M = 0.9M, SD = 0.9M) and 305M words (M = 15.2M, SD = 14.3M).

3.2 A selection of Swedish dogwhistle expressions

A sample of known-to-be Swedish DWEs are investigated (Åkerlund, 2022; Hertzberg, 2022; Lindgren et al., 2023), henceforth referred to as *S-DWE*:

(*S-DWE*) *berika* (enrich, verb), *kulturberika* (culture enrich, verb), *kulturberikare* (culture enricher, noun), *globalist* (globalist, noun), *återvandra* (re-migrate, verb), *återvandring* (re-migration, noun), and *hälpa på plats* (help at site, verb phrase).

This set is identified through exploration of frequent morphological variation of a set of "base forms" in corpus data, resulting in adjectives, nouns and verbs: "återvandr" (as in the verb *återvandra* 're-migration'), "(culture) berika" ([culture] enrich), "globalist" (globalist) and "hjälpa på plats" (help at site). With the exception of the VP *hjälpa*

[3] See: https://spraakbanken.gu.se/en

på plats, which is here explored as a fixed phrase (ignoring inflectional variation), *S-DWE* is a set of lexemes, i.e., abstractions over inflectional forms.

The in-group meanings of the terms in *S-DWE* can be listed at a general level, related to their base forms (Lindgren et al., 2023). This discussion ignores the systematic meaning variation resulting from morphological modifications of the base forms, for example, *kulturberika* (process) $\rightarrow$ *kulturberikare* (agent of that process). The terms related to re-migration are assumed to have in-group and out-group meanings based on the (in)voluntariness of the process, with a voluntary act as the out-group meaning, while 'deportation' is the in-group meaning. The DWE of *berika* (and its related terms) is a result of malevolent irony, in response to the positive opinions about multiculturalism. The in-group meaning of *berika* (and its related terms) is the opposite of enrichment (i.e. the out-group meaning), namely criminal and destructive activities (by immigrants). In a Swedish context and elsewhere, *globalist* (and related DWEs) is used with several different in-group meanings, including an anti-Semitic reference to Jews and a nationalistic reference to anti-nationalists (i.e., opponents of nationalism). Finally, *hjälpa på plats* (help at site) has as its in-group meaning non-acceptance of refugees coming to Sweden.

Below we present examples of the words *berika* and *återvandring* in context. The examples are selected from years of transitions where the terms exemplified have a higher rate of semantic change in *Flashback* than *Familjeliv*; i.e., transitions where there is a divergence of semantic change of the (potential) DWE in the two corpora. Examples are taken from the top five sentences that are most similar to the the average vector of the SBERT-PRT approach, as defined in detail below, where the similarity of the average vector and sentence representations has been measured by cosine similarity.

1. "jag tycker att relationen till min sambos ursprung **berikar** mig enormt!" (*Familjeliv*, 2004)
(I think that the relationship to my partner's origin enriches me enormously!)

2. "olikheter **berikar** också" (*Familjeliv*, 2005)
(differences enrich also)

3. "det har ju bildat en hel politisk / facklig rörelse uttryckligen med syftet att ta ifrån andra och **berika** sig själva" (*Flashback*, 2004)
(It has made a whole political / trade-union movement explicitly with the objective to take from others and enrich themselves)

4. "dessutom kan det ju vara så att detta inte är första gången någon **berikare berikar** en infödd" (*Flashback*, 2005)
(In addition, it can be the case that this not is the first time that some enricher enriches a native)

5. "i dessa fall, och det är många , så är jag övertygad att det samhällsekonomiskt är bäst att satsa på **återvandring**" (*Familjeliv*, 2021)
(In these cases, and those are many, I am convinced that it is socioeconomically best to go for re-migration)

6. "jag har skrivit det förr i en annan tråd: inom tio år är det '**återvandring**' som är modeordet nummer ett inom svensk politik ." (*Familjeliv*, 2022)
(I have written that before in another thread: within ten years it is 're-migration' that is the number one buzzword in Swedish politics)

7. "det viktigaste är att vi får **återvandring**, inte hur politiker motiverar det imho" (*Flashback*, 2021)
(The most important is that we get re-migration, not how politicians motivates it IMHO [i.e. English loan of In My Humble Opinion])

8. "sd talar om frivillig **återvandring**, men det som behövs är forcerad *återvandring*" (*Flashback*, 2022)
(SD [i.e., the Sweden Democrats] speaks of voluntary re-migration, but what is needed is forced re-migration)

While not sufficient for systematic analysis, these examples still illustrate potential shifts in meaning in *Flashback*, but not in *Familjeliv*. We interpret example 4 as a case of the malevolent irony characteristic of the in-group meaning of enrichment dogwhistles but not present in examples 1-3. Moreover, in example 8, re-migration is associated with (in)voluntariness, where the author argues for the need of deportation. This (in)voluntariness is not present in examples 5-7.

3.3 Frequency distributions

Three observations of the frequency distributions of the terms in *S-DWE* in the present data need

DWE	*Flashback* Total	*M*	*SD*	*Familjeliv* Total	*M*	*SD*
berika	20936	27.92	12.18	2047	8.02	2.94
globalist	31156	32.07	39.62	122	1.77	3.15
hjälpa på plats	1150	1.14	1.50	453	1.99	2.88
kulturberika	2445	2.88	2.75	101	0.21	0.38
kulturberikare	6133	9.88	8.41	202	0.42	0.58
återvandra	1449	1.51	1.84	66	0.12	0.25
återvandring	12999	13.19	22.20	384	3.27	5.73

Table 1: Total frequency and mean frequency per million per year

mentioning (Table 1). First, compared with each other they are very different in frequency. Second, their frequencies are very different in different years, reflected by high standard deviations. Third, the terms are more common in the *Flashback* data than in the *Familjeliv* data.

For semantic change of words in general, previous work has observed a correlation with word frequency (Hamilton et al., 2016). Also in the present data there are correlations of LSC and word frequency (see Appendix A). However, three comments can be made in this regard. First, LSC and frequency are not (significantly) related for all terms in *S-DWE*. Second, correlation measures are not consistent over the three approaches here explored to model semantic change (see next section for details). For example, for SBERT-CLT, there is only significant correlation between LSC and word frequency for one of the terms in *S-DWE*. Third, as expected, with the rectified measure of change to control for noise (defined below), fewer terms in *S-DWE* show a significant correlation of frequency and semantic change rates (Noble et al., 2021; Dubossarsky et al., 2017). So although frequency is a factor for LSC modelled here, these points suggest that our findings on semantic change of DWEs are not solely due to word frequency and corpus sizes. See Noble et al. (2021) for other factors than word frequency that can drive semantic change in online communities.

3.4 Preprocessing

Data for all experiments (SGNS, SBERT-PRT and SBERT-CLT) have been preprocessed by lowercasing and removing URLs and emojis. Data for the SGNS approach has been further processed by removal of numbers and punctuation; separation of compounds that have a term in *S-DWE* as its left-hand element, for example, "globalistelit" is replaced by "globalist elit" (with space); and lemmatization of terms in *S-DWE*, for example, "globalisten" (definite form of *globalist*) is replaced by "globalist" (lemma form). Regular expressions were used for lemmatization and separation of compounds. For the SBERT approaches, there is no additional step of preprocessing to the general steps listed above. However, the analysis still implements generalizations similar to those of lemmatization by pairing every sentence with with its "lexemes" in *S-DWE*, thereby generalizing over inflection and compounding. Again, regular expressions were used for this.[4]

4 Semantic change modeling

4.1 The SGNS approach

A corpus is a collection of sentences. Let C be a diachronic corpus that covers the ordered set T of consecutive time periods $t_1, \ldots\ t_n$. C consists of an ordered set of temporally defined sub-corpora $c_{t_1}\ , \ldots\ \ c_{t_n}$. In the present experiments, $T = \langle 2000, \ldots, 2022\rangle$. Consequently $C = \langle c_{2000}, \ldots, c_{2022}\rangle$. A SGNS model is trained for each sub-corpus in C, in the sorted order of T, from first to last. The vocabulary is restricted by a minimum frequency of 10. The weights of the model for the first time period, M_{2000}, are randomly initialized. For every other model, M_{t_i}, where $t_i > 2000$, the weights of M_{t_i} are initialized with the trained weights of $M_{t_{i-1}}$. For every consecutive pair in T, i.e. the set of transitions $R = \langle\langle t_1, t_2\rangle, \ldots \langle t_{n\text{-}1}, t_n\rangle\rangle = \langle\langle 2000, 2001\rangle, \ldots \langle 2021, 2022\rangle\rangle$, and for every word w existing in both models M_{t_i} and $M_{t_{i+1}}$ the vectors $\overrightarrow{w_{t_i}}$ and $\overrightarrow{w}_{t_{i+1}}$ are compared for two measures: (i) naive cosine change, and (ii) rectified

[4]Code for running experiments can be found at https://github.com/mboholm/dogwhistle-community-divergence.

change.

Naive cosine change for a word w in transition from t_i to t_j, i.e. $\Delta_{t_i,t_j}(w)$, is defined as the angular distance between $\overrightarrow{w}_{t_i}$ and $\overrightarrow{w}_{t_j}$ (Kim et al., 2014; Noble et al., 2021):

$$\Delta_{t_i,t_j}(w) = \frac{\arccos(cossim(\overrightarrow{w_{t_i}}, \overrightarrow{w_{t_j}}))}{\pi}$$

As argued by Dubossarsky et al. (2017), vectors of the same word w derived from different samples are expected to be different. Therefore when studying meaning change this general variation expected for w's vectors from different samples should be controlled for (Dubossarsky et al., 2017). To do so, we use a measure of *rectified change* (Noble et al., 2021). For another approach, see Liu et al. (2021). To measure rectified change we perform $n_Q = 10$ controls for every transition $\langle t_i, t_{i+1}\rangle$ (in R) such that: (1) c_{t_i} and $c_{t_{i+1}}$ are concatenated and then the combined list is shuffled; call this list of (shuffled) sentences $Q^{t_i,t_{i+1}}$. (2) $Q^{t_i,t_{i+1}}$ is split in half, resulting in subsets q_1 and q_2. (3) A SGNS model is trained for q_1 and q_2: M_1^Q and M_2^Q. (4) For every word w in both M_1^Q and M_2^Q, the angular distance of w's vectors in M_1^Q and M_2^Q are recorded. Next, *rectified change* is calculated as the t-statistic of the naive cosine change given the estimated noise distribution from the controls, with Bessel's correction (Noble et al., 2021). That is, for a given word w and a temporal transition from t_i to t_j, *rectified change* is defined as:

$$\Delta^*_{t_i,t_j}(w) = \frac{\Delta_{t_i,t_j}(w) - \bar{x}_{Q,w}}{s_{Q,w}\sqrt{1+1/n_Q}}$$

where $\bar{x}_{Q,w}$ and $s_{Q,w}$ are the mean and standard deviation of the naive cosine change measures of the controls ($\Delta_i^Q, \ldots, \Delta_{n_Q}^Q$). Rectified change can be interpreted as "a measure of how much higher (or lower) the measured naive cosine change is than would be expected if the word's underlying context distribution hadn't changed at all. In other words, it quantifies the strength of the evidence that the word has changed" (Noble et al., 2021). Put differently, rectified change quantifies the evidence that the observed change is a genuine one. As with any statistical test of significance, a significant (genuine) change can be small or large; significance is distinct from effect size.

4.2 The SBERT-PRT approach

The second and third approach use SBERT (Reimers and Gurevych, 2019), which is BERT (Devlin et al., 2019) fine-tuned for predicting the semantic similarity of two sentences (Reimers and Gurevych, 2019). SBERT uses a bi-encoder architecture to solve a problem with computational cost in the sentence pair-regression in original BERT, more precisely its cross-encoder architecture. Reimers and Gurevych (2019) show that a bi-encoder with fine-tuning reaches state-of the art performance on sentence similarity, while using the `[CLS]` token or averaging over tokens without fine-tuning does not. We use SBERT to represent DWEs. Thereby this work contrasts with previous work who uses (simple) BERT for LSC detection. The reason for using SBERT instead of BERT is (i) to give more prominence to the full context of DWEs in representing them, and (ii) to be able to represent words not in the vocabulary of BERT.

The implementation of SBERT-PRT approach is in many respects similar to the implementation of SGNS approach. However, a key difference is that in SBERT-PRT, word vectors are only build for the terms in *S-DWE*, not for the complete vocabulary of C as in SGNS. Thus for SBERT-PRT, let B be a diachronic corpus that covers the same consecutive time periods as in SGNS, i.e. T, but where every sub-corpus b_{t_i} in B is a subset of c_{t_i} such that b_{t_i} = sentence s: s is in c_{t_i} $\wedge$ at least one term from *S-DWE* is in s. Sentences in B are encoded by Swedish SBERT (Rekathati, 2021), resulting in 768-dimensional token vectors.

Swedish SBERT is trained using the method for transfer learning in Reimers and Gurevych (2020) where the objective is to make a student model (of an under-resources language, e.g., Swedish) match the sentence embeddings of a high performing teacher model (developed for a well-resourced language, mostly English) in a parallel corpus. Swedish SBERT is trained with the sentence transformer `paraphrase-mpnet-base-v2` hosted on Hugging Face[5] functioning as teacher model and Swedish BERT (Malmsten et al., 2020) functioning as a student model, using several parallel corpora (Rekathati, 2021).

For every term w in *S-DWE* and for every t_i in T, the mean vector (centroid) of the token vectors for w in t_i constitutes $\overrightarrow{w}_{t_i}$. *Naive cosine changes* for the terms in *S-DWE* are then calculated the same

[5]`https://huggingface.co/`

way as for SGNS (see equation above). Similar to the SGNS approach, controls for calculation of rectified change are construed as follows in the SBERT-PRT: for every transition $\langle t_i, t_{i+1} \rangle$ (in R) and for every term w in *S-DWE*: (1) token vectors from sentences in b_{t_i} and $b_{t_{i+1}}$ (which both contain w) are concatenated and then shuffled; the result being $Q^{t_i,t_{i+1}}$; (2) $Q^{t_i,t_{i+1}}$ is split in half, resulting in subsets q_1 and q_2; (3) the mean vectors (centroids) of the token vectors in q_1 and q_2 are calculated, being $\vec{w}_{q1}$ and $\vec{w}_{q2}$; (4) the angular distance (naive cosine change) of $\vec{w}_{q1}$ and $\vec{w}_{q2}$ is calculated and recorded. The calculations of rectified change change then follow the same procedure as in the SGNS approach.

4.3 The SBERT-CLT approach

Every sentence in B (defined above) is independently of its time stamp assigned a label from $l_1, \ldots, l_k$ through k-Means clustering where the value of k is determined by the silhouette method (Rousseeuw, 1987), where k is the number of clusters. After this atemporal labeling, labels are counted per time period. Next, the proportion of labels for a time period t is calculated relative the total counts of labels in t. That is, for every term w in *S-DWE* and every time period t (in T), the proportion of each label is calculated.

The proportions of $l_1, \ldots\ l_k$ at t, call it $L_{w,\,t}$, sums to 1 and can be treated as a probability distribution over labels. In SBERT-CLT, w at t is vectorized as $L_{w,\,t}$, i.e. $\vec{w}_t = L_{w,\,t}$. Next, in SBERT-CLT, w's change in meaning from t_i to t_{i+1} is measured by through *Jensen-Shannon distance* (JSD), which measures the similarity (difference) between two (or more) probability distributions. JSD is defined as the square root of the symmetrical and smoothed variant of Kullback–Leibler divergence (D_{KL}) of two probability distributions P and Q; see Appendix B.[6] The JSD-based measure of w's semantic change from t_i to t_{i+1}, is defined as follows:

$$\Delta^{JSD}_{t_i,t_{i+1}}(w) = JSD(L_{w,t_i} \parallel L_{w,t_{i+1}})$$

For SBERT-CLT there is no parallel to the shuffled controls to calculate rectified change as in the other two approaches described above.

Approach	Measure	D^{KS}	p
SGNS	naive	0.568	<0.001
SGNS	rectified	0.500	<0.001
SBERT-PRT	naive	0.750	<0.001
SBERT-PRT	rectified	0.318	<0.05
SBERT-CLT	JSD	0.636	<0.001

Table 2: Results of KS-tests (N = 44).

5 Results

For an approach A and a corpus Ω, let $S_{A,\Omega}$ be the series of measures of change at each word–transition combination, $\Delta_1, \ldots\ \Delta_N$, where N is the total number of combinations such that the frequency of w at t_i *and* t_{i+1} is at least 10 (minimum frequency).

H1 has multiple variants depending on which approach that is considered. Moreover, for the SGNS and SBERT-PRT approaches, variants are defined for both naive and rectified change. For SBERT-CLT, only the JSD measure of semantic change is tested. These combinations result in five variants of H1 being tested, one for each of: (1) SGNS with naive change, (2) SGNS with rectified change, (3) SBERT-PRT with naive change, (4) SBERT-PRT with rectified change, and (5) SBERT-CLT with JSD change.

To clarify, for each hypothesis, two series of change measures are defined by the same approach and the same change metric, but for data from different communities, i.e. *Flashback* and *Familjeliv*. Note that for every version of H1 there is a corresponding null hypothesis H0, that the two samples are equal.

Statistically, all variants of H1 are tested through the two-sample Kolmogorov–Smirnov test (KS-test), see Appendix C. The test-statistic D^{KS} of a KS-test provides a measure of the likelihood that two samples derive from the same distribution. Like other statistical testing, if D^{KS} reaches the critical value at the decided alpha-level (α = 0.05), H0 is considered unlikely and is rejected, in support of H1. The KS-tests are only based on transitions which fulfill the minimum frequency criterion in both samples (N= 44).

All versions of H1 are supported (Table 2). For each variant of hypothesis H1, a KS-test supports that the scores of semantic change measured in the *Flashback* data are different from those in the

[6] Here we compare the probability distributon over clusters by Jensen-Shannon *distance* implemented through the Python package *SciPy* (`scipy.spatial.distance.jensenshannon`). This diverges from others who compare probability distributions over clusters by Jensen-Shannon *divergence*, which is the square root of JSD, as defined here. For present purposes, the implementation of Jensen-Shannon divergence or distance does not really matter for the analysis.

Familjeliv data. Thus, semantic change of terms in *S-DWE* is community-dependent. The semantic changes of the terms observed in one community are significantly different from those observed in another community. This observation gives provisional support for the isolated change of DWEs hypothesis.[7]

5.1 Correlation of models

An auxiliary question is the extent to which the different modeling approaches are correlated with one another, which we test here on the *Flashback* data. If they are correlated, then it is more likely that all these measures are capturing the same generalizations about semantic change in this setting. If they are not correlated, then it suggests that they are capturing different aspects of semantic change, which could then motivate future work in determining which components of semantic change are captured by which method.

Correlation of models is measured by Spearman's correlation coefficient ρ of the series of semantic change values. For example, the *correlation*$(S^*_{A1,Flashb.}, S^*_{A2,Flashb.})$ is measured to test the correlation of SGNS and SBERT-PRT with respect to rectified change, with data from *Flashback*.

Results are shown in Table 3. There are two general observations here. First, the three approaches often disagree. With naive change, the SGNS, SBERT-PRT, and SBERT-CLT are mostly non-correlated or even negatively correlated with each other (Table 3). The first two approaches' relationship with the third approach is weak with rectified change as well (Table 3). Moreover, while the stronger correlations in Table 3 are in the range of 0.4 to 0.6, there is still a large proportion of the variance of the relationships that is not explained. The deeper insight here is that, deciding how to computationally model the semantic change of terms in *S-DWE* is far from trivial. In particular, SBERT-CLT does not have much in common with SBERT-PRT, despite that both approaches are based on Sentence-BERT. Clustering of data and differing distance metrics seem to have an effect, which is an observation in line with previous research.

Second, rectification clearly has an effect. The relationship between the SGNS approach and the SBERT-PRT approach goes from being negatively correlated when considering naive cosine change to being clearly positively correlated when considering rectified change. However, rectification does not have any effect on the first two approaches' relationship with SBERT-CLT. Remember that there was no control for noise in the third approach, but given the convergence of SGNS and SBERT-PRT when considering rectified change, the cluster based method (SBERT-CLT) is clearly "the odd one out". That is, by clustering token embeddings and using another distance measure (JSD instead of angular distance), quite different conclusions about the data seem to emerge.

6 Discussion

This study finds support for the isolated change of DWEs hypothesis. There is a detectable difference in the rate of semantic change of DWEs between the more politically polarized community and the less polarized community. It could have been possible that DWEs change to the **same** degree in the community more representative of the in-group and the community more representative of the out-group, even if they meant different things to the community participants. In that case, our measures would not have detected a difference. But there is a difference in degree likely driven by the communicative needs of the in-group community.

As such, this paper corroborates previous work that has emphasized the role of community in accounting for dogwhistle meanings (Henderson and McCready, 2018; Quaranto, 2022), but this finding must also be seen in the light of a previous emphasis on the importance of community for word meaning in general (Clark, 1996). Following Lewis (1969)'s notion of convention, Clark (1996) writes "conventional meaning hold not for a word *simpliciter*, but for a word *in a particular community*. You can't talk about conventional word meaning without saying what community it is conventional in" (p. 107, emphasis in original). Clark (1996) continues by defining a "communal lexicon" as the set of word conventions of an individual community and notes that such communal lexicons sometimes contain unique word forms (e.g., *quark* in the community of modern physicists), but more often the same word form is shared among different

[7] Correlation measures confirm this. Spearman's correlation (ρ) of S from *Flashback* and *Familjeliv* are close to zero and non-significant ($N = 44$): $\rho(S_{SGNS,Fla.}, S_{SGNS,Fam.}) = 0.120$, $p = 0.443$; $\rho(S^*_{SGNS,Fla.}, S^*_{SGNS,Fam.}) = 0.120$, $p = 0.439$; $\rho(S_{SBERT-PRT,Fla.}, S_{SBERT-PRT,Fam.}) = -0.074$, $p = 0.635$; $\rho(S^*_{SBERT-PRT,Fla.}, S^*_{SBERT-PRT,Fam.}) = 0.265$, $p = 0.080$; and $\rho(S^{JSD}_{SBERT-CLT,Fla.}, S^{JSD}_{SBERT-PRT,Fam.}) = 0.134$, $p = 0.386$.

	SGNS	SGNS*	SBERT-PRT	SBERT-PRT*	SBERT-CLT
SGNS	1.000	0.721	-0.306	0.385	0.037
SGNS*	0.721	1.000	-0.239	0.601	0.137
SBERT-PRT	-0.306	-0.239	1.000	-0.383	0.290
SBERT-PRT*	0.385	0.601	-0.383	1.000	0.126
SBERT-CLT	0.037	0.137	0.290	0.126	1.000

Table 3: Cross-correlation (Spearman) of the three approaches (N = 117). Asterix (*) for rectified measures; JSD is used for SBERT-CLT; otherwise, naive measure.

communal lexicons, but with different meanings. The latter case of shared form across communities, but with different meanings that evolve in relation to the local needs and interactions of particular communities is an important insight with clear relevance for an account of dogwhistle meaning.

Although Clark (1996) does not discuss his notion of communal lexicon in relation to semantic change, Noble et al. (2021) have expanded on Clark's ideas and did observe that meanings of terms evolve relative to the communities they are used in Noble et al. (2021). Our result is quantitative evidence in the Swedish online context of different communal lexicons evolving in parallel in relation to a political drive regarding messaging on a controversial topic, immigration and refugees.

Dogwhistle meaning can thus be understood partially in relation to some general principles of lexical meaning. However, whether DWEs' dependence on community for semantic change is especially strong in comparison with words not laden with the role of DWE is an interesting question for future research.

Another point should be noted with regard the isolated change of DWEs hypothesis. Its support has implications for the task of automated detection of dogwhistles, which is important to counteract hidden racist language online, by potential disclosure of concealed derogatory messages. The lesson here, from our experimental support for the isolated change of DWEs hypothesis, is that terms that change in one community, but not in another, are possible indicators of emerging dogwhistles. Although such community specific change of meaning is not a sufficient criterion for the identification of dogwhistles, it can be part of a solution to a complex problem of detecting dogwhistles and other concealed code words, which is gaining increasing attention in NLP (Gavidia et al., 2022; Hertzberg, 2022; Hertzberg et al., 2022; Xu et al., 2021; Zhu and Bhat, 2021).

There are a number of avenues for future work on this topic. One of these would be to address *how* the assumed DWEs change. This can include a more detailed qualitative analysis of the linguistic contexts of the dogwhistles in the years that they exhibit greater change difference between the two communities. Future studies can systematically address the extent that semantic change of these terms is related to their potential dogwhistle functions. For example, do changes reflect encoding of in-group meanings or do they rather reflect other forms of semantic drift, for example, with regard to various topics? Another avenue for future work would be an analysis of the differences between the change measurement approaches, since they are often poorly correlated with one another. A further, more ambitious agenda, would be to identify characteristics of DWE-related lexical semantic change that differ from non-DWE community-based semantic change, which would enable their detection and differentiation in large corpora. Part of this agenda, could be a systematic comparison DWEs and other words with regard to their community divergence of semantic change in order to determine the extent that community divergence is a feature of special importance for words functioning as DWEs compared with words in general.

Limitations

Our work applies to the Swedish political and media context. We believe that it should also apply to other languages, national political contexts, and media, but this will have to be tested by other work.

It is impossible to develop a sample of relevant DWEs that allow for a hypothesis to be tested over DWEs themselves as a general category, since DWEs emerge and disappear based on politically relevant current affairs. Consequently, our work demonstrates our hypothesis for the dogwhistles we present, but we cannot generalize to all dogwhistles everywhere. Nevertheless, showing that the effects are possible and strong is a contribution that makes the case for larger scale testing over newly emerging dogwhistles in different national contexts.

There are also significant differences in the frequencies and distributions of the tested expressions in the two communities of interest. Furthermore, we rely on the rectification approach to deal with the fact that we have a low frequency threshold for including a DWE in the analysis.

Ethics Statement

There is always a problem of dual use when creating a system to detect potentially negative social phenomena. Malicious actors can use the same technique to evaluate, e.g., their own attempts at manipulating political discourse. Nevertheless, we believe that such actors are motivated to do this anyway and that the public research should not be fully "disarmed" and have tools available for detecting these phenomena. Furthermore, this work is a part of the groundwork that will contribute to understanding this phenomenon, and not a full detector in itself.

The community corpus data used in this project was collected from a national repository charged with archiving Swedish political and cultural discourse. The DWE selection was motivated by published experiments conducted by other researchers under the supervision of an ethics review board.

Acknowledgements

Funding for this work was provided by the Gothenburg Research Initiative for Politically Emergent Systems (GRIPES) supported by the Marianne and Marcus Wallenberg Foundation grant 2019.0214. We wish to thank the anonymous reviewers for their constructive criticism and comments.

References

Mathilda Åkerlund. 2021. Influence Without Metrics: Analyzing the Impact of Far-Right Users in an Online Discussion Forum. *Social Media + Society*, 7(2):20563051211008831.

Mathilda Åkerlund. 2022. Dog whistling far-right code words: The case of 'culture enricher'on the Swedish web. *Information, Communication & Society*, 25(12):1808–1825.

Prashanth Bhat and Ofra Klein. 2020. Covert hate speech: White nationalists and dog whistle communication on twitter. *Twitter, the public sphere, and the chaos of online deliberation*, pages 151–172.

Helena Blomberg and Jonas Stier. 2019. Flashback as a rhetorical online battleground: Debating the (dis) guise of the Nordic Resistance Movement. *Social Media+ Society*, 5(1):2056305118823336.

Herbert H. Clark. 1996. *Using Language*. Cambridge university press.

Jacob Devlin, Ming-Wei Chang, Kenton Lee, and Kristina Toutanova. 2019. BERT: Pre-training of Deep Bidirectional Transformers for Language Understanding. In *Proceedings of the 2019 Conference of the North American Chapter of the Association for Computational Linguistics: Human Language Technologies, Volume 1 (Long and Short Papers)*, pages 4171–4186, Minneapolis, Minnesota. Association for Computational Linguistics.

Yadolah Dodge. 2008. Kolmogorov–Smirnov Test. *The Concise Encyclopedia of Statistics*, pages 283–287.

Haim Dubossarsky, Daphna Weinshall, and Eitan Grossman. 2017. Outta control: Laws of semantic change and inherent biases in word representation models. In *Proceedings of the 2017 Conference on Empirical Methods in Natural Language Processing*, pages 1136–1145.

J. R. Firth. 1957. A Synopsis of Linguistic Theory, 1930-1955.

Martha Gavidia, Patrick Lee, Anna Feldman, and Jing Peng. 2022. Cats are fuzzy pets: A corpus and analysis of potentially euphemistic terms. *arXiv preprint arXiv:2205.02728*.

Mario Giulianelli, Marco Del Tredici, and Raquel Fernández. 2020. Analysing Lexical Semantic Change with Contextualised Word Representations. In *Proceedings of the 58th Annual Meeting of the Association for Computational Linguistics*, pages 3960–3973, Online. Association for Computational Linguistics.

Robert E Goodin and Michael Saward. 2005. Dog whistles and democratic mandates. *The Political Quarterly*, 76(4):471–476.

William L. Hamilton, Jure Leskovec, and Dan Jurafsky. 2016. Diachronic Word Embeddings Reveal Statistical Laws of Semantic Change. In *Proceedings of the 54th Annual Meeting of the Association for Computational Linguistics (Volume 1: Long Papers)*, pages 1489–1501, Berlin, Germany. Association for Computational Linguistics.

Linnea Hanell and Linus Salö. 2017. Nine months of entextualizations: Discourse and knowledge in an online discussion forum thread for expectant parents. In *Entangled Discourses: South-North Orders of Visibility*, pages 154–170. Routledge, New York.

Ian Haney-López. 2014. *Dog Whistle Politics: How Coded Racial Appeals Have Reinvented Racism and Wrecked the Middle Class.* Oxford University Press.

Zellig S. Harris. 1954. Distributional structure. *Word*, 10:146–162.

Robert Henderson and Elin McCready. 2018. How dog-whistles work. In *New Frontiers in Artificial Intelligence: JSAI-isAI Workshops, JURISIN, SKL, AI-Biz, LENLS, AAA, SCIDOCA, kNeXI, Tsukuba, Tokyo, November 13-15, 2017, Revised Selected Papers 9*, pages 231–240. Springer.

Niclas Hertzberg. 2022. Semantic modeling of Swedish dog whistles. Master's thesis, University of Gothenburg.

Niclas Hertzberg, Robin Cooper, Elina Lindgren, Björn Rönnerstrand, Gregor Rettenegger, Ellen Breitholtz, and Asad Sayeed. 2022. Distributional properties of political dogwhistle representations in Swedish BERT. In *Proceedings of the Sixth Workshop on Online Abuse and Harms (WOAH)*, pages 170–175.

Internetstiftelsen. 2021. Svenskarna och Internet 2021. Technical report.

Yoon Kim, Yi-I Chiu, Kentaro Hanaki, Darshan Hegde, and Slav Petrov. 2014. Temporal analysis of language through neural language models. *arXiv preprint arXiv:1405.3515*.

Andrey Kutuzov and Mario Giulianelli. 2020. UiO-UvA at SemEval-2020 task 1: Contextualised embeddings for lexical semantic change detection. *arXiv preprint arXiv:2005.00050*.

Andrey Kutuzov, Lilja Øvrelid, Terrence Szymanski, and Erik Velldal. 2018. Diachronic word embeddings and semantic shifts: A survey. In *Proceedings of the 27th International Conference on Computational Linguistics*, pages 1384–1397, Santa Fe, New Mexico, USA. Association for Computational Linguistics.

Severin Laicher, Sinan Kurtyigit, Dominik Schlechtweg, Jonas Kuhn, and Sabine Schulte im Walde. 2021. Explaining and improving BERT performance on lexical semantic change detection. *arXiv preprint arXiv:2103.07259*.

David Lewis. 1969. *Convention: A philosophical study.* Harvard University Press.

Elina Lindgren, Björn Rönnerstrand, Ellen Breitholtz, Robin Cooper, Gregor Rettenegger, and Asad Sayeed. 2023. Can Politicians Broaden Their Support by Using Dog Whistle Communication? In *119th APSA Annual Meeting & Exhibition, August 31 – September 3, 2023, Held in Los Angeles, California*, Los Angeles, California.

Yang Liu, Alan Medlar, and Dorota Glowacka. 2021. Statistically Significant Detection of Semantic Shifts using Contextual Word Embeddings. In *Proceedings of the 2nd Workshop on Evaluation and Comparison of NLP Systems*, pages 104–113, Punta Cana, Dominican Republic. Association for Computational Linguistics.

Karl Malmqvist. 2015. Satire, racist humour and the power of (un) laughter: On the restrained nature of Swedish online racist discourse targeting EU-migrants begging for money. *Discourse & Society*, 26(6):733–753.

Martin Malmsten, Love Börjeson, and Chris Haffenden. 2020. Playing with Words at the National Library of Sweden–Making a Swedish BERT. *arXiv preprint arXiv:2007.01658*.

Matej Martinc, Syrielle Montariol, Elaine Zosa, and Lidia Pivovarova. 2020a. Capturing Evolution in Word Usage: Just Add More Clusters? In *Companion Proceedings of the Web Conference 2020*. ACM.

Matej Martinc, Syrielle Montariol, Elaine Zosa, and Lidia Pivovarova. 2020b. Discovery Team at SemEval-2020 Task 1: Context-sensitive Embeddings Not Always Better than Static for Semantic Change Detection. In *Proceedings of the Fourteenth Workshop on Semantic Evaluation*, pages 67–73, Barcelona (online). International Committee for Computational Linguistics.

Tali Mendelberg. 1997. Executing Hortons: Racial crime in the 1988 presidential campaign. *The Public Opinion Quarterly*, 61(1):134–157.

Tomáš Mikolov, Wen-tau Yih, and Geoffrey Zweig. 2013. Linguistic regularities in continuous space word representations. In *Proceedings of the 2013 Conference of the North American Chapter of the Association for Computational Linguistics: Human Language Technologies*, pages 746–751.

Bill Noble, Asad Sayeed, Raquel Fernández, and Staffan Larsson. 2021. Semantic shift in social networks. In *Proceedings Of* SEM 2021: The Tenth Joint Conference on Lexical and Computational Semantics*, pages 26–37.

Jeffrey Pennington, Richard Socher, and Christopher D Manning. 2014. Glove: Global vectors for word representation. In *Proceedings of the 2014 Conference on Empirical Methods in Natural Language Processing (EMNLP)*, pages 1532–1543.

Matthew E. Peters, Mark Neumann, Mohit Iyyer, Matt Gardner, Christopher Clark, Kenton Lee, and Luke Zettlemoyer. 2018. Deep Contextualized Word Representations. In *Proceedings of the 2018 Conference of the North American Chapter of the Association for Computational Linguistics: Human Language Technologies, Volume 1 (Long Papers)*, pages 2227–2237, New Orleans, Louisiana. Association for Computational Linguistics.

Anne Quaranto. 2022. Dog whistles, covertly coded speech, and the practices that enable them. *Synthese*, 200(4):330.

Nils Reimers and Iryna Gurevych. 2019. Sentence-bert: Sentence embeddings using siamese bert-networks. *arXiv preprint arXiv:1908.10084*.

Nils Reimers and Iryna Gurevych. 2020. Making monolingual sentence embeddings multilingual using knowledge distillation. *arXiv preprint arXiv:2004.09813*.

Faton Rekathati. 2021. The KBLab Blog: Introducing a Swedish Sentence Transformer.

Peter J. Rousseeuw. 1987. Silhouettes: A graphical aid to the interpretation and validation of cluster analysis. *Journal of Computational and Applied Mathematics*, 20:53–65.

Magnus Sahlgren. 2008. The Distributional Hypothesis. *The Italian Journal of Linguistics*, 20:33–54.

Jennifer Saul. 2018. Dogwhistles, political manipulation, and philosophy of language. In Daniel Fogal, Daniel Harris, and Matt Moss, editors, *New Work on Speech Acts*, pages 360–383. Oxford University Press, Oxford.

Dominik Schlechtweg, Barbara McGillivray, Simon Hengchen, Haim Dubossarsky, and Nina Tahmasebi. 2020. SemEval-2020 task 1: Unsupervised lexical semantic change detection. *arXiv preprint arXiv:2007.11464*.

Anna Schmidt and Michael Wiegand. 2017. A survey on hate speech detection using natural language processing. In *Proceedings of the Fifth International Workshop on Natural Language Processing for Social Media*, pages 1–10.

Jason Stanley. 2015. *How Propaganda Works*. Princeton University Press.

Nina Tahmasebi, Lars Borin, and Adam Jatowt. 2021. Survey of computational approaches to lexical semantic change detection. Language Science Press Berlin.

Nina Tahmasebi and Haim Dubossarsky. 2023. Computational modeling of semantic change. In Claire Bowern and Bethwyn Evans, editors, *Routledge Handbook of Historical Linguistics*, 2nd edition. Routledge.

Xuri Tang. 2018. A state-of-the-art of semantic change computation. *Natural Language Engineering*, 24(5):649–676.

K. Vani, Sandra Mitrovic, Alessandro Antonucci, and Fabio Rinaldi. 2020. SST-BERT at SemEval-2020 Task 1: Semantic Shift Tracing by Clustering in BERT-based Embedding Spaces. *ArXiv*, abs/2010.00857.

Thomas Viehmann. 2021. Numerically more stable computation of the p-values for the two-sample Kolmogorov-Smirnov test.

Wikipedia contributors. 2023. Kolmogorov–Smirnov test — Wikipedia, The Free Encyclopedia.

Canwen Xu, Wangchunshu Zhou, Tao Ge, Ke Xu, Julian McAuley, and Furu Wei. 2021. Blow the dog whistle: A Chinese dataset for cant understanding with common sense and world knowledge. *arXiv preprint arXiv:2104.02704*.

Wanzheng Zhu and Suma Bhat. 2021. Euphemistic phrase detection by masked language model. *arXiv preprint arXiv:2109.04666*.

A Correlation of LSC and word frequency

Table 4 shows correlation of semantic change and word frequency at the first year of transitions (only *Flashback* data).

B Jensen-Shannon distance (JSD)

For two probability distributions *P* and *Q*, Jensen-Shannon distance (JSD) is defined as follows:

$$JSD(P \parallel Q) = \sqrt{\frac{D_{KL}(P \parallel \frac{P+Q}{2}) + D_{KL}(Q \parallel \frac{P+Q}{2})}{2}}$$

where D_{KL} can be defined as follows:

$$D_{KL} = \sum_{x \in X} P(x) \log(\frac{P(x)}{Q(x)})$$

where *X* is the sample space (the labels in the present case).

C Kolmogorov–Smirnov test (KS-test)

Let $F_n(x)$ and $G_m(x)$ be the the empirical cumulative distribution function (ECDF) of two samples *X* and *Y*, then:

$$D_{n,m}^{KS} = \sup_x |F_n(x) - G_m(x)|$$

where *sup* is the supremum function, which for present purposes can be approximated by the *max* function (Viehmann, 2021). The null hypothesis ($X = Y$) is rejected at level α, if $D_{n,m}^{KS} > D_{n,m,\alpha}^{KS}$, where:

$$D_{n,m,\alpha}^{KS} = c(\alpha)\sqrt{\frac{n+m}{n \cdot m}}$$

Here $c(\alpha)$ is the inverse of the Kolmogorov distribution at α. For $\alpha = 0.05$, $c(\alpha) \approx 1.358$ (Wikipedia contributors, 2023).

The Mann-Whitney/Wilcoxon rank-sum test (MWW test) is another common non-parametric

	SGNS		SBERT-PRT		SBERT-CLT
DWE	Naive	Rect.	Naive	Rect.	JSD
berika	0.043	0.014	0.278	-0.048	0.386
globalist	-0.767***	-0.11	-0.615**	0.647**	-0.037
hjälpa på plats	-0.253	-0.571*	-0.692**	0.253	-0.275
kulturberika	0.579*	0.524*	-0.844***	0.103	-0.215
kulturberikare	0.279	0.372	-0.16	0.496*	-0.293
återvandra	0.532*	0.257	-0.796***	0.279	-0.386
återvandring	0.05	0.207	-0.638**	0.253	-0.571*

Table 4: Correlation (Spearman's rho) between semantic change (naive, rectified and JSD) and log-transformed fpm (at first year of transition) in the *Flashback* data. Statistical significance is denoted by *p<0.05, **p<0.01, ***p<0.001.

tests, which like the KS test, tests the null hypothesis that the underlying distributions of the two samples are equal. However, the MWW test detects a difference between the medians of the samples, while KS test considers the distribution functions collectively not restricted to differences in the central values of the samples (Dodge, 2008).

*ℰvo*Sem: A database of polysemous cognate sets

Mathieu Dehouck
LATTICE, CNRS–ENS-PSL–USN
mathieu.dehouck@ens.psl.eu

Alexandre François
LATTICE, CNRS–ENS-PSL–USN
alexandre.francois@ens.fr

Siva Kalyan
University of Queensland
s.kalyan@uq.edu.au

Martial Pastor
Radboud University Nijmegen
LATTICE, CNRS–ENS-PSL–USN
martial.pastor@ru.nl

David Kletz
LATTICE, CNRS–ENS-PSL–USN
david.kletz@sorbonne-nouvelle.fr

Abstract

Polysemies, or "colexifications", are of great interest in cognitive and historical linguistics, since meanings that are frequently expressed by the same lexeme are likely to be conceptually similar, and lie along a common pathway of semantic change. We argue that these types of inferences can be more reliably drawn from polysemies of cognate sets (which we call "dialexifications") than from polysemies of lexemes. After giving a precise definition of dialexification, we introduce *ℰvo*Sem, a cross-linguistic database of etymologies scraped from several online sources. Based on this database (publicly available at http://tiny.cc/EvoSem), we measure for each pair of senses how many cognate sets include them both—i.e. how often this pair of senses is "dialexified". This allows us to construct a weighted dialexification graph for any set of senses, indicating the conceptual and historical closeness of each pair. We also present an online interface for browsing our database, including graphs and interactive tables. We then discuss potential applications to NLP tasks and to linguistic research.

1 Introduction

Colexification is the structural pattern whereby two meanings are expressed by the same word in a given language: e.g., Spanish *pueblo* colexifies the meanings PEOPLE and VILLAGE. While polysemy is defined semasiologically, as a property of a word, colexification is defined onomasiologically, as a property of a pair of meanings. These are two sides of the same coin: if a pair of meanings is colexified, then this means they are senses of the same polysemous word.

The concept of colexification was introduced by François (2008) in the context of lexical typology, with the aim of discovering universal patterns of conceptual structure, adapting the semantic-map approach that had already proven fruitful in typological studies of grammar (Anderson, 1974; Haspelmath, 1997). Since then, a number of works have been published on the topic of colexification. Some of these suggest additional sources of data (e.g. Östling, 2016), while others look for universals in lexical semantics (e.g. Georgakopoulos et al., 2022), or try to predict patterns of colexification from properties of the meanings themselves (e.g. Xu et al., 2020; Di Natale et al., 2021; Brochhagen and Boleda, 2022; Brochhagen et al., 2023). The growing body of research into colexification has also led to the creation of the CLICS database (Rzymski et al., 2020, available at https://clics.clld.org), now in its third edition: the empirical dataset that it provides makes it possible to test hypotheses about cross-linguistic patterns of colexification. This in turn has led to recent applications in the field of NLP, with presentations at major venues such as Bao et al. (2021) (GWC2021) who question the universality of common colexifications by comparing different colexification databases, Chen and Bjerva (2023) (SIGMORPHON 2023) who use colexification to create cross-lingual resources and Chen et al. (2023) (NoDaLiDa 2023) who infuse language embeddings with semantic typology using colexification information.

While it yields some insight into universal constraints on semantic change, "strict colexification" (François 2008, 171), defined in terms of synchronic properties of lexemes, misses the semantic links that are synchronically absent, yet can be revealed by studies of etymology. Incorporating semantic change into the study of lexical typology would contribute to a growing body of research on computational approaches in this domain (e.g. Kutuzov et al., 2018; Tahmasebi et al., 2021).

This issue is addressed by the new concept of *dialexification* (François and Kalyan, 2023, in prep.), the structural pattern whereby two meanings are expressed by members of the same cognate set. For example, knowledge of regular sound change in the Indo-European family shows that Norwe-

Proceedings of the 4th Workshop on Computational Approaches to Historical Language Change, pages 66–75
December 6, 2023

gian *gård* 'land', Gothic *gards* 'house' and Polish *gród* 'city' are all cognate, since they all descend from the same Proto-Indo-European (p-IE) etymon $*g^h\acute{o}rd^h os$ (Mallory and Adams, 1997, 199). The historical relations that link these three concepts cannot be captured by the notion of colexification, since none of these words has more than one of these meanings; but they can be described as instances of dialexification. More specifically, we can say that the semantic pairs {LAND–HOUSE}, {LAND–CITY}, and {HOUSE–CITY} are *dialexified* by (or under) the p-IE form $*g^h\acute{o}rd^h os$.

If two meanings *A* and *B* are dialexified, this means that either *A* evolved into *B*, *B* evolved into *A*, or both *A* and *B* evolved from a common source. In other words, dialexification is always indicative of a historical relation between two meanings—one that may not have been captured by earlier conceptual tools.

In this paper, we present *EvoSem*, a database and a website (`http://tiny.cc/EvoSem`) dedicated to the study of dialexification. It consists of etymologies and definitions scraped from the English-language Wiktionary (`https://en.wiktionary.org`), itself a compilation of earlier scholarly work from various sources; as well as the *Austronesian Comparative Dictionary* or ACD (Blust and Trussel, 2013; Blust et al., 2023) and the *Sino-Tibetan Etymological Dictionary and Thesaurus* or STEDT (Matisoff, 2016). Among other features, *EvoSem* allows us to measure how often any given pair of meanings is dialexified across the world's languages.

This paper is organized as follows. Section 2 will define the notion of dialexification mathematically, and contrast it with colexification. Section 3 will describe the process of data collection and post-processing. Section 4 will discuss the visualization of the data on our companion website. Finally, section 5 will discuss potential applications of *EvoSem* to NLP tasks and to linguistic research.

2 Definitions

Let $\mathcal{L} = \{l_1, \ldots, l_n\}$ be a set of languages. For each language $l \in \mathcal{L}$, we have a vocabulary $\mathcal{V}_l = \{w_1, \ldots, w_{|\mathcal{V}_l|}\}$ of words and/or morphemes. Let $C(w)$ be the set of meanings (also called concepts or glosses) of the word $w \in \mathcal{V}_l$. Furthermore, let $e = a(w)$ be the earliest known ancestor (the "etymon") of w. We say that w is a *reflex* of e, and we call the set of all reflexes of e the *cognate set* to which w belongs.

Two concepts c_i and c_j are said to be "dialexified"—which we represent as "$\delta(c_i, c_j)$"—if there exist two words w_p and w_q such that w_p expresses c_i, w_q expresses c_j, and w_p and w_q are cognate (i.e., have the same etymon). Mathematically, dialexification is a symmetric and reflexive relation that can be formally defined as follows:

$$\begin{aligned}\forall c_i, c_j,\ \delta(c_i, c_j) &\iff \\ &\exists w_p, w_q : a(w_p) = a(w_q) \\ &\quad \wedge c_i \in C(w_p) \wedge c_j \in C(w_q).\end{aligned}$$

As for colexification, it corresponds to the situation where w_p and w_q are the same; in this case, w_p and w_q are obviously cognate, since they necessarily descend from the same etymon. We write the colexification relation as $\kappa(c_i, c_j)$, and define it as follows:

$$\begin{aligned}\forall c_i, c_j,\ \kappa(c_i, c_j) &\iff \\ &\exists w : c_i \in C(w) \wedge c_j \in C(w).\end{aligned}$$

Like dialexification, this relation is symmetric and reflexive. Also, $\kappa(c_i, c_j) \Rightarrow \delta(c_i, c_j)$ for all c_i and c_j: in other words, any relation of colexification is also a relation of dialexification, though the converse is not true.

Note that the etymon of a given word is not always attested: it may be a proto-form reconstructed using the comparative method (Weiss, 2015). Its exact form may thus be uncertain; but this does not affect our ability to identify cases of dialexification, since all that matters for the definition is whether two words have the *same* etymon, i.e. belong to the same cognate set.

To put it another way, the domain of dialexification is not, strictly speaking, the etymon itself, but rather the cognate set that descends from the etymon. Thus, to say that a given etymon dialexifies concepts *A* and *B* is not a direct claim about the semantics of the original etymon: it is simply a statement about the meanings of its descendants. Strictly speaking, we could have defined dialexification in terms of cognate sets. But since it is more convenient to refer to a cognate set by its etymon than to list out all the cognate forms (and since there is a one-to-one correspondence between etyma and the cognate sets that descend from them), we prefer the etymon-based definition.

We make a distinction between a *root*, which is the minimal unit of historical reconstruction (e.g. p-IE *$g^h erd^h$- 'enclose'), and an *etymon*, i.e. a proto-form that is morphologically derived from a root: e.g., the nouns *$g^h órd^h$-*os* and *$g^h r̥d^h$-*ós* (both glossed 'enclosure') are two distinct etyma derived from the root *$g^h erd^h$-. Strictly defined, relationships of dialexification are always assessed at the level of the etymon rather than its root.[1]

Note that "cognate sets", as we define them in this paper, include not only direct descendants of etyma, but also borrowings. For example, the cognate set that descends from p-IE *$g^h órd^h os$ includes not only Russian *gorod* 'city', but also Yakut (Turkic) *kuorat* 'city', which is borrowed from the Russian word. This differs from the way cognate sets are usually defined in historical linguistics (i.e. excluding borrowings); however, we see no principled reason to distinguish between semantic changes that affect borrowed forms and those that affect inherited forms, and so this distinction is not relevant for defining dialexification. Regardless, we retain information about the borrowed status of lexemes in our database, to allow for future analyses that are sensitive to this distinction.

3 Data collection

We now describe how we went about assembling the $\mathcal{E}vo$Sem dataset.

3.1 Wiktionary

The bulk of our data comes from the English Wiktionary (`https://en.wiktionary.org`). Due to differences in the way different language families are organised on Wiktionary, we used slightly different procedures for extracting data for Indo-European; Semitic and Uralic; and all the remaining language families represented on Wiktionary, especially in terms of how we identified lemmas in the respective proto-languages. We describe these procedures in turn.[2]

3.1.1 Indo-European

Initially, we started with pages from the category "Proto-Indo-European roots" (653 entries on `https://en.wiktionary.org/wiki/Category:Proto-Indo-European_roots`). On each page, we looked for the section titled "Derived terms", and extracted every etymon derived from this root (e.g. the etyma *$g^h órd^h$-*os*, *$g^h r̥d^h$-*yé-ti*, listed under the p-IE root *$g^h erd^h$-).

We then proceeded to extract entire cognate sets, by listing every reflex of each etymon – e.g. Albanian *gardh* from *$g^h órd^h$-*os*, or Proto-Germanic (p-Gmc) **gurdijaną* from *$g^h r̥d^h$-*yé-ti*. In the latter example, the reflex was itself a form from a proto-language (p-Gmc), the source of further reflexes. In such cases, the "Descendants" section of the relevant page was also scraped to yield further reflexes (e.g. Old English *gyrdan* and English *gird*, under p-Gmc **gurdijaną*). Descendants were crawled recursively until no more reflexes could be added. At every stage, relations of borrowing were noted (even though in our analyses, we do not treat borrowings separately from inherited forms).

While many p-IE lemmas in Wiktionary derive from a p-IE root, some are underived forms – i.e. morphologically simple rather than derived from a root (e.g. **oḱtṓw* 'eight'). We thus applied a similar scraping procedure to all underived p-IE lemmas to extract all of their reflexes.[3]

For each reflex of a given etymon, we then extracted all of its senses. The particular format of Wiktionary made it possible to design an approach based on the hyperlinks that usually appear in the (English-language) definitions of all entries. For example, Russian *grad* is defined as

> (poetic, archaic) town, city, used as a common city name suffix (Volgograd, Kaliningrad, Leningrad)

(where underlining indicates hyperlinks). We removed all parenthetical comments, and then extracted every hyperlinked word, with the idea that they would usually correspond to suitable English glosses;[4] in our example, this yielded a set of simple glosses {*town* | *city*}. Reducing the senses to

[1] In practice, the distinction between root and etymon only applies to Proto-Indo-European and Proto-Semitic, since for other proto-languages, the proto-forms listed in our sources are morphologically simple.

[2] All scraping of Wiktionary was done in R, using the `xml2` package (Wickham et al., 2023).

[3] In cases where the same reflex appeared under both a p-IE root and an underived p-IE lemma, only the entry with the root was kept.

[4] A limitation of this approach is that our use of English lemmas as glosses makes it hard to detect cases where a language distinguishes between two senses that are colexified in English: for example, German distinguishes between *kennen* 'to be acquainted with' and *wissen* 'to be aware of', but these are both glossed as *know* in Wiktionary. Ideally, we would be able to gloss the items in our database with WordNet synsets (Miller, 1995), for better granularity; but we are not aware of a reliable way to automate the matching of free-form definitions with synsets. We are grateful to an anonymous reviewer for highlighting this limitation, and acknowledge that it partially compromises the onomasiological perspective that motivates this work.

(mostly single-word) glosses would then make the meanings of different words easy to compare across languages—the very purpose of $\mathcal{E}$voSem.

However, this hyperlink-based approach led to a couple of difficulties. Firstly, the words that are hyperlinked in a given Wiktionary definition often include not only the key words in the definition, but also auxiliary words such as *be* or *become*; this was addressed by excluding stopwords (using the list built in to the `stopwords` package in R, Benoit et al. 2021), unless the *only* hyperlinked words are stopwords (so as to not exclude words whose meaning is 'to be', etc.).

Secondly, while the definitions of non-English words tend to be succinct, and only contain hyperlinks to direct translations of the word being defined, the definitions of English words tend to be verbose, and contain hyperlinks to a wide variety of related concepts, running the risk of collecting noisy data. For example, the English word *gird* is defined as

1. (*transitive*) To bind with a flexible rope or cord.
2. (*transitive*) To encircle with, or as if with a belt.
3. (*transitive, reflexive*) To prepare (oneself) for an action.

Clearly, the hyperlinked words include both acceptable glosses (*bind, encircle, prepare*) and words that are only thematically related to the word being defined (e.g. *flexible, rope, belt, action*). In the absence of a reliable way to distinguish between the two types of links, we addressed the problem by forcing the gloss of every English word to be identical to the word itself (so that *gird* would only be glossed as *gird*). This meant erasing all polysemies in English; but we found this to be an acceptable alternative to an otherwise noisy dataset.[5]

Another problem we encountered is that many languages have homographs, i.e. lexemes with the same spelling but different etymologies: each of these homographs derives from a different etymon, and covers a different set of senses. For example, the Dutch word *vorst* means 'prince', 'frost', 'forest', and 'ridgepole'; but each of these meanings derives from a different etymon (p-IE **pr̥h₂-is-*, **prustós*, **pr̥kʷ-éw-s*, and **perst-*, respectively). When extracting the reflexes of a given etymon, there was no easy way to ensure that in cases like this, only the meanings corresponding to the correct etymon would be returned, and instead all meanings of the word were extracted, regardless of the etymology. (Thus, for example, *vorst* meaning 'forest' was initially listed under p-IE **pr̥h₂-is-* as well as **pr̥kʷ-éw-s*.) To remedy this, we ran a separate deduplication step, where for every word definition that appeared under multiple etyma (e.g. *vorst* meaning 'forest'), we searched the wikitext of the etymology for the `{{inh}}` ("inherited") and `{{der}}` ("derived") templates, to find the oldest mentioned ancestral form (in this case, p-West Germanic **furhiþi*), and then recursively searched for ancestors of this form until we arrived at a p-IE etymon (**pr̥kʷ-éw-s*); this allowed us to eliminate cases where a definition of a word was listed under the wrong etymon.

In addition to extracting reflexes of p-IE roots and underived lemmas, we also extracted reflexes of proto-forms from each first-order descendant of p-IE (Proto-Germanic, Proto-Indo-Iranian, etc.), wherever these proto-forms are not themselves known to be descended from p-IE forms.

3.1.2 Semitic and Uralic

The same procedure that we applied to underived lemmas in p-IE was also applied to lemmas in Proto-Semitic and Proto-Uralic. We also deduplicated homographs in the same way.

For Semitic, we were able to have a domain expert (Chams Bernard) check the data manually, to correct errors in the extraction of glosses, and ensure that the etymologies reflect the state of the art in Semitic historical linguistics. We plan to also have the Indo-European and Uralic data manually checked by experts.

3.1.3 Other language families

To extract data from language families other than Indo-European, Semitic and Uralic, we first located all subcategories of "Lemmas by language" that have the form "Proto-[family] lemmas", exclud-

[5] In any case, English is just one of the 1,941 languages in our dataset, and accounts for only 2% of lemmas (though it is the most heavily-represented language in our dataset). An anonymous reviewer asks whether excluding English polysemies could lead to mis- or underidentification of cognate sets; this is not the case, as cognacy relations are determined purely by shared descent from a proto-form, which is not affected by our ability to accurately extract glosses from the definitions. Moreover, it does not introduce ambiguities into our results, beyond those that are inherent to the use of English lemmas as glosses. At some point, the glossing algorithm developed for non-Wiktionary sources (such as 3.2) could easily be applied to Wiktionary definitions as well, allowing us to recover a number of English polysemies; we plan to do this in future iterations.

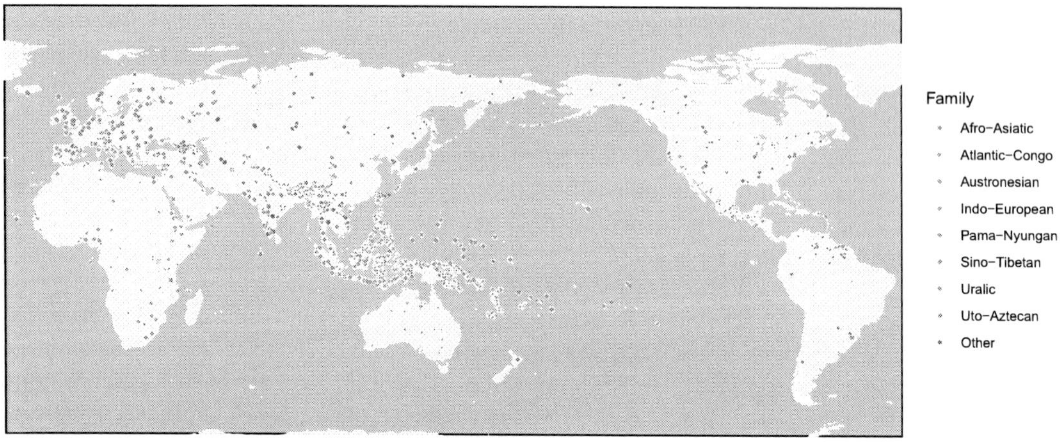

Figure 1: Geographic distribution of those languages covered by $\mathcal{E}$*vo*Sem for which metadata is available from the Glottolog reference database of the world's languages (Nordhoff and Hammarström, 2012). Languages are color-coded by language family, and their size is proportional to $\log_{10}$ of the number of dialexifications that involve each language.

ing Proto-Indo-European, Proto-Semitic, Proto-Uralic, and all their descendant proto-languages. For each remaining proto-language, we then applied the same scraping procedure as for p-IE underived lemmas. Finally, whenever the same reflex was listed under multiple proto-languages at different hierarchical levels of the same language family (e.g. Proto-Austronesian and Proto-Malayo-Polynesian), only the entry under the highest-level proto-language was retained.

3.2 ACD (Austronesian) and STEDT (Sino-Tibetan)

We primarily drew on Wiktionary, since it is a rich and reliable resource for several language families – notably Indo-European – and generally provides references to published etymological research. Another reason for using it is ease of access, particularly since for many language families, the only other available etymological resources are printed publications. However, $\mathcal{E}$*vo*Sem also incorporates data from other electronic sources when these are available. We thus added to our dataset two etymological resources we judged to be reliable: ACD and STEDT (see §1). (Other databases will be added to this list in the future, for other families.)

The ACD and STEDT databases were harvested using a web crawler that went through an index of their etyma. Each etymon was in turn associated with a cognate set, a list of reflexes for which our crawler collected all relevant details (language; family; form of the reflex; etymon; definitions).

Because these resources do not include hyperlinked words in their definitions like Wiktionary does, we developed a different parsing algorithm; in most cases, it proved able to convert wordy definitions into acceptable glosses. Our starting point was definitions such as the following description given by the ACD for the verb *a-kan* in the Kadazan Dusun language of Malaysia: {*to eat, consume, wear away; (in such games as chess) take a piece, destroy (as if by eating)*}.

Our first step is to identify key separators in the overall definition (e.g. ',' or ';'), so as to parse the text into separate glosses. Then all potential glosses are run through a regular expression that cleans out all non-essential lexicographic indications, such as content in parentheses, usage notes or special abbreviations. Likewise, we ignore certain stopwords at the beginning of a string, such as the article *a(n)* before nouns ('*a spoon*' → '*spoon*'), or the particle *to* before infinitives ('*to eat*' → '*eat*'). In the example of *a-kan* above, these first steps yield a set of separate strings, namely {*eat* | *consume* | *wear away* | *take a piece* | *destroy*}.

Next, a different parser attempts to isolate potential concepts for every clear gloss. In order to make sure that the glosses extracted from these databases are comparable to those extracted from Wiktionary, our parser matches every parsed string with the lemmas listed under `https://en.wiktionary.org/wiki/Category:English_lemmas` (which contains 729,370 entries). This matching operation recognizes '*eat*' and '*wear away*' as valid glosses, but not '*take a piece*', which is not listed as an English lemma, and is thus eliminated from our results. This process allows us to filter many verbose definitions into a simple set of lemmatized glosses: e.g., the definition '*to open, as the fist or a book; to spread out, as a folded paper or mat*' is correctly parsed as {*open* | *spread out*}, leaving out the noise from other strings.

While this filtering script gave satisfying results, we noted that certain English words were not correctly identified, due to being inflected. For instance, conjugated verbs or plural forms like *children* would go unrecognized, as they do not correspond exactly to an English lemma in Wiktionary (unlike uninflected forms such as *child*, which do count as lemmas). Since we judged that such glosses ought to be retained rather than deleted altogether, we chose to accept them as well, as long as they belonged to a reference list of English non-lemmas (444,072 entries from `https://en.wiktionary.org/wiki/Category:English_non-lemma_forms`).[6]

Finally, some additional rules were made necessary by the different typological profile of certain language families. It is a well-known observation that parts of speech differ cross-linguistically (Croft, 2005); e.g. in various language families, *adjectives* tend to behave like a sub-class of verbs (Dixon, 2004; Van Lier, 2016). As a corollary, many dictionary authors choose to gloss property words as if they were verbs, with such definitions as '*be small*' (static reading), '*become small*' (dynamic reading), or even '*to be or become small*'. In order to make glosses compatible across language families, we decided to suppress these copulas: as a result, '*to be or become small*' (along with all possible variations thereof) is now correctly converted into a simple gloss {*small*}.

3.3 Summary of data

Table 1 summarizes the amount and diversity of data we were able to extract from each data source. Figure 1 shows the geographic distribution of languages, with dots colored according to language family and sized by how many dialexifications involve each language.

	Wiktion.	ACD	STEDT	combined
Languages	1,537	461	227	1,941
Families	55	6	5	58
Proto-lang.	91	9	19	115
Etyma	9,471	7,279	1,777	18,527
Reflexes	95,840	55,208	18,936	169,256
Meanings	26,822	13,569	3,327	31,143

Table 1: Summary statistics for each data source in current $\mathcal{E}vo$Sem, as well as the combined dataset. Note that the statistics for the individual data sources do not always add up to the values in the "Combined" column, due to overlap in coverage between sources. The reason why ACD and STEDT cover more than one family each is that they both contain borrowings from Austronesian or Sino-Tibetan into other language families. The proto-languages covered by ACD include not only Proto-Austronesian, but also a number of proto-languages descended from it; likewise, the proto-languages covered by STEDT include not only Proto-Sino-Tibetan, but also a number of proto-languages descended from it, and Proto-Indo-Aryan.

4 Visualization

In this section, we present the tools provided on the $\mathcal{E}vo$Sem website for exploring the database.

4.1 Dialexification graphs

From the collected data, we generate a weighted dialexification graph $G = (V, E)$ where $V = \{c \mid \exists c' : \delta(c, c')\}$ is the set of semantic concepts that participate in at least one dialexification, and $E \subset V \times V$ is the set of weighted dialexification relations, such that $(c_1, c_2) \in E \iff \delta(c_1, c_2)$.

The weight of an edge (c_1, c_2) is equal to the number of etyma (or cognate sets) that dialexify that pair of concepts:[7]

$$\begin{aligned} w(c_1, c_2) &= |\{e \mid \delta_e(c_1, c_2)\}| \\ &= |\{e \mid \exists w_1, w_2 : e = a(w_1) = a(w_2) \\ &\qquad \wedge c_1 \in C(w_1) \wedge c_2 \in C(w_2)\}|. \end{aligned}$$

The graph G represents all the dialexification relations between concepts in our database. Because it currently contains tens of thousands of concepts and more than a million edges, it is impossible to represent visually in its entirety. Instead, we propose to display subgraphs based on specific subsets of the concept set.

[6] A reviewer asked why we did not use a lemmatizer to address this issue. The main reason is that we did not want to lose the information conveyed by the inflections; since most dictionary definitions present the key defining words in an uninflected form, the use of an inflected form is likely to carry crucial information about the semantics of the word being defined, e.g. the fact that Italian *prole*, glossed as 'children', is in fact a collective noun (whose meanings also include 'offspring' and 'progeny').

[7] Given a pair of concepts, the weight of its edge is also called *dialexification score*, or *delta* score.

Given the definition of dialexification, a possible way to restrict the graph is to only select the concepts that are lexified by a given cognate set, as defined by an etymon e in language l_p: $G_e = (V_e, E_e)$ with $V_e = \{c \mid \exists w : c \in C(w) \wedge a(w) = e\}$, and $E_e = E \cap (V_e \times V_e)$. We call G_e the *etymograph* of e. Fig. 2 shows part of the etymograph of the etymon **deḱs(i)wós* in Proto-Indo-European.

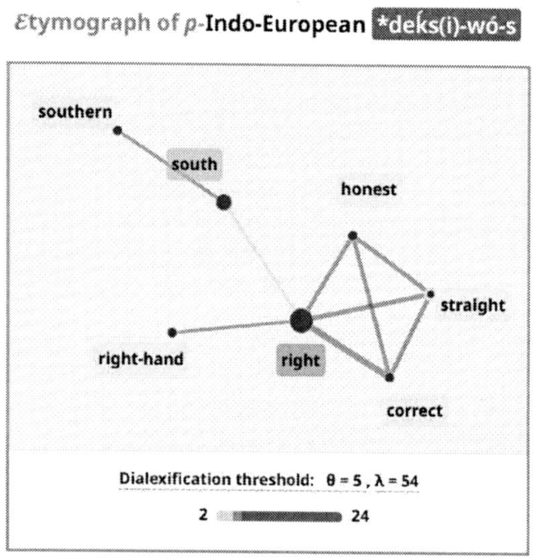

Figure 2: *Etymograph* of p-IE **deḱs(i)wós*, showing the concepts that are dialexified among its descendants. The highlighted edge indicates a pair of concepts {RIGHT–SOUTH} that is dialexified (according to *Ɛvo*Sem) by 6 distinct etyma from four different families: its dialexification score is $\delta = 6$. The thickness of each edge reflects logarithmically the δ score of the concept pair for *Ɛvo*Sem as a whole; for this etymon, the value of δ ranges from 2 to 24 (24 being the δ score of {RIGHT–CORRECT}. The current view has a threshold $\theta = 5$, i.e. it selects only those links whose dialexification score is $\delta \geq 5$; for this etymon, the number of dialex links displayed for $\theta = 5$ is $\lambda = 54$. As for the size of each vertex, it reflects the distribution of different concepts across the descendants of this etymon **deḱs(i)wós*: e.g. 5 of its reflexes have the sense RIGHT, but only one means HONEST.

Note that the weights of the edges are independent of the choice of etymon, since they are computed from the entire *Ɛvo*Sem database.

Since there is one etymograph for each etymon, there are tens of thousands of etymographs in *Ɛvo*Sem (see Table 1). However, each etymograph is of a limited size: the largest one (Proto-Austronesian **maCa*) has 292 nodes, and the median number of nodes in *Ɛvo*Sem is 5. This makes etymographs much easier to view than the entire dialexification graph.

Because all pairs of concepts in an etymograph G_e are dialexified by e, an etymograph is, by definition, a clique. For this reason, we choose not to represent edges of weight $\delta = 1$. More generally, not displaying edges of weight 1 tends to reduce the noise resulting from faulty gloss extraction.

Even with the exclusion of edges of weight 1, some etymographs still have too many edges for easy visualization. To improve legibility, we offer the user the ability to set the weight threshold θ, so as to reduce the number of edges displayed. For example, Figure 2 shows the etymograph of the p-IE etymon **deḱs(i)wós* with $\theta = 5$. Decreasing the threshold brings more senses into view; increasing it reduces the number of nodes displayed.

From a technical standpoint, we store the information necessary to build each etymograph (concepts, reflexes, glosses, links to external sources) in a dedicated JSON file. When the user opens the etymon's dedicated page, an SVG representation of the etymograph is generated using the D3 Javascript library (Bostock, 2012) for computing the vertex layout. The user can then explore the graph, either by interacting with it directly, or by browsing the tables presenting the underlying data.

4.2 Data tables

The data related to an etymograph and its cognate set are presented in three tables: the *etymon-to-concepts* (E2C) *table*, the *concept-to-etyma* (C2E) *table*, and the *dialexification table*.

The *etymon-to-concepts table*, which appears directly alongside the etymograph, lists all the concepts lexified by at least one member of the cognate set. For each concept, a collapsible list of the relevant reflexes is provided (see Fig. 3).

Clicking on a concept cell, or clicking on the concept label directly on the graph, selects the given concept and opens the corresponding C2E table. The table ranks concepts by their frequency of attestation among reflexes; this is shown by the number in the last column, and by the node size in the graph (see Fig. 2). When a concept is selected, its row changes colors, and the concepts that are not dialexified with it at least θ times have their rows grayed out (see Fig. 3). On the graph, this is also reflected by a color change of the edges incident to the corresponding vertex.

The *concept-to-etyma table* lists all the etyma

▾ 19 meanings dialexified by *deḱs(i)-wó-s

MEANINGS	▸ REFLEXES		#
right	▾ language data		5
	Cornish	dyghow	
	Greek	δεξιός - dexiós	
	Irish	deas	
	Old High German	zeso	
	Old Irish	dess	
right-handed	▸ language data		2
south	▾ language data		2
	Irish	deas	
	Old Irish	dess	
able	▸ language data		1
close	▸ language data		1
convenient	▸ language data		1
correct	▸ language data		1
courteous	▸ language data		1
fortunate	▸ language data		1
honest	▸ language data		1

Figure 3: *Etymon-to-concepts table* for the p-IE etymon **deḱs(i)wós*, corresponding to the graph in Fig. 2. The table shows the first 10 of the 19 meanings dialexified by its descendants: RIGHT, SOUTH, CORRECT, etc. Clicking on the concept RIGHT has turned the row to blue (Concept$_1$). The rows in white show senses (e.g. CORRECT) that are dialexified with that Concept$_1$ at least θ times (here, $\theta = 5$); those that are dialexified fewer times appear grayed out. The sense SOUTH was selected as Concept$_2$, and thus appears in red. The collapsible lists for both selected senses are seen unfolded; they show that while Irish *deas* means both RIGHT and SOUTH, Greek *dexiós* only means RIGHT.

79 sources of concept *right*

FAMILY	ETYMON	▸ REFLEXES	
Indo-European	*deḱs(i)-wó-s	▸ language data	
Afroasiatic	*yamin-	▾ language data	
		Akkadian	[illegible] - imnum
		Arabic	يمين - yamīn
		Aramaic	יַמִּינָא - yammīnā
		Hebrew	יָמִין - yamín, yāmîn
		Maltese	lemin
		Ugaritic	𐎊𐎎𐎐 - ymn
Algonquian	*keʔči-	▾ language data	
		Ojibwe	gichi-
Austronesian	*waNan	▸ language data	
Bantu	*-dònga	▸ language data	
Germanic	*garihtiją	▾ language data	
		Old English	ġerihte
Tibeto-Burman	*g-(yr)a	▸ language data	
Dravidian	*wal	▾ language data	
		Telugu	వల - vala
Indo-European	*deḱs(i)-teró-s	▸ language data	
Indo-European	*déḱs(i)-no-s	▾ language data	
		Bengali	দক্ষিণ - dokkhin
		Macedonian	десен - désen
		Old Church Slavonic	деснъ - desnŭ
		Pali	dakkhiṇa
		Sanskrit	दक्षिण - dákṣina
Indo-European	*h₃reǵ-tó-s	▸ language data	

Figure 4: *Concept-to-etyma table* for the concept RIGHT, opened by selecting that sense in the E2C table of p-IE **deḱs(i)wós* (blue row in Fig. 3). 79 etyma include reflexes that lexify the concept RIGHT, of which 11 are shown here. When unfolded, the reflex lists cite only those reflexes that have the target meaning.

that dialexify[8] the selected concept: e.g. the C2E table corresponding to RIGHT in Fig. 3 is given in Fig. 4. For each etymon, the C2E table provides the name of the language family to whose proto-language the etymon belongs; a link to the main source of data for that etymon; and a collapsible list of reflexes that lexify the concept of interest.

Clicking on a second (non-grayed out) concept has the effect of selecting the dialexification relation holding between Concept$_1$ (in blue) and Concept$_2$ (in red). Alternatively, the user can directly click on an edge of the graph. Selecting a dialexification edge replaces the C2E table with a new *dialexification table*: see Fig. 5.

The dialexification table lists all etyma that dialexify the pair of selected concepts. It works as if by combining together two C2E tables. The collapsible list of reflexes is now sorted and colored to reflect which concept is lexified by which reflex.

The top-most elements of the list (on a blue background) lexify only Concept$_1$, while the bottom-most elements (on a red background) lexify only Concept$_2$. The elements in the middle of the list, on a two-color striped background, are reflexes that colexify the two concepts.

It is always possible that some part of the list may be empty: e.g. in Fig. 5, no reflex of **deḱs(i)wós* means only SOUTH (red background). When a cognate set has no reflex that colexifies Concept$_1$ and Concept$_2$ together, one can speak of "pure dialexification". While the more common configuration is to find both dialex and colex in the same cognate set, cases of *pure dialexification* do occur.

5 Applications

*ℰvo*Sem allows us to observe historical connections between meanings that would be missed if we were to limit ourselves to looking at colexifications. For example, the meanings CHEST and

[8] Saying that an etymon dialexifies a concept implicitly means "with some other concept", since dialexification is a binary relation.

Figure 5: *Dialexification table* showing the six etyma that dialexify {RIGHT–SOUTH}. For each etymon, an unfolded list displays those reflexes that lexify only Concept$_1$ (blue background), or only Concept$_2$ (red background). When a reflex has both meanings at once, it is a case of colexification, made visible by the two-color stripe pattern. The clickable icon on each row (after the etymon) gives access to the online source.

STOMACH are dialexified 6 times in our data, but are not colexified even once.

Such instances of pure dialexification are useful to historical linguists, as they help to more accurately determine whether two forms with different meanings are potential cognates. They also provide insight into pathways of semantic change. Thus, while the pair {CHEST–STOMACH} is dialexified $\delta = 6$ times, {CHEST–HEART} has $\delta = 13$, and {HEART–STOMACH} has $\delta = 11$. From this, one can hypothesize that, if a form that once meant 'chest' later came to mean 'stomach', at some intermediate point it probably included 'heart' among its meanings.

Finally, dialexifications provide a way of measuring the similarities between concepts—much like colexifications, but in a manner that controls for shared descent. This opens up the possibility of using dialexifications to improve performance in similarity judgment tasks (as in Harvill et al., 2022), or to bootstrap the inference of semantic features in cross-lingual datasets (as in Chen and Bjerva, 2023).

References

Lloyd B. Anderson. 1974. Distinct sources of fuzzy data: ways of integrating relatively discrete and gradient aspects of language, and explaining grammar on the basis of semantic fields. In Roger W. Shuy and Charles-James N. Bailey, editors, *Towards Tomorrow's Linguistics*, pages 50–64. Georgetown University Press, Washington, D.C.

Hongchang Bao, Bradley Hauer, and Grzegorz Kondrak. 2021. On universal colexifications. In *Proceedings of the 11th Global Wordnet Conference*, pages 1–7, University of South Africa (UNISA). Global Wordnet Association.

Kenneth Benoit, David Muhr, and Kohei Watanabe. 2021. *stopwords: Multilingual Stopword Lists*. R package version 2.3.

Robert Blust and Stephen Trussel. 2013. The Austronesian comparative dictionary: A work in progress. *Oceanic Linguistics*, 52(2):493–523.

Robert Blust, Stephen Trussel, and Alexander D. Smith. 2023. CLDF dataset derived from Blust's "Austronesian Comparative Dictionary". Data set.

Mike Bostock. 2012. *D3.js - Data-Driven Documents*.

Thomas Brochhagen and Gemma Boleda. 2022. When do languages use the same word for different meanings? the goldilocks principle in colexification. *Cognition*, 226:105179.

Thomas Brochhagen, Gemma Boleda, Eleonora Gualdoni, and Yang Xu. 2023. From language development to language evolution: A unified view of human lexical creativity. *Science*, 381(6656):431–436.

Yiyi Chen, Russa Biswas, and Johannes Bjerva. 2023. Colex2Lang: Language embeddings from semantic typology. In *Proceedings of the 24th Nordic Conference on Computational Linguistics (NoDaLiDa)*, pages 673–684, Tórshavn, Faroe Islands. University of Tartu Library.

Yiyi Chen and Johannes Bjerva. 2023. Colexifications for bootstrapping cross-lingual datasets: The case of phonology, concreteness, and affectiveness. In *Proceedings of the 20th SIGMORPHON workshop on Computational Research in Phonetics, Phonology, and Morphology*, pages 98–109, Toronto, Canada. Association for Computational Linguistics.

William Croft. 2005. Word classes, parts of speech, and syntactic argumentation. *Linguistic Typology*, 9(3):431–441.

Anna Di Natale, Max Pellert, and David Garcia. 2021. Colexification networks encode affective meaning. *Affective Science*, 2(2):99–111.

Robert MW Dixon. 2004. Adjective classes in typological perspective. *Adjective classes: A cross-linguistic typology*, pages 1–49.

Alexandre François. 2008. Semantic maps and the typology of colexification: Intertwining polysemous networks across languages. In Martine Vanhove, editor, *From Polysemy to Semantic Change: Towards a typology of lexical semantic associations*, Studies in Language Companion Series, pages 163–215. John Benjamins.

Alexandre François and Siva Kalyan. 2023. Dialexification: A tool for studying cross-linguistic patterns of semantic change. 16th International Cognitive Linguistics Conference.

Alexandre François and Siva Kalyan. in prep. Dialexification and the typology of lexical change. *Bulletin de la Société de linguistique*.

Thanasis Georgakopoulos, Eitan Grossman, Dmitry Nikolaev, and Stéphane Polis. 2022. Universal and macro-areal patterns in the lexicon: A case-study in the perception-cognition domain. *Linguistic Typology*, 26(2):439–487.

John Harvill, Roxana Girju, and Mark Hasegawa-Johnson. 2022. Syn2Vec: Synset colexification graphs for lexical semantic similarity. In *Proceedings of the 2022 Conference of the North American Chapter of the Association for Computational Linguistics: Human Language Technologies*, pages 5259–5270, Seattle, United States. Association for Computational Linguistics.

Martin Haspelmath. 1997. *Indefinite Pronouns*. Oxford University Press, Oxford.

Andrey Kutuzov, Lilja Øvrelid, Terrence Szymanski, and Erik Velldal. 2018. Diachronic word embeddings and semantic shifts: a survey. In *International Conference on Computational Linguistics*.

James P Mallory and Douglas Q Adams. 1997. *Encyclopedia of Indo-European Culture*. Fitzroy Dearborn Publishers, London, Chicago.

James A Matisoff. 2016. *STEDT: Sino-Tibetan etymological dictionary and thesaurus*. University of California, Berkeley.

George A. Miller. 1995. Wordnet: A lexical database for english. *Commun. ACM*, 38(11):39–41.

Sebastian Nordhoff and Harald Hammarström. 2012. Cataloguing linguistic diversity: Glottolog/langdoc. Proceedings of Digital Humanities 2012.

Robert Östling. 2016. Studying colexification through massively parallel corpora. In Päivi Juvonen and Maria Koptjevskaja-Tamm, editors, *The lexical typology of semantic shifts*, pages 157–176. De Gruyter Mouton.

Christoph Rzymski, Tiago Tresoldi, Simon J. Greenhill, Mei-Shin Wu, Nathanael E. Schweikhard, Maria Koptjevskaja-Tamm, Volker Gast, Timotheus A. Bodt, Abbie Hantgan, Gereon A. Kaiping, Sophie Chang, Yunfan Lai, Natalia Morozova, Heini Arjava, Nataliia Hübler, Ezequiel Koile, Steve Pepper, Mariann Proos, Briana Van Epps, Ingrid Blanco, Carolin Hundt, Sergei Monakhov, Kristina Pianykh, Sallona Ramesh, Russell D. Gray, Robert Forkel, and Johann-Mattis List. 2020. The database of cross-linguistic colexifications, reproducible analysis of cross-linguistic polysemies. *Scientific Data*, 7(1).

Nina Tahmasebi, Lars Borin, Adam Jatowt, Yang Xu, and Simon Hengchen. 2021. *Computational approaches to semantic change*. Language Science Press, Berlin.

Eva Van Lier. 2016. Lexical flexibility in Oceanic languages. *Linguistic Typology*, 20(2):197–232.

Michael Weiss. 2015. The comparative method. In Claire Bowern and Bethwyn Evans, editors, *The Routledge handbook of Historical linguistics*, pages 127–145. Routledge, London.

Hadley Wickham, Jim Hester, and Jeroen Ooms. 2023. *xml2: Parse XML*. R package version 1.3.5.

Yang Xu, Khang Duong, Barbara C. Malt, Serena Jiang, and Mahesh Srinivasan. 2020. Conceptual relations predict colexification across languages. *Cognition*, 201:104280.

Multi-lect automatic detection of Swadesh list items from raw corpus data in East Slavic languages

Ilia Afanasev
University of Vienna
ilia.afanasev.1997@gmail.com

Abstract

The article introduces a novel task of multi-lect automatic detection of Swadesh list items from raw corpora. The task aids the early stage of historical linguistics study by helping the researcher compile word lists for further analysis.

In this paper, I test multi-lect automatic detection on the East Slavic lects' data. The training data consists of Ukrainian, Belarusian, and Russian material. I introduce a new dataset for the Ukrainian language. I implement data augmentation techniques to give automatic tools a better understanding of the searched value. The test data consists of the Old East Slavic texts.

I train HMM, CRF, and mBERT models, then test and evaluate them by harmonic F1 score. The baseline is a Random Forest classifier. I introduce two different subtasks: the search for new Swadesh list items, and the search for the known Swadesh list items in new lects of the well-established group. The first subtask, given the simultaneously diverse and vague nature of the Swadesh list, currently presents an almost unbeatable challenge for machine learning methods. The second subtask, on the other hand, is easier, and the mBERT model achieves a 0.57 F1 score. This is an impressive result, given how hard it is to formalise the token belonging to a very specific and thematically diverse set of concepts.

1 Introduction

The need for automatic tools that can aid human researchers has been pressing in computational linguistics for at least the last two decades (Mackay and Kondrak, 2005). There are turnkey solutions for the word list data (Jäger and Sofroniev, 2016; Jäger et al., 2017; Nath et al., 2022). However, when a researcher starts working with a new lect from scratch, they usually have nothing but raw data, from which they must extract this kind of a word list. This is where computational technologies may assist the researcher in the earlier stage of the study: they may execute preliminary detection of tokens that are of special interest – the Swadesh list items (Holman et al., 2008).

In this paper, I present a task of multi-lect automatic detection of Swadesh list items from raw corpus data. Swadesh list, named after its creator, Morris Swadesh, is a list of basic concepts that generally are universal among the human languages and may be used for historical linguistics purposes (Borin, 2012). I want to test, whether the computer can grasp the vague concept of *swadeshness* (Dellert et al., 2020), if even human researchers often struggle with its formalisation. I define swadeshness by the following set of criteria:

- **Historical stability**: lexical items that express Swadesh list concepts remain relatively unchanged during the history of language.
- **Frequency**: generally, Swadesh list concepts-expressing lexical units are among the more frequent ones of the language. However, it is a tendency, not a law. There is no distinct correlation, and by no means frequency should be considered the ultimate criterion (Burlak, 2021).
- **Stylistic neutrality**: concepts that represent Swadesh list items do not have a tendency to appear in a specific register or in statements with a specific sentiment.
- **Syntactic independence**: lexical items that express Swadesh list concepts should remain in the language not as a part of a bigger collocation, such as proverb (Kassian et al., 2010).
- **Semantic preciseness**: a member of the Swadesh list should have a distinct, easily identifiable meaning.

The multi-lect automatic detection of Swadesh list items from raw corpora is challenging. The tool

Proceedings of the 4th Workshop on Computational Approaches to Historical Language Change, pages 76–86
December 6, 2023 ©2023 Association for Computational Linguistics

(a rule-based, statistical, or neural network-based model) should be able to perform it zero-shot and from the first attempt: otherwise, human researchers are not going to need it at all. Ideally, the model should be able to grasp the concept of swadeshness and become proficient enough to perform the task on the languages, the relations of which to the others are completely unknown. Such a model ideally should be at the forefront, laying the groundwork for a human researcher. However, currently, automatic tools are not able to efficiently zero-shot detect Swadesh list items in the raw corpus of a randomly given language. It is only reasonable to start with an easier task, detecting Swadesh list items in the language for which there is a strong hypothesis of its genetic relationships. To carry out this detection, a researcher needs raw corpus material from this language and a model trained on the material of the language's hypothetical relatives. Thus, the task of multi-lect automatic detection of Swadesh list items from raw corpus data transforms into the task of multi-lect automatic detection of Swadesh list items from raw corpus data of a particular language group.

I propose to start with the East Slavic lects. In this paper, I use the term *lect* instead of dialect and/or language to denote any distinct variety without imposing any hierarchy, which generally distracts from the variation study. This is particularly relevant in the case of the Slavic group due to the political circumstances of the last three decades.

The East Slavic group seems especially well-fit for the task because a group is quite a small unit of language classification, for which the concept of swadeshness may be easier to grasp. The East Slavic group possesses some rather big corpora for both modern and historical data. I intend to train the models on the modern East Slavic data from different lects (Ukrainian, Russian and Belarusian) and to zero-shot test them on the historical data. I want to try different models, both simple probability-based tools and complex large linguistic models (LLMs).

1.1 Contributions

- I present a novel task of multi-lect automatic detection of Swadesh list items from raw corpora and its two subtasks: the search for new Swadesh list items and the search for the known Swadesh list items in new lects of a well-established group.
- I propose possible solutions for this task which achieve the highest score one may require from the computer, given that even the formalisation of swadeshness is quite hard for humans, as the definition I provide is far from being comprehensive.
- I prepare a new dataset for Ukrainian in the Universal Dependencies format, currently possessing silver morphological tagging, lemmatisation, and dependency parsing, performed with Stanza toolkit (Qi et al., 2018, 2020).

1.2 Paper structure

The second section is dedicated to the previous research, including works on automatic cognate detection, possible architectures, and evaluation in NLP. In the third section, I describe the dataset for the training models and the dataset to test them against. The fourth section includes a step-by-step description of the research method, including the architectures of the models I use and the metrics utilised to inspect the quality of their performance. In the fifth section, I report the results of the experiments. The conclusion provides an overall analysis of how well the models fulfilled the task and proposes possible ways to enhance their performance in the future.

2 Related Work

The desire to automatically extract Swadesh list items from new data manifested itself in historical linguistics almost as soon as the computing powers became sufficient for this type of task (Mackay and Kondrak, 2005). Generally, it falls within the greater historical linguistics trend of implementing computational methods as researcher's assistants (Dellert, 2019). HMM models are some of the most frequent solutions due to their simple yet effective architecture and overall dominance across the NLP horizon; with PairHMMs, adapted for working with parallel data (Wieling et al., 2007), being the most widely used. Further steps are connected with different techniques in multiple sequence alignment (List, 2012) and sequence comparison (List, 2014). After that, the automatic cognate detection and classification as a task emerges (Jäger and Sofroniev, 2016; Jäger et al., 2017; Nath et al., 2022). The methods to extract large Swadesh lists in the context of multi-lingual databases appear at this time (Dellert and Buch, 2016) and simultaneously the multi-lingual datasets for them to be tested on arise (Dellert et al., 2020). The formalisation of *swadeshness* has become an important part of the discussion in recent years (Dellert and Buch, 2016).

The multi-lect automatic detection of Swadesh list items requires other approaches, as it utilises raw corpus data rather than lexical databases. One such approach is part-of-speech tagging. Part-of-speech tagging is mostly dominated by universal methods, based on recurrent neural networks (Qi et al., 2018) (Qi et al., 2020). Yet the tasks conducted on different language varieties demand agile models that can both be tuned for the needs of a specific tagset and work in the context of low-resourced and sparse data (Scherrer, 2021). Hidden Markov Model (HMM)-based taggers present this opportunity (Schmid, 1994, 1995; Özçelik et al., 2019; Lyashevskaya and Afanasev, 2021). The other probabilistic tool used for part-of-speech tagging is conditional random fields (CRF) (Behera, 2017). Both these methods are regularly applied in the context of historical linguistics and language variation (Mackay and Kondrak, 2005; Wieling et al., 2007; Gillin, 2022; Camposampiero et al., 2022). CRF is also used in named entity recognition, where it is rivalled by methods based on the use of transformer models (Yang et al., 2021). Historical linguistics study often requires efficient resource utilisation. This fits the current NLP trend that gave rise to the distilled and tiny versions of transformers (Sanh et al., 2019).

Historical data is usually quite low-resourced, which provides an additional challenge to the detection of sparsely distributed Swadesh items. This requires using special metrics for imbalanced data (Dudy and Bedrick, 2020). The harmonic F1 score, traditionally used for such cases (Chinchor, 1992), still finds its application in the analysis of NLP tasks (Scherrer, 2021).

3 Data

The data consists of two subsets of different sizes and coming from different languages, one used to train the models and to test them on the first subtask, the search for new Swadesh list items, and another – for the second subtask, to test their performance on completely new material. Both datasets are stored in Universal Dependencies (UD) format (Zeman; et al, 2022). I use UD format as it contains information on the lemma, which makes it significantly easier to prepare the datasets for the experiments.

The first subset is a large Modern East Slavic multi-lect dataset. It was vital to maintain the balance between these groups for the model to learn as many features of Swadesh list items across the East Slavic lects as possible. I call the main principle of balance a parent-node one, which means that the amount of data from the lects under the same node (i.e., sharing the last common ancestor) should be approximately equal. For instance, in the case of this research, it means that Ukrainian and Belarusian, the closest relatives out of the three present lects, should have the same amount of tokens on their part. Russian, the sole representative of their sister group, should be presented with a corpus of the same size.

The first corpus I use, the Belarusian-HSE corpus (Shishkina and Lyashevskaya, 2022), consists of 305,000 tokens of different genres, such as fiction (including poetry), legal texts, non-fiction, news texts, Wikipedia, social networks texts.

Ukrainian UD (IU) corpus consists of only 122,000 tokens[1], so I need more data. For this purpose, I take the ua-gec corpus (Syvokon and Nahorna, 2021) and tag it with the existing Stanza model (Qi et al., 2018, 2020), acquiring silver data in UD format [2]. I get 183,961 samples of this corpus, and thus the Ukrainian-Belarusian branch of East Slavic remains in balance.

The Russian corpus Taiga (Shavrina and Shapovalova, 2017) consists of 197,000 tokens and is represented by a diverse set of genres, including poetry, fiction, non-fiction, Wikipedia, blogs, social media, and news. Taiga is designed to represent syntactic features of Russian lexical units (obviously, taking in Swadesh list items) in the best possible way.

To balance the Russian branch with the Ukrainian-Belarusian branch, I add data from SynTagRus (Droganova et al., 2018), a 1.5 million corpus of fiction, news, and non-fiction. I take 395,431 tokens, so the training corpus may achieve the balance.

One may point out that this makes the dataset imbalanced in favour of the Russian lect. However, it balances the Russian branch of the East Slavic tree with the Ruthenian branch, while the Ruthenian branch is still balanced within itself. This follows

[1]https://github.com/UniversalDependencies/UD_Ukrainian-IU/tree/master

[2]https://huggingface.co/datasets/djulian13/Swadesh-list-tagged-East-Slavic

Table 1: General characteristics of the training dataset.

Dataset	Language	Token number
IU	Ukrainian	122,000
UA-GEC	Ukrainian	183,961
Belarusian-HSE	Belarusian	305,000
Taiga	Russian	197,000
SynTagRus	Russian	395,431
Overall	**Various Slavic**	**1,203,392**

the historical-comparative principle of step-by-step reconstruction (see, for instance, Starostin (2019)). We illustrate this with Figure 1.

The corpora of the training dataset and their key features are presented in Table 1.

The test dataset is the two corpora of historical East Slavic lects, the Old East Slavic TOROT corpus (Eckhoff and Berdicevskis, 2015), containing nearly 246,000 tokens. The TOROT corpus is predominantly later Old East Slavic (Belarusian, Ukrainian and Russian ancestral lect continuum) and partly Middle Russian (when it split from Ukrainian and Belarusian) material. Its texts are mostly legal documents and non-fiction (chronicles). Old East Slavic being the ancestral form for all three modern East Slavic languages (thus containing within different texts proto-Belarusian, proto-Ukrainian, and proto-Russian features) is the main reason I use every one of them, and not only Russian.

Both datasets are additionally preprocessed to prepare them for the task. They are assigned a label *c* (non-Swadesh list item) or *i* (Swadesh list item). I use the 40-item Swadesh list (Holman et al., 2008), enriching it with some concepts from the 110-item list (Kassian et al., 2010), namely, *woman, kill, eat, all, man, me*, and *you (indirect)* (genitive stem). I chose these particular concepts as they are semantically close to the concepts of the 40-item list: *woman* to *breast*, *kill* to *die*, *eat* to *drink*, *all* to *full*, *man* to *person*, *me* to *I*, and *you (indirect)* to *you*. Hopefully, this aids the models to better grasp the semantic component of swadeshness. I tag each possible morphological form of Swadesh list items. Genitive stems of *you* and *I*, *you (indirect)* and *me* respectively, get the treatment of separate concepts. Yet this does not mean that I use only base forms for all the concepts in the dataset, as the East Slavic languages are highly inflective. I would risk losing a lot of forms, tagging only base forms as Swadesh list items. In this fashion, all the forms of *I* (я) and *me* (меня, мне, and мной) have an *i* (Swadesh list item) label. While picking the exact lexical item for a concept, I generally follow guidelines by Kassian et al. (2010).

The training dataset, while quite big, does not contain a lot of contexts for Swadesh list items for the model to learn on. The fully automatic generation of new examples, contrarily to grammatical error detection, currently seems impossible. However, I apply artificial augmentation, using token-level 3-grams that provide minimal left and right context. This is an approach that part-of-speech studies successfully implement (Lyashevskaya and Afanasev, 2021).

I wrote a script that generates 3-grams for each instance of the Swadesh list item in the text. These may be represented as *c i c*, where *i* is a Swadesh list item, and *c* is used for any other token, including *[CLS]* (this denotes fragment-starting token) and *[EOS]* (this denotes fragment-finishing token). An item of the dataset thus contains the original sentence and its labels and generated 3-grams with their labels. The script is also used for the test dataset. Artificial augmentations of the test dataset are not going to be used in the evaluation, as they may seemingly boost results for a poorer-performing model, and compromise the intention of evaluating the model on the raw data. Generated datasets are available on HuggingFace [3].

4 Method

4.1 Task

I treat multi-lect automatic Swadesh list items detection as a sequence labelling and information extraction task, placing it among the part-of-speech tagging (Behera, 2017) and named entity recognition (Tjong Kim Sang and De Meulder, 2003) tasks, as it shares common features (a clear split of all the items into categories with part-of-speech-tagging and a heavy imbalance of two classes with named entity recognition) with both. One may see it as a reduced information extraction task with the extracted entity restricted to a single token, or as an unbalanced sequence labelling task with two labels, one of which is significantly less frequent than another. These different ways imply using

[3]https://huggingface.co/datasets/djulian13/Swadesh-list-tagged-East-Slavic

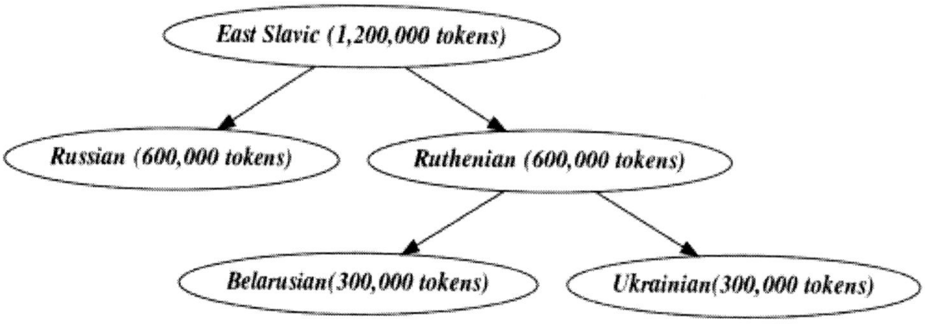

Figure 1: Application of step-by-step reconstruction principle to the training corpora size. On each historical division, the token number is equal between lects or groups of lects.

particular methods for both creating the tool and its evaluation.

Whether one frames the task as a reduced information extraction task or an unbalanced sequence labelling task, one should use metrics that fit the case of unbalanced classes the most. I propose to use the traditional harmonic F1 score between precision (the number of correctly predicted items of a particular class, divided by the number of all items) and recall (the number of correctly predicted items of a particular class, divided by the number of items that belong to this class) (Chinchor, 1992). The formula for harmonic F1 score is given in (1).

$$F = 2\frac{PR}{P + R} \quad (1)$$

I am going to provide information on precision and recall to present a clearer picture. As an evaluation method, I use only the F1 score for the Swadesh list items, as the average F1 score and F1 score for non-Swadesh list items, the dominating class, are going to be very high, and, at the same time, not informative.

4.2 Baseline

If I treat multi-lect automatic Swadesh list items detection as a sequence labelling task, the optimal methods are the ones used for part-of-speech tagging. Otherwise, if one sees the task as an information extraction one, the models, generally used for named entity recognition, are suitable.

Our intention to build the model able to generalise its knowledge on the previously unknown lects poses additional restrictions, making the use of rule-based methods, adjusted for a specific lect or set of lects, hard and probably not worthy of implementation. The possible tool is going to be based on machine learning methods.

As a baseline method, I use a random forest (Ho, 1995) classifier that utilises frequency (absolute and relative as different parameters), one of the most easily Swadesh list item quantifiable properties. The only tweaked parameter of classifier is random state, set to 1590.

4.3 Statistical methods

The first method I propose is a simple Hidden Markov Model (HMM), originally designed for part-of-speech tagging (Özçelik et al., 2019). It is a state machine that predicts the next state on the basis of the previous ones (Warjri et al., 2019). The particular implementation is enhanced with the Viterbi algorithm. Viterbi algorithm enhances HMM's ability to find the most likely tag sequence (Prajapati and Yajnik, 2019). The Hidden Markov Model nowadays almost never achieves state-of-the-art result quality and is not exactly well-adjusted for the unbalanced classification. However, it often demonstrates the ability to generalise on low-resourced heterogeneous datasets, sometimes exceeding modern state-of-the-art multi-lingual transformer neural networks (Lyashevskaya and Afanasev, 2021). This paper does not utilise any specific training setup, other than the one used in Lyashevskaya and Afanasev (2021)

Conditional Random Fields (CRF) is a model that also often performs part-of-speech tagging (Behera, 2017) and named entity recognition (Jie and Lu, 2019). This model is based on computing the probabilities, which makes it similar to HMM, though some detailed implementations are different (Behera, 2017). CRF is a simple statistical tool, yet these currently demonstrate high results after slight augmentations, often competing with recurrent and transformer neural networks: it is especially relevant in non-standard conditions (Gillin,

2022) (Camposampiero et al., 2022). There is no specific parameter tuning for CRF: preprocessing includes adding special tokens for marking start and end of sentences, and training parameters are mostly default. The final set is the following:

- L-BGFS as gradient descent method,
- L1 regularisation coefficient = 0.25,
- L2 regularisation coefficient = 0.3,
- maximum number of iterations is 100,
- generation of transition features for all possible combinations of attributes and labels. This is especially important, as there are only two classes, and one heavily outweighs another. It is extremely necessary for the model to get the grasp of what Swadesh list items are not, not only what they are.

4.4 BERT

I also fine-tune multilingual cased BERT-base (Devlin et al., 2018) on the data, as one may fine-tune it for the task of named entity recognition (NER). Transformers are nowadays often used for this kind of task, showing state-of-the-art results (Yang et al., 2021). I do not implement the hierarchical architecture of (Yang et al., 2021) designed for nested named entity recognition. As Swadesh list items are not nested ones, the advantages it gives are not going to be useful.

NER is a much simpler task than swadeshness detection, and there is a high probability that the model used for NER may fail, yet this is probably the best shot there is. Models trained for other tasks, such as machine translation (MT), may become confused even more. They aim at direct transformation, while NER models grasp a concept, and thus, hopefully, will not only learn to find the known Swadesh list items but the ones the model does not know beforehand as well.The model trains for 1 epoch with batch size being equal to 1, due to the hardware restrictions.

The code for each of these models is present on GitHub [4].

4.5 Swadesh list split

I split the prepared Swadesh list into two halves presented in Table 2. The parts are designed for the model to be able to at least partially rely on vectorised semantics and syntactic behaviour, with pairs such as *come - path, one - two, ear - hear*. This is the motivation behind the addition of items to list (Holman et al., 2008). Not all the concepts find a pair (*name*), and some pairs, such as *horn - nose* may prove not as informative as one hopes. I also try to assign an equal amount of part-of-speech items to each part of the dataset.

[4] https://github.com/The-One-Who-Speaks-and-Depicts/SlavNLP-23

5 Experiments and Results

The experiments start with splitting the modern dataset into three parts, α, β, and ω. ω is a full dataset, α and β contain sentences that include only tokens from the A part of the Swadesh list split, or the B one, respectively. I then augment each of the datasets with 3-gram addition. I train each architecture - HMM, CRF, BERT (but the baseline, random forest classifier) - separately on α, α-augmented, β, β-augmented, ω, and ω-augmented. The historical test dataset is not split, and later I refer to it as γ.

I cross-validate α- and β-trained models. This is the first subtask, the search for new Swadesh list items, and here the models are not going to show a high F1 score, as it is a hard task even for a human.

For the second subtask, I test the ω-trained model with the γ dataset. Here the results should be better, as there are obvious graphical similarities between modern and historical Swadesh list concepts, and their semantic and syntactic stability possibly may allow for an easier capture of historical Swadesh list concepts.

The models' results comparison should lead to the discussion of possible reasons why the model with the best performance was the most successful and why others failed.

5.1 Unknown Swadesh list items identification

The results of the experiments are in tables 3 and 4.

I provide only aggregated results, as with error rates this high there is no sense in the analysis of each concept precision/recall/F1-score. The numbers are going to be too low for us to get any valuable insights. I also do not attempt to simultaneously identify a token as a particular concept in addition to marking it as bearing swadeshness.

It is clearly easier for the models to predict β tokens than α. Mostly, this is due to the semantic closeness of *woman* and *person* concepts to *man*, and words that are very close to *one* (α-list) in β. It

Table 2: Swadesh list split.

Half	Concepts
α	*come, ear, see, fire, hand, horn, I, leaf, mountain, skin, one, star, tongue, louse, breast, die, drink, full, man, you (indirect), blood, fish, name, new, night, we*
β	*path, hear, eye, water, knee, nose, you, tree, stone, liver, two, sun, tooth, dog, woman, kill, eat, all, person, me, bone*

Table 3: Results on β-dataset of all the models trained on α-dataset rounded to the third decimal place. Best results here and afterwards are in **bold**.

Model	Precision	Recall	F1
Baseline	0	0	0
HMM	0.123	0.036	0.056
HMM (3-gram-augmented data)	0.02	0.036	0.026
CRF	0.011	0.003	0.005
CRF (3-gram-augmented data)	0.009	0.003	0.005
BERT	**0.795**	**0.082**	**0.149**
BERT (3-gram-augmented data)	0.5	0	0

Table 4: Results on α-dataset of all the models trained on β-dataset rounded to the third decimal place.

Model	Precision	Recall	F1
Baseline	0.01	0.004	0.005
HMM	0.034	0.012	0.018
HMM (3-gram-augmented data)	0.034	0.012	0.018
CRF	0	0	0
CRF (3-gram-augmented data)	0	0	0
BERT	**0.379**	**0.02**	**0.36**
BERT (3-gram-augmented data)	0.231	0	0

also seems that models may deduce that concept *eye* belongs to the Swadesh list.

Augmentation directly leads to overfitting, as the models trained on augmented datasets experience a significant drop in quality. HMM is probably the least influenced one, it seems to be heavily resistant to this kind of noise. Despite that, its precision gets down on β-dataset prediction.

The baseline model, a random forest classifier that is aware only of frequencies, is unable to predict new Swadesh tokens appearing in the dataset, which supports the theory that frequency is not a determining factor in choosing candidates for addition to lexicostatistical lists. There are, however, some words that may be interesting: месяц 'month', вы 'you (plural)', both from basic vocabulary lists. The baseline model clearly fails in the subtask - on the familiar data it achieves a much more optimistic 0.91 F1-score. In the same fashion CRF fails: it is good at memorising the exact tokens, not in generalisation over them.

The HMM model performs significantly better. HMM yet again proves that its simplistic design is exceptionally well-suited for classification tasks. In β-dataset, it detects наш 'our' that shares root with *we (indirect)*, a genitive stem of *we*, and хадзіць 'go', an aspectual pair for *come*. HMM also makes mistakes, tagging frequent words (such as м 'm') as Swadesh list items.

BERT is by far the best-performing model - probably, due to it being context-oriented, and thus able to grasp such properties of Swadesh list items as syntactic independence, stylistic neutrality, and semantic preciseness. It still has a low F1 score and its recall is not exactly high, but this is probably one of the best shots that a computer may have for a prediction of such a vague category. It also detects concepts, which are similar to the ones from the 110-item Swadesh list (Kassian et al., 2010), for instance, *somebody* (хтось is similar in form to хто 'who', a concept from the list).

Table 5: Results on γ-dataset of all the models trained on ω-dataset.

Model	Precision	Recall	F1
Baseline	0	0	0
HMM	0.384	0.36	0.371
HMM (3-gram-augmented data)	0.384	0.36	0.371
CRF	0.045	0.014	0.022
CRF (3-gram-augmented data)	0.045	0.014	0.021
BERT	0.734	**0.459**	**0.565**
BERT (3-gram-augmented data)	**0.737**	0.01	0.02

5.2 Swadesh list items identification for unknown lects

The results of the search for Swadesh list items in Old East Slavic texts are presented in Table 5.

The baseline score remains the same. It is probably due to the differences in size between ω- and γ-datasets and the distribution patterns of modern and historical East Slavic lects tokens. CRF architecture also lags behind the other models, barely beating the baseline.

Augmentation technique harms the results of Swadesh list items identification for unknown lects in a similar manner that it harms the results of the unknown Swadesh list items identification in the known lects. HMM yet again resists its negative effects, but the other models (even CRF, though slightly) do not.

Overall, the scores are significantly better than for the previous subtask. There are still choices that one may treat as mistakes. For instance, the model labels есми 'be-PRES.1.PL' as a Swadesh list item. At the same time, they find some tokens that may present interest as a potential Swadesh list material, for instance, ноць 'night'. Picking есми 'be-PRES.1.PL' here is more of an error, it is just very much alike to Ukrainian ми 'we'. However, ноць 'night' is a more interesting case: it is a historically stable, more or less frequent, stylistically neutral, syntactically independent and semantically precise unit. It is a Swadesh list concept (Kassian et al., 2010) in the East Slavic languages, and the model successfully discovered it. Cases like this prove that models generally may grasp the concept of swadeshness.

BERT performs the best out of all, mostly due to its ability to grasp the behaviour of the Swadesh list items and not their exact form. One additional explanation is that East Slavic languages are quite closely related, having started to split approximately 600 - 1,000 years ago (Starostin, 1989). BERT's F1 score steps over 0.5, which I see as a huge achievement, given the complexity and vagueness of the task presented even for humans (Burlak, 2021).

6 Conclusion

Automatic tools demonstrate modest yet inspiring results, achieving a maximum of 0.56 F1 score on the tokens they are familiar with in unfamiliar languages and a maximum of 0.15 F1 score on unfamiliar tokens in the familiar lects. This seems quite promising, as the Swadesh list items is a very sparsely distributed class of lexical units. The average probability of encountering them in raw text (across 1000 random samples, 100 lexical units each) is 0.02 for ω-dataset and 0.04 for γ-dataset. BERT outcompetes probabilistic tools, HMM and especially CRF, as it grasps the deep core properties of Swadesh list items, namely, syntactic independence, stylistic neutrality, and semantic preciseness. HMM, though, is the most stable one in terms of resisting the noise in the data. All the models perform better at memorising tokens than at generalising over the concept of swadeshness. This may still aid the search for concepts that are expressed by the forms most stable across the span of time, such as pronouns. They even sometimes find completely new candidates for Swadesh list items, such as *night*. Unfortunately, one still needs to deal with each case manually when a model labels something as a Swadesh list item. Effective evaluation systems are yet to appear. As for automatic evaluation, the last resort is still checking against an existing list.

Data augmentation, restricted to 3-gram generation from sentences, is harmful to both the probabilistic tools and the transformer models. It definitely leads to overfitting.

For the automatic tools to aid human researchers better, further enhancements must be provided in the future. The extension of the datasets and the implementation of new, effective data augmentation techniques, such as providing quantified information on the described features of Swadesh list items, are required. It seems crucial to add verification of the method on other language groups, not only East Slavic.

The task may also be approached with other methods based on other NLP tasks. I believe that at least a random forest classifier will become a much better baseline with information on syntactic independence, semantic precision, and stylistic neutrality. The other models are also going to benefit from this kind of feature engineering.

7 Acknowledgements

I owe Olga Lyashevskaya and George Starostin for insightful discussion on the nature of swadeshness. I am grateful to anonymous reviewers from VarDial 2022, Slavic NLP 2023, and CNLPS 2023, whose comments helped to shape the research in its current form. I thank the anonymous reviewers from the LChange'23 conference for their useful feedback. The remaining errors are my own.

References

Pitambar Behera. 2017. An experiment with the CRF++ Parts of Speech (POS) tagger for Odia. *Language in India*, 17:18–40.

Lars Borin. 2012. *Core Vocabulary: A Useful But Mystical Concept in Some Kinds of Linguistics*, pages 53–65. Springer Berlin Heidelberg, Berlin, Heidelberg.

Svetlana Burlak. 2021. Stability and frequency: is there a correlation? *Journal of Language Relationship*, 19(3-4):293–307.

Giacomo Camposampiero, Quynh Anh Nguyen, and Francesco Di Stefano. 2022. The curious case of logistic regression for Italian languages and dialects identification. In *Proceedings of the Ninth Workshop on NLP for Similar Languages, Varieties and Dialects*, pages 86–98, Gyeongju, Republic of Korea. Association for Computational Linguistics.

Nancy Chinchor. 1992. MUC-4 evaluation metrics. In *Fourth Message Uunderstanding Conference (MUC-4): Proceedings of a Conference Held in McLean, Virginia, June 16-18, 1992*.

Johannes Dellert. 2019. *Information-theoretic causal inference of lexical flow*. Language Science Press.

Johannes Dellert and Armin Buch. 2016. Using computational criteria to extract large Swadesh lists for lexicostatistics. In *Proceedings of the Leiden Workshop on Capturing Phylogenetic Algorithms for Linguistics*, Tübingen. Universitätsbibliothek Tübingen.

Johannes Dellert, Thora Daneyko, Alla Münch, Alina Ladygina, Armin Buch, Natalie Clarius, Ilja Grigorjew, Mohamed Balabel, Hizniye Isabella Boga, Zalina Baysarova, et al. 2020. NorthEuralex: A wide-coverage lexical database of Northern Eurasia. *Language resources and evaluation*, 54(1):273–301.

Jacob Devlin, Ming-Wei Chang, Kenton Lee, and Kristina Toutanova. 2018. BERT: pre-training of deep bidirectional transformers for language understanding. *CoRR*, abs/1810.04805.

Kira Droganova, Olga Lyashevskaya, and Daniel Zeman. 2018. Data conversion and consistency of monolingual corpora: Russian UD treebanks. In *Proceedings of the 17th International Workshop on Treebanks and Linguistic Theories (TLT 2018)*, pages 52–65, Oslo University, Norway. Linköping University Electronic Press.

Shiran Dudy and Steven Bedrick. 2020. Are some words worth more than others? In *Proceedings of the First Workshop on Evaluation and Comparison of NLP Systems*, pages 131–142, Online. Association for Computational Linguistics.

Hanne Eckhoff and Aleksandrs Berdicevskis. 2015. Linguistics vs. digital editions: The tromsø old russian and ocs treebank. *Scripta & e-Scripta*, 14-15:9–25.

Nat Gillin. 2022. Is encoder-decoder transformer the shiny hammer? In *Proceedings of the Ninth Workshop on NLP for Similar Languages, Varieties and Dialects*, pages 80–85, Gyeongju, Republic of Korea. Association for Computational Linguistics.

Tin Kam Ho. 1995. Random decision forests. In *Proceedings of 3rd International Conference on Document Analysis and Recognition*, volume 1, pages 278–282 vol.1.

Eric Holman, Søren Wichmann, Cecil Brown, Viveka Velupillai, André Müller, and Dik Bakker. 2008. Explorations in automated language classification. *Folia Linguistica*, 42:331–354.

Gerhard Jäger, Johann-Mattis List, and Pavel Sofroniev. 2017. Using support vector machines and state-of-the-art algorithms for phonetic alignment to identify cognates in multi-lingual wordlists. In *Proceedings of the 15th Conference of the European Chapter of the Association for Computational Linguistics: Volume 1, Long Papers*, pages 1205–1216, Valencia, Spain. Association for Computational Linguistics.

Gerhard Jäger and Pavel Sofroniev. 2016. Automatic cognate classification with a support vector machine. In *Conference on Natural Language Processing*.

Zhanming Jie and Wei Lu. 2019. Dependency-guided LSTM-CRF for named entity recognition. In *Proceedings of the 2019 Conference on Empirical Methods in Natural Language Processing and the 9th International Joint Conference on Natural Language*

Processing (EMNLP-IJCNLP), pages 3862–3872, Hong Kong, China. Association for Computational Linguistics.

Alexei Kassian, George Starostin, Anna Dybo, and Vasiliy Chernov. 2010. The Swadesh wordlist. An attempt at semantic specification. *Journal of Language Relationship*, 16(59):46–89.

J.-M. List. 2014. *Sequence Comparison in Historical Linguistics*. Walter de Gruyter GmbH & Co KG.

Johann-Mattis List. 2012. LexStat: Automatic detection of cognates in multilingual wordlists. In *Proceedings of the EACL 2012 Joint Workshop of LINGVIS & UNCLH*, pages 117–125, Avignon, France. Association for Computational Linguistics.

Olga Lyashevskaya and Ilia Afanasev. 2021. An HMM-based PoS Tagger for Old Church Slavonic. *Journal of Linguistics/Jazykovedný casopis*, 72(2):556–567.

Wesley Mackay and Grzegorz Kondrak. 2005. Computing word similarity and identifying cognates with Pair Hidden Markov Models. In *Proceedings of the Ninth Conference on Computational Natural Language Learning (CoNLL-2005)*, pages 40–47.

Abhijnan Nath, Rahul Ghosh, and Nikhil Krishnaswamy. 2022. Phonetic, Semantic, and Articulatory Features in Assamese-Bengali Cognate Detection. In *Proceedings of the Ninth Workshop on NLP for Similar Languages, Varieties and Dialects*, pages 41–53, Gyeongju, Republic of Korea. Association for Computational Linguistics.

Rıza Özçelik, Gökçe Uludoğan, Selen Parlar, Özge Bakay, Özlem Ergelen, and Olcay Taner Yıldız. 2019. User Interface for Turkish Word Network KeNet. In *2019 27th Signal Processing and Communications Applications Conference (SIU)*, pages 1–4.

Manisha Prajapati and Archit Yajnik. 2019. POS Tagging of Gujarati Text using VITERBI and SVM. *International Journal of Computer Applications*, 181(43):32–35.

Peng Qi, Timothy Dozat, Yuhao Zhang, and Christopher D. Manning. 2018. Universal Dependency parsing from scratch. In *Proceedings of the CoNLL 2018 Shared Task: Multilingual Parsing from Raw Text to Universal Dependencies*, pages 160–170, Brussels, Belgium. Association for Computational Linguistics.

Peng Qi, Yuhao Zhang, Yuhui Zhang, Jason Bolton, and Christopher D. Manning. 2020. Stanza: A python natural language processing toolkit for many human languages. In *Proceedings of the 58th Annual Meeting of the Association for Computational Linguistics: System Demonstrations*, pages 101–108, Online. Association for Computational Linguistics.

Victor Sanh, Lysandre Debut, Julien Chaumond, and Thomas Wolf. 2019. DistilBERT, a distilled version of BERT: smaller, faster, cheaper and lighter. *ArXiv*, abs/1910.01108.

Yves Scherrer. 2021. *Adaptation of Morphosyntactic Taggers*, Studies in Natural Language Processing, page 138–166. Cambridge University Press.

Helmut Schmid. 1994. Probabilistic part-of-speech tagging using decision trees. In *Proceedings of International Conference on New Methods in Language Processing*, Manchester, UL.

Helmut Schmid. 1995. Improvements in Part-of-Speech Tagging with an Application to German. In *Proceedings of the ACL SIGDAT-Workshop*, Dublin, Ireland.

Tatiana Shavrina and Olga Shapovalova. 2017. To the methodology of corpus construction for machine learning: «Taiga» syntax tree corpus and parser. In *Proceedings of the International Conference "CORPORA 2017"*, Saint-Petersbourg, Russia.

Yana Shishkina and Olga Lyashevskaya. 2022. Sculpting Enhanced Dependencies for Belarusian. In *Analysis of Images, Social Networks and Texts*, pages 137–147, Cham. Springer International Publishing.

George Starostin. 2019. *Reply to Pozdniakov' paper "On the threshold of relationship*, pages 215–220. Gorgias Press, Piscataway, NJ, USA.

Sergei A. Starostin. 1989. Sravnitel'no-istoricheskoe jazykoznanie i leksikostatistika. In *Lingvisticheskaja rekonstrukcija i drevnejshaja istorija Vostoka*, pages 3–39.

Oleksiy Syvokon and Olena Nahorna. 2021. Ua-gec: Grammatical error correction and fluency corpus for the ukrainian language.

Erik F. Tjong Kim Sang and Fien De Meulder. 2003. Introduction to the CoNLL-2003 shared task: Language-independent named entity recognition. In *Proceedings of the Seventh Conference on Natural Language Learning at HLT-NAACL 2003*, pages 142–147.

Sunita Warjri, Dr. Partha Pakray, Saralin Lyngdoh, and Arnab Maji. 2019. Identification of POS Tag for Khasi language based on Hidden Markov Model POS Tagger. *Computación y Sistemas*, 23.

Martijn Wieling, Therese Leinonen, and John Nerbonne. 2007. Inducing sound segment differences using pair hidden markov models. In *Proceedings of ninth meeting of the acl special interest group in computational morphology and phonology*, pages 48–56.

Zhiwei Yang, Jing Ma, Hechang Chen, Yunke Zhang, and Yi Chang. 2021. HiTRANS: A hierarchical transformer network for nested named entity recognition. In *Findings of the Association for Computational Linguistics: EMNLP 2021*, pages 124–132, Punta Cana, Dominican Republic. Association for Computational Linguistics.

Daniel Zeman; et al. 2022. Universal dependencies 2.11. LINDAT/CLARIAH-CZ digital library at the Institute of Formal and Applied Linguistics (ÚFAL),

Faculty of Mathematics and Physics, Charles University.

Anchors in Embedding Space: A Simple Concept Tracking Approach to Support Conceptual History Research

Jetske Adams[1], Martha Larson[1], Jaap Verheul[2], Michael Boyden[2]
[1]Centre for Language Studies, Radboud University
[2]Radboud Institute for Culture and History, Radboud University

Abstract

We introduce a simple concept tracking approach to support conceptual history research. Building on the existing practices of conceptual historians, we use dictionaries to identify "anchors", which represent primary dimensions of meaning of a concept. Then, we create a plot showing how a key concept has evolved over time in a historical corpus in relation to these dimensions. We demonstrate the approach by plotting the change of several key concepts in the COHA corpus.

1 Introduction

Conceptual history is the study of the abstract, sociopolitical concepts that are used to describe and understand history. The purpose of our work is to complement the computational methods that are available for research in conceptual history by introducing an approach specifically designed to be easily used by conceptual historians.

Conceptual historians are interested in the evolution over time of "key concepts" that have social or political relevance. Our approach follows the work of Reinhart Koselleck, a pioneer of conceptual history. While key concepts are necessarily expressed as words, not all words are concepts in the sense of Koselleck. In his introduction to *Geschichtliche Grundbegriffe*, a collaborative multivolume lexicon of key concepts during the period 1750-1850, Koselleck states, "a word becomes a concept when a single word is needed that contains—and is indispensable for articulating—the full range of meanings derived from a given sociopolitical context" (Koselleck and Richter, 2011, p. 19). Analysis of sociopolitical concepts aims to bring out the coexistence of meaning layers ("temporal strata") in a given concept (Koselleck, 2004).

One approach used by Koselleck is to analyze how definitions in dictionaries change over the years, e.g., in Koselleck and Richter (2006). A definition of a word in a dictionary explicitly expresses primary dimensions of meaning. Here, we do not analyze historical dictionaries, but rather investigate changes in the relative importance of primary dimensions of meaning derived from a contemporary dictionary. As such, our approach represents a way to base concept tracking on known, and explicitly expressed, dimensions of meaning, without relying on the existence and availability of multiple historical dictionaries. Note that dictionaries are not the only source that conceptual historians use to identify dimensions of meaning that are interesting for investigation. However, due to their importance and easy accessibility, we focus on them here.

Our approach uses two primary dimensions of meaning represented by words we refer to as "anchors". We use the contextual word embeddings of the two anchors to create a plot that visualizes how the meaning of a key concept has changed over time within a diachronic corpus of historical texts. We argue that this simple concept tracking approach is useful for conceptual history research. First, it yields a concise plot that is easily interpretable for historians. Second, contextual embeddings do not necessarily have to be trained on the specific data being analyzed, which in the case of conceptual history research might be quite limited.

2 Background and related work

2.1 Concepts in conceptual history

Key concepts, in the sense of Koselleck, display specific properties that can be analyzed on a formal level: they are abstract, freestanding terms that often function as political catchwords that can be mobilized by various ideologies and factions (Koselleck, 2002). Often, they also display a metahistorical quality (e.g., the concept "progress" captures a linear understanding of time). Because of their function in steering public debate, concepts of this sort are inherently ambiguous. Thus, although a word such as "bank" is polysemous, it does not

Proceedings of the 4th Workshop on Computational Approaches to Historical Language Change, pages 87–92
December 6, 2023

count as a key concept because its meanings can be distinguished on the basis of its immediate context of use and because it does not carry forward political discourse in the way that, for instance, "justice" or "democracy" do. The meanings of a polysemous word are often assumed by linguists to be "well behaved", whereas conceptual historians are interested in the "ungovernability" of meaning.

Although conceptual history should be understood as distinct from semantic history, the approach as it emerged has remained, as De Bolla et al. (2019, p. 70) have noted, "at base a semantically motivated field of inquiry". The computational study of language, however, allows us to disentangle conceptual and semantic history in ways not possible before. These methodological advances should make it possible to uncover deeper conceptual structures of the sort theorized by Koselleck (De Bolla et al., 2019).

2.2 Computational concept tracking

In contrast to our approach that uses contextual word embeddings, many of the computational approaches to tracking concept change split a text corpus into (possibly overlapping) time windows and train (or fine-tune) a static word embedding model on the data in each window. Then, given a target concept, for each time window, they determine the neighbors of the embedding of the target concept, i.e., they calculate the embeddings of the words that are semantically closest to the target concept in the time window. Changes in the identity of the closest neighbors and in their degree of closeness are then analyzed over time. This information is summarized with a neighborhood change measure (Hamilton et al., 2016a) or a meaning stability score (Azarbonyad et al., 2017), or it is visualized as a plot tracing the distance of the target concept to individual neighbors (Viola and Verheul, 2020), as a series of graphs centered on the target concept, one for each time window (Martinez-Ortiz et al., 2016; Verheul et al., 2022), as t-SNE embeddings (Hamilton et al., 2016b), or as a complex graph (Haase et al., 2021).

A common position, to our knowledge first expressed by Kenter et al. (2015), is that algorithms that track semantic change over time should be "ad hoc" in the sense that they should generate words that are similar to the concept being tracked on the fly from the data, and no input should be required by the user. In this paper, we argue that in the case of conceptual history it is useful to take the opposite starting point. Specifically, concepts should be tracked with respect to known dimensions of meaning that are derived from explicit knowledge. Here, we focus on knowledge captured by lexicographers in the form of dictionary.

The closest related work to our own is, to our knowledge, work by Martinc et al. (2020) on diachronic semantic shift, which also uses contextual word embeddings. However, this work uses the ad hoc approach, deriving semantic neighbors from the data rather than using a dictionary or other knowledge sources. Further, Martinc et al. (2020) plot individual word similarities, whereas our plots visualize the relative movement between two different primary meanings.

3 Our anchor-based approach

For each key concept to be tracked, we retrieve its dictionary definition and look at the different meanings (sub-definitions) there. We select the two major meanings and, for each, choose an "anchor", a term that captures that meaning (i.e., a keyword from the sub-definition). In the online Miriam-Webster dictionary that we used, such words are often bolded. If more than two major meanings are present, we choose the meanings that are most related to the research interests of the conceptual historian. Once we have two anchors, we plot the difference over time between the similarity of the key concept to one anchor and its similarity to the other. The data and the details of our implementation are described in this section.

3.1 Data

Our study uses the Corpus of Historical American English (COHA) (Davies, 2010), specifically, the data between 1900 and 2000. Pre-processing steps included removal of irrelevant characters such as the article number at the beginning of texts, removal of punctuation marks except for apostrophes, removal of numerical characters, splitting of the texts into sentences, and conversion to lowercase.

3.2 Implementation

The English BERT 'bert-base-uncased' (Devlin et al., 2019) was used as the model to acquire contextual embeddings. It was pre-trained on BookCorpus and English Wikipedia (a total of 3.3×10^9 running words). Since COHA is not domain-specific, we did not fine-tune the model for this study.

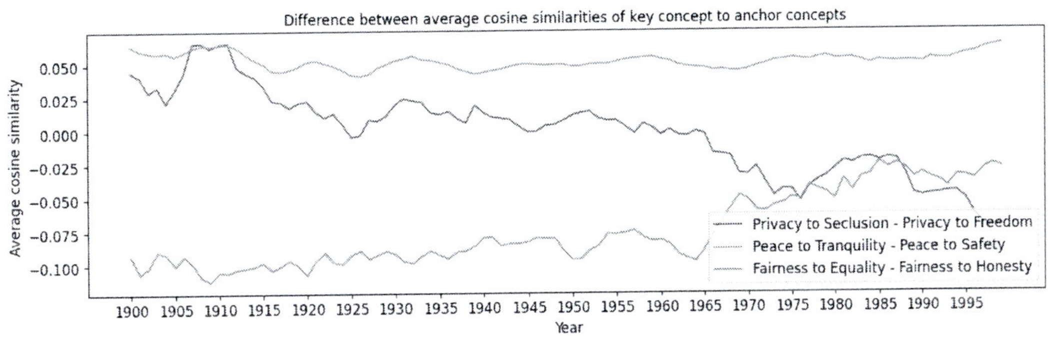

Figure 1: "Anchors" plot, which shows the difference in average cosine similarity per year between the key concept and the anchor concepts. The graph was smoothed by averaging the results over a period of 5 years.

Key Concept	Anchor Concepts	Mentions/year	Median std
Privacy	Seclusion - Freedom	27	0.078
Peace	Tranquility - Safety	455	0.041
Fairness	Equality - Honesty	164	0.066

Table 1: Information about the data for all three key concepts. Mentions per year gives the mean annual number of mentions of the key concept in the corpus. The median standard deviation is obtained from the difference values (similarity to anchor concept - similarity to other anchor concept) of all years.

To represent key concepts, we used contextual embeddings of the key concept's occurrences. The two sentences before and after the sentence in which the target occurred were added as context. This text window was chosen because it gives enough leeway even if the key concept word occurs in the first sentence of the text or if a surrounding sentence is very short. In case the context was longer than 512 tokens (infrequent) the remainder was left out. The final embeddings of the key concepts were obtained by extracting the hidden states from the last (12th) layer of the model. These hidden states yield embeddings of 768 dimensions.

For the two anchors, the steps described above were also followed to obtain embeddings. Then, the embeddings of all occurrences of the anchor word between 1900 and 2000 were averaged to obtain the two final anchor embeddings. Averaging of contextual embeddings is also used in Martinc et al. (2020). The cosine similarity between the embedding of each occurrence of a key concept in the text and both anchor embeddings was computed.

Next, for each anchor, the cosine similarities were averaged per year. We calculated the difference between the average similarity of the key concept to one anchor and the average similarity of the key concept to the other anchor and plotted this difference over time. We also calculated the standard deviation of the differences for each year.

3.3 Statistical testing

We used the Mann-Kendall test to identify monotonic trends in time series, either upwards or downwards. This test is frequently used for hydrometeorological time series (Wang et al., 2020). The trend is deemed statistically significant when the p-value is lower than 0.05. For this test to be effective it is not necessary that the trend is linear or that the data is normally distributed. Because the Mann-Kendall test can only deal with one score for a time period, we use the average difference in cosine similarity per year. We also apply a second statistical test, Spearman's rank correlation, since it has been used in the literature (Hamilton et al., 2016b).This test has the same significance threshold and gives a correlation coefficient that reflects the direction of the trend.

4 Tracking key concepts: Three examples

We illustrate our approach with the key concepts "privacy" (anchors: "seclusion"/"freedom"), "peace" (anchors: "tranquility"/"safety") and "fairness" (anchors: "equality"/"honesty"). Results are shown in table 2 and figure 1. The trends for both "privacy" and "fairness" are statistically significant, but "peace" has no overall trend. Spearman's correlation, used by Hamilton et al. (2016b), yielded the same significance result.

Key Concept	Anchor Concepts	Slope$_{MK}$	p-value$_{MK}$	Correlation$_{SP}$	p-value$_{SP}$
Privacy	Seclusion - Freedom	-9.97×10^{-4}	<.001	-0.767	<.001
Peace	Tranquility - Safety	-0.05×10^{-4}	.856	-0.051	.614
Fairness	Equality - Honesty	8.21×10^{-4}	<.001	0.707	<.001

Table 2: Results for all three key concepts. For the Mann-Kendall test, the slope and p-value are given. For the Spearman's rank correlation test, the correlation coefficient and p-value are given.

Sentence	Year	S_C Seclusion	S_C Freedom
"it wiould be better to have it out with the railway representative in the **privacy** of the council room"	1917	0.60	0.46
"our **privacy** is under attack not just from government but also from corporations and even ourselves"	1998	0.47	0.64

Table 3: Example sentences from COHA for key concept "privacy" given with the cosine similarity (S_C) of the "privacy" embedding to each anchor embedding. Both examples are from newspaper text.

"Fairness" consistently leans towards "honesty" rather than to "equality" in terms of similarity, although the difference becomes smaller over time. "Peace" remains closer to "tranquility" than to "safety". During the 1900s, "privacy" was more similar to "seclusion" than to "freedom", but this reversed around the 1960s. The two sentences in table 3 illustrate the difference.

Table 4 highlights two important points concerning our approach using the example "peace". First (top two rows), our plot does not reflect the case in which both anchor concepts' cosine similarity to the key concept move in the same direction. We advise historians not to abandon plots of the cosine between key concepts and individual terms, but to use them alongside our difference plots. Second (bottom two rows), before World War II, a slight but significant trend was found of "peace" towards "safety", followed by a small reversal. The Mann-Kendall test is not suited for detecting such changes without choosing a point to split up the data.

5 Connecting to conceptual history

In this section, we present an example illustrating how our anchor-based approach might connect to existing conceptual history research. Specifically, we look at work by Boyden et al. (2022) on how "climate" has emerged as a key concept. Before the rise of climate science, "climate" was undifferentiated from geography and weather associated with places. In early modern geography, "climate" was roughly identical to geodetic position. However, over the years "climate" has become *globalized*, i.e., associated with future weather conditions of the entire planet. We can explain the shift from "local" to "global" in terms of the difference between meteorology and climate science. The latter deals with weather patterns averaged over long periods of time and on a planetary scale.

Figure 2 shows a graph of the key concept "climate". We see "climate" moving further from "local" and closer to "global" over time. The Mann-Kendall test gave an increasing trend (slope = 5.42×10^{-4}, $p < 0.001$) so the shift was significant. In this time span, "climate" appeared an average of 48 times per year in the corpus, with a median standard deviation of the subtracted average cosine similarities of all years of 0.045. Particularly in the last quarter of the 20th Century, our analysis shows "climate" became increasingly associated with "global". However, before that time it was already evolving away from "local" and towards "global". These observations are consistent with the ideas and insights of Boyden et al. (2022). We note that Boyden et al. (2022) point to the Oxford English Dictionary as a source of support for older "local" meanings of "climate", but the choice of the anchors here is also based on other considerations, such the rise of climate science, mentioned above. Finally, we emphasize that our anchor-based approach is not intended to replace concept graphs, such as those also used by Boyden et al. (2022), but rather complements them.

6 Conclusion and outlook

In this study we have proposed a "Definitions as Anchors" approach to tracking the evolution of "key concepts", i.e., abstract sociopolitical concepts, which makes use of "anchors" drawn from dictionary definitions. Our approach maps key con-

Key Concept	Anchor Concept(s)	Years	Slope$_{MK}$	p-value$_{MK}$
Peace	Tranquility	1900-2000	-2.32×10^{-4}	<0.001
Peace	Safety	1900-2000	-2.10×10^{-4}	<0.001
Peace	Tranquility - Safety	1900-1945	-3.66×10^{-4}	<0.001
Peace	Tranquility - Safety	1945-2000	1.12×10^{-4}	0.032

Table 4: Further points about our approach demonstrated by key concept "peace"

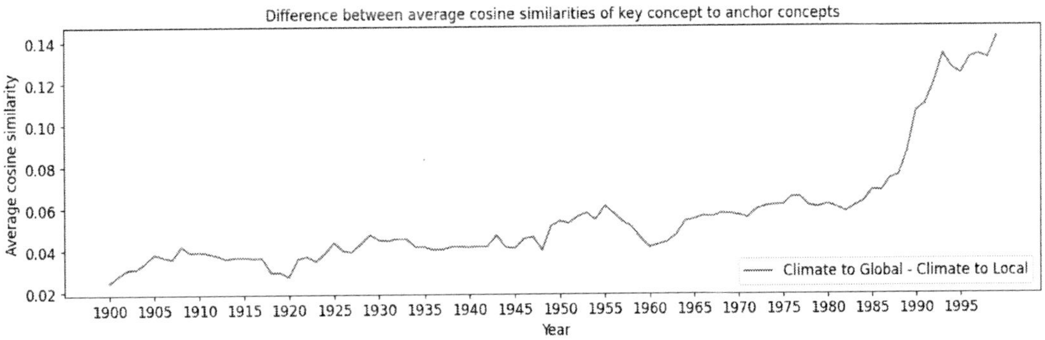

Figure 2: "Anchors" plot for the key concept "climate", with anchors "global" and "local". As above, the graph was smoothed by averaging the results over a period of 5 years.

cepts to a relative position in semantic space, much like approaches that build semantic graphs for individual time windows, e.g., Martinez-Ortiz et al. (2016). Instead of being positioned with respect to a larger number of ad hoc neighbors, key concepts are traced with respect to two pre-defined anchors, dramatically simplifying the interpretation and allowing straightforward calculation of the statistical significance of trends.

We have argued for pre-defined anchors because it builds on conceptual historians' established practices. However, we also note that using pre-defined anchors may help to address our concern that the neighbors of a key concept within a time window are determined more by the dominant topics in that time window, rather than by an actual shift in the semantics of the key concept. The importance of this concern should be investigated in future work.

Future work should also investigate the advantage that contextual word embeddings offer in leveraging more training data that non-contextual embeddings. Our word embedding model was pre-trained on the order of 10^9 running words. In contrast, if the COHA collection is split into year-length windows and a static word embedding model is built on each window, i.e., the approach of Martinez-Ortiz et al. (2016), each model is trained on only on the order of 10^6 words, three orders of magnitude fewer words.

In sum, our study enriches conceptual history with an approach that can statistically confirm monotonic changes of abstract sociopolitical concepts over time in a diachronic text corpus. It contributes to the practical understanding of how and over what time periods conceptual shifts occur.

7 Limitations

We present a simple concept tracking approach, which we have designed to be easy for conceptual historians to interpret and also relatively robust to variation (for example changes of topic) that is not relevant to underlying conceptual change. We have not, however, demonstrated experimentally that our approach has either of these properties. We have not compared non-contextual embeddings to show the advantage of contextual embeddings.

Further, as noted in section 3.2, the 'bert-base-uncased' model was not further trained or fine-tuned. Although COHA is broad in topic and genre (i.e., not domain specific) and fine-tuning may be inconvenient for historians, we do find that future work should test a model pre-trained on COHA, such as histBERT (Qiu and Xu, 2022).

Also, the stability of the anchor concepts requires additional evaluation. Finally, our statistical tests analyze monotonic trends. Future work should consider trends that change direction and also change point detection.

References

Hosein Azarbonyad, Mostafa Dehghani, Kaspar Beelen, Alexandra Arkut, Maarten Marx, and Jaap Kamps. 2017. Words are malleable: Computing semantic shifts in political and media discourse. In *Proceedings of the 2017 ACM on Conference on Information and Knowledge Management*, CIKM '17, page 1509–1518, New York, NY, USA. Association for Computing Machinery.

Michael Boyden, Ali Basirat, and Karl Berglund. 2022. Digital conceptual history and the emergence of a globalized climate imaginary. *Contributions to the History of Concepts*, 17(2):95 – 122.

Mark Davies. 2010. The corpus of historical American English: 400 million words, 1810-2009. http://corpus.byu.edu/coha/. Accessed: 2023-08-31.

Peter De Bolla, Ewan Jones, Paul Nulty, Gabriel Recchia, and John Regan. 2019. Distributional concept analysis: A computational model for history of concepts. *Contributions to the History of Concepts*, 14(1):66 – 92.

Jacob Devlin, Ming-Wei Chang, Kenton Lee, and Kristina Toutanova. 2019. BERT: Pre-training of deep bidirectional transformers for language understanding. In *Proceedings of the 2019 Conference of the North American Chapter of the Association for Computational Linguistics: Human Language Technologies, Volume 1 (Long and Short Papers)*, pages 4171–4186, Minneapolis, Minnesota. Association for Computational Linguistics.

Christian Haase, Saba Anwar, Seid Muhie Yimam, Alexander Friedrich, and Chris Biemann. 2021. SCoT: Sense clustering over time: a tool for the analysis of lexical change. In *Proceedings of the 16th Conference of the European Chapter of the Association for Computational Linguistics: System Demonstrations*, pages 198–204, Online. Association for Computational Linguistics.

William L. Hamilton, Jure Leskovec, and Dan Jurafsky. 2016a. Cultural shift or linguistic drift? comparing two computational measures of semantic change. In *Proceedings of the 2016 Conference on Empirical Methods in Natural Language Processing*, pages 2116–2121, Austin, Texas. Association for Computational Linguistics.

William L. Hamilton, Jure Leskovec, and Dan Jurafsky. 2016b. Diachronic word embeddings reveal statistical laws of semantic change. In *Proceedings of the 54th Annual Meeting of the Association for Computational Linguistics (Volume 1: Long Papers)*, pages 1489–1501, Berlin, Germany. Association for Computational Linguistics.

Tom Kenter, Melvin Wevers, Pim Huijnen, and Maarten de Rijke. 2015. Ad hoc monitoring of vocabulary shifts over time. In *Proceedings of the 24th ACM International on Conference on Information and Knowledge Management*, CIKM '15, page 1191–1200, New York, NY, USA. Association for Computing Machinery.

Reinhart Koselleck. 2002. *"Progress" and "Decline": An Appendix to the History of Two Concepts*, pages 218–235. Stanford University Press, Redwood City.

Reinhart Koselleck. 2004. *History, Histories, and Formal Time Structures*, pages 93–114. Columbia UP, New York.

Reinhart Koselleck and Michaela Richter. 2011. Introduction and prefaces to the Geschichtliche Grundbegriffe: (basic concepts in history: A historical dictionary of political and social language in Germany). *Contributions to the History of Concepts*, 6(1):1–37.

Reinhart Koselleck and Michaela W. Richter. 2006. Crisis. *Journal of the History of Ideas*, 67(2):357–400.

Matej Martinc, Petra Kralj Novak, and Senja Pollak. 2020. Leveraging contextual embeddings for detecting diachronic semantic shift. In *Proceedings of the Twelfth Language Resources and Evaluation Conference*, pages 4811–4819, Marseille, France. European Language Resources Association.

Carlos Martinez-Ortiz, Tom Kenter, Melvin Wevers, Pim Huijnen, Jaap Verheul, and Joris van Eijnatten. 2016. Design and implementation of ShiCo: Visualising shifting concepts over time. In *Proceedings of the 3rd International Workshop on Computational History (HistoInformatics2016) (CEUR Workshop Proceedings 1632)*.

Wenjun Qiu and Yang Xu. 2022. Histbert: A pre-trained language model for diachronic lexical semantic analysis.

Jaap Verheul, Hannu Salmi, Martin Riedl, Asko Nivala, Lorella Viola, Jana Keck, and Emily Bell. 2022. Using word vector models to trace conceptual change over time and space in historical newspapers, 1840-1914. *Digital Humanities Quarterly*, 16(2).

Lorella Viola and Jaap Verheul. 2020. One hundred years of migration discourse in The Times: A discourse-historical word vector space approach to the construction of meaning. *Frontiers in Artificial Intelligence*, 3:64.

Fan Wang, Wei Shao, Haijun Yu, Guangyuan Kan, Xiaoyan He, Dawei Zhang, Minglei Ren, and Gang Wang. 2020. Re-evaluation of the power of the Mann-Kendall test for detecting monotonic trends in hydrometeorological time series. *Frontiers in Earth Science*, 8.

ChiWUG: A Graph-based Evaluation Dataset for Chinese Lexical Semantic Change Detection

Jing Chen
The Hong Kong Polytechnic University
jing95.chen@connect.polyu.hk

Emmanuele Chersoni
The Hong Kong Polytechnic University
emmanuele.chersoni@polyu.edu.hk

Dominik Schlechtweg
University of Stuttgart
schlecdk@ims.uni-stuttgart.de

Jelena Prokic
Leiden University
j.prokic@hum.leidenuniv.nl

Chu-Ren Huang
The Hong Kong Polytechnic University
churen.huang@polyu.edu.hk

Abstract

Recent studies suggested that language models are efficient tools for measuring lexical semantic change. In our paper, we present the compilation of the first graph-based evaluation dataset for semantic change in the context of the Chinese language, covering the periods before and after the *Reform and Opening Up*.

Exploiting the existing framework DURel, we collect over 61,000 human semantic relatedness judgments for 40 targets. The inferred word usage graphs and semantic change scores provide a basis for visualization and evaluation of semantic change.

1 Introduction

Lexical semantic change detection, i.e. measuring meaning changes across different timespans, gained substantial popularity with the growing availability of historical corpora and language models (Hamilton et al., 2016; Tahmasebi et al., 2019; Montanelli and Periti, 2023; Kutuzov et al., 2018; Schlechtweg et al., 2020; Zamora-Reina et al., 2022), mostly for English and for other Indo-European languages.

The increasing number of published evaluation datasets further fostered the domain, enabling different models and hyperparameters to be quantitatively tested on the same benchmarks (Kutuzov et al., 2022; Schlechtweg et al., 2021; Aksenova et al., 2022; Chen et al., 2022; Zamora-Reina et al., 2022; Basile et al., 2019). These datasets are predominantly constructed within the framework of Diachronic Usage Relatedness (DURel), wherein changing scores are generated by calculating human ratings on semantic relatedness across a variety of usage pairs for targets (Schlechtweg et al., 2018; Rodina and Kutuzov, 2020; Chen et al., 2022). In the extended DURel framework, namely Diachronic Word Usage Graphs (DWUGs) (Schlechtweg et al., 2021, 2020), the usages could be further populated through *Word Usage Graphs* (WUGs) for visualization (McCarthy et al., 2016; Kutuzov et al., 2022).

To foster the development of lexical semantic change detection in Chinese, we constructed the first graph-based evaluation dataset, namely *ChiWUG*, following the DURel framework for the human judgments collection. Based on the collected 61k human judgments for 40 targets, we populated 40 WUGs to visualize usage changes preceding and following the context of the *Reform and Opening Up*, one of the most important milestones in the recent history of China. [1]

2 Related Work

Instead of categorizing words into *changed* and *unchanged* (Basile et al., 2020; Tang et al., 2013, 2016), the DURel framework adopted a graded view towards semantic change that words may exhibit varying degrees of semantic change. This is achieved by comparing the semantic relatedness targets in usage pairs on a scale of 1 to 4 (Schlechtweg et al., 2018), referring to semantic proximity from homonymy to identical usages. Specifically, usage pairs are assembled with contexts from periods of interest.

In the original DURel framework, three groups of usage pairs are assembled for a two-period setting, pairs consisting of two sentences from the same period and pairs having usages from each period (Schlechtweg et al., 2018). The extended

[1] The Reform and Opening Up period coincided with a series of policies implemented around 1978 to modernize the Chinese economy and engage with the global market.

Proceedings of the 4th Workshop on Computational Approaches to Historical Language Change, pages 93–99
December 6, 2023 ©2023 Association for Computational Linguistics

DWUGs allow us to categorize these usages into different groups by clustering, and groups proximately refer to different senses of a word. Through comparing the derived clusters from periods of interest, *DWUGs* allows us to easily measure the changes of sense distributions, i.e. loss and gain of senses and the turnover of usage dominance, which goes beyond the pure 'degree of changes' offered by the original DURel framework (Schlechtweg et al., 2021).

The DURel framework and its extension DWUGs have been applied to constructing evaluation datasets for a variety of languages, such as English, Swedish, German, and Latin released in the *SemEval 2020* (Schlechtweg et al., 2020), and later for Russian, Norwegian, Spanish, and Chinese (Rodina and Kutuzov, 2020; Kutuzov and Pivovarova, 2021; Kutuzov et al., 2022; Zamora-Reina et al., 2022; Chen et al., 2022). Since the nature of this paradigm is to measure usage differences between sentence pairs, it has also been extended to the construction of synchronic disambiguation datasets (Aksenova et al., 2022; Hätty et al., 2019) and to diatopic variation (i.e., usage differences across regional variations) (Baldissin et al., 2022).

3 Data

Building on the previous work by Chen et al. (2022), which collected human judgments for 20 targets following the DURel framework, we expand the data size and obtain the DWUGs to have a more comprehensive evaluation dataset for Chinese.[2]

3.1 Corpus

The corpus exploited in this study is derived from *People's Daily* [3], one of the most popular newspapers in China, which covers a wide range of topics. It is, to our knowledge, the largest continuous dataset with significant diachronic coverage that can be freely accessed. It covers the period from 1954 to 2003. All newspaper articles are in a Markdown format and are sorted into different temporal folders based on the release date.

More specifically, we take the year of the *Reform and Opening Up* as the borderline and divide all coverage into two subcorpora according to the releasing date information. One subcorpus contains all coverages from 1954 to 1978, and the other from 1979 to 2003. Table 1 summarizes word token/type information for the two sub-corpora. [4]

Period	Word Token	Word Type	TTR
1954 – 1978	1.27×10^8	46,743	0.368
1979 – 2003	1.66×10^8	58,376	0.351

Table 1: Statistics of two subcorpora. TTR = Type-Token ratio (Types/Tokens * 1000)

3.2 Target Words

To select targets, we first consulted Chinese linguistic studies on semantic change, with an emphasis on the period proceeding and following *Reform and Opening Up* (刁晏斌, 1995; 林伦伦, 2000; 于根元, 1992, 1994; 熊忠武, 1982; Tang et al., 2013, 2016; Tang, 2018). Considering the size and genre of our historical dataset, we only kept these candidates with validated senses recorded in the dictionaries. We do so by checking whether the mentioned emergent senses/usages were stabilized and absorbed into the standard Mandarin, relying on one of the most influential dictionaries in Modern Chinese (Department of Chinese Lexicography, 2019).

For example, '病毒'(bingdu, *virus*) developed a new sense roughly in the 1970s, relating to the computer virus, due to the introduction of the computer into the Chinese market (刁晏斌, 1995; Hamilton et al., 2016). However, 困难 'kun nan, *difficulty*' was recorded its usage as 'unattractive appearance' (刁晏斌, 1995), while such usage is neither much attested in the data nor recorded in dictionaries.

We further filtered those candidates with a normalized frequency of less than 1 in each period, specifically one from 1954 to 1978 (the EARLIER period) and the other from 1979 to 2003 (the LATER period).

Through such procedures, we identified a list of 20 changed words recorded in the linguistic literature as targets for constructing our evaluation dataset. Specifically, the list contains 11 verbs, 4 adjectives, and 5 nouns. We also selected an equal number of filler words as negative examples, only considering words of the same part of speech and comparable frequency in each period. Meanwhile, the same semantic field, with reference to

[2]Find the dataset at: `https://zenodo.org/records/10023263`.

[3]The *People's Daily Newspaper* Dataset: https://github.com/fangj/rmrb.

[4]Words averaging less than one occurrence in a one million tokens sample would be removed.

the dictionary 'Tongyici Cilin'(梅家驹, 1984), is also preferred if the first two criteria are met.

In sum, the evaluation dataset has 40 targets, including 20 changed words and 20 filler words. The changed words in this version have 9 out of 10 changed words in Chen et al. (2022) and the left one was filtered out due to frequency constraints. In general, the current *ChiWUG* dataset doubled the size of the target words.

3.3 Usage Pairs

To obtain semantic change scores, we first contextualized target words by providing actual usages in the historical dataset introduced in Section 3.1 and then asked native speakers to judge usage differences in the compared settings.

We first randomly sampled 40 sentences containing a target in each period from the dataset as sentence candidates and then removed those with insufficient contexts or/and having word segmentation errors after manual checking by the first author. In total, each target word has two groups of sampled sentences, containing 20 sentences from the EARLIER period and 20 from the LATER period [5]. Table 2 summarizes the general statistics regarding the sampled sentence pairs.

In theory, each sampled sentence would be automatically paired with each one of the other 39 sentences for comparison in the DWUG paradigm. Therefore, each target would have $(n(n-1))/2$ pairs, i.e. $(40 * 39)/2$, 780 pairs to be compared.

Targets	Sentences	Pairs	Avg Tokens per Sent.
40	1600	31,200	53.39

Table 2: Statistics of usage. *Avg Tokens per Sent.* refers to the average number of characters in sampled sentences.

4 Human Annotation

To collect human judgments, we recruited four native speakers of Mandarin as annotators. All the annotators are graduate students from the Faculty of Humanities, specializing in Chinese Linguistics. They were invited to experiment on the DURel platform after passing a tutorial specific to the Chinese lexical semantic change task [6]. Before the tutorial, we arranged a meeting for instructions.

After passing the tutorial, annotators were asked to indicate their intuitions on how semantically related a target was used in two displayed contexts in the 'official' annotation work. Targets would be highlighted, and options for judgments on a scale from identical (完全一致) to unrelated (不相关) are listed in the left bar, as shown in Figure 1. [7].

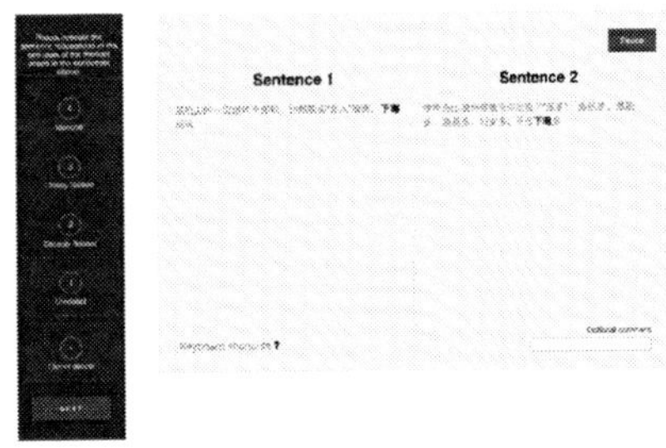

Figure 1: The annotation interface for Chinese

Besides assigning scores from 1 (unrelated meanings) to 4 (identical meanings) for semantic relatedness, they are also allowed to 'discard' usage pairs by giving the '0' score if the current pair is hard to understand due to the ambiguity of contexts or word segmentation errors. They are also encouraged to 'pause' the annotation process during the annotation after a period of annotation (around 30 minutes) to avoid excessively long sessions and keep their judgments as consistent as possible.

Due to the heavy load of annotation, the data was split in half, and each pair of annotators took one half consisting of 10 changed words and 10 fillers for annotation. We finally collected over 61,000 judgments from four annotators, after removing those judgments with a score of zero, that is, discarded pairs.

The weighted mean pairwise Spearman score for inter-rater agreements is 0.691, and the Krippendorff's alpha is 0.602, which are quite high if compared to other DURel datasets (Schlechtweg et al., 2021, 2020, 2018; Erk et al., 2013; Chen et al., 2022). For more statistics, see Table 3.

5 Graph Representations

Based on human judgments collected from the procedures described previously, we follow Schlechtweg et al. (2021, 2020) to aggregate the scores per usage pair as their median for populating

[5]The temporal information for all sentences is recorded in the meta-data, but would be invisible to annotators.

[6]The DURel interface: https://durel.ims.uni-stuttgart.de/. For the Chinese version of the guideline of this task: https://durel.ims.uni-stuttgart.de/guidelines?lang=ch

[7]More details: https://durel.ims.uni-stuttgart.de/guidelines?lang=zh

Periods	n	N/V/A	|U|	AN	JUD	AV	SPR	K
1954-2003	40	10/22/8	1,599	4	61k	2	.691	.602

Table 3: Statistics of target words in ChSemShift. n = the number of usages, $N/V/A$ = the number of nouns, verbs and adjectives, $|U|$ = the total number of usages. One usage pair was discarded during the annotation due to the context ambiguity. AN = the number of annotators, JUD = the number of judgments, AV = the average number of annotations per usage pair, SPR = weighted mean of pairwise Spearman score, K = Krippendorff's alpha.

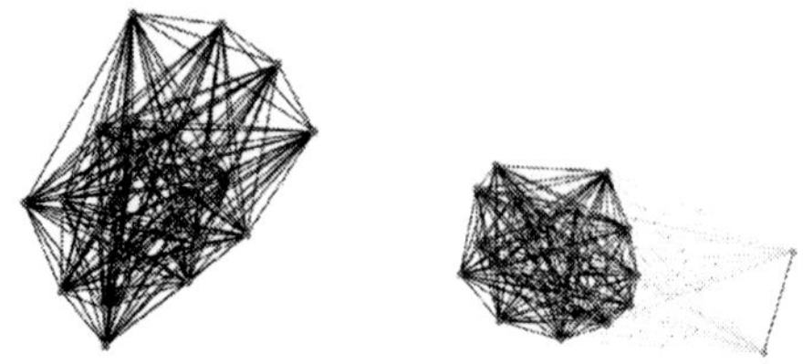

Figure 2: Word Usage Graphs of 病毒 *bingdu, 'virus'* in the EARLIER period *left* and the LATER period *right*). Colors label different clusters/senses, and nodes are different usages.

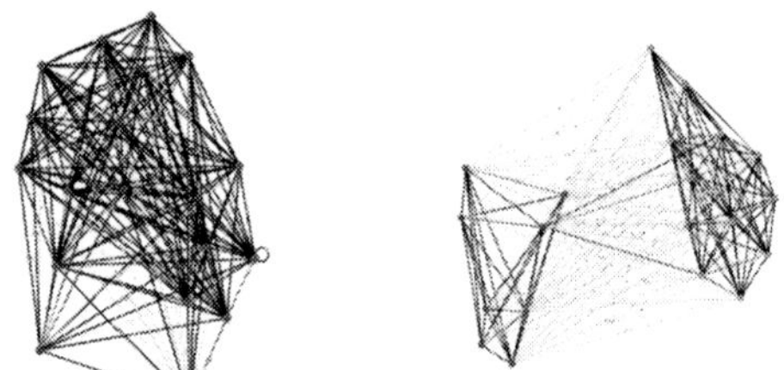

Figure 3: Word Usage Graphs of 下海 *xiahai, 'go into the sea' or 'to venture'* in the EARLIER period *left* and the LATER period *right*). Colors label different clusters/senses, and nodes are different usages.

WUGs, where usages with the same senses would be grouped together by performing the correlation clustering (Bansal et al., 2004). To populate WUGs with dense clusters, we took usage pairs with scores 3 and 4 as the same sense, while scores 1 and 2 were considered as different senses.[8]

Figure 2 and Figure 3 are inferred word usage graphs for 病毒 *bingdu* ('virus') and 下海 *xiahai* ('go into the sea' or 'to venture'), respectively. Nodes in the same color are clustered as the same sense, and subgraphs from the left to the right show the clusters/senses changes. In Figure 2, the right subgraph reveals the emergence of a new usage denoted by nodes in orange. By delving into the contexts associated with the orange-labeled usages [9], we discern that 病毒 (*bingdu*) acquired a fresh sense, namely 'computer virus', during the second period, diverging from its earlier associations with 'viral infections'.

Similarly, Figure 3 highlights the emergence of a new sense characterized by orange nodes, which are later confirmed as *'to venture'*, besides its original sense *'go into the sea'*. Furthermore, this emergent sense exhibits increased usage dominance in our samples, as evidenced by the greater presence of orange nodes in the LATER period.

6 Quantifying Changes: Metrics for Semantic Change

The DWUG paradigm obtains both graded change scores and binary change. We utilize two graded metrics: the Jensen-Shannon Distance on cluster frequency distributions (usually referred to as "graded change") as well as the COMPARE metric, calculated solely from edge weights. Binary change is instead based on the presence or absence of clusters across the two periods (Schlechtweg et al., 2018, 2020; Zamora-Reina et al., 2022).

COMPARE Metric The COMPARE metric C was proposed to directly compare the mean of weights where usages are from two different periods $W_{1,2}$, as shown in Eq. (1). A higher value yielded from the COMPARE metric indicates more stable words, while a lower value suggests a higher degree of meaning change (Schlechtweg et al., 2018; Schlechtweg, 2023).

$$C(W_{1,2}) = \frac{1}{|W_{1,2}|} \sum_{x \in W_{1,2}} x \qquad (1)$$

Jensen-Shannon Distance (Graded Change) After populating clusters, the frequency of sense distributions in two periods can be easily identified. To quantify the probability changes of sense distributions, the Jensen-Shannon Distance (JSD) is adopted to measure the change score between two normalized cluster frequency distributions (Schlechtweg, 2023), as shown in Eq. (2). The JSD is the symmetrized square root of the Kullback-Leibler Divergence (Lin, 1991). A higher JSD indi-

[8] We use the WUG pipeline with default opt parameters to generate graphs, cluster them and compute statistics and change scores: `https://github.com/Garrafao/WUGs`.

[9] Clicking the nodes in the DURel platform would display the full context embedded in each node.

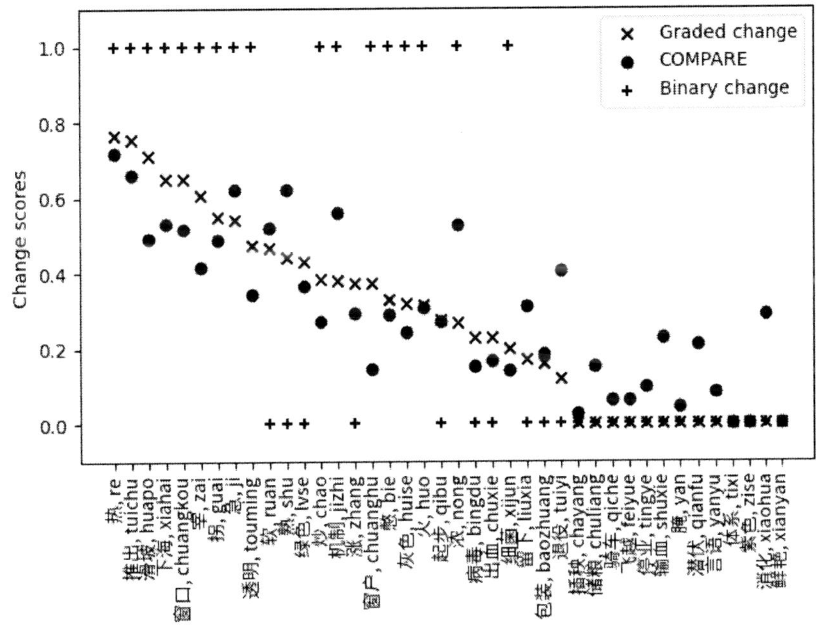

Figure 4: Change scores inferred on the WUGs resulting from our annotation. The COMPARE score was mapped with $f(x) = 1 - \frac{1}{3}(x-1)$ to fit the range of the other scores and to follow their direction (higher values mean more change).

cates a higher degree of usage change while a lower one suggests more stable usage across periods of interest.

$$JSD(P,Q) = \sqrt{\frac{KLD(P\|M) + KLD(Q\|M)}{2}} \tag{2}$$

where:

$$KLD(P\|Q) = \sum_{i}^{K} log_2(\frac{p_i}{q_i}), \quad M = \frac{(P+Q)}{2}$$

Binary Change The DWUG paradigm also enables us to detect binary change, defined as the gain or loss of clusters/senses. It is defined as:

$$B(w) = \begin{cases} 1 & \text{if for some } i, D_i \leq k \text{ and } E_i \geq n, \\ & \text{or vice versa.} \\ 0 & \text{otherwise} \end{cases}$$

where D_i and E_i respectively the frequency of sense *i* in the two periods, and k and n are lower frequency thresholds to control the handling of noise (Schlechtweg et al., 2020), which we set to $k = 1$ and $n = 3$.

Figure 4 demonstrates the change scores obtained on our data. Graded change and the COMPARE metric are strongly correlated (cf. Schlechtweg, 2023, pp. 63–64). Both scores in turn correlate with binary change. However, examples such as 软 *ruan* show that without binary change there can be considerable graded change. Similarly, words showing binary change can have varying degrees of graded change: 下海 *xiahai, 'go into the sea* or *'to venture'* demonstrate higher graded change than e.g. 病毒 'bingdu, *virus*' in Figure 4. Figure 2 and Figure 3 demonstrate their gaining of a new sense, respectively.

7 Conclusion

This study presents the first graph-based evaluation dataset for Chinese lexical semantic change constructed following the DWUG paradigm. It populates 40 word usage graphs based on more than 61k human judgments on contextual semantic relatedness between sentence pairs.

With its comparably high inter-rater agreement and dense clusters post-processed by clustering, we assume this high-quality evaluation dataset could be included in the shared evaluation datasets to foster Lexical semantic change detection in Chinese. Meanwhile, the inferred WUGs themselves are interesting for linguistic studies.

Limitations

We acknowledge that the periods we investigated were confined to a relatively short period of Chinese history, primarily spanning from the 1950s to the 2000s. Moreover, the analysis was concentrated on a specific regional source, utilizing a dataset derived from newspapers. While this scope is sufficient to unveil certain changes, it's imperative to acknowledge that the observed changes might merely represent a fraction of the broader evolutionary path. Changes identified within the current dataset could potentially be magnified or narrowed when explored within alternative data sources.

Acknowledgments

Dominik Schlechtweg has been funded by the project 'Towards Computational Lexical Semantic Change Detection' supported by the Swedish Research Council (20192022; contract 2018-01184) and by the research program 'Change is Key!' supported by Riksbankens Jubileumsfond (under reference number M21-0021).

References

Anna Aksenova, Ekaterina Gavrishina, Elisey Rykov, and Andrey Kutuzov. 2022. Rudsi: graph-based word sense induction dataset for russian. *arXiv preprint arXiv:2209.13750*.

Gioia Baldissin, Dominik Schlechtweg, and Sabine Schulte im Walde. 2022. DiaWUG: A Dataset for Diatopic Lexical Semantic Variation in Spanish. In *Proceedings of the 13th Language Resources and Evaluation Conference*, Marseille, France. European Language Resources Association.

Nikhil Bansal, Avrim Blum, and Shuchi Chawla. 2004. Correlation clustering. *Machine Learning*, 56(1).

Pierpaolo Basile, Annalina Caputo, Tommaso Caselli, Pierluigi Cassotti, and Rossella Varvara. 2020. DIACR-Ita @ EVALITA2020: Overview of the EVALITA2020 Diachronic Lexical Semantics (DIACR-Ita) Task. In *Proceedings of EVALITA*.

Pierpaolo Basile, Giovanni Semeraro, and A. Caputo. 2019. Kronos-it: a dataset for the italian semantic change detection task. In *Italian Conference on Computational Linguistics*.

Jing Chen, Emmanuele Chersoni, and Chu-ren Huang. 2022. Lexicon of changes: Towards the evaluation of diachronic semantic shift in Chinese. In *Proceedings of the 3rd Workshop on Computational Approaches to Historical Language Change*, pages 113–118, Dublin, Ireland. Association for Computational Linguistics.

Chinese Academy of Social Science Department of Chinese Lexicography, Institute of Linguistics. 2019. *Contemporary Chinese Dictionary (Xiandai Hanyu Cidian)*, the 7th edition. Commercial Press, Peking.

Katrin Erk, Diana McCarthy, and Nicholas Gaylord. 2013. Measuring word meaning in context. *Computational Linguistics*, 39(3):511–554.

William L. Hamilton, Jure Leskovec, and Dan Jurafsky. 2016. Diachronic word embeddings reveal statistical laws of semantic change.

Anna Hätty, Dominik Schlechtweg, and Sabine Schulte im Walde. 2019. SURel: A gold standard for incorporating meaning shifts into term extraction. In *Proceedings of the 8th Joint Conference on Lexical and Computational Semantics*, pages 1–8, Minneapolis, MN, USA.

Andrey Kutuzov and Lidia Pivovarova. 2021. Three-part Diachronic Semantic Change Dataset for Russian. In *Proceedings of the ACL International Workshop on Computational Approaches to Historical Language Change*.

Andrey Kutuzov, Samia Touileb, Petter Mhlum, Tita Ranveig Enstad, and Alexandra Wittemann. 2022. Nordiachange: Diachronic semantic change dataset for norwegian.

Andrey Kutuzov, Lilja vrelid, Terrence Szymanski, and Erik Velldal. 2018. Diachronic word embeddings and semantic shifts: a survey.

Jianhua Lin. 1991. Divergence measures based on the shannon entropy. *IEEE Transactions on Information Theory*, 37:145–151.

Diana McCarthy, Marianna Apidianaki, and Katrin Erk. 2016. Word sense clustering and clusterability. *Computational Linguistics*, 42(2):245–275.

Stefano Montanelli and Francesco Periti. 2023. A survey on contextualised semantic shift detection.

Julia Rodina and Andrey Kutuzov. 2020. RuSemShift: a dataset of historical lexical semantic change in Russian. In *Proceedings of the 28th International Conference on Computational Linguistics (COLING 2020)*. Association for Computational Linguistics.

Dominik Schlechtweg. 2023. *Human and Computational Measurement of Lexical Semantic Change*. Ph.D. thesis, University of Stuttgart, Stuttgart, Germany.

Dominik Schlechtweg, Barbara McGillivray, Simon Hengchen, Haim Dubossarsky, and Nina Tahmasebi. 2020. SemEval-2020 Task 1: Unsupervised Lexical Semantic Change Detection. In *Proceedings of the 14th International Workshop on Semantic Evaluation*, Barcelona, Spain. Association for Computational Linguistics.

Dominik Schlechtweg, Sabine Schulte im Walde, and Stefanie Eckmann. 2018. Diachronic Usage Relatedness (DURel): A framework for the annotation of lexical semantic change. In *Proceedings of the 2018 Conference of the North American Chapter of the Association for Computational Linguistics: Human Language Technologies*, pages 169–174, New Orleans, Louisiana.

Dominik Schlechtweg, Nina Tahmasebi, Simon Hengchen, Haim Dubossarsky, and Barbara McGillivray. 2021. DWUG: A large Resource of Diachronic Word Usage Graphs in Four Languages. In *Proceedings of the 2021 Conference on Empirical Methods in Natural Language Processing*, pages 7079–7091, Online and Punta Cana, Dominican Republic. Association for Computational Linguistics.

Nina Tahmasebi, Lars Borin, and Adam Jatowt. 2019. Survey of computational approaches to lexical semantic change.

Xuri Tang. 2018. A state-of-the-art of semantic change computation. *Natural Language Engineering*, 24(5):649–676.

Xuri Tang, Weiguang Qu, and Xiaohe Chen. 2013. Semantic change computation: A successive approach. In *Behavior and Social Computing*, pages 68–81, Cham. Springer International Publishing.

Xuri Tang, Weiguang Qu, and Xiaohe Chen. 2016. Semantic change computation: A successive approach. *World Wide Web*, 19.

Frank D. Zamora-Reina, Felipe Bravo-Marquez, and Dominik Schlechtweg. 2022. LSCDiscovery: A shared task on semantic change discovery and detection in Spanish. In *Proceedings of the 3rd International Workshop on Computational Approaches to Historical Language Change*, Dublin, Ireland. Association for Computational Linguistics.

于根元. 1992. *1991*汉语新词语. 北京语言学院出版社.

于根元. 1994. 现代汉语新词词典. 北京语言院出版社.

刁晏斌. 1995. 新时期大陆汉语的发展与变革. Hung Yeh Publishing, Taibei.

顾向欣 林伦伦, 朱永锴. 2000. 现代汉语新词语词典, *1978-2000*. 花城出版社.

梅家驹. 1984. 同林:. 商印; 上海.

熊忠武. 1982. 当代中国流行语词典. 吉林文史出版社.

Towards Detecting Lexical Change of Hate Speech in Historical Data

Sanne Hoeken[*1], **Sophie Spliethoff**[*2], **Silke Schwandt**[2], **Sina Zarrieß**[1] and **Özge Alaçam**[1,3]
[1]Computational Linguistics, Dept. of Linguistics, Bielefeld University
[2]Faculty for History, Philosophy and Theology, Bielefeld University
[3]Center for Information and Language Processing, LMU Munich
{sanne.hoeken, sophie_jasmin.spliethoff, silke.schwandt, sina.zarriess, oezge.alacam}@uni-bielefeld.de

Abstract

The investigation of lexical change has predominantly focused on generic language evolution, not suited for detecting shifts in a particular domain, such as hate speech. Our study introduces the task of identifying changes in lexical semantics related to hate speech within historical texts. We present an interdisciplinary approach that brings together NLP and History, yielding a pilot dataset comprising 16th century Early Modern English religious writings during the Protestant Reformation. We provide annotations for both semantic shifts and hatefulness on this data and, thereby, combine the tasks of Lexical Semantic Change Detection and Hate Speech Detection. Our framework and resulting dataset facilitate the evaluation of our applied methods, advancing the analysis of hate speech evolution.[1]

1 Introduction

The present research landscape on lexical change in NLP predominantly focuses on generic language evolution, targeting shifts in meaning for a set of words that span a wide spectrum of vocabulary (Schlechtweg et al., 2020; Basile et al., 2020). This approach falls short of modeling meaning shifts in specific domains or dimensions of meaning (e.g. hatefulness), which is often of interest when applying language change detection in disciplines beyond linguistics, i.e. in social sciences and humanities. For instance, historians investigating religious conflicts between Protestants and Catholics during the English Reformation may be particularly interested in the dynamics of polemical expressions (Steckel, 2018; Schwerhoff, 2020), which exist within a limited subset of the lexicon. In this paper, we present a first step towards the detection of meaning shifts within a particular subdomain.

"the **foxes** have hooles, the birdes of the aire have nestes, but the sonne of manne hathe not wherin to lay his heade."
Richard Tracy (1544)

"so these **foxes** conceive mischiefe and bring foorth most monstrous and cruel wickednesse; both by open violence and by secret treacherie."
Edwin Sandys (1585)

Figure 1: Example of 'foxes', for which our study found that the use of its hateful meaning *increased* between the periods of 1530-1553 and 1580-1603.

Specifically, our focus is on the domain of hate, aiming to uncover, for instance, change in hateful usage of the term 'foxes' during the 16th century as illustrated in Figure 1.

Lexical Semantic Change Detection (LSCD) is currently the predominant approach to modeling meaning shift in NLP. LSCD methods are typically designed to observe shifts in word usage, targeting a word's denotative meaning within evaluation data encompassing general language sources such as newspapers and books (Schlechtweg et al., 2020; Zamora-Reina et al., 2022). Target words are selected from the full vocabulary, often guided by etymological and historical dictionaries. Following this, well-developed techniques detect semasiological (from term to concept) variation by determining to what extend a word has shifted its meanings *somehow*. While certain more interpretable methods could offer deeper insights into the nature of individual shifts, by e.g. looking into usage clusters or word substitutes (Montariol et al., 2021; Card, 2023), current LSCD approaches have not demonstrated the ability to detect shifts within specific semantic subdomains, such as hate, which could be considered as an onomasiological perspective (from concept to term).

The development of Hate Speech Detection (HSD) systems, on the other hand, does address

[*]These authors contributed equally to this work.
[1]The published dataset and code used can be found at https://github.com/SanneHoeken/DigHist

Proceedings of the 4th Workshop on Computational Approaches to Historical Language Change, pages 100–111
December 6, 2023 ©2023 Association for Computational Linguistics

the identification of lexical items used to convey hateful meanings (e.g. Gitari et al., 2015; Bassignana et al., 2018; Davidson et al., 2017). However, the evolution of these expressions often remains unexplored (with McGillivray et al. (2022) being a rare exception). Although hate speech lexicons are frequently integrated into these systems, their application is most prevalent within limited temporal scopes, such as short-term social media data sets.

Our study introduces the task of detecting lexical semantic change of hate speech in historical texts. Such changes can involve an increase or decrease in hatefulness, or even the acquisition of an entirely new hateful sense. To address this task, we present an interdisciplinary framework, that brings together NLP and History. More specifically, we use and combine methods, annotation and evaluation procedures for Lexical Semantic Change Detection (LSCD) and Hate Speech Detection (HSD) in the context of historical data. The resulting dataset, consisting of 16th century Early Modern English religious writings in the context of the Protestant Reformation, is enriched with annotations of both lexical semantic changes and lexical hatefulness. In conclusion, our paper presents a 1) task, 2) dataset and 3) methodological framework facilitating the evaluation of computational approaches for identifying shifts in hateful word meanings.

2 Related Work

2.1 Historical text analysis

Semantic changes in historical polemical writing have not yet been targeted with the help of computational methods; instead, historians and literary researchers focused on qualitative approaches, such as close reading methods, in order to work out characteristics of polemical speech (Bevan Zlatar, 2011; Almasy, 2008). Moreover, Steckel (2018) and Schwerhoff (2020) provide first conceptualisations of historical polemics as a research instrument, and Dröse (2021) shows how interwoven these writings were with medial changes. Nevertheless, there have been approaches to apply NLP methods in the fields of Digital Humanities and Digital History already, which demonstrate that using digital methods to deal with historical texts does not only enable us to generate new findings and process larger amounts of textual data. As highlighted by Schwandt (2018), an interdisciplinary approach combining computational methods and practices with historical research also changes the way we perceive and interpret text and allows for new research questions.

2.2 Lexical Semantic Change Detection (LSCD)

In LSCD, a diverse range of methods has been employed, leveraging various language modeling techniques, including count-based models, static word embedding models, and contextualized language models. Tahmasebia et al. (2021) or Montanelli and Periti (2023) provides a comprehensive overview for further reading.

The evaluation of LSCD methods has been challenging due to the lack of large-scale annotated data. The first SemEval shared task on LSCD in 2020 provided one of the few available larger-scale human-annotated evaluation datasets (Schlechtweg et al., 2020). Interestingly, the results on this task demonstrated that methods utilizing static word embedding models, e.g. Hamilton et al. (2016), outperformed other approaches, including those using BERT-based models (Kutuzov and Giulianelli, 2020). More recently, several methods based on contextualized models have shown greater success, either by extracting representations from a Transformer-based model fine-tuned on Word Sense Disambiguation (Rachinskiy and Arefyev, 2022), or relying on the most probable substitutes for masked target terms (Card, 2023). In our study, we adopt a method loosely based on the latter approach, which we will elaborate on in Section 4.2.

2.3 Lexical Hate Speech Detection (LHSD)

Considering the potential application purposes of LSCD methods, addressing hate speech becomes a pressing concern, as neglecting changes in hateful meanings can lead to harmful consequences. While Hate Speech Detection (HSD) research has predominantly centered on identifying hate speech at the utterance level (Schmidt and Wiegand, 2017), a few works have addressed automatic detection at the lexical level, which is particularly relevant in the context of lexical change. Wiegand et al. (2018) presented an approach that utilizes a feature-based classification system to automatically expand a base lexicon of abusive words.

More recently, Hoeken et al. (2023) introduced a methodology for detecting lexical hate speech, involving the identification of a specific dimension within the embedding space of a language model that encodes hate. This dimension, estimated as the average difference vector of a set of lexical pairs that differ only with respect to the semantic dimension of hate, is then used to compare various word vectors. Using a pre-trained contextualized language model for generating lexical representation, this approach enables the prediction of hateful words within specific contexts.

2.4 Integrating HSD and LSCD

To our knowledge, the only contribution to the integration of hate speech detection and semantic change is done by McGillivray et al. (2022). Their study explores the feasibility of identifying offensive speech within data from 2020 using a model trained data from 2019. Their approach involves incorporating lexical semantic change scores as supplementary lexical features. Unlike our study, their primary focus is on contemporary hate speech detection and short-term meaning shifts. Nonetheless, their study illustrates the applicability of LSCD methods to a curated list of words that underwent shifts in offensive meanings. Still, the ability to filter out shifts that pertain solely to the semantic subdomain of hate remains unsolved.

A few other studies explore the shift of a specific dimension of meaning, that go beyond the predominant focus within LSCD on denotation. Charlesworth et al. (2022) employ static diachronic word embeddings trained on data reaching back to the 1800s (Hamilton et al., 2016) (in contrast to our contextualized LLM-based approach) and human-rated sentiment scores to explore to investigate how the social group representations and their perception have changed over time.

Another approach proposed by Basile et al. (2022) builds upon a 'connotative hyperplane' within embedding space, which is similar to the principle of an hate dimension. Shifts are quantified by measuring the difference in distances between word vectors and the hyperplane.

3 Data

3.1 Historical pamphlets as input data

Our study focuses on 16th century pamphlets, which provide a glimpse into conflicts and controversies associated with the Protestant Reformation in England and context-related language use. Pamphlets had been a new phenomenon in Early Modern England and were on the rise with the introduction of the printing press in the late 15th century. Much smaller, cheaper and faster in production than books at that time, pamphlets provided the opportunity to reach large audiences for the first time, which brought about a change in the dynamics of public debate (Dröse, 2021).

Although religious pamphlets came along in various shapes - poems, dialogues, sermons, treatises etc. - , a major shared characteristic is a polemical style in order to convince the readership of certain religious positions. Polemical language in the 16th century is described by historians and literary scholars as being persuasive, emotionally charged, and reactive (Almasy, 2008). The intention of Catholic and Protestant polemicists often was to argumentatively justify and demonstrate their sovereignty in interpreting religious issues. A major characteristic is a double audience (Steckel, 2018): not only were the pamphlets addressed at people sharing the same beliefs, but also at the respective opponents.

Thus, we find these texts riddled with derogatory language and hateful terms as we see in an illustrative statement made by Thomas Bell, an anti-Catholic author, in 1596, denoting Catholics as heretics: "the papistes are nothing else but flatte heretikes." Moreover, the historical writings already reflect a sense of different nuances of hatefulness. For instance, in his *Actes and Monuments*, first published in 1563, the Protestant clergyman and writer John Foxe made a qualitative differentiation between hateful terms in a religio-political context: "I had rather be counted a king foolish and simple, then to be iudged a tiraunt or a seeker of bloude". Hence, we can assume that hate speech constitutes a crucial feature of Early Modern English religious polemics and was subject to reflection at that time, too.

3.2 Period and text selection

Our data is sourced from Early English Books Online (EEBO)[2], an online database which provides the largest Early Modern English text corpus and includes publications from 1473 to 1700. Narrowing down the time frame to 1485-1603 allows us to look into possible changes in language use with the beginning of the English Reformation era. The texts were selected through an iterative keyword-based search, which ensured that they share the context of the Reformation. Appendix A lists the total set of keywords used. The data statistics of our final selection from EEBO are presented in Table 1.

The division into smaller periods of time is based

[2]https://www.proquest.com/eebo/index

Period	Phase	Texts	Sentences	Tokens
1485-1529	Catholic	14	31 692	852 823
1530-1552	Protestant	70	74 573	2 752 053
1553-1558	Catholic	20	24 846	809 885
1559-1579	Protestant	43	189 139	6 360 794
1580-1603	Protestant	162	477 896	16 768 865

Table 1: Statistics of texts per time period after final data selection.

on major political, societal and religious events and, as can be seen in Table 1, divided into periods of Catholic and Protestant monarchs: i. 1485-1529, ii. 1530-1552, iii. 1553-1558, iv. 1559-1579, and v. 1580-1603. The first phase marks the pre-reformation era under Henry VII. and Henry VIII (i.). With the 1530s, the Protestant Reformation in England gained momentum, Henry VIII. breaking with Rome and establishing Protestantism across England (ii.). After the reigns of Henry VIII. and Edward VI., Mary I. succeeded (iii.), who tried to re-establish the Catholic church. With Elizabeth I., a Protestant monarch followed again in 1558 (iv.). Anti-Catholic sentiments further increased and peaked during the 1580s (v.). Therefore, we can expect changes due to radicalization and changing political circumstances under which the texts were published.

For the present study, we chose to focus on only two of these time spans, taking into account 70 texts from 1530-1552 (ii.) and 162 texts from 1580-1603 (v.), in order to trace the diachronic change in Protestant polemical language. The difference in quantity aligns with the availability of publications, which continually increased from the beginning of the 16th century.

3.3 Cleaning and Normalization

Firstly, we removed both the header and footer sections, containing metadata, from the lowercased texts, along with the page numbers. Afterwards, we employed the sentence tokenizer provided by the Natural Language Toolkit (NLTK).

Initial analysis of the data showed significant spelling variations for identical words. Therefore we apply spelling normalization through a rule-based approach that generates a spelling dictionary which we apply to the whole corpus. A naive lookup technique like this showed most effective for historical text normalisation (in the case of in-vocabulary tokens) in the methodological evaluation conducted by Bollmann (2019). The details of our used method are specified in Appendix B.

4 Methods

4.1 Task and Procedure

In this paper we introduce an approach designed to tackle the task of **Lexical Semantic Hate Change Detection**, which we define as follows:

> Given a dataset D_0 from time period T_0, dataset D_1 from time period T_1, detect whether a target word gained or lost a hateful meaning between time T_0 and T_1.

Our approach ultimately yields a dataset with dual-aspect annotations: lexical semantic changes and lexical hatefulness. To capture potential changes of hateful meanings in our dataset (see Section 3), the selection of target words for the annotated dataset is guided by outcomes of both LHSD and LSCD methods. For both methods, we employ a historical BERT model, MacBERTh (Manjavacas Arevalo and Fonteyn, 2021)[3], which was trained on data spanning the years 1450 to 1950, also encompassing the EEBO database.

In the following, we present our method for LSCD (Section 4.2) and for LHSD (Section 4.3); a simple validation of LHSD on our historical data (Section 4.4). We also detail the manual annotation of lexical change and hatefulness (Section 4.5). The main idea of our approach is to first rank candidate words with respect to their semantic change and hatefulness score, and, based on the rankings, annotate a sample of potential target words to be able to evaluate the aumatic scoring.

4.2 LSCD

To measure changes in word meanings over time, we use a slightly simplified version of a recent methodology introduced by Card (2023). This method utilizes a BERT model's ability to predict masked words and involves the following steps for each target word. For a sample of contexts in which the target word occurs, we mask the target word and let the model predict its substitution. We gather the top 10 most probable substitutions for each instance (omitting stopwords, words with fewer than 3 characters or containing non-alphabetic characters). Across all target word instances, we calculate the frequency for each distinct substitute token, relative to the entire vocabulary of the model. Finally, the Jensen Shannon Divergence (JSD) is calculated

[3]We implemented the 'emanjavacas/MacBERTh' model using Hugging Face's *transformers* library (Wolf et al., 2020).

to quantify the difference in substitute frequency distributions between different time periods.

4.3 LHSD

To assess whether words carry a hateful connotation, we adopt the methodology introduced by Hoeken et al. (2023). Diverging from their approach, we apply it to a diachronic scenario. We create a hate dimension based on lexical pairs sourced from one time period. Subsequently, we project potential target terms from different time periods onto this dimension, allowing to determine the degree of hatefulness encoded in their representations and whether this has shifted over time.

Dimension creation. From the last time period (1580-1603), we create a set of lexical pairs of hateful terms and their neutral counterparts, i.e. terms referencing the same target group without any derogatory connotations. We extracted all unique nouns (using the Spacy library for POS tagging) from the texts in this period that occurred more than 10 times, ended with an 's' (potentially targeting references to (groups of) people) and consist of more than 3 characters, resulting in a list of 5976 nouns. From this list, 65 potential hateful terms were selected for further analysis. An expert historian manually examined the contexts in which these terms were used and selected 10 terms that consistently demonstrated a highly hateful connotation across the majority of contexts in which they appeared. For these 10 terms, we identified their neutral counterparts, resulting in our set of lexical pairs as displayed in Table 2.

	Hateful term	Neutral counterpart
1	heretikes	protestants
2	hipocrites	catholikes
3	idolaters	catholikes
4	papists	catholikes
5	popelings	catholikes
6	traitours	catholikes
7	shavelings	monkes
8	harlots	women
9	strumpets	women
10	whores	women

Table 2: 10 pairs of hateful terms and their neutral counterparts, used for dimension creation, from the 1580-1603 dataset.

Following Hoeken et al. (2023), we computed a dimension vector as the mean distance vector of the set of lexical pairs. For every pair, an averaged lexical representation is generated across 10 contexts in which they occur. We manually selected the contexts for each term ensuring that each context distinctly represents a hateful word as hateful and a neutral counterpart as neutral. This also guarantees that both parts of the lexical pair refer to the same entity, fulfilling the requirement of a difference, solely concerning the hateful dimension, between the two. We employed the MacBERTh model to extract each contextualized representation by averaging over all the hidden layers and the sentence positions of the subwords forming the pair.

Dimension projection. For a contextualized representation of a target word, the degree of hate encoded in it can be determined by projecting it on the hate dimension. This is established by computing the cosine distance between the two vectors. Positive angle values indicate a hateful connotation, while negative values do not.

4.4 Identifying historical hateful terms

To assess the applicability of the above-mentioned method for detecting lexical hate speech, originally devised for synchronic use, in the context of historical and diachronic data, we conduct a proof-of-concept validation analysis.

For the two periods under investigation, we extracted a list of terms adhering to the same criteria as those further employed throughout this study[4]. This yielded 1490 terms from the period 1530-1552 and 6338 terms from 1580-1603. Subsequently, we applied the hate projection method to 100 contextual representations of each noun, or fewer if a word occurred fewer than 100 times.

In Table 3, we present the top 25 words from each period, ranked by their average projection values, indicative of the degree of hate encoded in their representations. A historian further evaluated the hatefulness of these words, drawing on their historical expertise, historical dictionaries, or examination of the contexts in which the words occurred. The majority of these words (all but one to three per period) were confirmed to convey hateful meanings. This implies that, given a small sample of known hateful terms to create a dimension vector, this method can effectively detect hateful terms in *different* historical periods based on a small sample of known terms from *one* period.

[4]i.e. nouns occurring more than 10 times, ending with 's' and consisting of more than 3 characters.

1530-1552	1580-1603
extorcioners, liars, liers, buggerers, idolatres, stubburnes, fals, abusions, aulters, dregges, blasphemers, baudes, bablinges, *gobbettes*, deuelles, mischefes, idolatours, deuels, robbers, wrincles, sclaunders, persecutours, sorcerers, idolles, vnthankefulnes	liars, abhominations, inchaunters, *diotrephes*, libidinis, hipocrits, iuglers, backbiters, corrupters, impostures, extortioners, liers, iarres, whoredomes, puddles, lascivious, vilanies, bawdes, *iambres*, fornications, varlets, abusers, baudes, *paunches*, iuglings

Table 3: Top 25 words with highest average projection values in 1530-1552 and 1580-1603. The hatefulness of all but *italic* words were confirmed by an historian expert.

4.5 Annotation

4.5.1 Target word selection

To scale the validation of our approach sketched in Section 4.4, we select a larger set of words for annotation of lexical change and hatefulness. From the intersection of the vocabularies of D_0 and D_1 (corresponding to the data from 1530-1552 (T_0) and 1580-1603 (T_1) respectively), all nouns that fits to the selection criteria and not used for dimension creation are extracted, resulting in 1163 nouns.

For each of these nouns, we randomly extract up to 100 contexts per period. Then, both the LHSD method as well as the LSCD method are applied on all instances, as explained in Section 4.4. As a result, we obtain for each noun, one semantic change value and two projection values (reflecting their predicted hatefulness in each period). The difference between the two projection values is computed for each word to calculate the "hate change" score.

For the creation of the pilot dataset, a selection of 100 nouns (target words) is made. This selection includes the top 20 and bottom 20 words ranked by their semantic change value as well as the top 20 and bottom 20 words ranked by their hate change score. The resulting sets can be found in Appendix C. Additionally, we randomly 20 sample nouns to end up with a total set size of 100.

4.5.2 Annotation scheme & procedure

The annotation study serves two primary objectives: 1) publishing a dataset with rich annotations, and 2) providing a test-set for the computational approaches employed. For annotation we predominantly adopt the Diachronic Usage Relatedness (DURel) framework by Schlechtweg et al. (2018) that is designed for annotating lexical semantic changes. We extend this framework by incorporating annotations of hatefulness.

For each of the 100 target words, 10 contexts are randomly selected from each time period. From this set of 20 contexts, we randomly select 10 pairs of contexts either from the same period or from different ones. Consequently, the final test-set comprises a total of 1000 pair instances. For each text pair with a highlighted word, annotators are asked to evaluate the lexical semantic change and hatefulness. An example of an annotation instance is provided in Appendix C.

To annotate lexical semantic change, we employ the 4-point scale of relatedness as presented in the DURel framework. For the annotation of hatefulness we adopt the three-class scheme of Vigna et al. (2017), and add 'Cannot decide' to it, see Table 4.

4	Identical		
3	Closely related	**2**	Strongly hateful
2	Distantly related	**1**	Weakly hateful
1	Unrelated	**0**	Not hateful
-	Cannot decide	**-**	Cannot decide

Table 4: Four-level scale of semantic relatedness (Schlechtweg et al., 2018) (left) and three-level scale of hatefulness (Vigna et al., 2017) (right)

The annotations have been performed by two experts on medieval and early modern history. Both annotators were provided with the same instructions and illustrative examples[5]. For reasons of feasibility, the second annotator undertook the annotation of a subset of the data, encompassing half (50) of the target words, each with the same set of 10 sentence pairs as in the complete dataset. The subset retained the same distribution with respect to high and low JSD and projection difference values.

5 Results

5.1 Annotation outcomes

Agreement. We analyze the agreement of our two annotators[6] and report the inter-annotator agreement in Table 5. Both for semantic relatedness, which involves all sentence pairs rated by both annotators (total of 435), as well as the annotation of hatefulness, which involves all individual sentences rated by both annotators (total of 870), show a fair agreement in terms of Cohen's Kappa (0.247 and 0.315, respectively).

Semantic change. To transform the human annotations of semantic relatedness between pairs of sentences (from the same or different time periods) into values that indicate the semantic change

[5]The annotation instructions can be accessed on our GitHub repository.

[6]'Cannot decide' annotations are omitted. The first annotator flagged 88 out of 1000 instances with one or more 'Cannot decide'. For the second annotator this was 15 out of 500.

	Sem. rel (n = 435)	Hate (n = 870)
Cohen's κ	0.247	0.315
Pearson's r	0.576*	0.511*

Table 5: Inter-annotator agreement for the two annotators on their ratings of semantic relatedness and hatefulness (* = significant).

of target words between the two time periods we compute the COMPARE score. This score, also introduced within the DURel framework, is defined as the average between sentence pairs from different periods (Schlechtweg et al., 2018). To facilitate a more intuitive and straightforward analysis, we convert the scaled human ratings into binary values by applying boundary thresholds. For the COMPARE scores, any score below 4 is interpreted as change whereas a score of 4 as no change.

Hatefulness. In contrast to the change scores, which are analyzed on type level only, i.e. one aggregated result value for each target word, the hatefulness scores are also analyzed on token level, involving all unique sentence ratings from both time periods. For transformation to a binary classification of each target word, any *average* hate rating greater than 0 is interpreted as hateful, and 0 as not hateful.

Changes of hateful meanings. Combining the binary outcomes for semantic change and hatefulness annotations, allows to distinguish words that are (on average) classified as both hateful and having undergone semantic changes from those that are not. Table 6 reports the number of words on categorized as changed in meaning, conveying a hateful meaning and those falling into both categories simultaneously. Overall, we obtain 23 types that changed their meaning wrt. hatefulness, yet the distribution also indicates the challenging nature of the task that can be attributed to the sparseness of this case.

	Annotator		
	1 (all)	1 (n=50)	2 (n=50)
changed	26	14	31
hateful	13	7	35
hateful + changed	8	3	23
Out of	99	50	50

Table 6: Number of target words whose meaning is on average classified as changed, hateful, and both by the different annotators, n = number of observation

5.2 Methods evaluation

We leverage the created (pilot) dataset enriched with two-aspect annotations to evaluate the outcomes of the proposed computational methods.

Semantic change. When comparing the JSD values from the LSCD method with the human change scores (as previously explained), we expect a negative correlation, as higher JSD values indicate higher difference between time periods while lower human scores indicate the same. To transform the continuous JSD values into binary classes, we set the mean JSD value across all words considered for comparison as the threshold between change and no change (following the common practice in Schlechtweg et al. (2020)).

Hatefulness. The hate dimension method produced projection values between -1 and 1, for each contextualized instance of a target word. We compare these output values with the human hatefulness ratings for all unique sentences. For binary classification, all positive values are interpreted as hateful, and negative ones as not hateful.

Annotator	Semantic change			Hatefulness		
	binary	graded	n	binary	graded	n
1 (all)	0.61	-0.39	99	0.66	0.21	1297
1	0.68	-0.43	50	0.61	0.26	683
2	0.74	-0.54	50	0.62	0.28	687
Avg.	0.74	-0.52	50	0.62	0.33	683

Table 7: Pearson's r for graded and accuracy for binary outcomes of computational approaches compared with human annotations; n = number of observations; all evaluation values are significant.

Table 7 presents the results of the graded evaluation using the Pearson correlation, while for the binary classification, we provide the accuracy scores. To determine significance for the latter, we employ the chi-squared test. We report the evaluation scores for each annotator individually (1 and 2), as well as aggregated by comparing them with the average ratings provided by both annotators[7].

Overall, both the accuracy scores (ranging between 0.61 and 0.74) and the correlation scores (between 0.26 and 0.52), indicate moderate performance of the computational approaches. These results align with the the inherent complexity of the tasks as demonstrated by the fair inter-annotator

[7]We computed Pearson correlation and significance tests using the SciPy library and Cohen's Kappa and the classification report using the scikit-learn library, for Python

agreement. Furthermore, the task of predicting hatefulness yields lower scores compared to predicting semantic change, which implies a difference in the complexity of the two tasks, with the former being more complex than the latter.

Changes of hateful meanings. Similarly to the human annotations, we merge the binary outcomes from the two computational approaches. This enables us to evaluate the classification of words being both hateful and undergoing changes in meaning. In Table 8 the classification by computational approaches is compared with the human annotation outcomes, averaged across the two annotators.

	prec.	recall	F1	n
hateful + changed	0.73	0.42	0.53	19
not hateful + changed	0.72	0.90	0.80	31
macro avg	0.72	0.66	0.67	50

Table 8: Report on the classification of change of hateful meanings compared with average annotator outcomes.

Unsurprisingly, the performance on the combined tasks demonstrates a trade-off between the individual task performances as reported in Table 7. The results reveal that our methods accurately identify around half of the words categorized as shifting in hateful meanings. The low recall rate indicates that false negatives constitute the predominant error type.

5.3 Error analysis

Overall, a potential explanation for the discrepancy between the human annotations and LSCD method predictions (not the LHSD method) might be attributed to the fact that human annotators were tasked with rating an average of approximately 10 contexts per time frame for each target word, whereas the method outcomes derived their predictions from a sample of up to 100 contexts.

To gain a deeper understanding of the specific errors made by the methods we conducted a manual analysis of error cases demonstrated in the comparisons between the methods and *both* annotators. These cases concerned all error types, except for non-existing false negatives of semantic change detection.

Semantic change: false positives. Discrepancies in the detection of semantic change between the computational method and human annotations do not necessarily imply a failure of the method, but could be due to annotation granularity, with the target word 'swearers' being an example case. The method's subtle change detection might not align with the expert annotations differentiating only between "weakly" and "strongly hateful". Consequently, the erroneous detection of *semantic change* leads to 'duns' and 'swearers' being false positives for the classification of *change in hateful meanings*, too.

Hatefulness: false negatives. A potential reason for this error type is usage of metaphor. For instance, 'foxes' was frequently used by Protestants to refer to their opponents in a hateful manner, examplified by a statement made by Andrew Willet in 1592: "They are the foxes that destroy the lords vineyard." (For a deeper analysis of metaphors used in polemical Reformation writings, see Kelly (2015)). This consequently led to 'foxes' being a false negative in the classification of *change in hateful meaning*, too.

Hatefulness: false positives. The target words falsely detected as hateful by the method are: 'anselmus', 'higinus', 'nauclerus', 'sigebertus'. These all are names which do not carry hateful meanings themselves but predominantly occur within hateful contexts, which potentially leads our method to predict a hateful meaning.

6 Discussion & Conclusion

Our study introduces the novel task of detecting changes of hateful word meanings in historical texts. Our interdisciplinary approach combines Lexical Semantic Change Detection and Hate Speech Detection. We leverage historical expertise to generate a pilot dataset with two-aspect annotations, a valuable resource for the evaluation of computational methods. While our methods showed effective precision in detecting hateful words that changed their meaning throughout the 16th century, they also underscored the complexity of (the combination of) the tasks, as evidenced by the human interrater agreement scores.

The exploration of hate speech within historical discourse poses particular challenges. Most importantly, we acknowledge inherent limitations as we may never achieve a perfect reflection of historical connotations. Still, our framework aims at a closer grasp of the past by combining historical research and linguistic analysis. The bounded text selection and the limited annotated data (for reasons of feasibility) pose challenges to the robustness and generalizability of our findings, pertaining to the efficacy of the employed methods as well as the outcomes we have presented. Therefore, our conclusions should be further validated in follow-up research that incorporates more diverse textual sources and enhances the quantity (and quality) of the annotated data. We further propose to broaden the scope beyond nouns, as verbs and adverbial phrases can also convey hate in the form of devaluation of action. Moreover, our error analyses highlighted the prevalence of metaphors for expressing hateful meanings, suggesting another direction further research. Finally, expanding the focus to longer time-spans or conducting cross-language comparisons could also yield valuable insights.

In conclusion, our paper lays foundations for advancing the analysis of lexical change of a specific domain in historical data. Particularly, our interdisciplinary framework paves the way to an expanded dataset and the development of better computational methods for detecting the evolution of historical hate speech.

Limitations

Going beyond the reflection of our work in 6, we would like to further point to some methodological limitations in our study. Firstly, the decision for the used sentence split method appeared not well-suited for digitized historical texts, with punctuation to indicate sentence breaks often missing. This resulted in some flawed sentences, thereby providing limited context information as input for the model's predictions. For further research we would therefore either opt for manual sentence splitting or better trained sentence split algorithms for historical data.

Additionally, the employed spelling normalization method fails to encompass all possible variations, potentially resulting in overlooked or misinterpreted semantic changes that could be perceived as errors. For instance, the word 'sees', which in both time periods could denote 'seas', referring to the ocean; whereas in the later period, it was also utilized in the context of 'bishop's sees', referring to their realm of power. In this case, a gain in word meaning is wrongly identified as the secondary meaning already existed in the earlier period, albeit in the orthographic variant 'sedes'.

Lastly, the method also catches target words if they are part of another word: e.g. the target word 'gaines' also occurs as part of the word 'gainesayers'. Therefore, sentences mentioning both words are taken into account, while we are only interested in the former.

Ethics Statement

Investigating hate speech brings about ethical issues to reflect upon. Unlike modern data typically used for HSD, the textual data from the 16th century we are drawing on is publicly available along with metadata, such as the authors' names. There is no need for anonymization. On the contrary, it is of high value to be able to access context information to further work with the results of our method once it is fully developed. However, we are aware that filtering out hate speech, in our case hateful terms particularly used against Catholics, allows for reproduction in modern days, especially because we still face Anti-Catholicism in present-day societies. Therefore, it is crucial, also for future work, to ensure that the methods' results are always viewed with regards to their historical context and only used for improving NLP methods in order to detect and potentially avoid further usage of hate speech or as a data basis for historical and cultural studies.

Acknowledgements

The authors acknowledge financial support by the project "SAIL: SustAInable Life-cycle of Intelligent Socio-Technical Systems" (Grant ID NW21-059A), which is funded by the program "Netzwerke 2021" of the Ministry of Culture and Science of the State of Northrhine Westphalia, Germany.

Additionally, we would like to thank Melvin Wilde for his annotations, expertise and support.

References

Rudolph P. Almasy. 2008. *Rhetoric and Apologetics*, pages 121 – 150. Brill, Leiden.

Pierpaolo Basile, Annalina Caputo, Tommaso Caselli, Pierluigi Cassotti, and Rossella Varvara. 2020. Diacrita@ evalita2020: Overview of the evalita2020 diachronic lexical semantics (diacr-ita) task. *Evaluation Campaign of Natural Language Processing and Speech Tools for Italian*.

Valerio Basile, Tommaso Caselli, Anna Koufakou, and Viviana Patti. 2022. Automatically computing connotative shifts of lexical items. In *Natural Language Processing and Information Systems: 27th International Conference on Applications of Natural Language to Information Systems, NLDB 2022, Valencia,*

Spain, June 15–17, 2022, Proceedings, pages 425–436. Springer.

Elisa Bassignana, Valerio Basile, Viviana Patti, et al. 2018. Hurtlex: A multilingual lexicon of words to hurt. In *CEUR Workshop proceedings*, volume 2253, pages 1–6. CEUR-WS.

Antoinina Bevan Zlatar. 2011. *Reformation Fictions. Polemical Protestant Dialogues in Elizabethan England.* Oxford University Press.

Marcel Bollmann. 2019. A large-scale comparison of historical text normalization systems. In *Proceedings of the 2019 Conference of the North American Chapter of the Association for Computational Linguistics: Human Language Technologies, Volume 1 (Long and Short Papers)*, pages 3885–3898, Minneapolis, Minnesota. Association for Computational Linguistics.

Dallas Card. 2023. Substitution-based semantic change detection using contextual embeddings. In *Proceedings of the 61st Annual Meeting of the Association for Computational Linguistics (Volume 2: Short Papers)*, pages 590–602, Toronto, Canada. Association for Computational Linguistics.

Tessa E. S. Charlesworth, Aylin Caliskan, and Mahzarin R. Banaji. 2022. Historical representations of social groups across 200 years of word embeddings from google books. *Proceedings of the National Academy of Sciences*, 119(28):e2121798119.

Thomas Davidson, Dana Warmsley, Michael Macy, and Ingmar Weber. 2017. Automated hate speech detection and the problem of offensive language. In *Proceedings of the international AAAI conference on web and social media*, volume 11, pages 512–515.

Albrecht Dröse. 2021. Invektive Affordanzen der Kommunikationsform Flugschrift. *Kulturwissenschaftliche Zeitschrift*, 6(1):37–62.

Njagi Dennis Gitari, Zhang Zuping, Hanyurwimfura Damien, and Jun Long. 2015. A lexicon-based approach for hate speech detection. *International Journal of Multimedia and Ubiquitous Engineering*, 10(4):215–230.

William L. Hamilton, Jure Leskovec, and Dan Jurafsky. 2016. Diachronic word embeddings reveal statistical laws of semantic change. In *Proceedings of the 54th Annual Meeting of the Association for Computational Linguistics (Volume 1: Long Papers)*, pages 1489–1501, Berlin, Germany. Association for Computational Linguistics.

Sanne Hoeken, Sina Zarrieß, and Ozge Alacam. 2023. Identifying slurs and lexical hate speech via lightweight dimension projection in embedding space. In *Proceedings of the 13th Workshop on Computational Approaches to Subjectivity, Sentiment, & Social Media Analysis*, pages 278–289, Toronto, Canada. Association for Computational Linguistics.

Erin Katherine Kelly. 2015. Chasing the fox and the wolf. Hunting in the religious polemic of William Turner. *Reformation*, 20(2):113–125.

Andrey Kutuzov and Mario Giulianelli. 2020. UiO-UvA at SemEval-2020 task 1: Contextualised embeddings for lexical semantic change detection. In *Proceedings of the Fourteenth Workshop on Semantic Evaluation*, pages 126–134, Barcelona (online). International Committee for Computational Linguistics.

Enrique Manjavacas Arevalo and Lauren Fonteyn. 2021. MacBERTh: Development and evaluation of a historically pre-trained language model for English (1450-1950). In *Proceedings of the Workshop on Natural Language Processing for Digital Humanities*, pages 23–36, NIT Silchar, India. NLP Association of India (NLPAI).

Barbara McGillivray, Malithi Alahapperuma, Jonathan Cook, Chiara Di Bonaventura, Albert Meroño-Peñuela, Gareth Tyson, and Steven Wilson. 2022. Leveraging time-dependent lexical features for offensive language detection. In *Proceedings of the The First Workshop on Ever Evolving NLP (EvoNLP)*, pages 39–54, Abu Dhabi, United Arab Emirates (Hybrid). Association for Computational Linguistics.

Stefano Montanelli and Francesco Periti. 2023. A survey on contextualised semantic shift detection. *arXiv preprint arXiv:2304.01666*.

Syrielle Montariol, Matej Martinc, and Lidia Pivovarova. 2021. Scalable and interpretable semantic change detection. In *Proceedings of the 2021 Conference of the North American Chapter of the Association for Computational Linguistics: Human Language Technologies*, pages 4642–4652, Online. Association for Computational Linguistics.

Maxim Rachinskiy and Nikolay Arefyev. 2022. GlossReader at LSCDiscovery: Train to select a proper gloss in English – discover lexical semantic change in Spanish. In *Proceedings of the 3rd Workshop on Computational Approaches to Historical Language Change*, pages 198–203, Dublin, Ireland. Association for Computational Linguistics.

Dominik Schlechtweg, Barbara McGillivray, Simon Hengchen, Haim Dubossarsky, and Nina Tahmasebi. 2020. SemEval-2020 task 1: Unsupervised lexical semantic change detection. In *Proceedings of the Fourteenth Workshop on Semantic Evaluation*, pages 1–23, Barcelona (online). International Committee for Computational Linguistics.

Dominik Schlechtweg, Sabine Schulte im Walde, and Stefanie Eckmann. 2018. Diachronic usage relatedness (DURel): A framework for the annotation of lexical semantic change. In *Proceedings of the 2018 Conference of the North American Chapter of the Association for Computational Linguistics: Human Language Technologies, Volume 2 (Short Papers)*, pages 169–174, New Orleans, Louisiana. Association for Computational Linguistics.

Anna Schmidt and Michael Wiegand. 2017. A survey on hate speech detection using natural language processing. In *Proceedings of the Fifth International Workshop on Natural Language Processing for Social Media*, pages 1–10, Valencia, Spain. Association for Computational Linguistics.

Silke Schwandt. 2018. Digitale Methoden für die Historische Semantik. Auf den Spuren von Begriffen in digitalen Korpora. *Geschichte und Gesellschaft*, 44(1):107–134.

Gerd Schwerhoff. 2020. Invektivität und geschichtswissenschaft konstellationen der herabsetzung in historischer perspektive. ein forschungskonzept. *Historische Zeitschrift*, 311(1):1–36.

Sita Steckel. 2018. Verging on the polemical. Towards an interdisciplinary approach to medieval religious polemic. *Medieval Worlds*, 7(1):2–60.

Nina Tahmasebia, Lars Borina, and Adam Jatowtb. 2021. Survey of computational approaches to lexical semantic change detection. *Computational approaches to semantic change*, 6:1.

Fabio Del Vigna, Andrea Cimino, Felice Dell'Orletta, Marinella Petrocchi, and Maurizio Tesconi. 2017. Hate me, hate me not: Hate speech detection on facebook. In *Italian Conference on Cybersecurity*.

Michael Wiegand, Josef Ruppenhofer, Anna Schmidt, and Clayton Greenberg. 2018. Inducing a lexicon of abusive words – a feature-based approach. In *Proceedings of the 2018 Conference of the North American Chapter of the Association for Computational Linguistics: Human Language Technologies, Volume 1 (Long Papers)*, pages 1046–1056, New Orleans, Louisiana. Association for Computational Linguistics.

Thomas Wolf, Lysandre Debut, Victor Sanh, Julien Chaumond, Clement Delangue, Anthony Moi, Pierric Cistac, Tim Rault, Remi Louf, Morgan Funtowicz, Joe Davison, Sam Shleifer, Patrick von Platen, Clara Ma, Yacine Jernite, Julien Plu, Canwen Xu, Teven Le Scao, Sylvain Gugger, Mariama Drame, Quentin Lhoest, and Alexander Rush. 2020. Transformers: State-of-the-art natural language processing. In *Proceedings of the 2020 Conference on Empirical Methods in Natural Language Processing: System Demonstrations*, pages 38–45, Online. Association for Computational Linguistics.

Frank D. Zamora-Reina, Felipe Bravo-Marquez, and Dominik Schlechtweg. 2022. LSCDiscovery: A shared task on semantic change discovery and detection in Spanish. In *Proceedings of the 3rd Workshop on Computational Approaches to Historical Language Change*, pages 149–164, Dublin, Ireland. Association for Computational Linguistics.

A Keywords used for text selection

The corpus of texts we used as input data was generated through an iterative keyword-based search using the following keywords.

First selection: catholic*, church, faith*, invective*, libel*, protestant*, pamphlet*, pope, religio*, reformatio*, reformer*, religio*. (Asterisks represent wildcards in the search mask.)

Second selection: harlots, heretics, hypocrites, papists, strumpets, whores.

B Spelling normalization

We generated a substitution dictionary, tailored to our dataset, aiming to transform word forms into their most modern spelling variations within the corpus (e.g. transforming 'shauelyngs' and 'shauelings' to 'shavelings'). To achieve this, we created a set of rules for character substitutions, grounded in regular expressions. We applied these rules to all words in the vocabulary of the raw data collection. If a substitution resulted in an existing word in the (same) vocabulary, we included the before-and-after substitution pair in the dictionary. An overview of these rules and the corresponding procedure (in code) are presented below. We applied the mappings to the entire corpus.

```
import re

def get_variant(word):
  word = word.replace('ā', 'an')
  word = word.replace('ū', 'un')
  word = word.replace('ē', 'en')
  word = word.replace('ā', 'am')
  word = word.replace('ū', 'um')
  word = word.replace('ē', 'em')
  word = re.sub("uy", r"vi", word)
  word = re.sub("([^q])u([aeiou])", r"\1
     v\2", word)
  word = word.replace('vv', 'w')
  word = re.sub(r"^vh", "wh", word)
  word = re.sub(r"v([bgnprstx])", r"u\1"
     , word)
  word = re.sub(r"y", "i", word) if word
     != "i" else word
  word = re.sub(r"ie$", "y", word)
  word = re.sub("([aeiou])ie", r"\1y",
     word)
  word = re.sub(r"i$", "y", word) if
     word != "i" else word
  word = re.sub(r"^iou", "you", word)
  return word

for w in vocab:
  if w != get_variant(w) and get_variant
     (w) in vocab:
    dictionary[w] = get_modern_variant(w
      )
```

C Target words for test set

Method outcomes for hate & semantic change to guide target word selection. (Random sample is not included here)

Hate changes.

- Top 20 projection value differences (neutral to hateful) between 1530-1553 and 1580-1603: counsailours, abbayes, tailes, higinus, dainties, swearers, hornes, adonias, winchesters, founders, notes, autours, sins, ananias, pastoures, agnus, adversaries, ensamples, heremites, duns

- Bottom 20 projection value differences (hateful to neutral) between 1530-1553 and 1580-1603: dedes, honours, affections, companies, purenes, freres, theues, affectes, cerimonies, businesses, evilles, noes, sclaunders, fabianus, luthers, holines, fees, plays, lordshippes, fines

Semantic changes.

- Top 20 JSD values (most changed between 1530-1553 and 1580-1603): strokes, males, dainties, winchesters, provisions, doctores, gaines, hominibus, affectes, womens, accountes, foxes, bargaines, parsons, giles, strengthes, wais, faculties, sees, professions

- Bottom 20 JSD values (most stable between 1530-1553 and 1580-1603): dionisius, preestes, presbiteros, aulters, berengarius, galathians, otherwhiles, polidorus, anselmus, rechabites, lanfrancus, ciprianus, sigebertus, apocalips, cauillations, ezechias, nauclerus, fulgentius, chrisostoms

Semantic & hate changes.

- Intersection of Top 20 projection value differences (neutral to hateful) and Top 20 JSD values (most changed): dainties, winchesters

- Intersection of Bottom 20 projection value differences (hateful to neutral) and Top 20 JSD values (most changed): affectes

Figure 2 displays an example of an annotation instance.

D Annotation example

target	sentence1	sentence2	semantic relatedness	hate1	hate2
swearers	for if there be a god, as i am certenly persuaded ther is, i am sure that these abhominable swearers shall not escape vnponysshed, let then esteme their sinne as light & as litle as they list, yea i am sure, i e vengeaunce of god hangeth over their heades, wher so ever they be.	the lorde will not holde him gyltelesse that taketh his name in vayne. let not these swearers therfore glory in their wickednes, and thinke i • they shall escape vnponished, because god takethe not vengeaunce on them streight ways , but rather let them thincke that their damnaciō shall be so muche the more greuous, seing they escape so longe without punishment.	4	2	2

Figure 2: Example of annotation instance

Changing usage of Low Saxon auxiliary and modal verbs

Janine Siewert
University of Helsinki
janine.siewert@helsinki.fi

Martijn Wieling
University of Groningen
m.b.wieling@rug.nl

Yves Scherrer
University of Oslo
University of Helsinki
yves.scherrer@ifi.uio.no

Abstract

We investigate the usage of auxiliary and modal verbs in Low Saxon dialects from both Germany and the Netherlands based on word vectors, and compare developments in the modern language to Middle Low Saxon. Although most of these function words have not been affected by lexical replacement, changes in usage that likely at least partly result from contact with the state languages[1] can still be observed.

1 Introduction

Low Saxon[2] is an unstandardised West Germanic language primarily spoken in the north-eastern Netherlands and northern Germany. As the contact situation with the state languages Dutch and German has led to divergence of Low Saxon dialects at the border, the primary research question we want to investigate is whether the usage of certain auxiliary and modal verbs can also be found to diverge.

This study is part of our broader research into dialectal variation and change in Low Saxon, cf. Siewert et al. (2022), and constitutes a first exploration of the field of lexical variation. Auxiliary and modal verbs are a suitable starting point because they form a relatively closed group for which automatic annotation works more reliably than for many others.

We use word vector representations to compare certain auxiliary and modal verbs and investigate changes in usage from Middle Low Saxon to Modern Dutch Low Saxon and German Low Saxon. These vectors representations were trained on lemmata in concatenation with dependency relations and PoS (Part-of-Speech) information.

[1]'State languages' refers to Standard Dutch and Standard German here, because they are the only languages with statewide official status in the respective countries. Contact with regional official languages, such as the Frisian languages or Danish, is not taken into account here although this would certainly be an interesting research question as well.

[2]Also called 'Low German'.

2 Background

The divergence of Low Saxon dialects at the border has been investigated in the form of lexical replacement as well as changes at the phonological, morphological and syntactic level, e.g., by Niebaum (1990) and Kremer (1990). A more quantitative study looking at frequencies of local phonological, morphological and syntactic traits in contrast with state language traits is presented by Smits (2009), who examines the stability of dialectal characteristics. All three authors mention the lexical level as an area particularly susceptible to influence from the state languages. Instead of lexical replacement mostly referred to by them, we will however focus on changing usage of the same lexical items.

2.1 Auxiliary and modal verbs

The auxiliary and modal verbs included in the comparison are *dôn* 'to do', *dōren* 'to dare', *dörven* 'to dare, to be allowed to', *hebben* 'to have', *künnen* 'can', *mōgen* 'may, like', *mȏten* 'must', *schōlen* 'shall, will', *wērden* 'to be (+ past participle), will', *wēsen* 'to be' and *willen* 'want, will' [3]. In particular, we will focus on two groups of auxiliary or modal verbs that exhibit partly overlapping usage: future auxiliaries on the one hand and models of permission, prohibition and obligation on the other hand.

2.2 Future auxiliaries

The first group consists of the verbs *wērden*, *schōlen* and *willen*. While *wērden*, like its Dutch and German cognates *worden* and *werden*, has traditionally functioned as the auxiliary verb for forming the passive, it has developed the additional

[3]The English cognates are *do, dare, tharf*†, *have, can, may, must, shall, worth*†, *be* and *will*, with the forms marked with a † being dialectal or historical. The translations represent some common usages today. Due to the internal diversity and change over time, it is not possible to provide translations covering all varieties and time periods here.

Proceedings of the 4th Workshop on Computational Approaches to Historical Language Change, pages 112–118
December 6, 2023 ©2023 Association for Computational Linguistics

function of the future auxiliary in German. A similar development can be observed in German Low Saxon with first attestations already in Middle Low Saxon (Härd, 2000, 1458), but in older Modern Low Saxon texts, an inchoative reading is often still possible or the more likely interpretation (cf. Lindow et al., 1998, 101–103). In Dutch Low Saxon, on the other hand, we have not encountered usage of *wērden* as an auxiliary for the future tense. Therefore, we expect to see differences in the distance of *wērden* to *schōlen* and *willen*, of which *schōlen* already functioned as a future auxiliary in Middle Low Saxon (Härd, 2000, 1458) and can still do so in both Dutch Low Saxon and German Low Saxon (Lindow et al., 1998, 106). The usage of *willen* as a future auxiliary in German Low Saxon is described at least by Lindow et al. (1998, 104).

2.3 Modals of permission, prohibition and obligation

In the second group, we look at the distance of *dörven* to *dōren*, *môten* and *mōgen*. The verb *dōren* is especially interesting, because in Modern Low Saxon it has generally been either replaced by or merged with *dörven*. According to Lindow et al. (1998, 110), *dörven* originally carried the meaning 'to be allowed to', while *dōren* meant 'to dare', and these meanings are to varying degree found in *dörven* the modern language.

While negated *müssen* in German carries the meaning 'does not need to', negated *môten* in German Low Saxon can be used like the English equivalent *must not* (Lindow et al., 1998, 110). This usage is similar to negated *dörven*.

The main usages of *mōgen* in German Low Saxon according to Lindow et al. (1998, 112) are the expression of possibility, of an assumption and of a wish. These meanings can be found in German and Dutch as well, but they differ in which meanings dominate.

Since we have not found comparable descriptions for the Dutch Low Saxon verbs, our expectations are mostly based on the corresponding usage in Dutch and our own exposure to Dutch Low Saxon.

3 Data

The Modern Low Saxon data shown in Table 1 comes from the LSDC dataset (Siewert et al., 2020) and is split into two time periods: 1800–1939 and 1980–2022. Furthermore, we split the dataset into

Abbr.	Variety	Time span	Tokens
MLS	Middle Low Saxon	1200–1650	1 406 979
DLS1	Dutch Low Saxon	1800–1939	147 212
DLS2	Dutch Low Saxon	1980–2022	393 619
NLS1	German North Low Saxon	1800–1939	1 008 851
NLS2	German North Low Saxon	1980–2022	103 568
SLS1	German South Low Saxon	1800–1939	371 611
SLS2	German South Low Saxon	1980–2022	416 686

Table 1: Low Saxon varieties and their token counts.

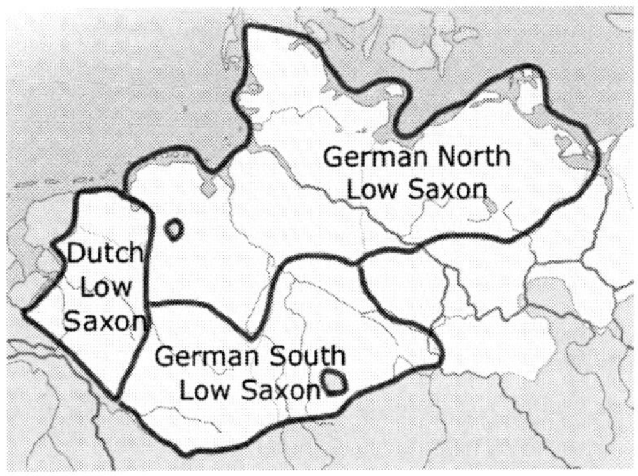

Figure 1: The three major Low Saxon dialect groups included.

three large geographical groups: Dutch Low Saxon (DLS), German North Low Saxon (NLS) and German South Low Saxon (SLS) as shown in Figure 1. All subcorpora contain a variety of genres, among others short stories, fairy tales, theatre plays, historical accounts, speeches, and letters.

The Middle Low Saxon (MLS) data is taken from the Reference Corpus Middle Low German / Low Rhenish (ReN-Team, 2021), and converted to CoNLL-U format including a conversion of the tags to the UD tagset[4] that is used in the LSDC dataset. The genres in the Reference Corpus are specified as prose, document, or verse.

3.1 Annotation

For this research, three layers of annotation are relevant: Lemmatisation, PoS tagging and dependency parsing.

The LSDC dataset comes with PoS tags, but does not include lemmata or dependency relations. The PoS tags are primarily annotated automatically, except for the around 300 sentences per dialect group that were manually corrected for finetuning annotation models.

The lemmata and PoS tags in the original version of the Reference Corpus have been annotated

[4]https://universaldependencies.org/u/pos

by human curators, but we needed to make some adaptations and add dependency parsing.

3.1.1 Lemmatisation

For comparison with the Reference Corpus, we needed to lemmatise Modern Low Saxon to Middle Low Saxon. Our lemmata follow the *Mittelniederdeutsches Handwörterbuch* (Lasch et al., 1928 ff.), but we removed superscript numbers and simplified a few graphemes, such as <ê^{i}> to <êi>, to speed up the manual lemmatisation of the training, development and test data for the lemmatiser. We furthermore slightly manually adapted the lemmata in the Reference Corpus in the same way as for the modern corpus.

We manually lemmatised these same around 900 sentences which contained gold standard PoS tags in order to train a lemmatiser. Of these, 700 were part of the train set and 100 each formed the development and the test set.

We trained a Stanza (Qi et al., 2020) lemmatiser on a train set that contained the whole Reference Corpus in addition to our small manually annotated Modern Low Saxon training data, whereas we only used Modern Low Saxon data for the development and test set. We reached an accuracy of 83% and lemmatised the remainder of the LSDC data with this model.

3.1.2 Dependency parsing

Due to time constraints, we only managed to annotate dependency relations for around 300 sentences of which 100 became part of the train set.

We used Stanza for dependency parsing[5] as well and complemented the small manually annotated Low Saxon train set with UD datasets in Afrikaans[6], Danish (Johannsen et al., 2015), Dutch (Bouma and van Noord, 2017), English (Zeldes, 2017), German (McDonald et al., 2013), Norwegian (Øvrelid and Hohle, 2016) and Swedish (Nivre and Megyesi, 2007). We included the mainland Scandinavian languages in addition to the West Germanic ones, because they were in close contact with and strongly influenced by Middle Low Saxon during the time of the Hanseatic League. Since Stanza does not allow for finetuning, the train set included all eight languages while the development and test set contained exclusively Low Saxon data. This parser reached an accuracy of 81% LAS for Modern Low Saxon and was used to parse both the Modern and the Middle Low Saxon corpus, but since it has only encountered Modern Low Saxon data during training, the parsing accuracy on Middle Low Saxon is likely lower.

The lemmatised and dependency-parsed Modern Low Saxon data is publicly available under a CC BY-NC license[7].

4 Methods

The word vectors were trained on the whole dataset – both the manually and the automatically annotated part – using fastText's (Bojanowski et al., 2016) skipgram model with a vector length of 100 and subwords[8] following these two set-ups: lemma + dependency relation (e.g., *dörven_aux*), and lemma + PoS tags (e.g. *wērden_AUX*). Our reason for using subwords during training is that, otherwise, the PoS or dependency information, that is part of the same string, could not be accessed.

Levy and Goldberg (2014) found dependency information to be beneficial for identifying words that behave in a similar way and not only occur in similar contexts. For comparison, we used PoS tags, because the PoS tagging in our dataset is more accurate than the dependency relations.

We initially also tested vectors based on lemmata only, but eventually excluded these, since they showed great fluctuations even within the same variety, when the vectors were trained with different mininum word counts. Furthermore, when working with fastText's function `.get_nearest_neighbors()`, we had observed that the suggested nearest neighbours tended to be more meaningful when dependency or PoS information was added, as otherwise the importance of uninformative subword units such as *nnen* or *llen* seemed to be overestimated.

We first trained common vectors with a mininum word count of 50 for both Middle and Modern Low Saxon to ensure a common initialisation for all variants. Subsequently we fine-tuned this model on Middle Low Saxon and Modern Low Saxon data separately, and finally, with a mininum word count of 25, retrained the general Modern Low Saxon model with data in the subgroups listed in table 1.

Due to the small size of the two subcorpora DLS 1 and NLS 2 (cf. Table 1), we also trained vectors

[5] https://universaldependencies.org/u/dep

[6] https://github.com/UniversalDependencies/UD_Afrikaans-AfriBooms/tree/master

[7] https://github.com/Helsinki-NLP/LSDC-morph/tree/main/lchange2023

[8] See training options here: https://fasttext.cc/docs/en/unsupervised-tutorial.html

with mininum counts of 5, 10 and 15 to check the stability of the results.

Subsequently, we used the Python libraries NumPy (Harris et al., 2020) and SciPy (Virtanen et al., 2020) to measure the Euclidean and cosine distances between the resulting word vectors. We will, however, only present the results based on Euclidean distance here, since the other approach produced comparable results.

Despite the common initialisation, the absolute distance values did not compare well across varieties. The reason for this might be found in the different sizes of the subcorpora. Therefore, we only discuss the relative closeness compared with the other modal or auxiliary verbs here.

5 Results

5.1 Future auxiliaries

We use *wērden* as a target verb and list the other auxiliary and modal verbs in order of closeness to *wērden* in Tables 2 and 3.

In both tables, we see that in German Low Saxon, NLS and SLS, *schōlen* is closer to *wērden* than in Middle Low Saxon and Dutch Low Saxon. Curiously, these verbs seem to grow closer in Dutch Low Saxon, but due to the small size of the DLS 1 corpus, one should not draw strong conclusions from this. The increase we see in German South Low Saxon in both tables is likely more reliable. For German North Low Saxon we find contradicting tendencies: While the dependency-based table shows continuity, we find a decrease in closeness in the PoS-based data.

Strikingly, while *willen* was still clearly closer to *wērden* than *schōlen* in Middle Low Saxon, the order has shifted in the modern language and *willen* has become less similar almost without exception.

5.2 Modals of permission, prohibition and obligation

Tables 4 and 5 present the verbs ordered by closeness to the target verb *dörven*. As mentioned in Section 2, *dōren* has mostly fallen out of use in the Modern Low Saxon period and is only represented by a handful of examples. As a result, the word vectors are largely inherited from the common pretrained vectors. Furthermore, the verb *dörven* has very few occurrences in the Dutch Low Saxon data. Therefore, vectors of this verb likely represent mostly the common Low Saxon pretrain-model.

The verb *dōren* is very close to *dörven* in Middle Low Saxon and Dutch Low Saxon[9], whereas the picture is less consistent in German Low Saxon: While closeness is high in the NLS 2 data, it is only the fourth or fifth most similar verb in the NLS 1 data. The number of occurrences of *dörven*, however, is small (only 10) in the newer data and, therefore, less reliable. Similarly, we observe a decrease in South Low Saxon, particularly in the dependency-based data.

The other verb that shows a contrasting development in Dutch Low Saxon and German Low Saxon is *mōgen*. Curiously, while the similarity compared to Middle Low Saxon seems to increase in Dutch Low Saxon in the dependency data, a decrease appears to occur in the PoS-based data. Nevertheless, in both cases the relative closeness is greater than in German Low Saxon. The only exception to this seems to be newer North Low Saxon (NLS 2) in table 5, but, in fact, the vectors trained with a smaller mininum word count showed a greater distance.

In case of *mōten*, we find a contrast between Dutch Low Saxon and German North Low Saxon on the one hand, and German South Low Saxon on the other hand: Whereas in German South Low Saxon, the closeness to *dörven* remains comparable to Middle Low Saxon over both time periods, the other two modern varieties show a decrease in both tables.

6 Discussion and future research

For *wērden*, we found partly expected and partly surprising results. The increased closeness of *schōlen* in German Low Saxon is in line with the development of *wērden* into a future tense auxiliary. The slight increase we see in German South Low Saxon when going from the older to the modern period might tell that this additional usage of *wērden* was not as widespread yet in the 19th and early 20th century.

On the other hand, we do not have an explanation for the decreased closeness of *willen*. However, at least for modern German Low Saxon, the greater distance might show that the usage of *willen* as a future auxiliary is in fact not very widespread.

While the similarity between *dörven* and *dōren*

[9]Due to the small number of occurrences, the Dutch Low Saxon vectors might represent mostly a copy of Middle Low Saxon.

MLS	DLS1	DLS2	NLS1	NLS2	SLS1	SLS2
wēsen	wēsen	wēsen	wēsen	wēsen	môten	wēsen
hebben	dörven	dȫren	**schȫlen**	**schȫlen**	künnen	môten
künnen	dȫren	dörven	dörven	dörven	dörven	**schȫlen**
willen	mȫgen	môten	môten	künnen	wēsen	mȫgen
môten	môten	mȫgen	künnen	dȫren	dȫren	dörven
dȫren	hebben	künnen	dȫren	hebben	**schȫlen**	hebben
dôn	künnen	dôn	hebben	môten	dôn	künnen
schȫlen	dôn	**schȫlen**	willen	willen	mȫgen	dȫren
mȫgen	**schȫlen**	willen	mȫgen	dôn	willen	willen
dörven	willen	hebben	dôn	mȫgen	hebben	dôn

Table 2: Auxiliar and modal verbs most similar to *wērden*, with dependency relation.

MLS	DLS1	DLS2	NLS1	NLS2	SLS1	SLS2
wēsen	hebben	wēsen	wēsen	wēsen	dȫren	wēsen
dôn	dȫren	dȫren	**schȫlen**	künnen	wēsen	dörven
willen	mȫgen	dörven	hebben	dȫren	môten	hebben
hebben	wēsen	dôn	môten	hebben	künnen	mȫgen
mȫgen	dörven	hebben	dȫren	**schȫlen**	dörven	**schȫlen**
dȫren	môten	môten	künnen	dörven	**schȫlen**	willen
schȫlen	künnen	**schȫlen**	dörven	dôn	dôn	dôn
môten	dôn	künnen	willen	mȫgen	hebben	môten
künnen	willen	mȫgen	dôn	willen	mȫgen	künnen
dörven	**schȫlen**	willen	mȫgen	môten	willen	dȫren

Table 3: Auxiliar and modal verbs most similar to *wērden*, with PoS information.

MLS	DLS1	DLS2	NLS1	NLS2	SLS1	SLS2
môten	môten	**dȫren**	künnen	schȫlen	schȫlen	môten
dȫren	**dȫren**	*mȫgen*	môten	**dȫren**	môten	willen
willen	*mȫgen*	willen	schȫlen	künnen	willen	künnen
mȫgen	künnen	môten	willen	willen	**dȫren**	dôn
schȫlen	dôn	künnen	**dȫren**	môten	künnen	**dȫren**
künnen	wērden	schȫlen	hebben	hebben	wēsen	wēsen
hebben	schȫlen	dôn	wēsen	*mȫgen*	dôn	hebben
dôn	hebben	wēsen	*mȫgen*	dôn	hebben	schȫlen
wēsen	wēsen	hebben	dôn	wēsen	*mȫgen*	wērden
wērden	willen	wērden	wērden	wērden	wērden	*mȫgen*

Table 4: Auxiliary and modal verbs closest to *dörven* based on lemmata with dependency relations.

MLS	DLS1	DLS2	NLS1	NLS2	SLS1	SLS2
dȫren	**dȫren**	**dȫren**	willen	**dȫren**	môten	môten
môten	wēsen	willen	hebben	schȫlen	**dȫren**	**dȫren**
mȫgen	wērden	schȫlen	môten	hebben	künnen	künnen
willen	*mȫgen*	dôn	**dȫren**	*mȫgen*	dôn	dôn
künnen	môten	*mȫgen*	schȫlen	willen	wērden	willen
schȫlen	künnen	hebben	künnen	künnen	schȫlen	wēsen
dôn	hebben	künnen	dôn	wēsen	wēsen	hebben
hebben	dôn	wēsen	wēsen	dôn	*mȫgen*	schȫlen
wērden	willen	môten	wērden	môten	willen	*mȫgen*
wēsen	schȫlen	wērden	*mȫgen*	wērden	hebben	wērden

Table 5: Auxiliary and modal verbs closest to *dörven* based on lemmata with PoS information.

in Dutch Low Saxon cannot be judged reliably due to data sparsity, we see an interesting decrease in German Low Saxon. This might be related to the usage of German *dürfen*, which generally does not carry the meaning 'to dare'.

A similar phenomenon can apparently be observed in case of *mȫgen*. While the meaning of 'to be allowed to' is still dominant in Dutch *mogen*, it has become less common for German *mögen*, and the distances we find in Table 4 and 5 suggest that the Low Saxon varieties might again follow the state languages.

Moreover, a shift in the usage of negated *môten* from 'must not / to not be allowed to' to 'do not need to' as in German might explain the decreased similarity in NLS.

In conclusion, we find that lexical change and divergence at the border is not only visible in the form of lexical replacement, but also at the level of word usage. For some of the developments described above, such as the increased closeness of *wērden* and *schȫlen* and the decreased closeness of *dörven* and *mȫgen* in German Low Saxon, state language influence likely plays a role.

6.1 Future Research

In order to increase the reliability of our results, we want to further improve dependency parsing accuracy. In particular, separate train, development and test data for Middle Low Saxon dependency parsing would be desirable.

We plan to also use these dependency relations for the detection of syntactic structures and a comparison of dialect similarity and change at the syntactic level, since this is often considered more stable than the lexical level.

Moreover, the reference corpus contains metadata information on place and time, so one might take a look at the internal variation of Middle Low Saxon as well.

Computing overall differences of the modal verbs to their Dutch and German cognates would be an interesting research direction as well, but on the one hand this might require subcorpora of more equal size, as discussed in Section 4 and on the other hand – and even more importantly – comparable Dutch and German corpora from the same time periods and with the same annotation.

Limitations

The Middle Low Saxon reference corpus does not cover the Netherlands, so our dataset does not include the predecessor to Modern Dutch Low Saxon. Unfortunately, to our knowledge, there is no reference corpus for the Middle Low Saxon varieties from today's Dutch side of the border.

Unlike in the Middle Low Saxon data, the lemmatisation and PoS tags of the modern data are not gold-standard, and the dependency parsing was done fully automatically for both. This needs to be kept in mind when judging the reliability of the results.

Acknowledgements

This work was partly funded by the COST Action CA21167: Universality, diversity and idiosyncrasy in language technology (UniDive), supported by COST (European Cooperation in Science and Technology).

In addition, this work was supported by the Fo-Tran project, funded by the European Research Council (ERC) under the European Union's Horizon 2020 research and innovation programme under grant agreement No 771113.

References

Piotr Bojanowski, Edouard Grave, Armand Joulin, and Tomas Mikolov. 2016. Enriching word vectors with subword information. *arXiv preprint arXiv:1607.04606*.

Gosse Bouma and Gertjan van Noord. 2017. Increasing return on annotation investment: The automatic construction of a Universal Dependency treebank for Dutch. In *Proceedings of the NoDaLiDa 2017 Workshop on Universal Dependencies (UDW 2017)*, pages 19–26, Gothenburg, Sweden. Association for Computational Linguistics.

Charles R. Harris, K. Jarrod Millman, Stéfan J. van der Walt, Ralf Gommers, Pauli Virtanen, David Cournapeau, Eric Wieser, Julian Taylor, Sebastian Berg, Nathaniel J. Smith, Robert Kern, Matti Picus, Stephan Hoyer, Marten H. van Kerkwijk, Matthew Brett, Allan Haldane, Jaime Fernández del Río, Mark Wiebe, Pearu Peterson, Pierre Gérard-Marchant, Kevin Sheppard, Tyler Reddy, Warren Weckesser, Hameer Abbasi, Christoph Gohlke, and Travis E. Oliphant. 2020. Array programming with NumPy. *Nature*, 585(7825):357–362.

John Evert Härd. 2000. Syntax des Mittelniederdeutschen. In Werner Besch, Anne Betten, Oskar Reichmann, and Stefan Sonderegger, editors, *Sprachgeschichte – Ein Handbuch zur Geschichte der deutschen Sprache und ihrer Erforschung*. Walter de Gruyter, Berlin and New York.

Anders Johannsen, Héctor Martínez Alonso, and Barbara Plank. 2015. Universal dependencies for danish. In *International Workshop on Treebanks and Linguistic Theories (TLT14)*, page 157.

Ludger Kremer. 1990. Kontinuum oder Bruchstelle? Zur Entwicklung der Grenzdialekte zwischen Niederrhein und Vechtegebiet. In Ludger Kremer and Hermann Niebaum, editors, *Germanistische Linguistisk 101-103*, pages 85–123. Olms.

Agathe Lasch, Conrad Borchling, Gerhard Cordes, Dieter Möhn, Ingrid Schröder, Jürgen Meier, and Sabina Tsapaeva. 1928 ff. *Mittelniederdeutsches Handwörterbuch*. Wachholtz Verlag, Neumünster.

Omer Levy and Yoav Goldberg. 2014. Dependency-based word embeddings. In *Proceedings of the 52nd Annual Meeting of the Association for Computational Linguistics (Volume 2: Short Papers)*, pages 302–308, Baltimore, Maryland. Association for Computational Linguistics.

Wolfgang Lindow, Dieter Möhn, Hermann Niebaum, Dieter Stellmacher, Hans Taubken, and Jan Wirrer. 1998. *Niederdeutsche Grammatik*. Verlag Schuster Leer.

Ryan McDonald, Joakim Nivre, Yvonne Quirmbach-Brundage, Yoav Goldberg, Dipanjan Das, Kuzman Ganchev, Keith Hall, Slav Petrov, Hao Zhang, Oscar Täckström, Claudia Bedini, Núria Bertomeu Castelló, and Jungmee Lee. 2013. Universal Dependency annotation for multilingual parsing. In *Proceedings of the 51st Annual Meeting of the Association for Computational Linguistics (Volume 2: Short Papers)*, pages 92–97, Sofia, Bulgaria. Association for Computational Linguistics.

Hermann Niebaum. 1990. Staatsgrenze als Bruchstelle? Die Grenzdialekte zwischen Dollart und Vechtegebiet. In Ludger Kremer and Hermann Niebaum, editors, *Germanistische Linguistisk 101-103*, pages 49–83. Olms.

Joakim Nivre and Beata Megyesi. 2007. Bootstrapping a swedish treebank using cross-corpus harmonization and annotation projection. In *Proceedings of the 6th international workshop on treebanks and linguistic theories*, pages 97–102. Association for Computational Linguistics Pennsylvania, PA.

Peng Qi, Yuhao Zhang, Yuhui Zhang, Jason Bolton, and Christopher D. Manning. 2020. Stanza: A Python natural language processing toolkit for many human languages. In *Proceedings of the 58th Annual Meeting of the Association for Computational Linguistics: System Demonstrations*.

ReN-Team. 2021. Reference Corpus Middle Low German/Low Rhenish (1200–1650); Referenzkorpus Mittelniederdeutsch/Niederrheinisch (1200–1650).

Janine Siewert, Yves Scherrer, and Martijn Wieling. 2022. Low Saxon dialect distances at the orthographic and syntactic level. In *Proceedings of the 3rd Workshop on Computational Approaches to Historical Language Change*, pages 119–124, Dublin, Ireland. Association for Computational Linguistics.

Janine Siewert, Yves Scherrer, Martijn Wieling, and Jörg Tiedemann. 2020. LSDC - a comprehensive dataset for Low Saxon dialect classification. In *Proceedings of the 7th Workshop on NLP for Similar Languages, Varieties and Dialects*, pages 25–35, Barcelona, Spain (Online). International Committee on Computational Linguistics (ICCL).

Tom F.H. Smits. 2009. Prinzipien der Dialektresistenz – Zur Bestimmung einer dialektalen Abbauhierarchie. In Alexandra N. Lenz, Charlotte Gooskens, and Siemon Reker, editors, *Low Saxon Dialects across Borders – Niedersächsische Dialekte über Grenzen hinweg*, pages 317–338. Franz Steiner Verlag.

Pauli Virtanen, Ralf Gommers, Travis E. Oliphant, Matt Haberland, Tyler Reddy, David Cournapeau, Evgeni Burovski, Pearu Peterson, Warren Weckesser, Jonathan Bright, Stéfan J. van der Walt, Matthew Brett, Joshua Wilson, K. Jarrod Millman, Nikolay Mayorov, Andrew R. J. Nelson, Eric Jones, Robert Kern, Eric Larson, C J Carey, İlhan Polat, Yu Feng, Eric W. Moore, Jake VanderPlas, Denis Laxalde, Josef Perktold, Robert Cimrman, Ian Henriksen, E. A. Quintero, Charles R. Harris, Anne M. Archibald, Antônio H. Ribeiro, Fabian Pedregosa, Paul van Mulbregt, and SciPy 1.0 Contributors. 2020. SciPy 1.0: Fundamental Algorithms for Scientific Computing in Python. *Nature Methods*, 17:261–272.

Amir Zeldes. 2017. The GUM corpus: Creating multilayer resources in the classroom. *Language Resources and Evaluation*, 51(3):581–612.

Lilja Øvrelid and Petter Hohle. 2016. Universal dependencies for norwegian. In *Proceedings of the Tenth International Conference on Language Resources and Evaluation (LREC 2016)*, Paris, France. European Language Resources Association (ELRA).

Semantic Shifts in Mental Health-Related Concepts

Naomi Baes[Φ] **Nick Haslam**[Φ] **Ekaterina Vylomova**[λ]
[Φ] Melbourne School of Psychological Sciences
[λ]School of Computing and Information Systems
The University of Melbourne
{n.baes, nhaslam, vylomovae}@unimelb.edu.au

Abstract

The present study evaluates semantic shifts in mental health-related concepts in two diachronic corpora spanning 1970–2016, one academic and one general. It evaluates whether their meanings have broadened to encompass less severe phenomena and whether they have become more pathology related. It applies a recently proposed methodology (Baes et al., 2023) to examine whether words collocating with a sample of mental health concepts have become less emotionally intense and develops a new way to examine whether the concepts increasingly co-occur with pathology-related terms. In support of the first hypothesis, mental health-related concepts became associated with less emotionally intense language in the psychology corpus (*addiction*, *anger*, *stress*, *worry*) and in the general corpus (*addiction*, *grief*, *stress*, *worry*). In support of the second hypothesis, mental health-related concepts came to be more associated with pathology-related language in psychology (*addiction*, *grief*, *stress*, *worry*) and in the general corpus (*grief*, *stress*). Findings demonstrate that some mental health concepts have become normalized and/or pathologized, a conclusion with important social and cultural implications.

1 Introduction

Mental health has become more culturally salient in recent years. Concurrently, concepts of mental illness have expanded their meanings to include new and milder phenomena (Haslam, 2016, 'concept creep'). Critics have argued that psychiatry has transformed everyday sadness into major depression (Horwitz and Wakefield, 2007) and adaptive worries and inhibitions into anxiety disorders (Horwitz and Wakefield, 2012). Others argue that this pattern extends to colloquial language, where people use 'depression' to refer to ordinary sadness or low mood (Bröer and Besseling, 2017). Brinkmann (2016) explains this trend as an ongoing cultural process of 'pathologization', where traits and behaviors that were once considered normal human problems (e.g., inattentiveness) are now conceptualized as mental disorders (e.g., attention-deficit/hyperactivity disorder) to be diagnosed and treated. Critics argue that pathologization leads to increasing vulnerability, which can partly be explained by the adoption of illness identities (Furedi, 2004), and to false positive diagnoses, resulting in the misallocation of treatment resources (Wakefield, 2010). Despite these arguments, whether people are indeed normalizing mental illness and pathologizing everyday life remains a largely untested empirical question.

The present study aims to clarify the nature of these semantic shifts in a new sample of mental health-related concepts: *addiction*, *anger*, *distress*, *grief*, *stress*, and *worry*. It first investigates whether they have undergone vertical concept creep (come to include less severe phenomena) and then tests whether they have become pathologized using a new index based on a dictionary of pathology-related terms. It hypothesizes that words collocating with mental health-related concepts have (1) become less emotionally severe (vertical concept creep) and (2) come to co-occur with pathology-related terms (pathologization).

2 Concept Creep Theory

According to concept creep theory (Haslam, 2016), harm-related concepts are susceptible to two kinds of semantic expansion, broadening to encompass qualitatively new phenomena (horizontal creep) and quantitatively less severe phenomena (vertical creep). Linguistically, horizontal creep resembles semantic widening, including via metaphorical extension, while vertical creep resembles hyperbole, where words shift from a stronger to a weaker meaning (Vylomova and Haslam, 2021). Both forms of creep can occur simultaneously. Theorized causes of concept creep include cultural

Proceedings of the 4th Workshop on Computational Approaches to Historical Language Change, pages 119–128
December 6, 2023 ©2023 Association for Computational Linguistics

shifts towards greater sensitivity to harm, post-materialist values and diminished exposure to adversity (Haslam et al., 2020). As with other harm concepts, the consequences of inflated concepts of mental illness are mixed. Negative consequences include excessive self-diagnosis, prescription of inappropriate health services and treatments (Xiao et al., 2023) and heightened emotional vulnerability (Jones and McNally, 2022). Positive consequences include recognizing and addressing previously neglected forms of suffering (Tse and Haslam, 2021; Foulkes and Andrews, 2023).

3 Related Work

Advances in computational linguistics have facilitated the detection and quantification of diachronic lexical semantic shifts (Tahmasebi and Dubossarsky, 2023), as outlined in pioneering survey papers (Kutuzov et al., 2018; Tahmasebi et al., 2021). New techniques to digitize, process, store, and quantify written language worldwide have enabled non-computational disciplines to use text corpora to explore questions with a social dimension. For instance, linguist Price (2022) used methods from computational linguistics to track the construction of mental illness in the UK press. In psychological science, text mining approaches are gaining traction as researchers begin to harness the advances in modern computational technologies and digital data sources by using natural language processing (NLP) as a tool to understand people and culture at an unprecedented scale. For reviews explaining this paradigm shift in psychology, see Berger and Packard (2022); Jackson et al. (2022); Pennebaker (2022); Demszky et al. (2023). Nevertheless, the field is only beginning to reap the benefits of using NLP to examine social and cultural change (Charlesworth et al., 2023; Leach et al., 2023).

Concept creep research provides an innovative engagement between social psychology and NLP. As the only theory in social psychology with a focus on lexical semantic change and its non-linguistic (societal, politically motivated, and cultural) causes and social consequences, researchers have employed NLP techniques to characterize and to track the theorized causes of concept creep (Haslam et al., 2020). Studies have revealed increases in the relative frequency of words reflecting harm-based morality since 1900 in the Google Books English corpus (Wheeler et al., 2019), and of prejudice-denoting terms in popular U.S. newspapers (Rozado et al., 2023). These trends align with the claims of concept creep theory regarding an increase in harm-based morality (Graham et al., 2013) and a rising cultural sensitivity to harm. Prior empirical work characterizing concept creep has focused on evaluating its horizontal expansion as increases in the semantic breadth of target concepts, evaluated as the average cosine (dis)similarity of a concept's semantic vectors. It has demonstrated that *addiction*, *bullying*, *empathy*, *harassment*, *prejudice*, *racism*, and *trauma* have broadened in recent decades (Vylomova et al., 2019; Haslam et al., 2020; Vylomova and Haslam, 2021).

Baes et al. (2023) recently developed a non-computationally intensive method to evaluate vertical creep by capturing whether a concept has come to be used in less severe contexts. It tests whether words collocating with a centre term have become less intensely negative in their connotation. Research using this new method has yielded mixed findings to date. *Trauma* came to be used in less emotionally severe semantic contexts from 1970–2019 in a corpus of psychology article abstracts (Baes et al., 2023, >133 million words). However, *anxiety* and *depression* showed the opposite trend in the abstracts corpus and in a corpus of everyday American English (Xiao et al., 2023, >500 million words). Subsequent analyses suggested a rising tendency to view these terms through a pathological (i.e., disease-related) lens in academic psychology and society at large.

4 Materials

4.1 Corpora

Two corpora enabled an analysis of shifts in the meaning of mental health-related terms in academic psychology and in the wider society. The psychology corpus contained 871,340 abstracts from 875 psychology journals, ranging from 1930 to 2019, sourced from E-Research and PubMed databases (Vylomova et al., 2019). The journal set was distributed across all subdisciplines of psychology. The final corpus of psychology abstracts was limited to 1970-2016 data due to the relatively small number of abstracts outside this period (Vylomova et al., 2019).

The general corpus combines two corpora: the Corpus of Historical American English (Davies, 2008, CoHA) and the Corpus of Contemporary American English (Davies, 2008, CoCA). CoHA contains approx. 400 million words from 1810–2009, from 115,000 texts distributed across everyday publications (fiction, magazines, newspapers, and non-fiction books). CoCA contains approx. 560 million words from 1990–2019 from 500,000 texts (extracted from spoken language, TV shows, academic journals, fiction, magazines, newspapers, and blogs). Some CoCA texts were removed, before merging CoCA with CoHA, to prevent overlap with the psychology corpus (removing academic journal texts) and due to missing year data (blogs). The combined general corpus has previously been demonstrated to be reliable (Haslam et al., 2021b; Xiao et al., 2023). It contains magazines (36%), newspapers (31%), spoken language (16%), fiction books (10%), TV shows (7%), and non-fiction books (<1%). Pre-processing both corpora involved tokenization (lowercasing, removing punctuation and stop words) and lemmatization.

4.2 Mental Health Terms

Six mental health-related terms were chosen for analysis: *addiction*, *anger*, *distress*, *grief*, *stress*, *worry*. None of the terms are mental illnesses but all refer to common emotional or behavioral states that can be construed as abnormal or pathological. Critics have argued that concepts such as these are increasingly understood in this manner (e.g., Ridner, 2004; Wakefield and First, 2013). Figure 1 shows that all the terms increased in their relative frequency in the psychology corpus and, for some, the general corpus, making them good candidates to use as centre terms. Analyses expected to indicate they had undergone semantic inflation (vertical creep) and/or pathologization (rising association with illness-related terminology).

4.3 Warriner Norms Data

Affective meaning norms from a dataset published by Warriner et al. (2013) were used to evaluate the emotional severity of the contexts in which target mental health-related words (i.e., 'centre terms') appeared. It contains norms for valence, arousal, and dominance ratings of 13,915 English lemmas provided by 1,827 United States residents. While reading a word, participants rated how they felt on a series of scales ranging from 1 (low) to 9 (high). For the present study, only valence and arousal ratings were used. For the valence rating (n = 723, M = 5.1, SD = 1.7), 1 corresponded to feeling extremely "annoyed", "bored", "despaired", "melancholic", "unhappy", or, "unsatisfied", and 9 corresponded to feeling extremely "contented", "happy", "hopeful", "pleased", or "satisfied". For the arousal rating (n = 745, M = 4.2, SD = 2.3), 1 represented feeling "calm", "dull", "relaxed", "sleepy", "sluggish", or "unaroused", while 9 indicated feeling "agitated", "aroused", "excited", "frenzied", "jittery", "stimulated", or "wide-awake".

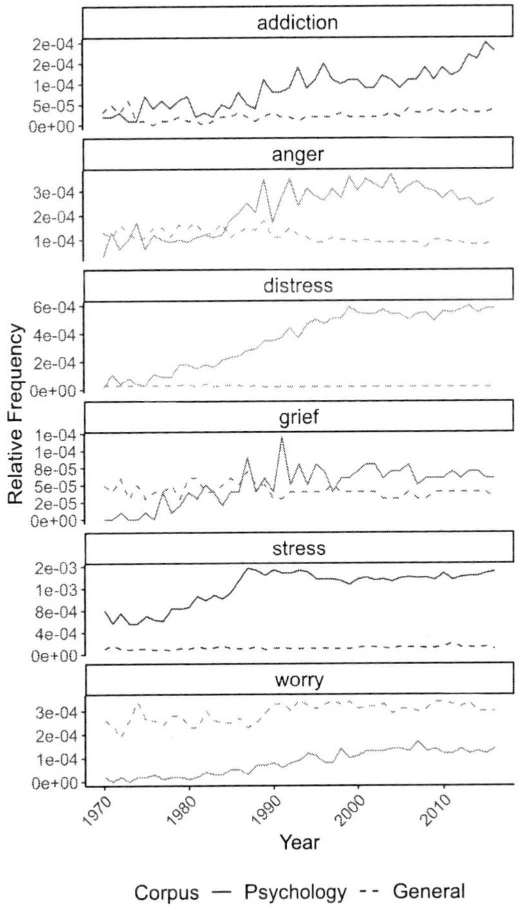

Figure 1: Relative frequencies of mental health-related terms over the study period (1970–2016).

5 Method

5.1 Severity Index

A procedure developed by Baes et al. (2023) was used to compute an index for evaluating annual changes in the mean emotional severity of mental health-related terms. For each preprocessed corpus, collocates within a ±5-word context window of the centre terms and their annual count statistics were extracted and linked to their ratings on valence and arousal. Ratings were then summed to generate an index of emotional severity for each collocate ranging from 2–18. The simplest approach was taken to approximate severity by summing negative valence and arousal ratings measured on the same scale. Valence ratings were reverse scored (1 = happy; 9 = unhappy), arousal ratings were not (1 = calm, 9 = aroused). Words judged as emotionally positive and calm had low scores; words judged as unpleasant and intense had high scores. The index was computed by calculating the weighted average collocate severity for each year (S), weighting the severity rating (x_i) for each collocate (n) by the number of times it appeared in the year (w_i). See the index formula below representing the mean emotional intensity of terms collocating with centre terms. For each centre term, we calculated its annual severity index as follows:

$$S = \frac{\sum_{i=1}^{n} w_i x_i}{\sum_{i=1}^{n} x_i} \tag{1}$$

The Warriner-matched dataset provided at least 80% coverage for each collocate in psychology (addiction: 82%, anger: 83%, distress: 83%, grief: 84%, stress: 80%, worry: 82%) and at least 77% coverage for each collocate in the general corpus (addiction: 81%, anger: 79%, distress: 80%, grief: 81%, stress: 81%, worry: 77%). Furthermore, in most decades, the same terms appeared among the top 10 collocates in each decade when comparing overall collocates to the Warriner-matched ones (with a 0-8% difference across all decades). See the link in the Supplementary materials for the top 10 ranked collocates in each grouping: overall collocates, Warriner-matched collocates, and non-Warriner-matched collocates.

5.2 Pathologization Index

To compute the pathologization index, a list of terms reflecting disease and illness were selected. First, six unambiguously disease-related words with restricted range in meaning (e.g., excluding "condition") were generated: "clinical", "disorder", "symptom", "illness", "pathology", "disease". Next, their 'Small World of Words' associations (De Deyne et al., 2019) were listed and duplicates were removed. See Appendix A for the final list.

Specifically, forward associations (participant responses to a cue word) for each disease-related term were documented using a web user interface. It graphs word association norms from the English Small World of Words project (SWOW-EN)[1] which contains data collected between 2011 and 2018 for 12,929 cues made by more than 90,000 fluent English speakers – making it the largest existing English-language resource.

[1]https://smallworldofwords.org

Authors filtered the list for terms reflecting pathologization (i.e., to view or characterize as medically or psychologically abnormal), leaving 17 terms: "ailment", "clinical", "clinic", "cure", "diagnosis", "disease", "disorder", "ill", "illness", "medical", "medicine", "pathology", "prognosis", "sick", "sickness", "symptom", "treatment". Next, the collocates for each centre term were searched for the final list of 17 pathologization terms and their appearances were summed across each year before being divided by the total sum of all collocates in that year.

Figure 2 shows that the pathology-related terms appeared in both corpora, making them good candidates to test the hypothesis that pathology-related terms increasingly accompany the target terms (words representing mental-health related concepts). Furthermore, as might be expected, pathology-related terms had higher total relative frequency and rose more steeply in the psychology corpus compared to the general corpus.

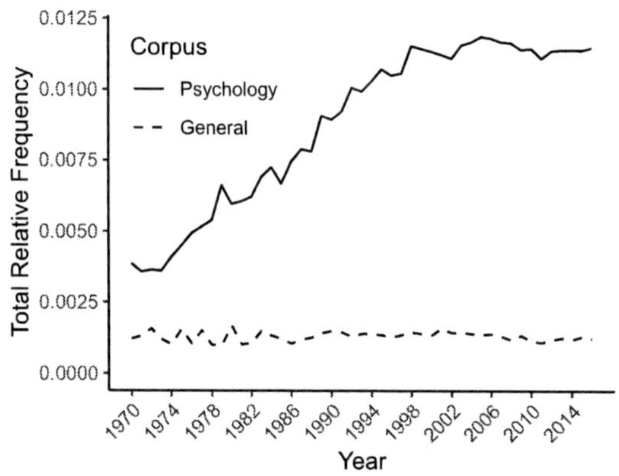

Figure 2: Total relative frequency of pathologization-related terms over the study period (1970-2016).

5.3 Analytic Strategy

Linear regression analyses were performed to test the statistical significance of the predicted trends in the first two hypotheses. An ordinary least squares estimator was used, unless autocorrelation was present (Durbin Watson test: $p < .05$), in which case the outcome variable was fit with a generalized least squares estimator to account for autocorrelated residuals.

6 Results

The linear regression models testing the hypothesized declining trend for the severity index showed some support for the concept creep hypothesis (see Figure 3). Irregularities in the data in earlier years are due to low sample size. In the psychology corpus, there was a significant declining trend in the severity of words related to two of the six concepts: *addiction* and *anger*, and a significant increasing trend in the severity of words related to *stress*. In the general corpus, there was a significant declining trend in the severity of words related to four of the six concepts: *addiction*, *grief*, *stress*, *worry*.

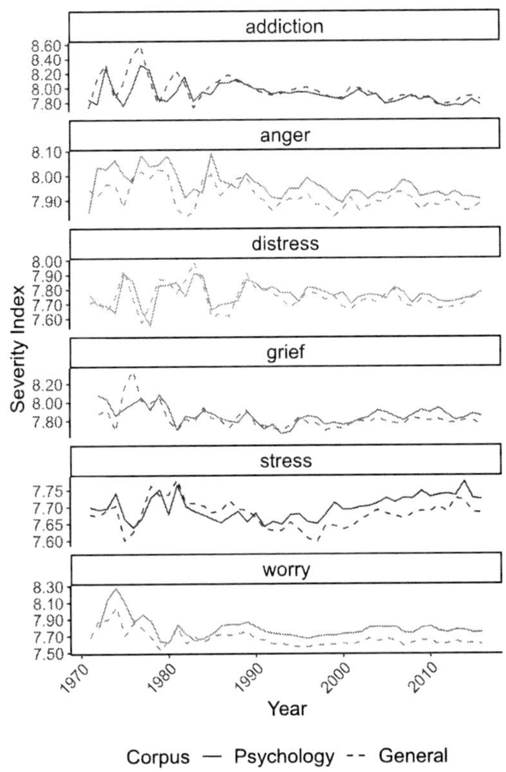

Figure 3: Severity index (3-year rolling mean) of mental health-related terms over the study period (1970-2016).

The linear regression models testing the hypothesized rising trend for the pathologization index showed some support for the hypothesis that mental health-related terms have become pathologized, as Figure 4 illustrates. Irregularities in the data in earlier years are due to low instances of pathology terms in respective context windows. In the psychology corpus, there were significant increases in the pathologization index for four of the six concepts (*addiction*, *grief*, *stress*, *worry*). For the general corpus, there was a significant increasing pathologization trend for two of the six concepts (*grief*, *stress*).

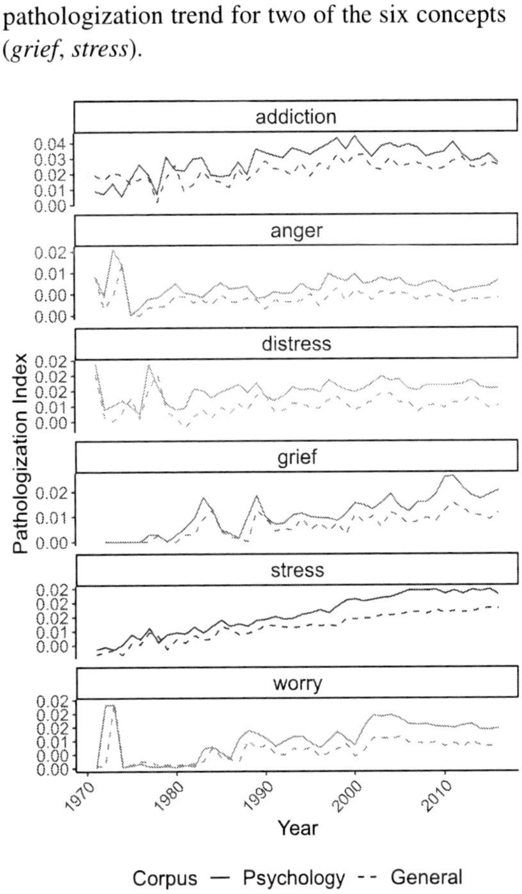

Figure 4: Pathologization index (3-year rolling mean) of mental health-related terms over the study period (1970-2016).

Control analyses were then run, holding the pathologization index and then the severity index constant (see Table 1 for predictive effects). These analyses were conducted because the two indices were partially confounded: terms in the pathologization dictionary tended to have above-average severity index scores (8.92) compared to the average severity index score of collocates for mental health concepts.[2] In the psychology corpus, holding the pathologization index constant showed significant decreases in the severity of four of the six concepts: *addiction*, *anger*, *stress*, *worry* (revealing the significant normalizing effect for worry and reversing the direction of the trend for *stress*). The

[2] *addiction* (psychology: 7.87; general: 8.02), *anger* (psychology: 8.00; general: 7.87), *distress* (psychology: 7.78; general: 7.73), *grief* (psychology: 7.90; general: 7.78), *stress* (psychology: 7.72; general: 7.66), *worry* (psychology: 7.91; general: 7.54)

general corpus showed the same significant effects when controlling for pathologization (with severity trends for four concepts: *addiction*, *grief*, *stress*, *worry*). Furthermore, when holding the severity index constant in the psychology corpus, the same four concepts showed significant increases in pathologization: *addiction*, *grief*, *stress*, *worry*. Similarly, in the general corpus, the same two concepts became associated with pathology-related language: *grief* and *stress*. Appendix B documents tables with summary statistics for all analyses.

Term	β(sev)	β(sev)+	β(path)	β(path)+
addict	-0.004*	-0.005*	0.0007*	0.0008*
	-0.008*	-0.008*	0.00004	-0.000002
anger	-0.002*	-0.002*	0.00002	0.000007
	-0.0009	-0.0009	0.00002	0.00002
distress	0.0007	0.004	0.0001	0.0001
	-0.002	-0.002	-0.000007	-0.000007
grief	-0.002	-0.004	0.0007*	0.0007*
	-0.005*	-0.006*	0.00006*	0.00007*
stress	0.002*	-0.001*	0.0006*	0.0006*
	-0.002*	-0.003*	0.0002*	0.0002*
worry	-0.004	-0.006*	0.0005*	0.0005*
	-0.005*	-0.005*	1.1139	0.00001

Table 1: Standardized Regression Coefficients for Year Predicting Severity Index (sev) and Pathologization Index (path) (row 1 = psychology; row 2 = COHCA). + = control analysis. * = $p < .05$. *addict* = addiction.

Post hoc correlation analyses indicated no relationship between rising pathologization and decreasing severity, except for in the psychology corpus for stress-related terminology, where there was a significant positive association (see Appendix C), likely influenced by the presence of high severity pathology terms (e.g., "disorder", "symptom") among top ranked collocates in later decades. Results indicate that the two indices rise and fall independently, apart from when (high severity) pathologization terms make up part of the severity index.

7 Discussion

The present findings support the concept creep hypothesis, which predicted that mental health concepts are increasingly used in the context of less emotionally intense language. *Addiction*, *stress*, and *worry* were normalized in this way within academic psychology and in the general corpus, whereas *anger* was only normalized in the former, and *grief* only in the latter. Only *distress* did not support the hypothesis in either corpus.

Findings also support the pathologization hypothesis, which predicted that mental health-related concepts are increasingly associated with pathology-related terminology. *Grief* and *stress* became pathologized in both academic psychology and the general corpus, whereas *addiction* and *worry* only became pathologized in the psychology corpus. *Anger* and *distress* showed no signs of pathologization.

Our findings indicate that the meanings of some mental health-related concepts have broadened to be used in less emotionally intense contexts and in more pathology-related contexts. This pattern can be observed in academic and general language. The semantic expansion of some mental health concepts in psychology (*addiction*, *anger*, *worry*) may have contributed to similar trends for these concepts and others (*grief*, *stress*) in non-academic language use. Previous work on the cultural dynamics of concept creep (Haslam et al., 2021b) demonstrates that semantic shifts of harm related concepts in psychology can influence those observed in society at large.

Trends like these have social and cultural implications. Concept creep and a rising tendency to view unpleasant emotional states through the lens of pathology may lead people to self-diagnose inappropriately and to seek unnecessary or even harmful treatments. Some evidence indicates that rates of mental illness have risen, alongside increased mental health service utilization, over-diagnosis, over-treatment, and over-prescription (Paris, 2020). Critics argue that the 'psychiatrization' of society (Haslam et al., 2021a) leads people to view ordinary problems in living as medical illnesses (Beeker et al., 2021). Growing awareness of mental ill health may be causing mental health concepts to broaden in ways that may have some benefits (e.g., reductions in stigma) but it may have significant costs as well (Foulkes and Andrews, 2023).

Conclusion

In conclusion, the findings from the present study lend support to the vertical concept creep hypothesis (Haslam, 2016) for mental health-related concepts and concerns that everyday life has become pathologized (Horwitz and Wakefield, 2007, 2012) in academic psychology and society at large. The severity index proved reliable for capturing the emotional intensity of mental health concepts, and future work will ideally apply it to pathological concepts to explore whether they have also become normalized. The newly developed pathologization index offers a way to quantify a cultural trend, which future work can use to explore whether it influences or tracks alongside the semantic shifts of certain concepts. A key task for future research is to disentangle the relationship between vertical and horizontal forms of concept creep and to quantify their social and cultural factors in corpora representing other disciplines and languages.

Limitations

Limitations inspire future directions. First, future work could explore alternative ways of combining the valence and arousal components in the severity index using different functions. For example, it could (i) sum standardized valence and arousal ratings, rather than summing raw mean scores on the two components or (ii) weight valence more heavily than arousal when combining them, under the assumption that valence is more central to severity. Second, while the severity index tracks historical patterns in the emotional intensity of collocates, it cannot reveal which words or classes contribute to these trends. To examine underlying dimensions in the collocate data, future work could reduce the dimensions of the collocate data with a bottom up dimensionality reduction technique (e.g., k-means clustering) or top-down approach (e.g., using WordNet; Fellbaum, 2010) to capture word sense disambiguation). Third, while the severity index robustly evaluates shifts in the emotional intensity of a concept's meaning, other linguistic shifts might be at play. Future work could parse the text into syntactic dependencies and examine whether there has been a rise in the use of intensifiers, a proxy for hyperbole (Bloomfield, 1933), to modify the centre terms and examine how this relates to severity and pathologization. Finally, count-based co-occurrence methods cannot represent word meaning as comprehensively as word embeddings can, given that their bag-of-words approach disregards grammar, word order, and other contextual signals like metaphor. Future work should compare the present method to a word embeddings approach and evaluate the performance of each method.

Acknowledgements

This research is supported by Australian Research Council Discovery Project DP210103984, and by an Australian Government Research Training Program Scholarship.

References

Baes, N., Vylomova, E., Zyphur, M., and Haslam, N. (2023). The semantic inflation of "trauma" in psychology. *Psychology of Language and Communication*, 27(1):23–45.

Beeker, T., Mills, C., Bhugra, D., te Meerman, S., Thoma, S., Heinze, M., and von Peter, S. (2021). Psychiatrization of society: A conceptual framework and call for transdisciplinary research. *Frontiers in Psychiatry*, 12:645556.

Berger, J. and Packard, G. (2022). Using natural language processing to understand people and culture. *American Psychologist*, 77(4):525.

Bloomfield, L. (1933). *Language*. Compton Printing Works Ltd., London.

Brinkmann, S. (2016). *Diagnostic cultures: A cultural approach to the pathologization of modern life*. Routledge, New York.

Bröer, C. and Besseling, B. (2017). Sadness or depression: Making sense of low mood and the medicalization of everyday life. *Social Science & Medicine*, 183:28–36.

Charlesworth, T. E., Sanjeev, N., Hatzenbuehler, M. L., and Banaji, M. R. (2023). Identifying and predicting stereotype change in large language corpora: 72 groups, 115 years (1900–2015), and four text sources. *Journal of Personality and Social Psychology*.

Davies, M. (2008). The corpus of contemporary american english (coca). Available online at `https://www.english-corpora.org/coca/`.

De Deyne, S., Navarro, D. J., Perfors, A., Brysbaert, M., and Storms, G. (2019). The "small world of words" english word association norms for over 12,000 cue words. *Behavior research methods*, 51:987–1006.

Demszky, D., Yang, D., Yeager, D. S., Bryan, C. J., Clapper, M., Chandhok, S., Eichstaedt, J. C., Hecht, C., Jamieson, J., Johnson, M., et al. (2023). Using large language models in psychology. *Nature Reviews Psychology*, pages 1–14.

Fellbaum, C. (2010). Wordnet. In *Theory and applications of ontology: Computer applications*, pages 231–243. Springer.

Foulkes, L. and Andrews, J. L. (2023). Are mental health awareness efforts contributing to the rise in reported mental health problems? a call to test the prevalence inflation hypothesis. *New Ideas in Psychology*, 69:101010.

Furedi, F. (2004). *Therapy culture: Cultivating vulnerability in an uncertain age*. Routledge Taylor Francis, London.

Graham, J., Haidt, J., Koleva, S., Motyl, M., Iyer, R., Wojcik, S. P., and Ditto, P. H. (2013). Moral foundations theory: The pragmatic validity of moral pluralism. In *Advances in experimental social psychology*, volume 47, pages 55–130. Elsevier.

Haslam, N. (2016). Concept creep: Psychology's expanding concepts of harm and pathology. *Psychological Inquiry*, 27(1):1–17.

Haslam, N., Dakin, B. C., Fabiano, F., McGrath, M. J., Rhee, J., Vylomova, E., Weaving, M., and Wheeler, M. A. (2020). Harm inflation: Making sense of concept creep. *European Review of Social Psychology*, 31(1):254–286.

Haslam, N., Tse, J. S., and De Deyne, S. (2021a). Concept creep and psychiatrization. *Frontiers in Sociology*, 6:806147.

Haslam, N., Vylomova, E., Zyphur, M., and Kashima, Y. (2021b). The cultural dynamics of concept creep. *American Psychologist*, 76(6):1013.

Horwitz, A. V. and Wakefield, J. C. (2007). *The loss of sadness: How psychiatry transformed normal sorrow into depressive disorder*. Oxford University Press, New York.

Horwitz, A. V. and Wakefield, J. C. (2012). *All we have to fear: Psychiatry's transformation of natural anxieties into mental disorders*. Oxford University Press, New York.

Jackson, J. C., Watts, J., List, J.-M., Puryear, C., Drabble, R., and Lindquist, K. A. (2022). From text to thought: How analyzing language can advance psychological science. *Perspectives on Psychological Science*, 17(3):805–826.

Jones, P. J. and McNally, R. J. (2022). Does broadening one's concept of trauma undermine resilience? *Psychological Trauma: Theory, Research, Practice, and Policy*, 14(S1):S131.

Kutuzov, A., Øvrelid, L., Szymanski, T., and Velldal, E. (2018). Diachronic word embeddings and semantic shifts: A survey. *arXiv preprint arXiv:1806.03537*.

Leach, S., Kitchin, A. P., and Sutton, R. M. (2023). Word embeddings reveal growing moral concern for people, animals and the environment. *British Journal of Social Psychology*.

Paris, J. (2020). *Overdiagnosis in psychiatry: how modern psychiatry lost its way while creating a diagnosis for almost all of life's misfortunes*. Oxford University Press, New York, 2nd edition.

Pennebaker, J. W. (2022). Computer-based language analysis as a paradigm shift. In Dehghani, M. and Boyd, R. L., editors, *Handbook of Language Analysis in Psychology*, pages 576–587. The Guilford Press.

Price, H. (2022). *The language of mental illness: corpus linguistics and the construction of mental illness in the press*. Cambridge University Press, Cambridge.

Ridner, S. H. (2004). Psychological distress: Concept analysis. *Journal of advanced nursing*, 45(5):536–545.

Rozado, D., Al-Gharbi, M., and Halberstadt, J. (2023). Prevalence of prejudice-denoting words in news media discourse: A chronological analysis. *Social Science computer review*, 41(1):99–122.

Tahmasebi, N., Borin, L., and Jatowt, A. (2021). Survey of computational approaches to lexical semantic change detection. In Tahmasebi, N., Borin, L., Jatowt, A., Xu, Y., and Hengchen, S., editors, *Computational approaches to semantic change*, pages 1–91. Language Science Press.

Tahmasebi, N. and Dubossarsky, H. (2023). Computational modeling of semantic change. *arXiv preprint arXiv:2304.06337*.

Tse, J. S. and Haslam, N. (2021). Inclusiveness of the concept of mental disorder and differences in help-seeking between asian and white americans. *Frontiers in Psychology*, 12:699750.

Vylomova, E. and Haslam, N. (2021). Semantic changes in harm-related concepts in english. In Tahmasebi, N., Borin, L., Jatowt, A., Xu, Y., and Hengchen, S., editors, *Computational approaches to semantic change*, pages 93–121. Language Science Press.

Vylomova, E., Murphy, S., and Haslam, N. (2019). Evaluation of semantic change of harm-related concepts in psychology. In *Proceedings of the 1st International Workshop on Computational Approaches to Historical Language Change*, pages 29–34.

Wakefield, J. C. (2010). Misdiagnosing normality: Psychiatry's failure to address the problem of false positive diagnoses of mental disorder in a changing professional environment. *Journal of Mental Health*, 19(4):337–351.

Wakefield, J. C. and First, M. B. (2013). Clarifying the boundary between normality and disorder: a fundamental conceptual challenge for psychiatry.

Warriner, A. B., Kuperman, V., and Brysbaert, M. (2013). Norms of valence, arousal, and dominance for 13,915 english lemmas. *Behavior Research Methods*, 45(4):1191–1207.

Wheeler, M. A., McGrath, M. J., and Haslam, N. (2019). Twentieth century morality: The rise and fall of moral concepts from 1900 to 2007. *PLOS ONE*, 14(2):e0212267.

Xiao, Y., Baes, N., Vylomova, E., and Haslam, N. (2023). Have the concepts of 'anxiety' and 'depression' been normalized or pathologized? a corpus study of historical semantic change. *PLOS ONE*, 18(6):e0288027.

A Appendix A

'Small World of Words' Associations for selected terms ("clinical", "disorder", "symptom", "illness", "pathology", "disease")": "ailment", "aids", "anxiety", "bad", "bacteria", "bed", "bipolar", "cancer", "cause", "clean", "clinical", "cold", "conduct", "contagious", "cough", "cure", "death", "diagnosis", "disease", "doctor", "epidemic", "fever", "green", "hospital", "ill", "illness", "infection", "list", "malaria", "medical", "medicine", "mental", "pain", "panic", "physical", "plague", "precise", "problem", "psychology", "research", "sad", "sickness", "sick", "surgery", "symptom", "tired", "treatment", "unhealthy", "unwell", "virus", "vomit", "white", "study", "sterile".

B Appendix B

Term	β	*p*	*SE*	Accuracy
addict	-0.004	.043	0.002	0.07
	-0.008	.010	-0.008	0.12
anger	-0.002	.034	0.001	0.08
	-0.0009	.329	.0009	-0.0005
distress	0.0007	.510	0.001	-0.01
	-0.002	.130	0.002	0.03
grief	-0.002	.459	0.003	-0.01
	-0.005	.005	0.002	0.15
stress	0.002	<.001	0.0005	-134.48*
	-0.002	.034	0.0008	-89.18*
worry	-0.004	.129	0.002	0.03
	-0.005	<.001	0.0007	0.48

Table 2: Regression Summary Statistics for Year Predicting Severity Index (row 1 = psychology; row 2 = general). Accuracy (model fit) = Adj. R^2. * = AIC. *addict* = addiction.

Term	β	*p*	*SE*	Accuracy
addict	0.0007	<.001	0.0001	-236.57*
	0.00004	.704	0.0001	-0.02
anger	0.00002	.757	0.00006	-0.02
	0.00002	.078	0.000009	-491.49*
distress	0.0001	.142	0.00008	0.03
	-0.000007	.905	0.00006	-0.02
grief	0.0007	<.001	0.00008	0.60
	0.00006	.002	0.00002	0.17
stress	0.0006	<.001	0.00003	-386.27*
	0.0002	<.001	0.00003	0.43
worry	0.0005	.0003	0.0001	0.24
	1.11	.919	0.00001	-473.42*

Table 3: Regression Summary Statistics for Year Predicting Pathologization Index (row 1 = psychology; row 2 = general). Accuracy (model fit) = Adj. R^2. * = AIC. *addict* = addiction.

Term	β year	*p* year	β path	*p* path	Accuracy
addict	-0.005	.04	1.33	.491	0.06
	-0.008	.012	-5.90	.166	0.14
anger	-0.002	.038	-3.09	.206	0.89
	-0.0009	.347	0.52	.975	-0.02
distress	0.004	.695	2.38	.247	-0.004
	-0.002	.135	0.02	.996	0.007
grief	-0.004	.333	3.20	.514	-0.02
	-0.006	.002	15.41	.244	0.15
stress	-0.001	.035	6.03	.012	-142.49*
	-0.003	.007	6.03	.094	-94.42*
worry	-0.006	.030	5.23	.082	0.08
	-0.005	<.001	9.74	.303	0.48

Table 4: Regression Summary Statistics for Year Predicting Severity Index, controlling for Pathologization (row 1 = psychology; row 2 = general). Accuracy (model fit) = Adj. R^2. * = AIC. *addict* = addiction. *stress* (psychology)** = independent variables have VIF: 11.91.

Term	β year	*p* year	β path	*p* path	Accuracy
addict	0.0008	<.001	0.008	.491	-228.00*
	0.00002	.871	-0.007	.166	0.003
anger	0.000007	.921	-1.17	.206	-0.006
	0.00002	.084	0.00005	.975	0.03
distress	0.0001	.175	0.012	.247	0.03
	-0.000007	.909	0.00002	.996	-0.05
grief	0.0007	<.001	0.004	.514	0.577
	0.00007	.001	0.002	.244	0.18
stress	0.0006	<.001	0.02	.012	-383.09*
	0.0002	<.001	0.01	.094	0.45
worry	0.0005	<.001	0.013	.082	0.25
	0.00001	.425	0.002	.303	-462.26*

Table 5: Regression Summary Statistics for Year Predicting Pathologization Index, controlling for Severity (row 1 = psychology; row 2 = general). Accuracy (model fit) = Adj. R^2. * = AIC. *addict* = addiction.

C Appendix C

Term	*r*	*df*	*p*
addiction	-0.09	45	.543
	-0.21	45	.149
anger	-0.19	45	.199
	-0.03	45	.824
distress	0.19	45	.199
	0.005	45	.974
grief	-0.02	42	.881
	-0.03	45	.828
stress	0.66	45	<.001
	-0.03	45	.851
worry	0.11	44	.451
	0.09	45	.505

Table 6: Correlation Statistics for Severity Index and Pathologization Index (row 1 = psychology; row 2 = general).

D Supplementary Material

The data and code are available at the following repository link: `https://osf.io/hbzmc/?view_only=f6e3d36f89204eae9c6ecaa501f0015e`

Access the spreadsheet with tables of the highest-ranked collocates for concepts related to mental health at the following link: `https://osf.io/hbzmc/files/osfstorage/652ddf3728274506adb867cc`

Automating Sound Change Prediction for Phylogenetic Inference: A Tukanoan Case Study

Kalvin Chang[1*] **Nathaniel R. Robinson**[1,2*] **Anna Cai**[1*]
Ting Chen[1] **Annie Zhang**[1] **David R. Mortensen**[1]
[1]School of Computer Science, Carnegie Mellon University
[2]Center for Language and Speech Processing, Johns Hopkins University
kalvin1204@alumni.cmu.edu, nrobin38@jhu.edu,
{annacai, tingc2, ruoxinz, dmortens}@cs.cmu.edu

Abstract

We describe a set of new methods to partially automate linguistic phylogenetic inference given (1) cognate sets with their respective protoforms and sound laws, (2) a mapping from phones to their articulatory features and (3) a typological database of sound changes. We train a neural network on these sound change data to weight articulatory distances between phones and predict intermediate sound change steps between historical protoforms and their modern descendants, replacing a linguistic expert in part of a parsimony-based phylogenetic inference algorithm. In our best experiments on Tukanoan languages, this method produces trees with a Generalized Quartet Distance of 0.12 from a tree that used expert annotations, a significant improvement over other semi-automated baselines. We discuss potential benefits and drawbacks to our neural approach and parsimony-based tree prediction. We also experiment with a minimal generalization learner for automatic sound law induction, finding it less effective than sound laws from expert annotation. Our code is publicly available.[1]

1 Introduction

Languages and biological species evolve in interestingly analogous ways. Both display variation in space and time that may be inherited or innovated. As in biology, each node in a linguistic phylogenetic (family) tree corresponds to one or more innovations ("mutations"). Typically, linguists infer these phylogenies by finding patterns of innovations in pronunciation, or sound changes.

Sound laws, or rules that define sound changes and the contexts in which they occur, apply to all instances of a sound in a given context. (For example, all instances of Proto-West Germanic [*t] became [t͡s] (written as z) at the beginning of words in High German, while English was unaffected. This resulted in the English-German cognate pairs *zehn* : ten, *Zoll* : toll, and *Zahn* : tooth.) Because these laws have few exceptions, they can work as a basis for modeling historical language change. Linguists typically infer phylogenies by constructing the tree that maps from the ancestor language at the root to the daughter languages via the most probable system of these sound laws (Hoenigswald, 1960). Existing partially automated approaches to this method require multiple sets of expert annotations. We attempt to alleviate this via proposed methods that incorporate even more automation. Below we discuss the necessity of both sound laws and sound changes in predicting phylogenies, which we automatically infer in our proposed methods.

Linguists induce sound laws by aligning cognates (words with a common ancestor) by phoneme. From this alignment they extract sound correspondences, or sets of sounds in the same context that likely evolved from the same sound in the proto-language. (For example, at the beginning of words, there is a correspondence between High German [t͡s], Dutch [t], English [t], Swedish [t], and Icelandic [t]). They then reconstruct protophonemes for each set of aligned cognates (in our Germanic example, this happens to be [*t]). The posited sound laws from this process enable deterministic derivation of the daughter forms from the reconstructed protoforms, or words in the protolanguage. Inducing sound laws is central to sound change-based phylogenetics. We experiment with both algorithms that predict these sound laws automatically and those that need them to be provided by a linguist. Beyond sound laws alone, however, phylogenetic inference algorithms must consider how sounds evolve and branch off through intermediate sound changes over time.

*Authors contributed equally.
[1]https://github.com/cmu-llab/aiscp

Proceedings of the 4th Workshop on Computational Approaches to Historical Language Change, pages 129–142
December 6, 2023 ©2023 Association for Computational Linguistics

Sound change emerges from phonetic variation, as speakers modify their pronunciation along acoustic or articulatory dimensions (Garrett et al., 2015; Garrett and Johnson, 2013; Lindblom et al., 1995). Because some variations in pronunciation occur more frequently than others, not all sound changes are equally probable. In particular, the probability of a sound change (e.g. [p] becoming [f]) is often different from that of its reverse (e.g. [f] becoming [p]), a property known as the DIRECTIONALITY of sound change (Campbell, 2013; Chacon and List, 2016). Because phonetic variation is gradual (with few ARTICULATORY FEATURES—or fundamental characteristics of pronunciation—changing at a time) (Sievers, 1901; Brugmann and Osthoff, 1878; Paul, 2010), sound change often results in phonetically similar sounds across cognates and their corresponding protoform. Larger apparent jumps in pronunciation from PROTO-PHONEME (ancestral sound) to REFLEX (descendant sound) are often the result of smaller changes over time, or intermediate sound changes (Garrett et al., 2015; Beguš, 2016). For example, k > t͡ʃ ([k] becomes [t͡ʃ]) may encompass the chain of sound changes k > kʲ > c > t͡ʃ. Intermediate paths from a proto-sound to different daughter reflexes can overlap, which enables identifying innovations that are shared among daughters (SHARED INNOVATIONS).

1.1 Contribution

We automate portions of Chacon and List (2016)'s phylogenetic inference method via our novel Automatic Intermediate Sound Change Prediction (AISCP) method, and attempt further automation via a novel method for Automatic Sound Law Induction (ASLI) in some experiments.

Chacon and List (2016) rely on expert judgements for Tukanoan sound changes, which we replace at different stages of their algorithm. Our main contribution is replacing expert-provided intermediate sound changes with AISCP—essentially "invent[ing]" proto-sounds not seen in reflexes, which many unsupervised protoform reconstruction models cannot do (List, 2022). These AISCP predictions rely on (1) a PHONOLOGICAL PRIOR based on articulatory distances (Mortensen et al., 2016) and (2) TYPOLOGICAL GROUNDING learned by a neural network from a database of multilingual sound changes. The phonological prior captures the tendency for sounds to change into sounds that are pronounced similarly, while the typological grounding encodes the direction and frequency of sound changes. Our results show that phylogenetic inference with AISCP approaches expert performance in a computational paradigm requiring expert knowledge only for cognate sets, sound laws, and protoforms.

In additional experiments, we further automate the process via ASLI: predicting not just intermediate sound changes, but sound laws from protoforms and reflexes. We induce these laws via methods from Albright and Hayes (2003) and Wilson and Li (2021), newly applied for ASLI.

We conduct experiments on data from Tukanoan languages, spoken in Columbia, Brazil, Peru, and Ecuador. The data contain Proto-Tukanoan reconstructions from a leading Tukanoan linguist, Chacon (2013, 2014). We take their reconstruction and sound changes as our gold standard, as did Chacon and List (2016). In summary, we contribute:

1. A training paradigm by which a neural network can produce phonetically natural intermediate sound changes as a typological grounding for AISCP
2. Experimental evidence that AISCP can approach expert phylogenetic inference, with automatic correct groupings of West Tukano and East-Eastern Tukano
3. Ablations indicating that intermediate sound changes and directional weighted sound transition costs are useful to predict phylogeny
4. An ASLI method for phylogenetic inference
5. Analysis suggesting parsimony-based phylogenetic inference may be unreliable

2 Related work

Unlike our work, prior phylolinguistic work mostly inferred a tree from a boolean cognacy matrix that shows which synonymous words come from the same ancestral word (Greenhill et al., 2020). However, cognacy is complicated by language contact that leads to the borrowing of words, as opposed to their inheritance (Ryskina et al., 2020; Francis et al., 2021). Campbell (2013) criticized such use of cognacy information in phylogenetic inference, and called on computational methods to use shared innovations as linguists do. Zheng (2018) heeded this call and manually derived shared innovations for Proto-Min and its modern daughters, finally running a maximum parsimony algorithm from Felsenstein (2013) on these shared innovations. However, their shared innovation matrix is binary and does not encode the direction and frequency of sound changes as our methods do.

Hruschka et al. (2015) jointly inferred phylogeny and reconstructed protoforms with Markov Chain Monte Carlo (MCMC) using phonological data from Turkic languages, where the tree likelihood was conditioned on reconstructed protoforms. However, their sound laws are all context-free. Clarté and Ryder (2022) perform joint phylogenetic, protoform reconstruction, and cognate inference for 14 Polynesian languages using MCMC, but the expressive power of their model is limited to only CVCV sequences for alignment without insertions or deletions or sound law contexts. Unlike these approaches, our methods (both with and without ASLI) include in-context sound laws and can process all sound sequences.

We are also not the first researchers to explore neural modeling of phonetic features. Hartmann (2019, 2021) showed that neural networks can predict features of Proto-Indo-European phones given the features of a trigram context, which reflect SYNCHRONIC (applying at a particular stage in a language's history) phonetic phenomena. Our neural network, on the other hand, predicts the probability of feature changes in a sound change, given DIACHRONIC data (data that represents change over time).

In recent years, there has also been existing work on ASLI. Luo (2021) used reinforcement learning with hierarchical Monte Carlo tree search to induce sound laws for Germanic, Romance, and Slavic. To our knowledge, they are the first to propose an ASLI method. List (2019) also attempted automatic induction of sound correspondences, though these correspondences lacked the contexts associated with actual sound laws. The minimum generalization learner we employ for ASLI (Albright and Hayes, 2003), in contrast, was originally designed to induce synchronic morphological rules and is deterministic.

3 Methodology

We incorporate AISCP and ASLI into Chacon and List (2016)'s DiWeST method for phylogenetic inference, which involves directed, weighted phone transitions. The authors describe it as a directed version of Sankoff parsimony (Sankoff, 1975). Their maximum parsimony algorithm searches for trees by trying different sound transitions (intermediate sound changes) along the branches of trees that minimize the total transition cost. By making the cost of sound changes asymmetrical in a sound change transition matrix, their method captures the directionality of sound change, yielding a rooted tree. To search the large space of possible trees, they used a genetic search algorithm that balances exploration (iterating through a subset of possible trees) and exploitation (incrementally mutating the current best trees). Chacon and List (2016)'s algorithm follows this framework:

1. Align protoforms with reflexes (performed by an expert)
2. Learn sound laws between protoforms and reflexes (performed by an expert)
3. Create a sound change transition matrix (largely performed by an expert)
   (a) Identify intermediate sound changes (Section 3.2)
   (b) Assign a weight to intermediate sound change transitions (Section 3.2.1)
4. Perform maximum parsimony-based phylogenetic inference using the transition matrix from the step above
5. Obtain a consensus tree

Our algorithm follows this same framework. Our contribution is to automate the expert's annotations in step 3, and in steps 1-2 in some experiments. Section 3.1 outlines the way both Chacon and List (2016)'s algorithm and our modifications of it incorporate intermediate sound changes via a sound transition matrix. Section 3.2 elaborates on replacing the expert in step 3 with AISCP. Section 3.3 outlines replacing the expert in steps 1-2 with ASLI.

3.1 Creating the sound change transition matrix

Chacon and List (2016)'s transition matrix specifies the cost of intermediate sound changes that the parsimony algorithm tries. It is constructed by creating a directed graph (with phones as nodes) of the possible intermediate sound changes given by a linguist for each sound correspondence.[2] (In this context, we use the term CORRESPONDENCE to mean a proto-phoneme and its reflexes.) The expert may identify more than one possible path of intermediate phones between the proto-phoneme and reflex (e.g. k > kʲ > c > t͡ʃ and k > x > h > ʃ

[2]See Figure 5 in Chacon and List (2016) for a diagram of the process.

> t͡ʃ). The transition cost from one phone (source) to another (target) on an intermediate path is simply the length (in edges) of the shortest path from source to target in the directed graph for the correspondence. This value is encoded in the transition matrix at the row corresponding to the source index and the column corresponding to the target index. Pairs of source and target phones with no connecting path in the graph are penalized with a high transition cost. Paths are all directed from the proto-phoneme towards the reflex, encoding sound change directionality. Our AISCP algorithm's transition matrix is also directional, but the intermediate sound changes and edge weights are derived from the probability of articulatory features changing, as predicted by a neural network.

3.2 Automatic intermediate sound change prediction (AISCP)

To automate intermediate sound change prediction, we create a fully connected graph using a mapping x that encodes each phone p as a ternary vector of N articulatory features (such as [voice] or [syllabic]), where each feature in position f is encoded as -1 (not present), 0 (not applicable), or 1 (present); $x(s)_f \in \{-1, 0, 1\}$. This encoding lets us consider information shared by phones. Encodings for [d] and [t] differ in only one articulatory feature: $x([\text{d}])_{[\text{voice}]} = 1$, while $x([\text{t}])_{[\text{voice}]} = -1$. We can quantify such phonetic similarity between sounds using Mortensen et al. (2016)'s feature edit distance (FED). FED is Levenshtein edit distance, where the cost of an edit is the proportion of articulatory features changed. It reflects phonetic similarity between sounds: FED([t], [k]) has four times the value of FED([t], [d]), since the former pair requires four feature edits. For our phonological prior, we create a graph where the nodes are IPA phones, and all node pairs are joined by an undirected edge with weight equal to the FED. In this graph, intermediate phones are interpreted as the phones on the least-weighted paths between the proto-sound and the reflex. There can be multiple least-weighted paths between nodes, just as there can be multiple transition paths in a correspondence.

3.2.1 Neurally weighted FED for AISCP

The way we modify FED is central to our approach. FED has undesirable traits for modeling sound change — it is not directional (e.g. there is no way to encode whether p > f or f > p is more likely), and it gives an equal cost to every feature change, regardless of the source phone. This neglects information about sound change tendencies: for example, [d] is more likely to change its [voice] feature and become [t] than to change its [sonorant] feature and become a sonorant (like [l] or [r]).

We propose directional weighted feature edit distance (DWFED) to model these realities, by training a neural network to predict the cost of each feature change, given the source phone. The network learns each feature's *directional* change costs: i.e. the cost of the [voice] feature increasing (*voicing*) may differ from the cost of [voice] decreasing (*devoicing*). We interpret a feature edit's cost as one minus the probability of its occurring. Thus we train the neural network to model the *probability* of each directional feature edit, conditioned on the source phone, e.g. $P(voicing \mid source = [\text{p}])$.

The network predicts this for all articulatory features. It uses the encoding function x described in Section 3.2 to encode each source phone s as a vector of feature values in positions f. For an arbitrary target phone t, the network predicts both probabilities $P(x(t)_f > x(s)_f \mid s)$ and $P(x(t)_f < x(s)_f \mid s)$, for each s and f. (We write these in shorthand as $P(f\uparrow)$ and $P(f\downarrow)$, respectively.) It does this by learning the mapping $M : \{0,1\}^{3N} \rightarrow \{0,1\}^{2N}$, where $M(v) = \sigma(\text{NN}(v))$, a series of linear layers with ReLU activations followed by a sigmoid activation at the end. The input is a one-hot encoding of the source phone's N articulatory features (each having value -1, 0, or 1), resulting in a binary vector of length $3N$. The output contains the two directional sound change probabilities mentioned, for each of the N features f, resulting in a length-$2N$ vector with values between 0 and 1.

Hence for a single-layer neural network, the model weights are a single $2N \times 3N$ matrix, where each entry encodes a feature's importance in determining another feature's probability of increasing or decreasing. For example, if $N = 24$, the weight matrix's [0,47] entry encodes the importance of the source phone's first feature equaling -1 in predicting whether its 24th feature will decrease. This also ensures some continuity: source phones with many common features will elicit similar output probabilities. However, because a feature value's probability of increasing or decreasing may depend on a combination of the source phone's features, we experiment with deeper neu-

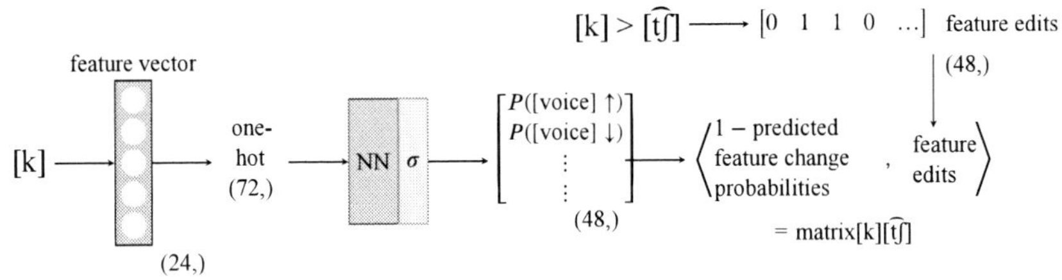

Figure 1: Calculation of the edge weights for the phone transition graph via DWFED

ral networks to capture more intricate relationships (Section 4.2).

These networks can be trained on a database of real sound changes (the typological grounding mentioned in §1.1), by converting each sound change with source phone s and target t into a length-$3N$ binary vector encoded from s and one length-$2N$ binary vector representing the ground-truth sound change direction (i.e. whether each feature increased and whether it decreased from $s \rightarrow t$). We use the length-$3N$ vector as the network's input and the length-$2N$ vector to compute loss with its output. In this way, the neural network learns which features tend to change in which directions for each source phone in natural languages. Refer to Figure 1 for a diagram of our method in the case $N = 24$. Since the length-$2N$ vector representing a direction of sound change is binary, using the dot product to multiply it with the output of the neural network at inference time extracts the relevant probabilities needed to calculate the DWFED of transitioning from a source phone to a target.

3.3 Automatic sound law induction (ASLI)

In addition to automating step 3 of the algorithm in Section 3 via AISCP, we experiment with ASLI via a minimal generalization learner from Wilson and Li (2021), instead of using sound laws from an expert in steps 1 and 2. This can be done by aligning the phones in protoforms and daughters (still provided by an expert) via Needleman-Wunsch alignment (Needleman and Wunsch, 1970), a Levenshtein edit distance alignment algorithm used in computational biology. We adapt the algorithm so that the substitution cost between two phones is the FED rather than a constant. This ensures that similar phones like [t] and [d] will align rather than more distant phones like [t] and [k]. See Figure 2 for an example of our *alignment* process.

Our ASLI method uses Albright and Hayes (2002, 2003)'s *minimal generalization* algorithm, as adapted by Wilson and Li (2021). These methods were developed for synchronic sound rules. However, since such rules reflect sound changes (Ohala, 2003), we repurpose the method for diachronic sound laws. Albright and Hayes generate the base rules by taking the longest common prefix and longest common suffix from each word pair as the context and treating the remaining strings as a rule, then iteratively generalizing the set of rules based on shared contexts. Because sound changes usually involve individual phones, we generate a base rule for every phone-level change in the aligned protoform and daughter instead. The *rule induction* process in Figure 2 shows sound law extraction, prior to iterative generalization.

4 Experiments

4.1 Dataset

In all our experiments we used Tukanoan expert annotations from two sources. For AISCP (without ASLI), we use expert-provided sound laws from 33 sound correspondences for 21 Tukanoan languages from Chacon and List (2016). Unfortunately, the phonological and lexical data needed for alignment and ASLI is not available for all 21 varieties. Thus for our ASLI experiment (Section 3.3) we used Chacon (2014)'s dataset of 15 Tukanoan languages.[3] This version contains phonetic transcriptions of daughters, cognacy, expert alignment (for manual evaluation and debugging), and reconstructed protoforms for 149 cognate sets, totalling 1,542 entries.

4.2 Implementation

As outlined in Section 3.2, our AISCP method consists of (1) encoding phones as vectors of features and (2) training a neural network to calculate DWFED between the feature vectors, to weight the transition edges in a phone graph. We used

[3] `https://github.com/lexibank/chacontukanoan/`

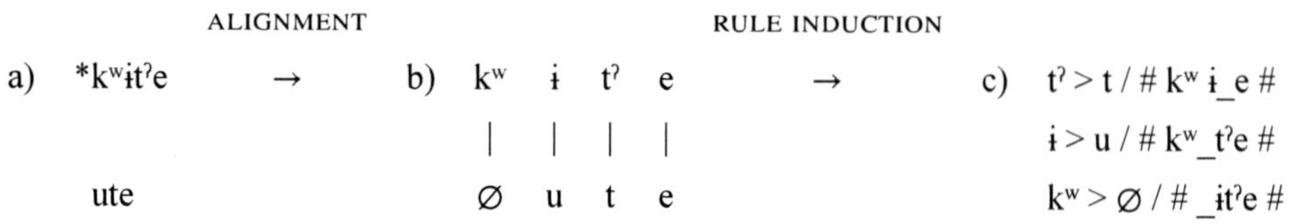

Figure 2: Alignment and induction of sound changes. A protoform and a daughter form are aligned, allowing the induction of base sound laws that can then be iteratively generalized using the minimal generalization learner.

PanPhon (Mortensen et al., 2016) as our mapping x from phones to $N = 24$ articulatory features. To compute DWFED, we trained neural networks on 7,042 sound changes in multiple language families[4] from *Index Diachronica*[5] (Anonymous, 2016). Training on actual sound correspondences collected by linguists ensures that the model learns the directionality of sound change. Because PanPhon has $N = 24$ articulatory features, all our neural networks accept length-72 vectors as input and output length-48 sound change probability vectors. We used Binary Cross Entropy Loss since the reference length-48 sound change vectors are binary. We trained multilayer perceptrons of differing depths: 1 layer, 4 layers, 8 layers, and 16 layers (the latter two with skip connections).

Using neural DWFED we produce a phone graph containing a subset of the phones supported by PanPhon.[6] We include the null phone ∅ to model insertions and deletions in sound changes. These we penalize with a cost multiplier (15 for insertions and 10 for deletions), since substitutions are more common along intermediate paths. We find the graph's shortest paths using NetworkX (Hagberg et al., 2023) to produce intermediate paths for the sound transition matrix of each correspondence in the data.

For our experiments with ASLI (as outlined in Section 3.3), we (1) align protoforms with daughters via Needleman-Wunsch alignment, (2) extract sound laws as in Figure 2, and (3) perform iterative generalization. We modified FED slightly for our alignment: we penalized substitutions between vowels ([+syl, -cons]) and non-syllabic consonants ([-syl, +cons]) to prevent unnatural substitutions. We also filtered out sound laws with raw accuracy ≤ 0.6 before iterative generalization, since our approach to single-phone law extraction generated superfluous laws otherwise.

When running the parsimony-based algorithm, we searched through 10,000 trees, though Chacon and List (2016) found that most best trees can be found within the first 5,000. When the algorithm resulted in multiple trees with the same score, we obtained a consensus tree with the `consense` program from PHYLIP (Felsenstein, 2013).

We also included two ablation experiments: *standard FED* and *direct paths*. Our *standard FED* ablation consists of applying AISCP with standard FED, rather than neural DWFED. Although FED is not directional and treats all articulatory features as the same, it does not preclude the directionality of sound change in our algorithm, since the sound change matrix encodes direction by only considering paths that lead from the proto-phoneme to the reflex (as mentioned in Section 3.1). Our *direct paths* ablation does not use AISCP or expert-provided intermediate sound changes. It uses sound laws from the Tukanoan expert directly without any intermediate sound changes. We performed this experiment to probe whether intermediate paths are necessary for the inference algorithm. In this ablation, we also used standard FED as the weight of transition directly from proto-phonemes to reflexes.

4.3 Baselines

We compare our adaptations of Chacon and List (2016)'s algorithm (Section 3) using AISCP and ASLI to two baseline inference methods: *cognacy* and *shared innovations*. Both of these baselines use undirected binary matrices for parsimony-based phylogenetic inference. The first uses a cognacy matrix, indicating simply which daughter languages have entries for which cognate sets Chacon (2014). This is commonly used in phylogenetic inference (Greenhill et al., 2020), but it only consid-

[4]We manually removed Altaic sound correspondences from the database, since the proposed family is controversial.

[5]We chose *Index Diachronica* instead of the more authoritative KonsonantalWandel (Kümmel, 2007) because the latter lacks a public LaTeX source and only includes consonants.

[6]To ensure matrix curation was computationally tractable, we excluded all phones with diacritics other than those marking length, aspiration, and glottalization.

ers lexical innovations and not phonological innovations. The second baseline uses a shared innovation matrix that indicates which languages participate in each sound law, i.e. innovate on the proto-phoneme in the conditioning environment of the law For both baselines we used PHYLIP's `Penny` program (Felsenstein, 2013) for parsimony-based phylogenetic inference, as it accepts binary matrices more readily than Chacon and List (2016)'s method.

4.4 Evaluation

We take the consensus tree from Chacon and List (2016) as the gold tree, which is a consensus between their DiWeST phylogenetic inference and the tree from (Chacon, 2014). To measure the distance between the gold and predicted trees, we use Generalized Quartet Distance (GQD), which groups leaf nodes (daughter languages) into *stars* and *butterflies* (Pompei et al., 2011). A *star* is a group of four leaves such that the most recent common ancestor of any pair among them is also the most recent common ancestor of all four. A *butterfly* is any quartet of leaves that is not a *star*[7]. GQD is the difference between the number of butterflies in the gold tree and the number of shared butterflies in both hypothesis and gold, normalized by the number in the gold. Because it does not penalize *stars*, GQD is well-suited to non-binary trees such as phylogenies (where *stars* persist, barring enough evidence to binarize them) (Sand et al., 2013; Pompei et al., 2011; Rama et al., 2018). For each experiment we report the minimum and mean GQD across ten runs of 10,000 trees each (which we found comparable to searching 100,000 trees).

5 Results and Discussion

Table 1 shows all experimental results. The *cognacy* baseline diverged greatly from the gold tree, while the *shared innovations* baseline captured about two-thirds of the gold tree butterflies, affirming the usefulness of phonological information. Our best tree overall reproduced 88% of gold butterflies, using AISCP with DWFED instead of an expert. (We discuss this tree in Section 5.1; see Figure 5.) Our *standard FED* ablation achieved worse mean GQD than any experiments using expert sound laws, suggesting DWFED is more effective in creating the sound transition matrix. The *direct paths* ablation performed worse than shallow networks using expert sound laws but outperformed deeper networks and ASLI approaches, indicating that intermediate sounds can be useful, but the quality of the sounds matters. (See Section 5.2.)

Our findings suggest that parsimony does not correlate with GQD, with Spearman's $\rho = -0.04$ across our experiments (Figure 6). The parsimony of our best tree overall was not even better than the median across the 10 runs of its experiment. It seems relying only on parsimony to predict phylogenies is not guaranteed—or perhaps even likely—to produce optimal trees.

The high variance across experiments is likely due to Chacon and List (2016)'s genetic search algorithm starting with random trees and at times getting stuck in sub-optimal areas of the search space.

5.1 Recovering major Tukanoan groupings

We analyze the best tree's recovery of subgroups proposed by Chacon (2014), which largely recur in the consensus tree from Chacon and List (2016). Our algorithm correctly groups "Western Tukano" and "East-Eastern Tukano" varieties into their respective subgroups but not "West-Eastern" Tukano. Within the correctly grouped subgroups, the relative chronology of the branch is incorrect. (See Appendix B for details.) Overall, the larger subgroups within Tukanoan are correctly displayed, showing that our method can capture broad phylogenetic relationships as a linguist would. Additionally, our parsimony method from Chacon and List (2016) produces binary trees with all language pairs split in an overly specific way, even though linguists often lack sufficient evidence to establish such binary splits.

5.2 Analyzing AISCP's intermediate paths

Intermediate paths from the phone graph using our best performing, 1-layer network are phonetically and typologically natural. We predict *k > *c > *t͡ɕ > t͡ʃ for proto-sound *k and reflex t͡ʃ, with [c] and [t͡ɕ] not observed in the daughters but plausible as intermediate phones. Another predicted path is *p > *f > h, where [f] is unobserved; p > f appears 16 times in our subset of *Index Diachronica*, and f > h is acoustically motivated since [f] and [h] are both characterized by low-amplitude aperiodic nose. This shows the viability of using articulatory features to model phonetically motivated interme-

[7]See `https://cran.r-project.org/web/packages/Quartet/vignettes/Quartet-Distance.pdf` for a visualization of the 3 possible arrangements of butterflies.

	Section	Experiment	GQD (Min) ↓	GQD (Mean ±σ) ↓
1	§4.3	Baseline: cognacy	0.533	0.533
2		Baseline: shared innovations	0.355	0.355
3	§4.2	C+L, w/ AISCP (*standard FED* ablation)	0.325	0.440 ±0.0623
4		C+L, w/ AISCP (*direct paths* ablation)	0.281	0.397 ±0.0719
5	§3.2	C+L w/ AISCP, 1 layer NN	**0.120**	**0.295** ±0.118
6		C+L w/ AISCP, 4 layer NN	0.191	0.309 ±0.0960
7		C+L w/ AISCP, 8 layer NN	0.402	0.439 ±0.0211
8		C+L w/ AISCP, 16 layer NN	0.248	0.435 ±0.0801
9	§3.3	C+L w/ AISCP + ASLI 1 layer NN	0.384	0.437 ±0.0314
10		C+L w/ AISCP + ASLI, 4 layer NN	0.451	0.600 ±0.0561
11		C+L w/ AISCP + ASLI, 8 layer NN	0.423	0.513 ±0.0799
12		C+L w/ AISCP + ASLI, 16 layer NN	0.426	0.529 ±0.0427

Table 1: Result of experiments across 10 runs. C+L refers to Chacon and List (2016)'s parsimony method outlined in (Section 3).

diate sound changes in future research. As a comparison, Chacon and List predicted *k > *kʲ > t͡ʃ (or *k > kʰ > t͡ʃ) and *p > *pʰ > *ɸ > h. (Note that they skipped a palatalization step or two in the former.) DWFED does not reproduce these expert paths perfectly, since it prefers paths matching feature change tendencies learned from *Index Diachronica*.

We find that many intermediate paths predicted in our *standard FED* ablation are also phonetically plausible, e.g. k > k͡x > t͡ɕ > t͡ʃ and j > ʒ > d͡ʒ > t͡ʃ. However, unweighted FED produces unreasonably many intermediate paths and many sound changes per path, resulting in phonetically unnatural paths, such as tˀ > ɗˀ > zˀ > ˀɾ > rˀ > r. For this same sound correspondence, our ablation includes all phonetic variants with the same FED, with no typological intuition. DWFED instead restricts the number of intermediate paths by favoring more typologically usual ones. While this results in plausible paths, DWFED yields only one unique intermediate path (Table 2) for each proto-phoneme and reflex pair. This is not entirely desirable, as proto-phonemes and reflexes may have multiple plausible paths. (The average number of paths in expert transition matrices is > 1; see Table 2.) The ideal setting is to include some of the most plausible paths, since this allows paths with higher DWFED that are in fact attested to be considered.

All neural approaches and the expert produce intermediate paths with an average of ∼ 2 edges (compared to 3.47 for our *standard FED* ablation.) The different networks also have similar expert sound change recall to each other. Thus their ability to replicate the length or phones of the expert intermediate paths cannot explain the ∼ 0.1 difference in GQD between the shallower and the deeper networks. (Indeed, the *standard FED* ablation has higher recall but performs worse.) This suggests that simply replicating the expert's intermediate paths is not sufficient without correctly reflecting the relative weights of the sound changes.

A naive alternative to weighting edit distances neurally is down-weighting the absolute FED between phones for attested sound changes. Our neural approach, however, is preferable. The naive approach is analogous to connecting cities (phones) with roads (edges), where distance represents FED, and then increasing certain speed limits. This fails because phones are not distributed uniformly; *Index Diachronica* has more attested occurrences of vowels than of consonants. So, the allegorical speed limits between "vowel cities" become so high that the paths between them act as "freeways." In analogous manner, the shortest paths between consonants tend to travel unnaturally through several vowels (e.g. k > g > w > u > o > a > ɛ > e > i > j > ʒ > d͡ʒ > t͡ʃ), in the same way that drivers may take a freeway to a neighboring city, even if the freeway entrance is not on the way. Our neural approach mitigates this by weighting the features of FED via probabilities between 0 and 1.

5.3 Hyper-specific sound laws from ASLI

Replacing the expert's sound laws with ASLI only reproduced ∼60% of expert *butterflies* and often lost to both baselines, indicating the quality of the sound laws generated by the minimal generalization learner is too low to have significant genetic signal. Within this set of experiments, the high GQD prevents us from drawing conclusions about the differences in the neural network architectures. As mentioned in §4.2, we filter out generated sound laws with low accuracy. However, these tend to be laws with more general contexts, which would be desirable if not for their lack of applicability to the data. This leaves us with many hyper-specific sound laws that only apply to single examples in the dataset. These specific contexts may limit the potential shared innovations explored by the genetic search algorithm. While the problem of insufficiently general sound laws may be due to our small dataset size, the lack of consideration for rule order could also play a role, as minimal generalization is designed for learning morphological rules that apply in a specific order.

6 Conclusion and Future Work

We propose a novel method to automatically predict intermediate sound changes for phylogenetic inference, via neural weighting of feature-based edit distance between phones. When we apply our method with a single-layer network, we accurately predict 88% of binary-branching language quartets (*butterflies*) in a gold Tukanoan phylogeny. Furthermore, our typologically informed neural approach based on articulatory features produces intermediate sound changes that capture expert intuitions on phonetic naturalness. Our analysis shows that not only does phonetic plausibility matter, but so does the accuracy of sound transition costs for successful phylogenetic inference. We also present a method to predict sound laws automatically via minimal generalization, which creates less generalizable sound laws than the expert.

Future work in this vein may involve exploration of other ASLI approaches (List, 2019; Luo, 2021), pruning the phone graph using PHOIBLE to focus on cross-linguistically frequent phonemes (Moran et al., 2014), generalization of our approach to other language families such as Polynesian, and incorporation of MCMC methods to jointly reconstruct protoforms and phylogenies.

Limitations

Distinctive feature theory does not take some aspects of acoustic similarity into account. For instance, the common sound change p > ʔ is motivated by acoustic factors, such as [p] having a weak burst. In addition, Schweikhard and List (2020) caution that *Index Diachronica* (Anonymous, 2016) does not always cite reliable sources. As such, we may wish to decrease the effect of our TYPOLOGICAL GROUNDING and instead include more language family-specific information a linguist would have just by analyzing its phoneme inventory. Historical linguists actually value rare sound changes that regularly occur since they are less likely to be parallel innovations and thus provide phylogenetic signal. Additionally, none of the methods we mention handle borrowing or parallel innovations (homoplasy in Chacon and List (2016)), which means the methods here would not generalize well for Chinese and Romance. Furthermore, our baseline involves a different maximum parsimony method (Wagner parsimony) than Chacon and List (2016)'s modified Sankoff parsimony, which muddies the comparison between the two. That our shared innovations baseline outperforms the cognacy baseline cannot actually tell us that shared innovations outperforms cognacy information in general, because our gold tree was generated in part using shared innovations. Another limitation is that the genetic search algorithm does not scale well with more languages. Finally, the rules we learn in our minimal generalization learner also do not consider the relative chronology of the sound laws, as a historical phonologist would.

Acknowledgement

We thank Maggie Huang for her independent study on phylogenetic inference that informed this work, Gašper Beguš for directing us to KonsonantalWandel (Kümmel, 2007), Edwin Ko for sharing his expertise in phylogenetic inference, Abhishek Vijayakumar for providing feedback on our initial phone graph ideas and for proofreading our paper, Melinda Fricke for answering our questions regarding the acoustic motivations behind sound change, and Leon Lu for proofreading our paper.

This material is based on research sponsored in part by the Air Force Research Laboratory under agreement number FA8750-19-2-0200. The U.S. Government is authorized to reproduce and distribute reprints for Governmental purposes notwithstanding any copyright notation thereon. The views and conclusions contained herein are those of the authors and should not be interpreted as necessarily representing the official policies or endorsements, either expressed or implied, of the Air Force Research Laboratory or the U.S. Government.

References

Adam Albright and Bruce Hayes. 2002. Modeling English past tense intuitions with minimal generalization. In *Proceedings of the ACL-02 Workshop on Morphological and Phonological Learning*, pages 58–69. Association for Computational Linguistics.

Adam Albright and Bruce Hayes. 2003. Rules vs. analogy in English past tenses: a computational/experimental study. *Cognition*, 90(2):119–161.

Anonymous. 2016. Index Diachronica v.10.2.

Gašper Beguš. 2016. Post-nasal devoicing and a probabilistic model of phonological typology. *MS, Harvard University*.

Karl Brugmann and Hermann Osthoff. 1878. *Morphologische Untersuchungen auf dem Gebiete der indogermanischen Sprachen*, volume 1. Hirzel.

Lyle Campbell. 2013. *Historical Linguistics: an Introduction*. Edinburgh University Press.

Thiago Chacon. 2013. On proto-languages and archaeological cultures: pre-history and material culture in the Tukanoan family. *Revista Brasileira de Linguística Antropológica*, 5(1):217–245.

Thiago Chacon. 2014. A revised proposal of Proto-Tukanoan consonants and Tukanoan family classification. *International Journal of American Linguistics*, 80(3):275–322.

Thiago Costa Chacon and Johann-Mattis List. 2016. Improved computational models of sound change shed light on the history of the Tukanoan languages. *Journal of Language Relationship*, 13(3-4):177–204.

Grégoire Clarté and Robin J. Ryder. 2022. A phylogenetic model of the evolution of discrete matrices for the joint inference of lexical and phonological language histories.

Joseph Felsenstein. 2013. Phylip (phylogeny inference package), version 3.695. Department of Genome Sciences, University of Washington, Seattle.

David Francis, Ella Rabinovich, Farhan Samir, David Mortensen, and Suzanne Stevenson. 2021. Quantifying cognitive factors in lexical decline. *Transactions of the Association for Computational Linguistics*, 9:1529–1545.

Andrew Garrett, Claire Bowern, and Bethwyn Evans. 2015. Sound change. *The Routledge handbook of historical linguistics*, pages 227–248.

Andrew Garrett and Keith Johnson. 2013. Phonetic bias in sound change. *Origins of sound change: Approaches to phonologization*, 1:51–97.

Simon J Greenhill, Paul Heggarty, and Russell D Gray. 2020. Bayesian phylolinguistics. *The handbook of historical linguistics*, 2:226–253.

Aric Hagberg, Dan Schult, and Pieter Swart. 2023. NetworkX: Network analysis in Python.

Frederik Hartmann. 2019. Predicting historical phonetic features using deep neural networks: A case study of the phonetic system of Proto-Indo-European. In *Proceedings of the 1st International Workshop on Computational Approaches to Historical Language Change*, pages 98–108.

Frederik Hartmann. 2021. The phonetic value of the proto-indo-european laryngeals: A computational study using deep neural networks. *Indo-European Linguistics*, 9(1):26–84.

Henry M. Hoenigswald. 1960. Language change and linguistic reconstruction.

Daniel J Hruschka, Simon Branford, Eric D Smith, Jon Wilkins, Andrew Meade, Mark Pagel, and Tanmoy Bhattacharya. 2015. Detecting regular sound changes in linguistics as events of concerted evolution. *Current Biology*, 25(1):1–9.

Martin Kümmel. 2007. *Konsonantenwandel: Bausteine zu einer Typologie des Lautwandels und ihre Konsequenzen für die vergleichende Rekonstruktion*. Reichert Verlag.

Björn Lindblom, Susan Guion, Susan Hura, Seung-Jae Moon, and Raquel Willerman. 1995. Is sound change adaptive? *Rivista di linguistica*, 7:5–36.

Johann-Mattis List. 2019. Automatic inference of sound correspondence patterns across multiple languages. *Computational Linguistics*, 45(1):137–161.

Johann-Mattis List. 2022. Computational approaches to historical language comparison. [Preprint not peer reviewed]. Leipzig: Max Planck Institute for Evolutionary Anthropology.

Jiaming Luo. 2021. *Automatic Methods for Sound Change Discovery*. Ph.D. thesis, Massachusetts Institute of Technology.

Steven Moran, Daniel McCloy, and Richard Wright. 2014. Phoible online.

David R Mortensen, Patrick Littell, Akash Bharadwaj, Kartik Goyal, Chris Dyer, and Lori Levin. 2016. Panphon: A resource for mapping IPA segments to articulatory feature vectors. In *Proceedings of COLING 2016, the 26th International Conference on Computational Linguistics: Technical Papers*, pages 3475–3484.

Saul B. Needleman and Christian D. Wunsch. 1970. A general method applicable to the search for similarities in the amino acid sequence of two proteins. *Journal of Molecular Biology*, 48(3):443–453.

John J. Ohala. 2003. *Phonetics and Historical Phonology*, chapter 22. John Wiley & Sons, Ltd.

Hermann Paul. 2010. *Prinzipien der sprachgeschichte*, volume 6. Walter de Gruyter.

Simone Pompei, Vittorio Loreto, and Francesca Tria. 2011. On the accuracy of language trees. *PloS one*, 6(6):e20109.

Taraka Rama, Johann-Mattis List, Johannes Wahle, and Gerhard Jäger. 2018. Are automatic methods for cognate detection good enough for phylogenetic reconstruction in historical linguistics? *arXiv preprint arXiv:1804.05416*.

Maria Ryskina, Ella Rabinovich, Taylor Berg-Kirkpatrick, David Mortensen, and Yulia Tsvetkov. 2020. Where new words are born: Distributional semantic analysis of neologisms and their semantic neighborhoods. In *Proceedings of the Society for Computation in Linguistics 2020*, pages 367–376, New York, New York. Association for Computational Linguistics.

Andreas Sand, Morten K Holt, Jens Johansen, Rolf Fagerberg, Gerth Stølting Brodal, Christian NS Pedersen, and Thomas Mailund. 2013. Algorithms for computing the triplet and quartet distances for binary general trees. *Biology*, 2(4):1189–1209.

David Sankoff. 1975. Minimal mutation trees of sequences. *SIAM Journal on Applied Mathematics*, 28(1):35–42.

Nathanael E Schweikhard and Johann-Mattis List. 2020. Handling word formation in comparative linguistics. *SKASE Journal of Theoretical Linguistics*, 17(1):2–26.

Eduard Sievers. 1901. *Grundzüge der Phonetik: zur Einführung in das Studium der Lautlehre der indogermanischen Sprachen*, volume 1. Breitkopf & Härtel.

Colin Wilson and Jane S.Y. Li. 2021. Were we there already? Applying minimal generalization to the SIGMORPHON-UniMorph shared task on cognitively plausible morphological inflection. In *Proceedings of the 18th SIGMORPHON Workshop on Computational Research in Phonetics, Phonology, and Morphology*, pages 283–291, Online. Association for Computational Linguistics.

Zhijun Zheng. 2018. A new proposal for Min subgrouping based on a maximum-parsimony algorithm for generating phylogenetic trees. *Lingua*, 206:67–84.

A Experimental Details

A.1 Neural network hyperparameters

- num_epochs = 25
- batch_size = 5
- optimizer = Adam
- learning_rate = 0.001
- train_test_split = 0.9
- seed = 411

B Best tree analysis

Our algorithm correctly groups Western Tukano (`Kue, Kor, Mai, Sek, and Sio`) varieties in the same branch, with `Kue/Kor` and `Sio/Sek` paired (and `Mai` by itself), correctly (though it does not predict the correct chronology of the branching). "East-Eastern Tukano" varieties (`Tuk, Wan, Pir, Tuy, Yur, Pis, Kar, Tat,` and `Bar`) are also grouped in the same branch, with `Tuk` correctly splitting off the earliest and `Pir/Wan` and `Yur/Tuy` paired correctly. However, `Pis, Kar, Bar`, and `Tat` are predicted in an incorrect order. As for "West-Eastern" Tukano (`Bas, Mak, Yup, Des`, and `Sir`), our tree's grouping is wrong: `Des/Sir` and `Yup` are correct relative to each other but are in the wrong branch, `Mak/Bas`, `Tan`, and `Kub` are grouped correctly, but our predicted tree splits `Kub` and `Tan`, while the gold tree does not. Refer to Chacon and List (2016) for the original names of each variety.

C Example sound laws

Examples of sound laws from our ASLI method:

- sufficiently general: e →ẽ / (n|m) __
- too specific: p →m / (#) (pˀ|ˀp) (o) __ (a) (#)

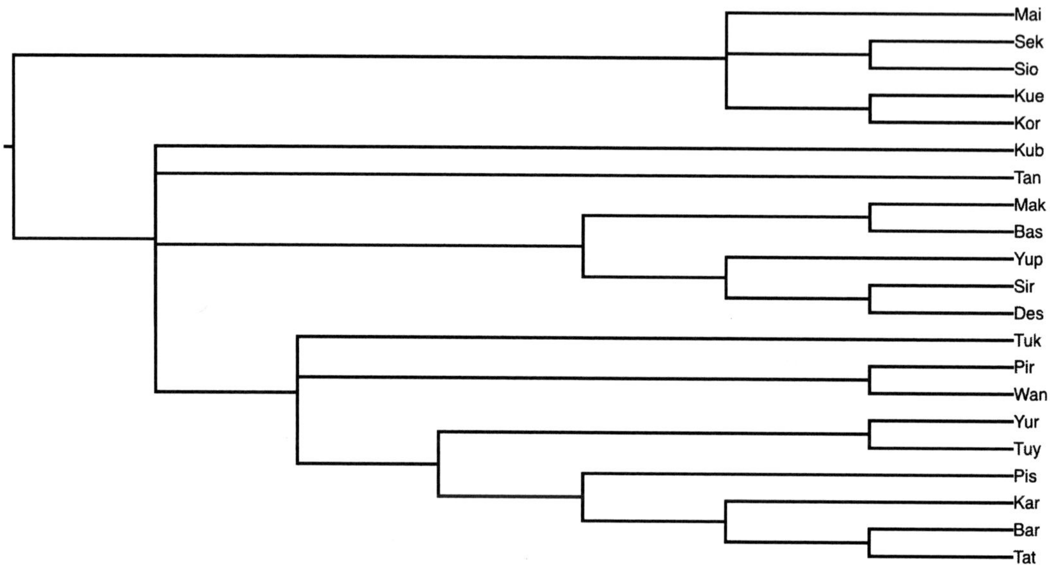

Figure 3: Gold Tukanoan phylogeny from Chacon and List (2016), which is a consensus of Chacon (2014) and their DiWeST tree

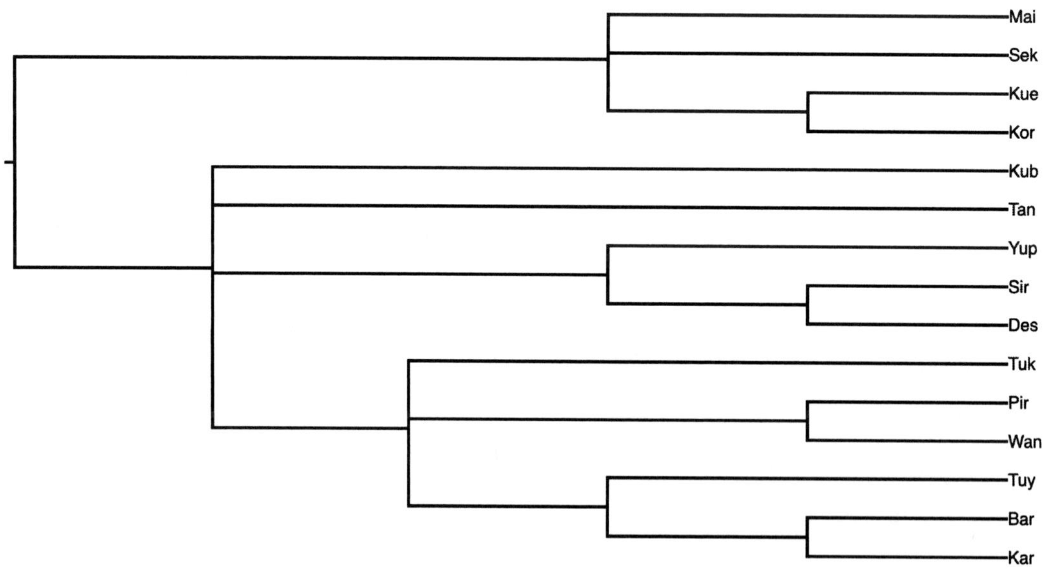

Figure 4: Gold Tukanoan phylogeny from Chacon and List (2016) but with only the 15 varieties in Chacon (2014)

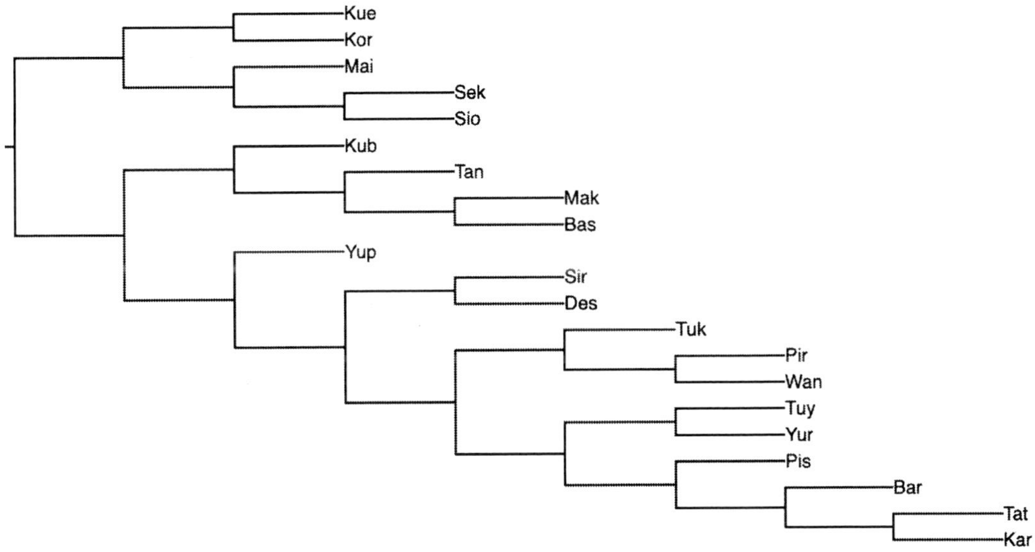

Figure 5: The predicted tree with the lowest GQD when compared to the gold tree (Figure 3), generated from the main experiments with a 1 layer neural network and using expert sound laws

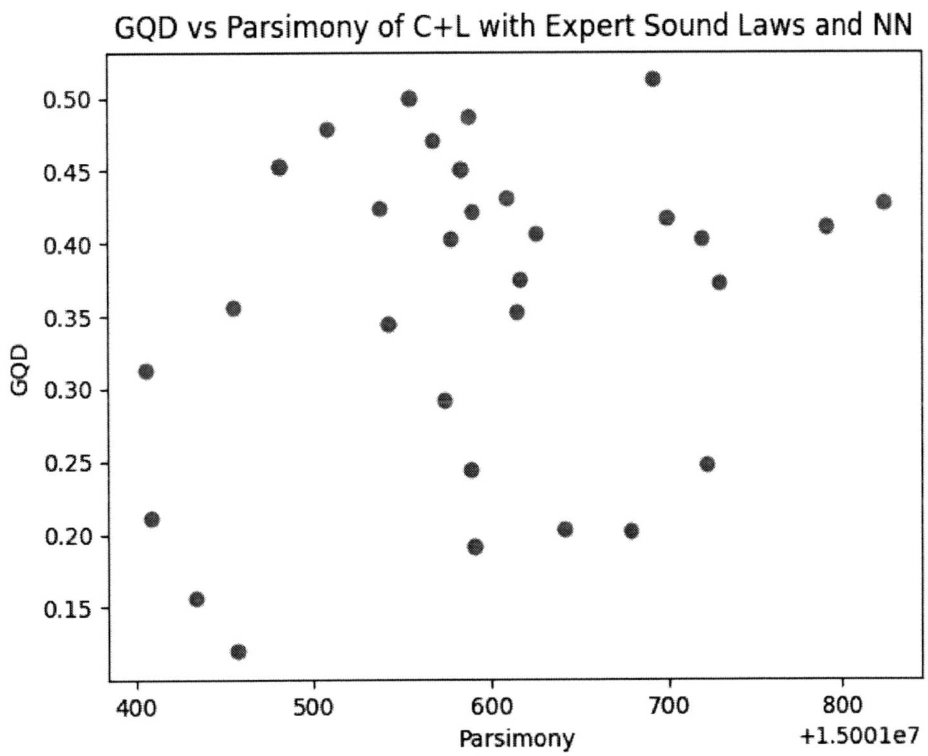

Figure 6: GQD vs parsimony of all 40 runs of C+L with expert sound laws and various NNs. The Spearman's coefficient between GQD and parsimony is -0.0373 (p = 0.819).

	Experiment	Shortest paths (corr. 6)	Shortest paths (corr. 13)	Avg. Num. Paths	Avg. Num. Edges/Path	Recall
3	C+L, w/ AISCP (*FED* ablation)	k > k͡x > t͡ɕ > t͡ʃ	p > h	1.78	3.47	0.522
5	C+L, w/ AISCP, 1 layer NN	k > c > t͡ɕ > t͡ʃ	p > f > h	1.0	2.10	0.342
6	C+L, w/ AISCP, 4 layer NN	k > c > t͡ʃ	p > h	1.0	1.94	0.366
7	C+L, w/ AISCP, 8 layer NN	k > c > t^j > t͡ʃ	p > f > h	1.0	2.16	0.354
8	C+L, w/ AISCP, 16 layer NN	k > c > t͡ʃ	p > f > h	1.0	2.01	0.329
	gold, expert sound laws	k > k^j > t͡ʃ, k > k^h > t͡ʃ	p > *p^h > *ɸ > h	1.31	1.86	-

Table 2: Comparison of the intermediate sound changes predicted in our main experiments using our DWFED method, with the unweighted ablation and the expert's posited sound changes included for comparison. Corr. 6 and 13 each refer to the index of the sound correspondence in Chacon and List (2016)'s dataset of annotated sound correspondences. Avg. # Paths refers to the average number of unique intermediate paths between proto-sound and reflex pairs in the dataset. Avg. # Edges/Path denotes the average number of edges in a shortest path. For Chacon and List's expert sound laws, we consider all paths in the calculation, since their paths are unweighted. Recall is the number of phones in the expert's proposed intermediate sound changes that appear in our predicted sound correspondences.

Scent and Sensibility: Perception Shifts in the Olfactory Domain

Teresa Paccosi,[1,2] Stefano Menini,[1] Elisa Leonardelli,[1]
Ilaria Barzon,[3] Sara Tonelli,[1]
[1]Fondazione Bruno Kessler, Trento, Italy
[2]Dept. of Cognitive Science, University of Trento, Italy
[3]Dept. of Humanities, University of Pavia, Italy
{tpaccosi, menini, eleonardelli, satonelli}@fbk.eu

Abstract

In this work, we investigate olfactory perception shifts, analysing how the description of the smells emitted by specific sources has changed over time. We first create a benchmark of selected smell sources, relying upon existing historical studies related to olfaction. We also collect an English text corpus by retrieving large collections of documents from freely available resources, spanning from 1500 to 2000 and covering different domains. We label such corpus using a system for olfactory information extraction inspired by frame semantics, where the semantic roles around the smell sources in the benchmark are marked. We then analyse how the roles describing *Qualities* of smell sources change over time and how they can contribute to characterise perception shifts, also in comparison with more standard statistical approaches.

1 Introduction

Over the past few decades, there has been a proliferation of studies in the realm of linguistics and perception (Winter, 2019; Bagli, 2021). However, there remains a distinct shortage of research dedicated to the tracking of perceptual changes over time. Although it has been already highlighted how much sensory language can be informative in terms of cultural attitudes (Majid and Burenhult, 2014), there has been a relatively limited exploration of how perceptual experiences are linguistically encoded over an extended period of time. A first attempt concerning the diachronic analysis of the olfactory domain using NLP has been presented in Menini et al. (2023), although this study was rather exploratory and relied on an existing approach utilizing word embeddings.

One of the reasons of the scarcity of studies using automatic approaches in this area is the difficult assessment of perceptual shifts due to the limited availability of suitable evaluation benchmarks. Therefore, in this paper, we first introduce a manually created benchmark containing a list of smell sources (mainly objects) that underwent some changes in the way their odour was described over time. This benchmark is based upon existing literature in historical studies and olfactory cultural heritage. We then present some analyses of perception shifts that compare standard statistical approaches to a novel framework based on the output of a system for olfactory information extraction. Our approach involves modelling perception shifts as changes in the association between a given smell source and its description in terms of (olfactory) quality. We show that focusing the analysis on text spans that the system identifies as being smell qualities makes the output more precise and tailored to the domain of interest. The results are validated on a selected set of smell sources from the benchmark, which is available at `https://github.com/dhfbk/scent-change`.

2 Related Work

There is limited research involving the diachronic analysis of sensory language, and the use of computational methods to study this phenomenon are even scarcer. Among the few works investigating this research direction, Strik Lievers (2021) proposes an analysis of the possible variations of olfactory lexicon in the transition from Latin to Italian. The results of the study show that olfactory lexicon did not present substantial alterations in its overall size and differentiation. However, there is evidence suggesting that it did evolve towards a more negatively-oriented lexicon. In Lievers and De Felice (2019), the authors test the hypothesis of the directionality of sensory adjectives in Latin and Italian from a diachronic perspective. This study provides evidence for the fact that the primary meanings of sensory adjectives and the hierarchy of synaesthetic metaphors did not undergo variations over time.

As regards the development of structured re-

Proceedings of the 4th Workshop on Computational Approaches to Historical Language Change, pages 143–152
December 6, 2023 ©2023 Association for Computational Linguistics

sources to investigate the evolution of sensory language, Menini et al. (2022a) present a multilingual taxonomy for olfactory-related terms, which was created semi-automatically, with the goal to describe the evolution of odours and smell sources' descriptions. Furthermore, in Menini et al. (2022b), the authors present a multilingual benchmark, manually annotated with smell-related information, to support the development of olfactory information extraction systems. Nevertheless, the first exploratory analysis of shifts in olfactory descriptors based on word embeddings between two time periods is introduced in Menini et al. (2023). The approach is inspired by the method for semantic change detection in El-Ebshihy et al. (2018), which was adapted to detect *perception shifts* rather than semantic ones. The hypothesis is that methods employed to detect how the meaning of a word changes over time (i.e. *semantic shift*) (Tahmasebi et al., 2021) can be adapted to analyse possible variations in the way sensory items are perceived and therefore described over time (i.e. *perception shifts*). The work we present in this paper further investigates this phenomenon by introducing a novel benchmark to study olfactory perception shifts. We also present a comparison between a 'traditional' PMI-based approach to shift detection (Hamilton et al., 2016) and our contribution that introduces an intermediate layer focusing on specific semantic roles.

3 Benchmark of Smell Perception Shifts

Given the difficulty to evaluate shifts in language use, we first develop a benchmark with the purpose to trace the history of some selected odors over time. This resource can be used as a test set for the evaluation of systems analysing possible changes in the way specific odors have been described in the past. We rely on historical studies in the olfactory domain (Tullett, 2019; Tullett et al., 2022) and on the Online Encyclopedia of Smell History and Heritage[1] to identify 16 words that domain experts consider particularly related to smell and whose perception may have changed over time: *asphalt, candle, brewing, car, chloride of lime, coffee, (perfumed) gloves, incense/frankincense, lavender, ozone, pomander, plastic, sulphur, tea, tobacco, wig*. For each of the above items, we then gather information on the **perception shift** it underwent, trying to address when this happened, whether it involved some changes in smell quality, whether it is connected to a change in location, and what type of shift it was. Indeed, we identify four possible types of perception shift, manually checked by two experts in olfactory language:

(a) **appearance**: in a mainly Eurocentric perspective, an odor that was not initially mentioned and that manifests itself at a certain point either due to trades and new habits (e.g. *coffee*) or as the outcome of inventions (e.g. *asphalt*);

(b) **disappearance**: in contrast with *appearance*, an odor associated with a particular era that slowly fades away over time. For instance, the pomander, a widely used item during the 16th century for carrying and diffusing fragrances, which eventually diminishes its presence, until its disappearance;

(c) **topic shift**: a change of environment/location in which a certain smell can appear, as the conditions of use or the meaning changes from a cultural point of view (e.g. *incense*, which disappears from Protestant churches after the Reformation of Henry the VIIIth, but which has been used in houses since the 18th century);

(d) **quality shift**: a change in the perception of the olfactory quality of a given odor over time, for instance the smell of candles that changes its olfactory connotation due to the different materials used to make them.

For each item in the benchmark, we specify one of the above types of perception shift, as well as the time period when the shift happened, the bibliographic or sitographic references, and in some cases the associated places for each period. Note that for each term in the benchmark different time periods may be related to a perception shift. In Table 1, we report an example of shift related to five smell sources with a brief description.

4 Olfactory Information Extraction

Our approach to analyse perception shifts in the olfactory domain relies on two components: *i)* a system for olfactory information extraction, and *ii)* a historical corpus of English, possibly well-balanced across topics and time periods, which is processed with the above system.

[1] https://odeuropa.eu/encyclopedia/

Smell source	Type of Shift	Brief Shift Description
Candle	*Quality*	From negative to positive perception due to materials' choice
Gloves	*Disappearance*	From being an object related to olfactory domain to not
Incense	*Topic*	A shift in the locations of usage
Ozone	*Quality*	From a connotation related to electricity to an healthy one
Tobacco	*Quality*	With the rise of snuff consumption, from positive to negative

Table 1: Selected smell sources from the benchmark

4.1 System Description

We develop a system for olfactory information extraction able to recognise smell-related information in a text. In particular, we detect olfactory events, typically evoked by smell words such as 'stink', 'odour', 'stench', 'whiff', 'stink', and the two semantic roles (or *frame elements*) that are more frequently mentioned in relation to these olfactory events, i.e. *Smell source* (items from where a smell comes from) and *Quality* (how such smell is described). For instance, in the sentence 'The tobacco has a pungent smell', 'The tobacco' would be *Smell source* and 'pungent' a *Quality*, while 'smell' would be the smell word evoking the olfactory event. This annotation framework, inspired by frame semantics (Fillmore and Baker, 2001) is described in detail in Tonelli and Menini (2021) and has been adopted to annotate an English benchmark (Menini et al., 2022b), which we use to train our system for olfactory information extraction.

For the supervised classifier, we adopt a multi-task learning approach (Caruana, 1993, 1997). In this configuration each task updates the model's shared parameters, leading to a more robust representation with less over-fitting. Each task corresponds to the classification of a single olfactory element, namely *Smell Word*, *Smell Source* and *Quality*.

We adopt a multi-task approach, since it performs better than a single multiclass classifier (see Table 2 for a comparison), and because simpler tasks, as can be smell word detection, can act as auxiliary task and share information for the classification of olfactory elements, which are more challenging to detect. To fine-tune the models, we use the MaChAmp framework (van der Goot et al., 2021), a toolkit for multi-task learning. The classification of each olfactory element was configured as a BIO task. Indeed, the tokens in the frame elements (that often span over multiple words) are marked with either B-FRAME_ELEMENT (beginning of a span), I-FRAME_ELEMENT (inside of a span) or O (outside the frame element).

All the results reported in Table 2 are the average of the experiments done with 10 different data splits, with each data split having 80% of the smell words and related olfactory elements as training data, 10% for validation and 10% as test. The splits are not completely random, as we keep the same temporal and domain distribution in every run.

We run a hyperparameter search[2] on one of the data splits and the best performance was obtained with a learning rate of $1e-4$ and a batch size of 32, and all the loss weight set to 1, which yield the best performance.

We report in Table 2 the performance of the multitask classifier on each of the three olfactory elements of interest, and compare it with a baseline obtained by fine-tuning the model with a single-task approach for multiclass classification. In both the configurations the fine-tuned model is bert-base-cased[3] (Devlin et al., 2019).

	Smell Word	Smell Source	Quality
Multitask	**0.871**	**0.571**	**0.758**
Multiclass	0.821	0.461	0.652

Table 2: Results of olfactory information extraction. Each result (F1) is the average of 10 different runs on 10 different data splits

4.2 Corpus Labelling

We launch the information extraction system on a set of historical corpora of English. We focus on seven freely available corpora:

<u>*Project Gutenberg*</u>:[4] A volunteer effort to digitize and archive cultural works, it contains different repositories, mainly in the literary domain.

[2]Search space: learning rate $[1e-3, 1e-4, 1e-5]$, batch size $[16, 32]$, training epochs $range(1, 20)$.

[3]https://huggingface.co/bert-base-cased

[4]https://www.gutenberg.org/

Early English Books Online (EEBO):[5] A collection containing documents published between 1475 and 1700 in different domains such as literature, philosophy, politics, religion, geography, history, politics, mathematics.
British Library:[6] A collection of 65,227 digitised volumes from the 16th to the 19th Century.
London Pulse Medical Reports:[7] A collection of 5800 Medical Officer of Health reports from the Greater London area from 1848 to 1972.
Wikisource:[8] An online digital library of free-content textual sources managed by the Wikimedia Foundation.
Eighteenth Century Collections Online (ECCO) :[9] A collection of over 3,000 titles printed in the United Kingdom during the 18th century.
UK Medical Heritage Library:[10] A collection of books and pamphlets from 10 research libraries in the UK, focused on the 19th and early 20th century history of medicine and related disciplines.

In Table 3 we provide an overview of the *Smell Sources* and *Qualities* instances extracted from the above set of corpora. Note that we report only the instances of smell sources present also in the benchmark (Section 3) that according to the system were part of an olfactory event. Qualities are less frequent than smell sources because they may not be necessarily mentioned when describing an odour.

Frame Element	Extracted Instances
Smell Sources	40,191
Qualities	39,521

Table 3: Number of *Smell Sources* from the benchmark extracted from the corpus and associated *Qualities*.

5 Analysis of Perception Shifts

In our analysis, we aim at detecting possible variations in the way specific smell-related concepts are described over time. For the sake of brevity, we focus our investigation on five *Smell Sources* selected from the benchmark (Section 3) that undergo some sort of change in terms of perception over time: *candle*, *gloves*, *incense/frankincense*, *ozone*, *tobacco*. Nevertheless, our approach to perception shift analysis can be generalised to any *Smell Source*. To conduct our study we use the corpus presented in Section 4.2, which was processed with the system for olfactory information extraction (Section 4.1).

5.1 Frequency Analysis of Smell-related Terms

The first analysis we perform is aimed at showing when specific items have become smell-related, i.e. when they started to be considered *smell sources* in olfactory descriptions. For instance, history scholars showed that leather *gloves* in the 17th Century used to be scented with perfumes to temper their bad smell coming from compounds used to make leather softer (Marx et al., 2022). Thus they were seen as strong olfactory objects at the time, while nowadays they are not considered 'smelly' items. In order to analyse the variations in the perception of items as being smell-related or not, for each of the five smell sources we compute the percentage of mentions in our corpus that are labeled also as Smell Source. Each time point (1 time point = 1 year) is calculated as the average percentage of a time range of 20 years centered around the time point. The results are plotted in the graph reported in Figure 1. Intuitively, a peak in the graph corresponds to a time period in which a term was strongly associated with the olfactory domain.

If we compare the plots for the five terms of interest, we observe that *incense* is the item that is overall more associated with the olfactory domain, in particular around 1860 and 1970, when almost 40% of its mentions are smell-related. The graph for *candle(s)*, instead, displays a growth after 1960, probably related to the widespread use of scented candles. As regards *glove(s)*, the graph shows that it stops being perceived as an olfactory object after 1950, as already mentioned before, but that nevertheless it was characterised as smell-related only rarely before that date (less than 2% of the mentions). Finally, *tobacco* and *ozone* are more 'modern' smells, in particular the latter, which was first used to characterise the aroma resulting from experiments with electricity around 1840.

5.2 PMI-based Analysis of Smell Qualities

While the analysis displayed in Figure 1 shows when a specific item was used in relation to the olfactory domain, it does not show *how* this rela-

[5] https://textcreationpartnership.org/tcp-texts/eebo-tcp-early-english-books-online/
[6] https://data.bl.uk/digbks/
[7] https://wellcomelibrary.org/moh/about-the-reports/about-the-medical-officer-of-health-reports/
[8] https://en.wikisource.org/
[9] https://textcreationpartnership.org/faq
[10] https://ukmhl.historicaltexts.jisc.ac.uk/home

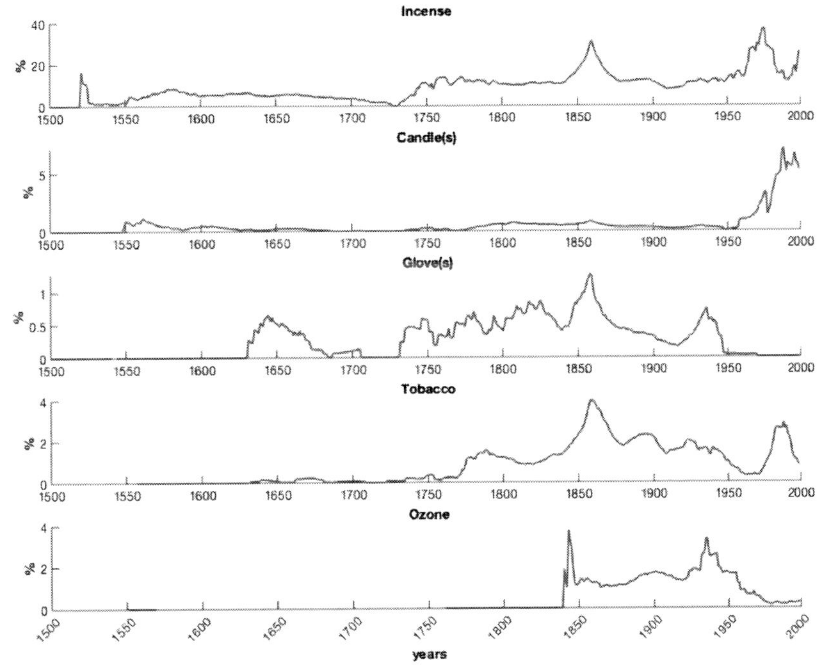

Figure 1: Percentage of term occurrences in our corpus that are also labeled as *Smell source*

tion was described, i.e. how an item's smell was characterised. To further address this aspect, we perform an analysis based on PMI with the goal to investigate more in detail the type of perception shifts of smell sources over the time. We opt for a PMI-based approach because it is a solution that can be straightforwardly combined with information from olfactory elements, usually consisting of few tokens, while other solutions like contextualized embeddings would require longer texts to be effective (Giulianelli et al., 2020). Furthermore, comparing a PMI-based analysis with and without olfactory element information gives us the possibility to assess the actual contribution of the latter to capture perception shifts.

We compute the association strength between a smell source and the words labelled as being their *Quality* by the information extraction system. The analysis is performed across different time periods marked as turning points in perception or attitudes towards these items, as identified in the benchmark. We calculate the PMI of a given smell source (w_1) and its associated qualities (w_2) in the following way:

$$PMI\,(w_1; w_2) = \log_2 \frac{P(w_1, w_2)}{P(w_1)P(w_2)}$$

where $P(w_1, w_2)$ is the probability of the smell source and a word/quality to co-occur, while $P(w_1)$ and $P(w_2)$ are their independent probabilities. We report in Table 4 the top-five qualities ranked by PMI for each smell source of interest in each time span. As a comparison, we also compute PMI for each of the five items in the whole corpus, dividing the analyses by the same time intervals, without considering the spans labeled as qualities. This comparison should highlight the difference between standard PMI-based analysis of shifts (see for example Hamilton et al. (2018)) and our approach, which targets the olfactory domain and is therefore carried out on specific text spans. We adopt the same setting as Hamilton et al. (2018) by considering a window of 4 terms before and after w_1. The top-ranked adjectives and nouns obtained without considering the olfactory annotation are reported in gray in Table 4. We report only these grammatical categories because they are prevalent also for *Qualities*.

We observe that in some cases the olfactory aspect is prevalent also if we do not consider only smell qualities, see for example the occurrences of 'perfumed/perfuming' in gray for all time periods related to *incense*. For *candle*, instead, PMI computed on raw text shows an alternation between the olfactory and the visual dimension, while focusing only on olfactory qualities allows us to capture the negative characterisation of candle smells in the past. Indeed, candles before 1800 were made from animal fats (pig tallow until 1700, followed by whale fat), resulting in a predominantly unpleasant odor (Muchembled, 2020). It wasn't until around 1830 that candles began to be fashioned from paraffin wax, leading to a likely shift in odor towards a more neutral quality. With the advent of kerosene lamps and the incandescent light bulbs, which rendered candles obsolete for illumination, these items found new purposes as decorations, ambient fragrance enhancers or votive offerings (Phillips, 1999).

As regards *ozone*, it is a peculiar element since it has no strongly associated smell qualities after 1950. Indeed, starting from 1840, the term "ozone" emerged to characterize the aroma resulting from experiments with electricity, often associated with thunder and lightning (Forster, 1813). However, as the 20th century unfolded, its connotation underwent a complete transformation and ozone was considered accountable for the healthful qualities found in mountainous and seaside air (Anonymous, 1910), while it was not perceived as an odorous element anymore. After this period, we have no data in our olfactory corpus since its primary role as a descriptor of scents diminishes until disappearing. Instead, it starts to be associated with atmospheric phenomena, particularly in relation to the ozone depletion event.

5.3 Perception Shift Analysis using PMI Vectors

We further use PMI to analyse the perception shifts involving the smell sources in different time periods. We first create vector embeddings containing the PMI value between each smell source in the benchmark and the fixed set of their context words, following an approach similar to the one presented in Hamilton et al. (2018). We consider as context only the spans labeled as *Qualities* of smell sources with a frequency higher than 3. In this way, for each item of the benchmark in each period, a vector was calculated, obtaining 56 vectors with 1,416 values. After keeping only the vectors containing more than 5 non-zero values, Pearson correlation between the vectors was used to calculate similarity/dissimilarity between them. We then utilized the correlations with the 'linkage' function within the MATLAB software to calculate the hierarchical clustering and finally represent it in a dendrogram (Figure 2 above). A high similarity between the vectors of the same smell source in two different time periods shows that the perception shift was limited. Moreover, different smell sources clustered together indicate that the qualities associated to them are similar. As a comparison, we create similar PMI-based embeddings but without considering the *Smell Source* and *Quality* information and using simple co-occurences in text in a window of 4 words between and after the occurence of the terms presented as Smell Sources in the benchmark (see approach presented in Section 5.2). This time the size of each embedding vector increased to 84,378 non-zero values and we calculate the dendogram in a similar way to what described above (Figure 2 below).

The above representation (PMI-embeddings based on *Smell Sources* and *Qualities*), shows that the vectors of the same Smell Source in different time periods tend to be more far apart and belong to different clusters, as can be observed for *gloves*, *ozone* and *incense / frankincense*. The last two terms, in particular, were considered interchangeable in the past (see yellow and green cluster), but from the beginning of the twentieth century frankincense seems to be used in different contexts (red cluster). On the contrary, the graph below tends to just group the vectors of the same smell sources across different periods, and seems therefore less suitable to capture shifts in time, see for example how *incense* and *frankincense* have all been clustered in the same group (red). This suggests that focusing the analysis only on elements that are relevant to the shift domain is beneficial to the quality of the outcome, enhancing its precision.

6 Discussion

Our analyses provide insights into the olfactory changes that were identified by domain experts, validating them from a quantitative point of view. However, we observe some differences in the outcome of our analyses. The results which better reflect the shifts manually identified in our benchmark are those whose changes were labeled as *quality shift*, namely 'candle', 'ozone' and 'tobacco'. This is not surprising considering that we focus on text spans classified as *Quality*. When it comes instead to'incense' and 'gloves', whose changes in perception are identified respectively as *topic shift*

Smell Source	Time period							
	1530 – 1600		1601 – 1800		1801 – 1900		1901 – 2000	
	aromatical	*perfume*	vernal	*dragge*	noisomely	*nidorous*	somnolent	*donative*
incense	perfume	*odours*	breathe	*breezy*	frank	*sepulchred*	sacerdotal	*exasperate*
(8,310)	sweet	*perfumed*	acceptable	*perfumed*	sanguinary	*perfuming*	frank	*wafting*
	fragrant	*fuming*	strange	*odours*	raptourous	*sweetsmelling*	sacred	*perfuming*
	odoriferous	*burnt*	holy	*perfume*	murky	*lawny*	heavenly	*enrage*
	1500 – 1700		1701 – 1829		1830 – 1900		1901 – 2000	
	abominable	*lighted*	ferous	*snuffing*	salutary	*guttering*	fragrance	*fumigating*
candle	ill	*lighting*	offensive	*lighted*	corrupt	*arsenicated*	scented	*relighted*
(1,186)	fetid	*blinking*	ill	*cerifera*	filthy	*relighted*	nauseous	*lighting*
	stink	*tallow*	odoriferous	*stationery*	snuff	*fumigating*	scent	*lighted*
	odoriferous	*cereus*	olfactory	*suppurating*	unsavoury	*sputtering*	perfume	*flickering*
	1500 – 1750		1751 – 1900		1901 – 2000			
	excellent	*perfumed*	perfume	*perfuming*	perfume	*gauntleted*		
gloves	venomous	*fringed*	spanish	*pictured*	scented	*buttoning*		
(670)	fine	*imbroidered*	remarkable	*cuticular*	scent	*boxing*		
	rich	*itchy*	costly	*worded*	odoriferous	*unbuttoning*		
	sweet	*scented*	excellent	*worshipful*	odorous	*rubber*		
	1600 – 1730		1731 – 1800		1801 – 1900		1901 – 2000	
	hateful	*smoaked*	olfactory	*smoky*	undiminished	*pipeful*	homely	*latakia*
tobacco	fulsom	*nicotian*	perfume	*chewing*	hateful	*negrohead*	indefinable	*unmanufactured*
(7,516)	ungrateful	*fulling*	peculiar	*fulling*	superficial	*unmanufactured*	spirituous	*chewing*
	offensive	*heroically*	grateful	*narcotick*	snug	*superexcellent*	stale	*carcinogenic*
	bad	*spicery*	pungent	*chewed*	vilest	*smoaking*	medicinal	*snuffing*
	1840 – 1899		1900 – 1950		1951 – 2000			
	restorative	*allotropique*	refresh	*ozonized*		*photochemical*		
ozone	inexhaustible	*oxidiser*	odorless	*allotropique*	None	*diurnal*		
(830)	denser	*ozonized*	peculiar	*triatomic*	found	*antarctic*		
	electrical	*sterilizes*	fresh	*ultraviolet*		*nickelic*		
	obvious	*vigorating*	pungent	*transboundary*		*spheric*		

Table 4: Words most associated with a given smell source (left), ranked by PMI, in different time periods associated to time shifts in the benchmark. Terms in normal font belong to *Qualities*, while those in gray have been extracted regardless of olfactory information. Below each smell source the number of total occurrences in the corpus has been reported.

and *disappearance*, the results are less evident compared to the defined changes in the benchmark. Our findings suggest that different types of shifts may require distinct approaches for proper detection. Indeed, if we want to capture shifts mostly due to *disappearance*, an analysis like the one displayed in Figure 1 is probably more effective than the one based on PMI, in particular because we identify to what extent an item is considered a smell source, see for example the graph for 'gloves' after 1950.

Nevertheless, qualities associated with gloves in the olfactory analysis closely align with the way perfumed gloves were described during their historical use. Adjectives such as 'venomous' or 'spanish' are indeed part of the practice to perfume gloves, since venom is hidden by the perfume and has been used to kill monarchs, while 'spanish' recalls the origin of glove-perfuming tradition from Spain and Italy. This observation provides further confirmation that this analytical approach effectively identifies qualities exclusively related to the olfactory domain with a precision that faithfully reflects the actual historical data. On the contrary, with regards to 'incense', its pronounced olfactory significance, as previously observed in Section 5.1, presented a challenge in detecting noteworthy changes through the quality-based methodology. To uncover *topic shifts* in textual data, further research is needed.

7 Conclusions

In this paper, we describe a range of analyses to investigate changes in the perceptual descriptions of five selected smell-related objects in textual data. We first present a frequency-based analysis aimed at delineating the olfactory relevance of these items over time. We then perform a PMI-based analysis to identify the qualities linked to smell sources during specific time periods, with the attempt to uncover changes in descriptions that reflect actual

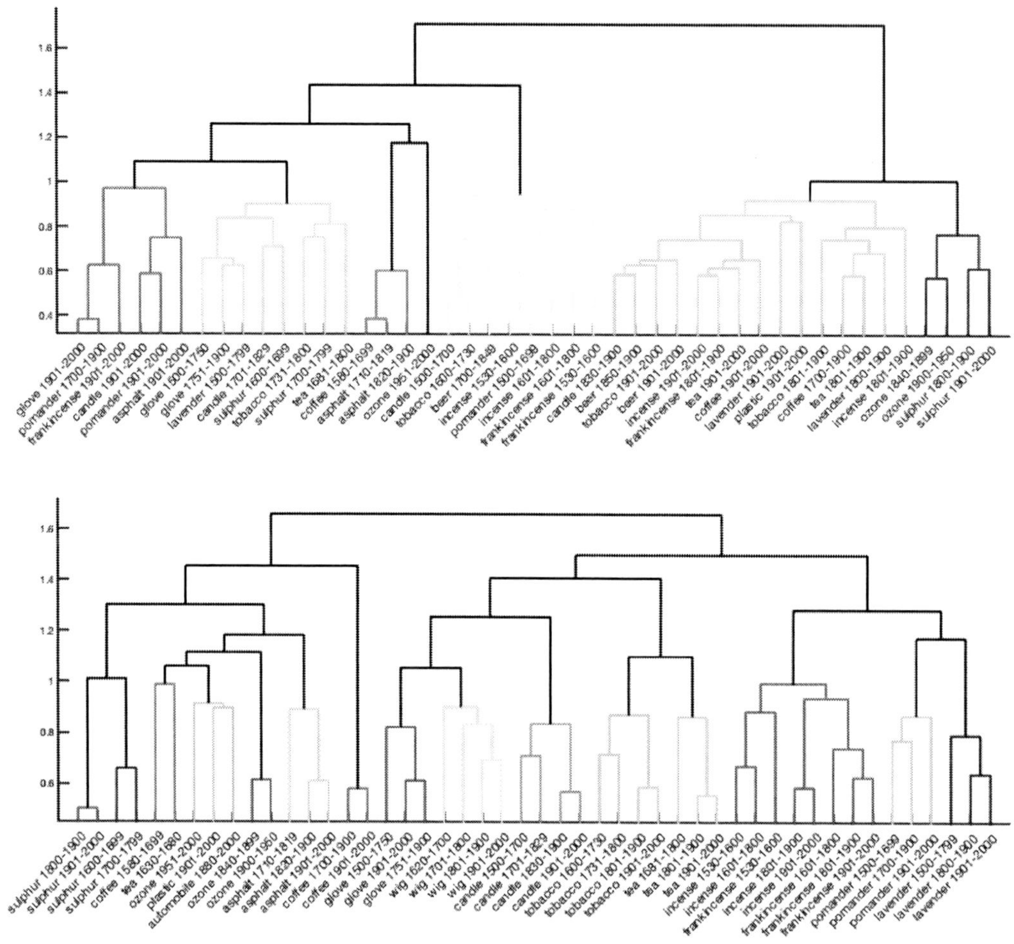

Figure 2: *Above*: Dendrogram clustering the PMI-embeddings of specific smell sources computed only on olfactory qualities for different time periods. *Below*: Dendrogram of the PMI-embeddings of the same words for the same time periods regardless of olfactory information.

shifts in perception. Additionally, we carry out a further analysis using PMI to represent the items of interest with vectors. The outcomes of these analyses support a twofold observation. On the one hand, the approaches previously used to detect diachronic semantic change prove effective in identifying variations also with regards to perceptual descriptions. On the other hand, the effectiveness of this adaptation is also due to the systematic encoding of the olfactory information offered by the frame-based approach. This work shows a novel approach which combines the power of frames in depicting semantic context and the tradition of semantic change detection to explore the evolution of olfactory language from a diachronic perspective. As previously discussed in Section 6, it would be worthwhile to expand our investigations by employing alternative frame elements to identify *topic shifts* associated with specific smell objects. Additionally, in the light of the observation made in Section 5.3, extending also the embedding-based approach to this type of shift detection could represents a promising path for prospective research. In future, we plan to further develop this methodology aiming towards a comprehensive approach for the study of perceptual shifts in texts.

Limitations

Like every corpus-based analysis, our work is strongly dependent on the corpus we were able to collect for this study. Although we tried to cover different domains and time periods, the limited availability of historical texts in good digital format is a major factor affecting our results.

Ethics Statement

No ethical issues are related to the current work.

Acknowledgements

This research has been supported by the European Union's Horizon 2020 program project ODEUROPA under grant agreement number 101004469.

References

Anonymous. 1910. Some recent applications of ozone. *Nature. 83, 47.*

Marco Bagli. 2021. *Tastes we live by: The linguistic conceptualisation of taste in English*, volume 50. Walter de Gruyter GmbH & Co KG.

R Caruana. 1993. Multitask learning: A knowledge-based source of inductive bias1. In *Proceedings of the Tenth International Conference on Machine Learning*, pages 41–48. Citeseer.

Rich Caruana. 1997. Multitask learning. *Machine learning*, 28(1):41–75.

Jacob Devlin, Ming-Wei Chang, Kenton Lee, and Kristina Toutanova. 2019. Bert: Pre-training of deep bidirectional transformers for language understanding. In *Proceedings of NAACL-HLT*, pages 4171–4186.

Alaa El-Ebshihy, Nagwa M El-Makky, and Khaled Nagi. 2018. Using google books ngram in detecting linguistic shifts over time. In *KDIR*, pages 330–337.

Charles J. Fillmore and Collin F. Baker. 2001. Frame semantics for text understanding. In *In Proceedings of WordNet and Other Lexical Resources Workshop*.

Thomas Forster. 1813. Meterological observations made at cambridge from march 18 to april 8, 1813. *The Philosophical Magazine. 41.*

Mario Giulianelli, Marco Del Tredici, and Raquel Fernández. 2020. Analysing lexical semantic change with contextualised word representations. In *Proceedings of the 58th Annual Meeting of the Association for Computational Linguistics*, pages 3960–3973, Online. Association for Computational Linguistics.

William L Hamilton, Jure Leskovec, and Dan Jurafsky. 2016. Diachronic word embeddings reveal statistical laws of semantic change. In *Proceedings of the 54th Annual Meeting of the Association for Computational Linguistics (Volume 1: Long Papers)*, pages 1489–1501.

William L. Hamilton, Jure Leskovec, and Dan Jurafsky. 2018. Diachronic word embeddings reveal statistical laws of semantic change.

Francesca Strik Lievers and Irene De Felice. 2019. *Metaphors and perception in the lexicon*. John Benjamins Publishing Company.

Asifa Majid and Niclas Burenhult. 2014. Odors are expressible in language, as long as you speak the right language. *Cognition*, 130(2):266–270.

Lizzie Marx, Sofia Collette Ehrich, William Tullett, Inger Leemans, Cecilia Bembibre, IFF (www. iff. com) Odeuropa, and Museum Ulm. 2022. Making whiffstory: A contemporary re-creation of an early modern scent for perfumed gloves. *The American Historical Review*, 127(2):881–893.

Stefano Menini, Teresa Paccosi, Serra Sinem Tekiroglu, and Sara Tonelli. 2022a. Building a multilingual taxonomy of olfactory terms with timestamps. In *Proceedings of the Thirteenth Language Resources and Evaluation Conference*, pages 4030–4039. European Language Resources Association.

Stefano Menini, Teresa Paccosi, Serra Sinem Tekiroğlu, and Sara Tonelli. 2023. Scent mining: Extracting olfactory events, smell sources and qualities. In *Proceedings of the 7th Joint SIGHUM Workshop on Computational Linguistics for Cultural Heritage, Social Sciences, Humanities and Literature*, pages 135–140, Dubrovnik, Croatia. Association for Computational Linguistics.

Stefano Menini, Teresa Paccosi, Sara Tonelli, Marieke Van Erp, Inger Leemans, Pasquale Lisena, Raphael Troncy, William Tullett, Ali Hürriyetoğlu, Ger Dijkstra, Femke Gordijn, Elias Jürgens, Josephine Koopman, Aron Ouwerkerk, Sanne Steen, Inna Novalija, Janez Brank, Dunja Mladenic, and Anja Zidar. 2022b. A multilingual benchmark to capture olfactory situations over time. In *Proceedings of the 3rd Workshop on Computational Approaches to Historical Language Change*, pages 1–10, Dublin, Ireland. Association for Computational Linguistics.

Robert Muchembled. 2020. *Smells: a cultural history of odours in early modern times*. pages 53-92, John Wiley & Sons.

Gordon Phillips. 1999. *Seven Centuries of Light: The Tallow Chandlers Company*. Book Production Consultants plc. p. 74.

Francesca Strik Lievers. 2021. Smelling over time. the lexicon of olfaction from latin to italian. pages 369–397. John Benjamins, Amsterdam.

Nina Tahmasebi, Lars Borin, and Adam Jatowt. 2021. Survey of computational approaches to lexical semantic change detection. *Computational approaches to semantic change*, 6(1).

Sara Tonelli and Stefano Menini. 2021. FrameNet-like annotation of olfactory information in texts. In *Proceedings of the 5th Joint SIGHUM Workshop on Computational Linguistics for Cultural Heritage, Social Sciences, Humanities and Literature*, pages 11–20, Punta Cana, Dominican Republic (online). Association for Computational Linguistics.

William Tullett. 2019. *Smell in Eighteenth-Century England: A Social Sense*. Oxford University Press.

William Tullett, Inger Leemans, Hsuan Hsu, Stephanie Weismann, Cecilia Bembibre, Melanie A. Kiechle, Duane Jethro, Anna Chen, Xuelei Huang, Jorge Otero-Pailos, and Mark Bradley. 2022. Smell, history, and heritage. *American historical review*, 127(1):261–309.

Rob van der Goot, Ahmet Üstün, Alan Ramponi, Ibrahim Sharaf, and Barbara Plank. 2021. Massive choice, ample tasks (MaChAmp): A toolkit for multi-task learning in NLP. In *Proceedings of the 16th Conference of the European Chapter of the Association for Computational Linguistics: System Demonstrations*, pages 176–197, Online. Association for Computational Linguistics.

Bodo Winter. 2019. *Sensory linguistics: Language, perception and metaphor*, volume 20. John Benjamins Publishing Company.

From Diachronic to Contextual Lexical Semantic Change: Introducing Semantic Difference Keywords (SDKs) for Discourse Studies

Isabelle Gribomont
KBR (Royal Library of Belgium)
CENTAL (Centre de Traitement Automatique du Langage)
UCLouvain
isabelle.gribomont@uclouvain.be

Abstract

This paper introduces the concept of Semantic Difference Keywords (SDKs). We define SDKs as keywords selected because of a comparatively high semantic difference between their use in two or more corpora. They are extracted by applying methods developed to identify diachronic Lexical Semantic Change. Like statistical keywords, most commonly used in quantitative discourse studies, SDKs capture the distinctiveness of a target corpus. However, they do not do so because they are used significantly more often or more consistently, but because they are used significantly differently. The case study presented in this paper shows that SDKs are successful in identifying concepts which are contested, i.e., sites of "semantic struggles" (Kranert, 2020). SDKs are therefore a useful contribution to (computational) discourse studies and text-based Digital Humanities more broadly.

1 Introduction

In discourse studies, a keyword is a central concept to the comparative study of corpora. However, the identification of such keywords is most often predetermined by the researcher, or, in the case of corpus linguistics studies, by statistical measures based on frequency and/or dispersion. Scholars have wondered how to identify keywords which are sites of "semantic struggles", i.e., which are at the centre of societal controversies and whose meaning is therefore contested (Jeffries and Walker, 2017).

This paper proposes the concept of Semantic Difference Keywords (SDKs), defined as words or multi-word expressions (MWEs) whose semantic difference between two or more corpora is comparatively large. SDKs are extracted with methods developed for the study of diachronic Lexical Semantic Change (LSC). This novel application of such methods is relevant to Computational and Digital Humanities.

As a case study, the discourse from Latin American guerrilla movements from the Cuban Revolution onward was investigated. More specifically, the words whose meaning in the discourse issued by the EZLN (Zapatista Army of National Liberation) most differs from their meaning in discourses issued by the other movements in the corpus were studied by training a Word2Vec model where two different embeddings were learned for candidate SDKs: one representing their use in the EZLN corpus, and one representing their use in the rest of the corpus. This analysis highlights that this concept shows promises to identify words which are sites of contestation within a specific discourse. It also underlines that high semantic difference can be explained by a variety of factors and that their relevance is therefore dependant on the initial research question. Stylistic markers, polysemy, context-dependant lexicon and ideological differences can all lead to variance in the context where words are being used by a specific group.

2 Background and related works

2.1 Quantitative and qualitative approaches to keywords in discourse studies

In corpus-driven discourse analysis, including computational literary studies, lexical "keyness" is a ubiquitous concept. It is most often based on frequency and represents the above-chance occurrence of the term in the corpus under investigation in comparison to another. Dispersion is another keyness measure which takes the distribution of the word across the corpus into account (Du et al., 2021; Egbert and Biber, 2019; Gries, 2008, 2021; Schöch et al., 2018).

From a computational discourse analysis perspective, keywords highlight what is distinctive at the lexical level in a target corpus. Through statistical keyword analysis, researchers have studied diplomatic letters (Pranoto and Yuwono, 2017),

Proceedings of the 4th Workshop on Computational Approaches to Historical Language Change, pages 153–160
December 6, 2023 ©2023 Association for Computational Linguistics

court proceedings (Potts and Kjær, 2016), academic writing (Paquot and Bestgen, 2009), gender differences in language use (Newman et al., 2008), political manifestos (Skorczynska, 2016), online COVID discourse (Joharry, 2023), and the representation of minorities or events in the press (Baker et al., 2013; Mohammed et al., 2022; Taylor, 2014).

However, keywords in (qualitative) discourse studies more globally refer to words which are central to a discourse. Schröter (2008) argues that studying the semantics and use of such expressions is key to understanding these discourses, particularly the ways in which "the meaning of the word change relative to the group that uses it". For instance, Kranert (2020) identifies "populism" as one such sociopolitical keyword in politics, news coverage and academic discourse. These keywords are sites of contestation or "semantic struggle". Their rhetorical role is therefore highly context dependent.

Previous research projects have combined quantitative and qualitative understandings of keywords. Kranert (2020) uses corpus linguistics methods to examine the pre-selected sociopolitical keyword "populism". Jeffries and Walker (2017), similarly drawing from research on cultural/sociopolitical keywords (Williams, 2014) and corpus linguistics keywords (O'Halloran, 2010; Stubbs, 2001), propose to identify keywords of interest by filtering statistical keywords, instead of focusing on a predetermined selection. To do so, they explicitly filter out statistical keywords that were "uncontested", "uncontroversial" and "least likely to actually demonstrate a change in their semantics between the two corpora".

This paper proposes a method that partially fulfills the same goals as the methodology proposed in Jeffries and Walker (2017). However, instead of filtering statistical keywords manually, relying on contextual knowledge and close readings of concordances and collocation lists, keywords are automatically extracted using NLP methods developed to recognise semantic difference.

2.2 Word embeddings and discourse studies

Because of their ability to map and formalise relationships between words within specific discourses, word embeddings are increasingly used in the field of Critical Discourse Analysis. See Wiedemann and Fedtke (2022) for a relevant survey of the topic. Such studies usually focus on one corpus (see, for instance Mandenaki et al. (2022) and Durrheim et al. (2023)). When the study is comparative, it usually investigates diachronic discourse change. For instance, Rodman (2020) tracked the changing meanings of political concepts in a dataset of 161 years of newspaper coverage and Viola and Verheul (2020) studied the evolution of the concept of migration in *The Times Archive* from 1900 to 2000.

Comparative synchronic semantic change analyses in discourse studies are rare. However, Schlechtweg et al. (2019) argue for the relevance of LSC for synchronic studies and apply it to detect sense divergence in domain-specific corpora (see also (Ferrari et al., 2017)). In addition, Gruppi et al. (2023) utilize semantic shift as an indicator of agreement among synchronic sources in the context of a method for news veracity classification. Yehezkel Lubin et al. (2019) use the concept of top changing words between synchronic corpora in the context of the alignment of vector spaces with noisy supervised lexicons, and Yin et al. (2018) investigate domain-specific linguistic shifts using word embeddings, also in the context of the development of a new vector space alignment method.

In the context of discourse studies specifically, a notable contribution is Dénigot and Burnett (2021), who use word embeddings to compare the discourses of the supporters and detractors of the legalisation of same-sex marriage at the French Assemblée Nationale in 2013. They conclude by arguing that embeddings have potential for the comparative analysis of synchronic corpora. The concept of SDK is part of the same impulse to expand the exploitation of word embeddings for discourse studies to synchronic investigation.

3 Defining Semantic Difference Keywords

SDKs are terms whose meaning differs substantially between two corpora. Otherwise stated, they are the words for which the semantic difference between their manifestation in one corpus and another is largest. In analogy with frequency or dispersion-based keywords, SDKs capture the distinctiveness of a target corpus, not because they are used significantly more often or more consistently, but because they are used significantly differently. Like frequency and dispersion-based keywords, they highlight the locations where the language of the two corpora differs at the lexical level. However, words which have similar relative frequencies and dispersions in two corpora, by definition, will not be selected as key, even if they are used in largely different ways, and therefore hold clues to fundamental differences in language use between the two corpora (Dénigot and Burnett, 2021).

In corpus linguistics, collocations are used to contrast how a word has different meanings or connotations in different contexts, but the words whose collocations are investigated are selected either because of underlying research questions, or according to frequency or statistical keyness criteria. In addition, they do not allow to measure how stable the meaning of the word under investigation is between the two corpora.

The concept of SDK is therefore useful to automatically extract words or phrases whose meaning is most unstable across two or more corpora. Not only can they contribute to identifying terms around which sociopolitical debates take place, but, like quantitative keywords, they could be leveraged for literary analysis, stylistic studies, authorship attribution, etc.

4 Case Study

As a case study, the discourse of Latin American leftist armed movements from the Cuban Revolution onward is investigated. The language of Latin American guerrilla discourse is relatively repetitive and heavily relies on fixed expressions and clichés. However, it has been argued that the EZLN (Zapatista Army of National Liberation), active from 1994 until today, offered a renovation of revolutionary leftist language in Latin America (Marcos and Le Bot, 1997; Gribomont, 2019). Identifying SDKs by comparing the EZLN corpus and a comparison corpus of texts written by other Latin American guerrilla movements from 1953 onward contributes to assess the ways in which this renovation takes place.

4.1 Data

The corpus was assembled by scraping the CeDeMa archive (Centro de Documentacion de los movimientos armados),[1] documents issued by the 26th of July Movement (the leading organisation of the Cuban Revolution),[2] and the archive of the Zapatista Army of National Liberation (EZLN).[3] The corpus totals more than 26 million Spanish words, of which more than 4 millions belong to the EZLN corpus. As part of pre-processing, the corpus was lower-cased, lemmatised and segmented into sentences.

4.2 Method

In theory, all methods developed to identify semantic change can be adapted to extract such sites of "semantic struggle". For a general survey of computational approaches to lexical semantic change, see Tahmasebi et al. (2021). See Kutuzov et al. (2018) for a survey focused on word embeddings.

The approach selected for this experiment relies on static word embeddings. With this method, a Word2Vec model (Mikolov et al., 2013) is trained with the whole data, but we append a context specific string to target words, i.e., words which are pre-selected as potential SDKs. This method is equivalent to the Temporal Referencing method described in Dubossarsky et al. (2019), where time-specific tokens are added to target words to model LSC. As demonstrated in the paper, this method has advantages in comparison to other embedding-based methods which learn a different semantic vector space for each time period before aligning them so as to minimise the distances between the time-specific embeddings of the same word (Hamilton et al., 2016). In addition, it shows that Temporal Referencing leads to models which are less noisy in comparison to alignment-based embeddings methods (Levy et al., 2015). Finally, it is more likely to perform well with smaller corpora since the words which are not selected for referencing are learned once, thereby minimizing the robustness issues caused by low frequency word embeddings (Dubossarsky et al., 2019). However, it does not account for the potential semantic difference between different contextual uses of the context words, which likely introduces biases into the semantic space.

To select the potential SDKs, the corpus was compared to the general Web Spanish corpus esTenTen18 available in Sketch Engine which contains 16.9 billion words of both European and American Spanish (Kilgarriff and Renau, 2013; Kilgarriff et al., 2014).[4] The words which obtained a simple maths keyness score higher than 1 (Kilgarriff, 2009) and whose frequency was greater than 400 in the EZLN corpus and 1000 in the rest of corpus were selected, resulting in 151 words.

Instead of the time period, the context is ref-

[1] https://cedema.org/digital_items

[2] http://www.fidelcastro.cu/es/biblioteca/documentos/

[3] https://enlacezapatista.ezln.org.mx/

[4] http://www.sketchengine.eu

erenced. In this case, the string *_EZLN* was appended to the pre-selected words so that different embeddings are learned for their manifestation in the EZLN corpus and the comparison corpus. The cosine similarity between vector pairs is calculated for all potential SDKs. They are then ranked from smallest to highest similarity.[5]

4.3 Results

Table 1 shows the top ten SDKs, i.e., the ten words for which the cosine similarity between the embedding pairs is the smallest. A full analysis is beyond the scope of this paper. However, the first word, "revolution" is particularly interesting. Its ten nearest neighbours include "independence", "1910", "1810" and "PRI". PRI is the acronym of the Mexican Institutional Revolutionary Party, a right-wing party which has been in power from 1929 to 2000. This party co-opted the imagery of the 1910 Mexican Revolution, which included a peasant rebellion against unjust agrarian laws, thereby "institutionalising" the concept of revolution. In doing so, they have rendered the word unusable for the EZLN. By naming their party "revolutionary", the PRI essentially altered the meaning of the word "revolution" for a segment of the Mexican population. Within the Mexican context, "revolution" is a site of semantic struggle at the centre of societal conflicts.

The second word, "class", reveals the EZLN's departure from the dominant language and ideology of Latin American guerrilla discourse. It is most commonly used in the context of "class struggle", "class conscience" and "working class" in the reference corpus, but used mostly to refer to the "political class" in the EZLN discourse. The approach proposed by the EZLN is intersectional and the redefinition of the word class is part of an abandonment of stereotypical Marxist vocabulary, symptomatic of a detachment from past guerrilla movements.

The third word, "citizen", is used to address "citizen rights", "citizen security" and "innocent citizens" in the reference corpus. In the EZLN corpus, it refers to "citizen initiatives", "citizen organizations" and "citizen movements". This semantic shift reflects the discrepancy in the perceived role of citizens in the social struggles and, more specifically, the key role of civil society in the Zapatista movement. In effect, the word "citizen" means something different in the two discourses, but semantics reflects a diverging ideology and mode of action.

Word	Translation	cosine sim.
revolución	revolution	0.2183
clase	class	0.2239
ciudadano	citizen	0.2299
plan	plan	0.2304
comandante	commandant	0.2351
frente	front	0.2462
terreno	piece of land/field	0.2540
dirección	direction/address/ management	0.2600
pensamiento	thought	0.2641
principio	principle/beginning	0.2657

Table 1: Top ten SDKs for the EZLN corpus and the comparison corpus.

It is also interesting to note that several words from this list are polysemic. It is the case of *principio*, for instance, which is used most often in the sense of "values" or "norms" in the reference corpus and in the sense of "beginning" in the EZLN corpus. This difference is again symptomatic of the Zapatistas' rhetoric, which is based on revolutionary practices more than revolutionary principles, but it also reflects the more narrative and oral writing styles adopted by Zapatista representatives.

The words whose meaning is the least different in the two corpora (negative SDKs) reveal the area where there is a strong continuity between the EZLN language and other movements. "Hand", "blood", "land", "money" and "wealth" are the top five negative keywords. For each of these, the nearest neighbour for the EZLN vector is the corresponding vector in the comparison corpus. Conversely, the EZLN vector is in the top five nearest neighbours of the comparison corpus vectors.

5 Discussion and future work

The method is successful in pointing to words which are used differently in different corpora. However, for the sake of illustrating the concept of SDKs, this pilot study relied on a single model and did not address potential robustness issues linked to the variability of word embeddings. For a fully-fledged analysis of the corpus, additional steps will be undertaken to increase reliability. First, im-

[5]The content of the scraped websites/archives is publicly available, but cannot be reproduced elsewhere. However, the code, frequency files and link to the resulting Word2Vec embeddings are available on GitHub: https://github.com/isag91/Semantic-Difference-Keywords.

plementing recommendations proposed by scholars who investigated the instability of Word2Vec models (Zhou et al., 2020; Pierrejean and Tanguy, 2018), especially those learned from comparatively small amount of data, will contribute to mitigate this issue. Antoniak and Mimno (2018) demonstrated that word embeddings are sensitive to small variations in the source documents, including their position in the corpora, suggesting that they are not trustworthy to study word associations. They recommend to average distance calculations over multiple bootstrap samples instead of relying on a single model. In addition, finetuning an existing model trained on a larger corpus instead of training a new model from scratch has proven to be a useful measure (Howard and Ruder, 2018).

Second, the influence of the algorithm, hyperparameters, word frequencies and length difference between sub-corpora on the results should be investigated. To truly assess performance and validate results, the creation of ground-truth datasets for such tasks would be valuable, whether via the annotation or existing data or the creation of simulated data (Hengchen et al., 2021). See Rodman (2020) for details on the creation of a gold standard for the evolution of meanings of political concepts.

As mentioned above, this pilot study aimed at illustrating the concept of SDKs. However, by limiting the contextual referencing to the EZLN corpus, the power of the methodology is limited. In future works, potential SDKs will be referenced for all movements (frequency permitting) and divided into three periods informed by historical research of Latin American leftist guerrilla movements (Wickham-Crowley, 2014). Some movements have been active for several decades and significantly evolved over time. This more granular referencing will be used to identify ideological clusters as well as patterns of continuity and rupture in the discourse of insurgency in Latin America (Chasteen, 1993). From a methodological viewpoint, by calculating all pairwise semantic similarities for potential SDKs, we will be able to extract keywords which are most susceptible to semantic variability across the board, rather than focusing on one movement. In addition, when focusing on one movement, it will be interesting to look at words whose pairwise distances is abnormally large in comparison to the pairwise distances involving the other movements.

Beyond this specific adaptation of LSC metholologies, relying on contextualised instead of static embeddings to investigate semantic difference (see Wiedemann and Fedtke (2022); Montanelli and Periti (2023)) would be productive for this area of research, since it would allow for the assessment of the stability of word meaning within one (sub-)corpus as well as across different corpora. For instance, examining the variance within different sub-corpora would be useful to track patterns of influence and cross-fertilisation between different social groups.

6 Conclusions

This paper introduced the concept of SDKs, i.e., keywords or key terms which are used most distinctively between two or more corpora. This concept is useful for the field of discourse studies, where researchers are interested in the ways in which terms are leveraged for differing rhetorical purposes by different groups. The extraction of SDKs bypasses the need for a predetermined shortlist of keywords. Nevertheless, the reason behind semantic difference cannot be assumed and close reading is necessary to interpret results.

In addition, researchers in the humanities and social sciences have to be wary of the potential instability or word embeddings (Sommerauer and Fokkens, 2019). Implementing recommended mitigating measures and reporting on variability metrics is key (Antoniak and Mimno, 2018). Ultimately, for this avenue of research to grow, the creation of more ground-truth datasets would be helpful.

Finally, like Dénigot and Burnett (2021), this paper wishes to argue that methods developed for the identification of LSC can productively be used for synchronic semantic difference in discourse studies as they have unique capabilities to extract language patterns which would be difficult to decipher with other quantitative or qualitative discourse studies methods.

Acknowledgements

This work was supported by a FED-tWIN grant (Prf-2020-026_KBR-DLL) funded by BELSPO (Belgian Science Policy). I thank my colleagues at CENTAL for the helful discussions and the three anonymous reviewers for their feedback and suggestions for improvements.

References

Maria Antoniak and David Mimno. 2018. Evaluating the stability of embedding-based word similarities. *Transactions of the Association for Computational Linguistics*, 6:107–119.

Paul Baker, Costas Gabrielatos, and Tony McEnery. 2013. Sketching muslims: A corpus driven analysis of representations around the word 'muslim'in the british press 1998–2009. *Applied linguistics*, 34(3):255–278.

John Charles Chasteen. 1993. Fighting words: the discourse of insurgency in latin american history. *Latin American Research Review*, 28(3):83–111.

Quentin Dénigot and Heather Burnett. 2021. Using word embeddings to uncover discourses. In *Proceedings of the Society for Computation in Linguistics 2021*, pages 298–312.

Keli Du, Julia Dudar, Cora Rok, and Christof Schöch. 2021. Zeta & eta: An exploration and evaluation of two dispersion-based measures of distinctiveness. *Proceedings http://ceur-ws. org ISSN*, 1613:0073.

Haim Dubossarsky, Simon Hengchen, Nina Tahmasebi, and Dominik Schlechtweg. 2019. Time-out: Temporal referencing for robust modeling of lexical semantic change. In *Proceedings of the 57th Annual Meeting of the Association for Computational Linguistics*, pages 457–470, Florence, Italy. Association for Computational Linguistics.

Kevin Durrheim, Maria Schuld, Martin Mafunda, and Sindisiwe Mazibuko. 2023. Using word embeddings to investigate cultural biases. *British Journal of Social Psychology*, 62(1):617–629.

Jesse Egbert and Doug Biber. 2019. Incorporating text dispersion into keyword analyses. *Corpora*, 14(1):77–104.

Alessio Ferrari, Beatrice Donati, and Stefania Gnesi. 2017. Detecting domain-specific ambiguities: An nlp approach based on wikipedia crawling and word embeddings. *2017 IEEE 25th International Requirements Engineering Conference Workshops (REW)*, pages 393–399.

Isabelle Gribomont. 2019. The zapatista linguistic revolution: A corpus-assisted analysis. *Discourses from Latin America and the Caribbean: Current Concepts and Challenges*, pages 139–171.

Stefan Th Gries. 2008. Dispersions and adjusted frequencies in corpora. *International journal of corpus linguistics*, 13(4):403–437.

Stefan Th Gries. 2021. A new approach to (key) keywords analysis: Using frequency, and now also dispersion. *Research in Corpus Linguistics*, 9(2):1–33.

Maurício Gruppi, Panayiotis Smeros, Sibel Adalı, Carlos Castillo, and Karl Aberer. 2023. Scilander: Mapping the scientific news landscape. In *Proceedings of the International AAAI Conference on Web and Social Media*, volume 17, pages 269–280.

William L. Hamilton, Kevin Clark, Jure Leskovec, and Dan Jurafsky. 2016. Inducing domain-specific sentiment lexicons from unlabeled corpora. In *Proceedings of the 2016 Conference on Empirical Methods in Natural Language Processing*, pages 595–605, Austin, Texas. Association for Computational Linguistics.

Simon Hengchen, Nina Tahmasebi, Dominik Schlechtweg, and Haim Dubossarsky. 2021. Challenges for computational lexical semantic change. *Computational approaches to semantic change*, 6:341.

Jeremy Howard and Sebastian Ruder. 2018. Universal language model fine-tuning for text classification. In *Proceedings of the 56th Annual Meeting of the Association for Computational Linguistics (Volume 1: Long Papers)*, pages 328–339, Melbourne, Australia. Association for Computational Linguistics.

Lesley Jeffries and Brian Walker. 2017. *Keywords in the press: The New Labour years*. Bloomsbury Publishing.

Siti Aeisha Joharry. 2023. Faith in the time of coronavirus: A corpus-assisted discourse analysis. *Intellectual Discourse*, 31(1):211–232.

Adam Kilgarriff. 2009. Simple maths for keywords. In *Proc. Corpus Linguistics*, volume 6.

Adam Kilgarriff, Vít Baisa, Jan Bušta, Miloš Jakubíček, Vojtěch Kovář, Jan Michelfeit, Pavel Rychlý, and Vít Suchomel. 2014. The sketch engine: ten years on. *Lexicography*, 1:7–36.

Adam Kilgarriff and Irene Renau. 2013. estenten, a vast web corpus of peninsular and american spanish. *Procedia-Social and Behavioral Sciences*, 95:12–19.

Michael Kranert. 2020. When populists call populists populists:'populism'and 'populist'as political keywords in german and british political discourse. *Discursive Approaches to Populism Across Disciplines: The Return of Populists and the People*, pages 31–60.

Andrey Kutuzov, Lilja Øvrelid, Terrence Szymanski, and Erik Velldal. 2018. Diachronic word embeddings and semantic shifts: a survey. In *Proceedings of the 27th International Conference on Computational Linguistics*, pages 1384–1397, Santa Fe, New Mexico, USA. Association for Computational Linguistics.

Omer Levy, Yoav Goldberg, and Ido Dagan. 2015. Improving distributional similarity with lessons learned from word embeddings. *Transactions of the Association for Computational Linguistics*, 3:211–225.

Katerina Mandenaki, Catherine Sotirakou, Constantinos Mourlas, and Spiros Moschonas. 2022. Topic models and word embeddings for ideological analysis: A case study in neoliberal discourse. *The International Journal of Communication and Linguistic Studies*, 21(1):37.

Subcomandante Marcos and Yvon Le Bot. 1997. El sueño zapatista. *Entrevistas con el Subcomandante Marcos, el.*

Tomas Mikolov, Ilya Sutskever, Kai Chen, Greg S Corrado, and Jeff Dean. 2013. Distributed representations of words and phrases and their compositionality. *Advances in neural information processing systems*, 26.

Tawffeek AS Mohammed, Felix Banda, and Mahmoud Patel. 2022. The topoi of mandela's death in the arabic speaking media: A corpus-based political discourse analysis. *Frontiers in Communication*, 7:849748.

Stefano Montanelli and Francesco Periti. 2023. A survey on contextualised semantic shift detection. *arXiv preprint arXiv:2304.01666*.

Matthew L Newman, Carla J Groom, Lori D Handelman, and James W Pennebaker. 2008. Gender differences in language use: An analysis of 14,000 text samples. *Discourse processes*, 45(3):211–236.

Kieran O'Halloran. 2010. How to use corpus linguistics in the study of media discourse. In *The Routledge handbook of corpus linguistics*, pages 563–577. Routledge.

Magali Paquot and Yves Bestgen. 2009. Distinctive words in academic writing: A comparison of three statistical tests for keyword extraction. In *Corpora: Pragmatics and discourse*, pages 247–269. Brill.

Bénédicte Pierrejean and Ludovic Tanguy. 2018. Predicting word embeddings variability. In *Proceedings of the seventh joint conference on lexical and computational semantics*, pages 154–159.

Amanda Potts and Anne Lise Kjær. 2016. Constructing achievement in the international criminal tribunal for the former yugoslavia (icty): A corpus-based critical discourse analysis. *International Journal for the Semiotics of Law-Revue internationale de Sémiotique juridique*, 29:525–555.

Budi Eko Pranoto and Untung Yuwono. 2017. Leader's attitude towards terrorism: A critical discourse analysis of dr. mahathir mohamad's diplomatic letters. In *Cultural dynamics in a globalized world*, pages 65–73. Routledge.

Emma Rodman. 2020. A timely intervention: Tracking the changing meanings of political concepts with word vectors. *Political Analysis*, 28(1):87–111.

Dominik Schlechtweg, Anna Hätty, Marco Del Tredici, and Sabine Schulte im Walde. 2019. A wind of change: Detecting and evaluating lexical semantic change across times and domains. In *Proceedings of the 57th Annual Meeting of the Association for Computational Linguistics*, pages 732–746, Florence, Italy. Association for Computational Linguistics.

Christof Schöch, Daniel Schlör, Albin Zehe, Henning Gebhard, Martin Becker, and Andreas Hotho. 2018. Burrows' zeta: Exploring and evaluating variants and parameters. In *DH*, pages 274–277.

Melani Schröter. 2008. Discourse in a nutshell: Key words in public discourse and lexicography. *German as a foreign language*, (2):42–57.

Hanna Skorczynska. 2016. The emerging parties' manifestos for the 2015 spanish general elections: a comparative analysis of lexical choices. *EPiC Series in Language and Linguistics*, 1:372–380.

Pia Sommerauer and Antske Fokkens. 2019. Conceptual change and distributional semantic models: an exploratory study on pitfalls and possibilities. In *Proceedings of the 1st International Workshop on Computational Approaches to Historical Language Change*, pages 223–233, Florence, Italy. Association for Computational Linguistics.

Michael Stubbs. 2001. *Words and phrases: Corpus studies of lexical semantics*. John Wiley & Sons.

Nina Tahmasebi, Lars Borin, and Adam Jatowt. 2021. Survey of computational approaches to lexical semantic change detection. *Computational approaches to semantic change*, 6(1).

Charlotte Taylor. 2014. Investigating the representation of migrants in the uk and italian press: A cross-linguistic corpus-assisted discourse analysis. *International journal of corpus linguistics*, 19(3):368–400.

Lorella Viola and Jaap Verheul. 2020. One hundred years of migration discourse in the times: A discourse-historical word vector space approach to the construction of meaning. *Frontiers in Artificial Intelligence*, page 64.

Timothy Wickham-Crowley. 2014. Two "waves" of guerrilla-movement organizing in latin america, 1956–1990. *Comparative Studies in Society and History*, 56(1):215–242.

Gregor Wiedemann and Cornelia Fedtke. 2022. From frequency counts to contextualized word embeddings: The saussurean turn in automatic content analysis. In *Handbook of Computational Social Science, Volume 2*. Taylor & Francis.

Raymond Williams. 2014. *Keywords: A vocabulary of culture and society*. Oxford University Press.

Noa Yehezkel Lubin, Jacob Goldberger, and Yoav Goldberg. 2019. Aligning vector-spaces with noisy supervised lexicon. In *Proceedings of the 2019 Conference of the North American Chapter of the Association for Computational Linguistics: Human Language Technologies, Volume 1 (Long and Short Papers)*, pages 460–465, Minneapolis, Minnesota. Association for Computational Linguistics.

Zi Yin, Vin Sachidananda, and Balaji Prabhakar. 2018. The global anchor method for quantifying linguistic shifts and domain adaptation. *Advances in neural information processing systems*, 31.

Xuhui Zhou, Zaixiang Zheng, and Shujian Huang. 2020. Rpd: a distance function between word embeddings. *arXiv preprint arXiv:2005.08113*.

Author Index

Association for Computational Linguistics
209 N. Eighth Street
Stroudsburg, Pennsylvania 18360

ISBN 978-1-7138-8601-3

CURRAN ASSOCIATES INC.
proceedings.com